D0053835

To my two sons, Geoffrey and Lowell Gibbs,
with the fervent hope that equal justice
under the law will become a reality in their lifetime
and
To the memory of my brother Julian,
and my brother-in-law,
James Brown, Jr.,
who did not live to see this dream realized.

race and justice

race and justice

RODNEY KING AND O. J. SIMPSON IN A HOUSE DIVIDED

JEWELLE TAYLOR GIBBS

Foreword by Cornel West

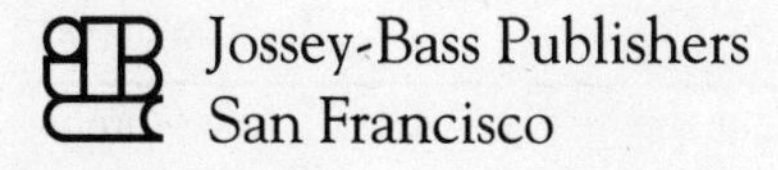
Jossey-Bass Publishers
San Francisco

For sales outside the United States, please contact your local Simon & Schuster International office.

Manufactured in the United States of America on Lyons Falls Pathfinder Tradebook. This paper is acid-free and 100 percent totally chlorine-free.

Library of Congress Cataloging-in-Publication Data

Gibbs, Jewelle Taylor.
Race and justice : Rodney King and O. J. Simpson in a house divided / Jewelle Taylor Gibbs ; foreword by Cornel West.
p. cm.
Includes bibliographical references and index.
ISBN 0-7879-0264-0
1. King, Rodney. 2. Trials (Police misconduct)—California—Los Angeles. 3. Simpson, O. J., 1947- —Trials, litigation, etc. 4. Discrimination in criminal justice administration—United States. I. Title.
KF220.G53 1996
364.3'0973—dc20 96-21545

HB Printing 10 9 8 7 6 5 4 3 2 1 FIRST EDITION

Contents

Foreword ix
by Cornel West
Preface xi
Prologue xix

Part One: Rodney King

1. Los Angeles: From Watts to South Central 3
2. Rodney King: Gentle Giant or Gorilla in the Mist? 22
3. The Color of Justice, I: The Trial, the Victim, the Verdict 38
4. Days of Rage: No Justice, No Peace 54
5. Two Commissions and Three Trials: Community Conflict and Concepts of Justice 76

Part Two: O. J. Simpson

6. O. J. Simpson: The Man, the Myth, the Marriage 115
7. The Crime, the Chase, the Arrest 140
8. *The People* v. *O. J. Simpson:* The Trial Begins 149
9. Ambushing the Prosecution: Playing the Race Card 180

10. The Color of Justice, II: The Verdict, the Response, the Aftermath 204

Part Three: Race and Justice

11. "Bad Blood": Conspiracy Theories and the Black Community 235
12. A House Divided: Healing the Wound, Restoring the Dream 265

Epilogue 279
Appendix A: Research Note 303
Appendix B: People Interviewed 307
Notes 313
Index 342
About the Author 348

Foreword

Race remains America's most explosive issue and the rawest nerve as we approach the twenty-first century. Race also continues to be the most difficult and most delicate matter to discuss. More than ever, we need candid and critical voices to help us confront our shortcomings, expose our blind spots, and strengthen our better selves. Jewelle Taylor Gibbs's powerful book is such a voice in our time.

In stark contrast to the sensational stories and superficial analyses of the Rodney King and O. J. Simpson trials and verdicts, Gibbs takes us on a poignant journey of painstaking facts and subtle interpretations of these two nation-shaking events in our recent past. For the first time since our media-saturated treatments of these events, we get a detailed examination of what happened in light of a sophisticated framework that discloses the meaning of these happenings for the country. In short, Gibbs has written the first major work on the most radically divisive trials at the close of our century—in the spirit of honest truth-telling and courageous nation-healing.

From the founding of the City of Los Angeles by a group of African, Indian, and Spanish settlers in 1781 to the most diverse urban metropolis of 1996, Gibbs provides a rich historical narrative of invasion, immigration, segregation, subordination, resistance, and hope for substantive cooperation. This narrative revolves around the central themes of race and justice. She allows the common folk of Los Angeles to speak even as she solicits the great voices of

W.E.B. Du Bois, Abraham Lincoln, and Martin Luther King, Jr. She grounds her narrative in the everyday realities of black Los Angeles alongside the institutional and structural dynamics of white supremacy in sunny Southern California. She demystifies the myth of racial harmony in the city's past and demands that we wrestle with the racism of its present. And she leaves no critical stone unturned—race, gender, and class are intertwined so as to illuminate the night side of L.A.'s bright lights.

Gibbs scrutinizes perceptions and practices on both sides of the color curtain, in both the black world and the white. We learn much about ourselves as a nation and Los Angeles as a city in regard to the color of justice. We are also forced to grapple with the depths of black disillusionment with this "justice."

Yet Gibbs refuses to succumb to any form of debilitating bitterness or paralyzing cynicism, even as she reveals a heart of darkness in Southern California. She provides great wisdom and insight for healing our painful wounds and restoring our precious dreams. In the great tradition of passionate democrats like Fanny Lou Hamer and Ella Baker, she calls for substantive accountability by our police departments, mass media, criminal justice system, and economy if our divided house is to be united. But this national unity must be rooted in a deep sense of justice—a sense of justice that confronts and overcomes the paranoia and poverty produced largely by the role of race in our past and present. Let us hope that America harkens to her prophetic voice!

Cambridge, Massachusetts Cornel West
July 1996

Preface

On April 30, 1992, the acquittal of white police officers accused of beating black motorist Rodney King set off four days of civil disorder in South Central Los Angeles. As a social scientist, I wondered about the impact of that civil disorder on the lives of young African-Americans in the area. I designed, and in September 1993 launched, an ethnographic study that would enable me to develop a multilayered understanding of the effects of those traumatic events on the attitudes, experiences, and aspirations of black youth in the fifteen-to-thirty age range living in South Central.

As a scholar whose research had always focused on the psychosocial adaptation of minority youth to a majority society, I viewed this as an opportunity to gain some valuable insights into the responses of these black youth to the inequities in the criminal justice system, the realities of racism, and the social and economic problems they faced in their inner-city community. As a mental health professional, I was particularly interested in assessing their capacities to develop healthy personalities and realistic goals in the midst of a distressed community, to maintain positive identities in the face of negative social forces, and to cope with daily challenges in overcoming barriers and boundaries to their self-realization.

During the ten months of interviewing for the study, I seized every opportunity to familiarize myself with the community, to observe its dynamics, to engage in informal interactions with its people, to worship in its churches, and to absorb its ambience through participating in a range of social, cultural, and political activities. My role as an observer-participant in these activities served to sharpen my sensibilities about the feelings and attitudes of a broad cross section of African-Americans about race and justice in Los Angeles. This dual role also helped me understand the shock and anger experienced in the community when it was learned in June 1994, shortly after the brutal murders of Nicole Brown Simpson and Ronald Goldman, that O. J. Simpson, Nicole's former husband and black celebrity sportscaster, was the leading suspect. I did not realize immediately how that event would alter the course of my study.

On June 17, 1994, I was driving south on the 405 freeway to the Los Angeles airport after completing my final interview for the study when a bulletin interrupted the regular news program to announce that the police had spotted O. J. Simpson's white Ford Bronco on the San Diego Freeway, apparently trying to evade arrest. Like so many millions of other Americans, I could not wait to arrive home to turn on my television set and watch the climax of the chase and the arrest. Somehow, the timing seemed strangely coincidental to the conclusion of my study, but O. J.'s arrest also resonated with many of the issues about black males in the criminal justice system that had provoked so much anger and hostility in the focus group discussions and my interviews with young and old alike in South Central.

Over the next year, as I analyzed the data from my study and began writing a book about the impact of the Rodney King beating and its aftermath on the black youth in South Central, the O. J. Simpson case was never far from my consciousness. As the media began to transform the story into a daily soap opera, they also began to transform O. J.'s image from the quintessential "crossover" sports superhero to the sinister black superstud. From profiles of O. J.'s early years in San Francisco and his teenage scrapes with the law, it also became clear that there were surprising parallels in the backgrounds of O. J. Simpson and Rodney King. By the time the trial began on September 26, 1994, I was more than an interested observer; I had become a critical analyst trying to look beneath the surface reports of the legal gamesmanship and the media circus to the subtexts of racial tensions, class conflicts, and gender antagonisms.

In late May, my editor, Alan Rinzler, called me to suggest that I abandon my original plan for a book on general issues facing black youth in South Central and radically shift the focus to black males in the criminal justice system, illustrated by the cases of Rodney King and O. J. Simpson. Although initially reluctant to take on such a daunting task, it took only a few days for me to realize that these two men really represented two sides of the same coin of the black male experience in America. Rodney King, the blue-collar high school dropout and ex-felon versus O. J. Simpson, the self-made celebrity businessman and sports superstar. Despite their superficial differences in lifestyle, success, and status, O. J. Simpson and Rodney King were treated as immediate suspects by the police, reduced to stereotyped symbols in the press, and manipulated by powerful interest groups in the community to advance their own agendas.

As the Simpson case progressed, it became increasingly clear that much of the media had abandoned their neutrality and the presumption of innocence for O. J. and that the trial had spawned a mini-industry of legal analysts, celebrity commentators, and creative entrepreneurs. The trial had also polarized blacks and whites, who had very different perspectives on the case and attitudes about O. J.'s possible complicity in the crime.

Less obvious but also interesting were three other patterns that emerged in this case: the complex relationship between the prosecutors and the police; the equally complex relationship among the prosecutors, the defense lawyers, and the judge; and the relationship between both teams of lawyers, the judge, and the press. The mass media played a significant role, not only in reporting the case, but also in becoming a central actor in the case itself, as well as manipulating public opinion about the case with an orchestrated series of negative stories about O. J. Simpson and his private life.

The major goal of this book is to compare and contrast the King and Simpson cases in terms of the involvement of two black males in the criminal justice system. Their experiences with the Los Angeles Police Department (LAPD) and the justice system are analyzed in the context of the recent history of black males in the criminal justice system in Los Angeles and the broader sociopolitical history of race relations in American society. Through the use of documentary evidence, case histories, and social protest activities, the very different experiences of blacks and whites with the police and the criminal justice system are delineated—from the decades of hundreds of unsolved lynchings to the killings of scores of civil rights workers, the repression of radical protest groups, and the criminalization of young black males in late twentieth-century America.

The "not guilty" jury decisions in the Simi Valley trial for three of the four white officers charged in the King beating and for O. J. Simpson on double murder charges in the downtown Los Angeles trial are analyzed to illustrate how the very different life experiences and perspectives of a predominantly white and a predominantly black jury shaped the way they perceived and processed the evidence in the cases and ultimately led to decisions that were quite logical and consistent based on their worldview, their evaluation of the evidence, and their predisposition to believe or disbelieve police testimony.

The intense responses of blacks and whites to both of these cases have reignited the long-smoldering debate about race and class in America, particularly since the ultimate decisions in both of these cases may have been significantly influenced by relative access to legal counsel and other resources. Three other cases that were related to the original Rodney King beating trial—the civil rights trial of the four officers accused of using excessive force, King's civil rights trial against the LAPD, and the trial of the black assailants of white truck driver Reginald Denny during the riots—are discussed briefly to highlight the pervasive influence of the race of both defendants and victims on jury decisions and judicial actions.

Ironically, all of these cases have played themselves out in a city founded by a multiracial, multicultural band of settlers and celebrated for its tolerance of racial and cultural diversity. Within that very contradiction lies the disillusionment and despair of African-Americans that their hope for equality and justice in the Golden West has not materialized in Los Angeles. While this book focuses on the impact of the criminal justice system on the African-American community in Los Angeles, many of these issues are equally problematic for other communities of color, particularly recent immigrants and refugees who are coping with their own issues of acculturation, discrimination, and economic opportunities. The proposed remedies for improving the relations between blacks and the police are also relevant to other oppressed minority groups in Los Angeles.

The Prologue of the book is a very brief account of the founding of Los Angeles in 1781 by a group of racially mixed soldiers, farmers, and laborers, invoking an author's license to interpret their vision of a multiracial, multicultural community with equal opportunity and justice for all of its citizens.

The book is then organized into major sections to reflect the impact of these two highly publicized cases on the Los Angeles community and, ultimately, on the nation. The five chapters in Part One begin with a brief history of African-Americans in Los Angeles, focusing on the period between the Watts riots in 1965 and the South Central riots in 1992 (Chapter One), followed by three chapters about the police beating of Rodney King (Chapter Two), the first trial of the four white police officers (Chapter Three), and the community's violent response to the acquittal of the officers (Chapter Four). The last chapter in Part One reports the findings of the two commissions that investigated the LAPD and the uprising and describes the three subsequent trials that resulted from the King beating and the postverdict riots: the civil rights trial of the four police officers, Rodney King's civil suit against the LAPD, and the trial of the assailants of Reginald Denny (Chapter Five).

Part Two contains five chapters describing the background of O. J. Simpson, his career, and his two marriages (Chapter Six), the murders of Nicole Brown Simpson and Ronald Goldman (Chapter Seven), and the lengthy trial of O. J. Simpson for the crime (Chapters Eight, Nine, and Ten). The first of the two chapters in Part Three, Chapter Eleven presents an analysis of the power of conspiracy theories in the African-American community, particularly those that impugn the motives of the government or its official representatives (such as the police, the FBI, and the CIA). Chapter Twelve proposes strategies for healing the painful wounds of racial prejudice and paranoia and restoring the dream of equal opportunity and justice for all Americans.

Following Chapter Twelve is the Epilogue, which presents an updated account of the activities and current whereabouts of the principal figures involved in both the Rodney King and O. J. Simpson cases.

There are two appendixes. Appendix A is a research note describing the author's research design and methodology for her study after the 1992 civil disturbances in Los Angeles following the acquittals of the police officers in the beating of Rodney King and her research methods on the Simpson case. Appendix B lists the participants in the community study conducted after the King-related incidents.

It is my fervent hope that this book will help illuminate the dark abyss of racial misunderstanding and mistrust and that it will also make a significant contribution to the healing of the racial wounds in Los Angeles and to the dialogue about race in America.

ACKNOWLEDGMENTS

I would like to express my sincere appreciation and gratitude to the following persons for their important contributions to this book:

To the leaders and activists who serve the African-American community and other communities of color in Los Angeles with such generosity and compassion, for sharing their valuable time with me and providing me with valuable information and insights about the impact of these two cases on the city and its diverse groups.

To the staff members of the agencies and organizations that assisted me in recruiting African-American youth from South Central Los Angeles for the first phase of this study, for their wholehearted support of this research project.

To the African-American youth who voluntarily participated in individual and group interviews to share their hopes, fears, and dreams about growing up black in racially divided Los Angeles.

To the individuals in Los Angeles and the San Francisco Bay Area who participated in the survey before and after the verdict in the O. J. Simpson case, for their thoughtful, candid, and often provocative comments.

To John Burris, Oakland civil rights attorney and co-counsel in Rodney King's civil case against the City of Los Angeles, for sharing his insider perspective and valuable insights about the implications of the case and its symbolic significance.

To my editor, Alan Rinzler, whose perspicacity helped shape the vision of this book, for his sharp eye, firm hand, and steady encouragement of this project.

To the Zellerbach Family Fund for its generous support of this project, and particularly to Ed Nathan, the former executive director of this San Francisco foundation, for his friendship, wise counsel, and long-term commitment to racial equality.

To Teiahsha Bankhead-Greene, a doctoral student in the School of Social Welfare at Berkeley, who served as my research assistant on the Rodney King case, for her unflagging enthusiasm, energy, and empathic insights about the study and the community.

To Joseph R. Merighi, a 1996 Ph.D. recipient from the School of Social Welfare, who served as my research assistant on the O. J. Simpson case, for his cheerful competence, computer expertise, and conscientiousness.

To Sharon M. Ikami, my secretary and confidant, whose support and loyalty help me manage a complex schedule, meet my deadlines, and keep my sense of humor.

To my husband, James Lowell Gibbs, Jr., for his consistent support, creative cuisine, and patient endurance of my total commitment to this project for nearly three years.

To Harry Specht, late dean of the School of Social Welfare, University of California, Berkeley, for his contribution to my professional development as a mentor and colleague and for his faith in my nontraditional route to an academic career.

To all my family, friends, and colleagues who expressed their encouragement and support of this project in countless unexpected and unrequited ways. To paraphrase the African proverb that it takes a whole village to raise a child, it takes a caring community to create an author. For nourishing my creativity and sustaining my faith in this project, I will be forever indebted to them all.

Berkeley, California Jewelle Taylor Gibbs
July 1996

Prologue

At sundown on September 4, 1781, a group of eleven settlers and their families, recruited from Sinaloa, Mexico, established a pueblo on the banks of the Porciuncula River and named it El Pueblo de Nuestra Señora de la Reina de los Angeles, the Pueblo of Our Lady, the Queen of the Angels. Having arrived at Mission San Gabriel in mid August after an arduous journey by land and sea from Loreto, this tired and dispirited band of pioneers had been held in quarantine until several of their children recovered from smallpox, which had already claimed one of their original members. This unremarkable group had responded to an invitation from Don Felipe de Neve, the first Spanish governor to establish his headquarters at Monterey in Alta California, to found a farming town at this site in order to supply the growing presidios of Santa Barbara and San Diego.

As they finally approached the selected site and stood on the banks of the narrow river, looking over the fertile plains, these settlers must have shared a vision of building a new community, the promise of a prosperous future, and a dream of racial harmony and justice for all their descendants. These *pobladores*, the founders of this "pueblo of the angels," were eleven male settlers with Spanish surnames, but one historian notes that these "first citizens were mainly of Indian and African blood, with only a moderate admixture of Spanish." In fact, these male settlers included two Spaniards, two blacks, two mulattos, one mestizo, and four Indians. By March 21, 1782, three of this original group had been dropped from the founder's list, for unclear reasons, leaving the remaining eight male settlers, along with their families, to be recorded as a total population of thirty-two official founders of the City of Los Angeles.

This multiracial, multicultural, and multilingual group managed to get along so well that by 1784, three years after the town's founding, "this motley band of colonists had replaced their first rude huts with adobe houses and laid the foundations for a church and other public buildings. Two years afterwards, when land titles were finally issued them, each Angeleno affixed his cross to the documents; apparently not one of Los Angeles' first citizens could write his name." For the Spanish governor, these founders deserved equal treatment in the granting of land titles. For these early settlers, justice was not determined by the color of their skin, their racial heritage, or the level of their literacy.

More than two hundred years later, after the City of Angels had been torn asunder in 1992 by racial conflict and violence, a young black man named Rodney King, the major symbol of that upheaval, plaintively asked, "Can we all get along?" Three years later, in 1995, Los Angeles would again be polarized by racial divisions over the acquittal of a black man named O. J. Simpson in the murder of his former wife and her male friend, both of whom were white.

Perhaps Rodney King and O. J. Simpson had never heard the story of the founding of Los Angeles. But as the twentieth century drew to a close, these two black males had become symbols of the social, political, and cultural conflicts dominating American society, where race was a primary factor in the distribution of justice. And it is ironic that these two black men had once shared the hopes for justice and the dreams of racial harmony of the Spaniards, blacks, mestizos, and Indians who had founded the pueblo on the banks of the Porciuncula River at sundown on that hot autumn day in 1781.

Part I

Rodney King

1

Los Angeles

From Watts to South Central

> Our nation is moving toward two societies, one black, one white, separate and unequal.
>
> National Advisory Commission on Civil Disorders (Kerner Report), March 1968

If the motley band of *pobladores* who founded Los Angeles in 1781 had been transported in a time capsule to Parker Center, the police department's headquarters in downtown Los Angeles, on October 3, 1995, they would have been awestruck by the square, fortress-like glass-and-concrete building, surrounded by dozens of black-and-white cars with flashing lights and tall, muscular men and women with skin and hair colors in all shades of the rainbow, wearing smartly pressed blue uniforms equipped with guns, batons, and an array of strange-looking metal gadgets. Even more fascinating would have been the conversations they overheard, mainly in a language they did not understand. But they could see in the strangers' faces and hear in their voices angry expressions, harsh words, and feelings of frustration.

Two names and two words were repeated over and over in the strangers' intense conversations: the names were O. J. Simpson and Rodney King; the terms were *race* and *justice*—not immediately understandable, although the Spanish-speaking time travelers might have found them vaguely familiar from their own language.

This impoverished group of Spanish and mulatto soldiers, Indian peasants, and African laborers, surveying this scene with their wives and families, would have been greatly disappointed and disheartened had they been able to comprehend who these uniformed strangers were, why they were so angry, and what the significance of those two names and terms had for their beloved City of Angels. In their wildest imaginings, they could never have guessed how the names of Rodney King and O. J. Simpson were linked or how the people in blue uniforms had altered the fate of each of these men. Most surprising of all, they could never have conceived that their city, with its multiracial and multicultural roots and its vision of harmony, had come to symbolize the most contentious and divisive schism in urban America between whites and blacks, between rich and poor, and between native-born and immigrants in the second half of the twentieth century.

THE CITY OF ANGELS: THE DREAM AND THE PROMISE

The vision and the promise of Los Angeles have beckoned generations of migrants and immigrants, refugees and renegades, merchants and misfits, all chasing dreams of success, freedom, wealth, even fame. Waves of migrants gravitated to Los Angeles—from early Spanish landholders to Mexican farm laborers, from poor white Okies and Arkies to rural blacks from Texas and Louisiana, from Japanese farmers to Chinese garment workers, from Korean shopkeepers to Southeast Asian refugees, from survivors of Central American political violence to survivors of the Ethiopian wars and famines. And as group after group of these newcomers swelled the city, Los Angeles welcomed them, nurtured them, and absorbed them, expanding its boundaries to create niches for each group to establish its own businesses, its places of worship, and its unique cultural ambience.

The movies and the media, capitalizing on the vision of Los Angeles as a dynamic, glamorous city, disseminated this unique

American dream around the world—the promise of diversity and opportunity, of fame and fortune, of a better life. What these media images did not show in their seductive movies and superficial TV sitcoms was the grimy underbelly of Los Angeles, the increasing spatial separation of whites and nonwhites, the continuing exploitation of immigrant laborers, the escalation of police harassment and brutality against blacks and Latinos, the growing unemployment in the inner city, and the growing gap between the rich and famous in Beverly Hills and the poor and powerless in South Central Los Angeles.

The dream has been shattered twice in the second half of this century—in 1965, when Watts exploded in a frenzy of frustration and anger over police harassment of two young black males, and in 1992, when South Central exploded in rage and resentment over police brutality directed against one young black male. Despite the somber warnings of the Kerner Report in 1968 that the United States was becoming a dual society divided by race and inequality of opportunity, the riots in 1992 exposed the fissures of a Los Angeles deeply divided by race and class, for blacks were joined by poor Latinos, Asians, and whites in the rioting and looting that terrorized the city for four days and four nights.

And in 1995, less than four years after the uprising in South Central, the dream was shattered again in the wake of the acquittal of another black man charged with the crime of murdering his former wife and her male friend, both whites. The riots this time were waged between whites and blacks with the weapons of angry words and hostile actions in the media and in the community, revealing the deep racial schisms lying just below the surface of the multicultural mosaic of the City of Angels.

FROM THE GOLDEN YEARS TO THE DEPRESSION

> Los Angeles is wonderful. Nowhere in the United States is the Negro so well and beautifully housed. Out here in this matchless

> Southern California there would seem to be no limit to your opportunities, your possibilities.
>
> W.E.B. DuBois, NAACP leader, 1913

The years between 1900 and 1929 have been called the Golden Era for Los Angeles's blacks, whose numbers had increased from 3,131 in 1900 to 15,579 by 1920, when they still accounted for less than 3 percent of the city's population. During those years, the black community experienced steady growth and prosperity, jobs were plentiful, home ownership increased to over 36 percent by 1910, numerous small businesses were established, and blacks were scattered in at least six residential areas throughout the city, from Boyle Heights in the East to Pico Heights in the South. Relations between the races were generally friendly, and African-Americans in Los Angeles were viewed with a mixture of admiration and envy by blacks in less hospitable areas of the nation.

Blacks had achieved so much in those first three decades of the twentieth century, yet none could foresee the losses they would endure after the stock market crashed on October 29, 1929, the day ironically called "Black Tuesday."

THE DEPRESSION YEARS

> The Great Depression crippled White America but it devastated Black America. Millions of Americans found themselves unemployed and unemployable—there just were not any jobs. Many of these citizens took to the roads in search of a chance, an opportunity. Black Americans joined that stream of the California bound. . . . Black residents and migrants alike found themselves restricted to the lowest paying positions, when finding a job was possible.
>
> California African-American Museum Foundation, *Black Angelenos*

The Great Depression years were devastating for the nation but particularly tragic for blacks, already at the bottom of the economic and social ladder. By 1930, over 70 percent of Los Angeles's black population was crowded into one assembly district, evidence of the increasingly rigid racial barriers in housing and the ghettoization of the black community. During the next ten years, black Angelenos suffered a triple loss—the failure of many black businesses, the loss of thousands of jobs, and the increased competition for scarce employment and housing with the massive influx of black and white migrants from the rural South and the Dust Bowl, all seeking relief from crushing poverty and unemployment.

Along with the southern migrants came their history of racial segregation, the legacy of racial inferiority, and the residue of racial antagonisms.

As the leader of the LAPD during the Depression years 1933–1938, Chief James Davis not only reflected those attitudes in his treatment of the black community but also refused to allow interracial police patrols. Chief Davis was widely credited with creating the "dragnet," an unofficial license for the police to stop and search anyone who looked vaguely suspicious. Though his colorful personality and controversial policies inspired the popular *Dragnet* television series in the 1950s, he also left a legacy of police harassment and injustice against minorities that was to shape the philosophy and the practice of the LAPD for the next fifty years.

WORLD WAR II AND UPWARD MOBILITY

With the onset of World War II, the fortunes of the black community were once again on the rise as jobs in war industries opened up, small businesses were revitalized, and blacks were drafted into the armed services. Despite the initial attempts of defense-related industries to exclude black workers, President Franklin Roosevelt's Executive Order 8802 in 1941 forbade discrimination in companies with government contracts, thus creating unparalleled opportunities for men and women alike, not only to obtain highly skilled jobs at good wages but also to develop, for the first time in American history, a true skilled black working class. Having enjoyed the benefits of higher wages in the factories and the promise of freedom in the Allied victory, blacks in Los Angeles shared with their brothers and sisters all over the country the expectation that the postwar society would finally bring them the freedom, the equality, and the justice denied them previously. This dream, too, was to be short-lived and bittersweet.

> Every time there's a war, black soldiers are sent to fight for some-body's else's freedom. My uncle fought in Europe in a segregated unit and even believed all that bullshit propaganda about making the world safe for democracy. Hell, he came back from the war with his mind messed up and a Purple Heart. Couldn't get a decent job and started hitting the bottle. He was worse off after the war than he ever was before it started.
>
> L. V., educator, Los Angeles

Soon after World War II ended, the defense industries began downsizing, with blacks the first to be fired or replaced with returning white veterans. Black families that had established a tenuous foothold in the middle-class world of home and car ownership by having both parents working now found themselves with both unemployed, unable to pay their mortgages, having their cars and furniture repossessed, giving up their aspirations of upward mobility.

Black veterans who had fought to restore freedom in Europe found themselves treated like second-class citizens at home. The equality and justice they had sought as a reward for their wartime service was still a distant dream, as they coped with the grim reality of an increasingly repressive police force that was determined to keep them "in their place."

DEINDUSTRIALIZATION AND THE DEATH OF THE DREAM

> Initially, the black community was very defined geographically and it was a fairly homogeneous community, but then some tremendous changes caused a decline in the economic status of blacks. People started losing their jobs, then their housing deteriorated, and then the middle-class blacks started migrating to the suburbs.
>
> Joycelyn M. Crumpton, social worker, Center on Child Welfare, UCLA

By the mid 1950s, the residential segregation of the black community was an established fact as boundaries had expanded to include the adjacent communities of Watts and Inglewood and were moving westward toward the Crenshaw district. Unemployment was rampant, many black businesses were unable to sustain themselves, and crime was becoming a visible problem in the community as young men without jobs and without skills were beginning to form loosely organized gangs, preying on the successful, the vulnerable, and the elderly to fulfill their own fantasies and dreams.

The LAPD had in 1950 appointed a new police chief, William Parker, who ushered in the modern era of a paramilitary force equipped with an arsenal of high-tech weapons and high-powered tactics in law enforcement. Chief Parker took a hard line against urban crime, social change, and racial integration. During Chief Parker's sixteen-year tenure, the LAPD escalated its war against the black community, amassing a record of harassment, brutality, and misconduct that fueled African-Americans' sense of injustice and contributed to their growing sense of anger and rage at these blatant violations of their civil rights.

However, another movement was emerging in the 1950s that served to recast and reinforce the realities of life for black Angelenos throughout the postwar period. Between 1954 and 1964, a series of judicial and legislative actions, beginning with the Supreme Court's *Brown* v. *Board of Education of Topeka* decision outlawing school segregation in May 1954 and culminating in the Civil Rights Act of 1964, ushered in a civil rights movement that forever changed the relations between blacks and whites in America and forever altered the hopes and aspirations of black youth, who believed they could now participate fully in the American dream. Two presidents, Kennedy and Johnson, had made promises to them, the Supreme Court had guaranteed their rights under the Constitution, and Congress had even passed legislation to enforce these hard-won rights. A war had been declared on poverty, and salvation was just around the corner—or so they naively believed.

> The brothers and sisters from the sixties got the opportunity to go to college and have somebody pay for it. . . . Go through college, get educated, get into the mainstream then you find out—guess what? You're still a nigger—no matter what you do.
>
> G. J., black alumnus, California State University, Northridge

---

But in the 1960s, the Los Angeles economy was stagnant, and blacks were the first to feel the impact of industrial plant closings, defense industry downsizing, and mass layoffs. As these factories closed and these jobs disappeared, "deindustrialization" resulted in much more than economic devastation for these communities. It also resulted in demoralization of the black men and women who had mortgaged their futures for a piece of the American dream and were threatened with the loss of their homes, their cars, and their savings. Most damaging of all, the deindustrialization of Los Angeles contributed significantly to the destabilization of the black community, which quickly came to realize that it was geographically and economically cut off from the city's newly emerging economic base of high-rise financial institutions and corporations in the downtown business center and the mushrooming high-technology information and communication service industries on the fashionable West Side.

With more whites and blacks competing for fewer skilled and semiskilled jobs, racial tensions increased and police hostility toward the black community escalated. The police clearly understood that it was their role to "keep Negroes in their place," and they relished every opportunity to carry it out.

By the mid 1960s, Chief Parker's invincible "blue knights," praised and publicized in the white community, were viewed with suspicion and distrust in the black community. Under Chief Parker's leadership, justice was just a seven-letter word that didn't apply to people of color in Los Angeles.

> Police malpractice is a very real thing, a routine of false arrests, illegal searches, rousts, beatings, intimidations, verbal abuse and official sanction by inaction, and no Negro is immune.
>
> American Civil Liberties Report on the Los Angeles Police Department, 1968

PROMISES, PROMISES

There were some signs of change, a new industry of poverty professionals, more rhetoric about equal opportunity and equal access for minorities, a few more blacks in window-dressing positions, more politicians making more promises to crowds eager for change and searching for solutions. Yet these changes were more superficial than structural; they benefited the few and bypassed the many; they raised expectations but denied realities.

> You know, I was a very young person in 1965, but I do recall some of the things that led to the Watts riot. Well, I really mean the revolt . . . from the injustice by your local law enforcement agencies and the things they were able to get away with and cover up. The

> same things that took place then led to the revolt just as after the Rodney King verdict. Nothing I see has really changed. There were a lot of programs that emerged in the early sixties, but a lot of promises were made and then broken—things like summer jobs for teenagers.
>
> E. B., probation officer, Los Angeles

As the 1960s progressed, the promises had begun to sound empty on the street corners and in the backyards of Watts. Yes, there was a poverty program, but how many real jobs did it generate for unskilled black males? Yes, there was a community health center, but where were the drug treatment facilities? Yes, there were training programs for unemployed single mothers, but why were the schools still failing to educate black children? Yes, there was much talk about equal rights for southern blacks, but what was being done about police brutality toward blacks right there in Los Angeles?

In his definitive history of the 1965 Watts riots, Gerald Horne quotes a white police officer describing the "Negrophobia" of the LAPD in the 1960s: "Some officers randomly and arbitrarily beat and tortured black men, even those who were not suspected of anything. . . . Overwhelmingly, their illegalities were perpetrated against black men, who were perceived to be least able to protest effectively." The complacency of the police in inflicting injustice on the black community, and brutalizing black males in particular, was shattered on a hot summer night in August 1965 when police officers mishandled a young black male in Watts.

THE WATTS RIOTS: DAYS OF RAGE

> People had a long history of tension over justice not being served. When you keep being deprived of your right to be equal in this society, it just sits heavy on your chest, and it finally exploded.
>
> C. A., social worker, Los Angeles

If you can understand how disappointed young blacks were by the summer of 1965, if you can understand how betrayed they felt by their government and all of its institutions, if you can understand how frustrated and angry they were over the lack of jobs, the poor schools, the police brutality, the many injustices—then you can understand why Watts exploded on a summer night in 1965.

Contemporary accounts attribute the cause of the Watts riot to an encounter between Marquette Frye, a twenty-one-year-old unemployed black male, and three white California highway patrol officers who were trying to arrest him on a drunk driving charge. On that sultry summer evening of August 11, 1965, after enjoying a few drinks with his brother and a friend, this young black male was driving somewhat erratically down Avalon Boulevard in the heart of Watts, speeding beyond the posted limit, attracting the attention of a motorcycle cop. When he was stopped, he got out of the car in a jovial mood, bantered playfully with the police, and even danced a little jig when the officer asked him for identification.

The incident occurred at the corner of Avalon Boulevard and 118th Street about 7:00 P.M., shortly after the dinner hour when people were sitting on their porches and strolling down the street. When Frye apparently tried to resist arrest, the officers overreacted, called for reinforcements, and pulled their guns on a small crowd of people who had gathered to watch the events unfold. After one officer had assaulted Frye and his brother with a riot baton, their mother, Rena Frye, had hit the officer, who then struck Mrs. Frye and put all three of them in the patrol car.

The crowd became incensed at this unnecessary brutal treatment. People began to shout defiant racial epithets at the officers and soon got out of control. By 7:45 P.M., after several confrontations between angry blacks in the crowd and police reinforcements, the Watts riot had begun as the crowd turned into a mob and hurled a hail of bricks, cans, bottles, sticks, and garbage at police cars leaving the area at 116th Street and Avalon. At that moment, all of the years of pent-up frustration over the discrimination, the brutalization, the humiliation, and the injustice they had endured erupted into an explosion of rage, bitterness, and violence.

Without plan or pattern, the riot spread quickly beyond that block as news of the arrests was fueled by rumors that a pregnant woman had been beaten by the cops, ignited by earlier incidents of police harassment and brutality in the community and inflamed by purported eyewitness accounts. The community was like an overripe watermelon, needing only one quick blow to expose its raw, red, jagged insides.

WAITING TO EXPLODE

Since the days of the Dust Bowl migration, the police force had been the major route to mobility and the perfect institutional vehicle for spreading attitudes of racial superiority and customs of racial segregation for poor white Okies and Arkies in Los Angeles. So it was that mainly white southern-bred cops were responsible for law and order in mainly black southern-bred Watts.

Their record was not good. Young black males complained that they were frequently stopped, searched, and harassed by white cops for no apparent reason. Young black women complained that they were often verbally abused, mistaken for prostitutes, and sometimes even forced to have sex with cops who picked them up on flimsy excuses. Black families complained that cops often invaded their homes and apartments, without a search warrant, on the pretext of looking for drugs or stolen goods, then leaving their belongings scattered and furniture destroyed without so much as a brief apology. Elderly blacks complained that the police were slow to respond to their calls if they had been robbed or mugged, so they did not feel reassured when they felt vulnerable to the gangs. The list of complaints included the penchant of some white cops to refer to blacks with racial epithets, calling them "niggers," "jigaboos," "jungle bunnies," and other terms of contempt. When blacks in Watts encountered the police, they did not expect justice or mercy; they simply hoped to avoid a violent or humiliating interaction.

In the two years before the summer of 1965, there had been several particularly egregious encounters between blacks and the police in Watts. Several young black males had been killed in police custody, sometimes as the result of choke holds and sometimes from beatings allegedly administered because they were "resisting arrest." This was the Southern California equivalent of the southern lynching, always justified by the police and always tolerated by the politicians, the press, and the nonblack people of Los Angeles.

Black civil rights organizations had been lobbying for more black police, but the LAPD was not a hospitable place for black officers, and few blacks were interested in law enforcement careers in that "rampant redneck" environment. Complaints about police brutality were routinely denied by the police department, disavowed by the politicians, and downplayed by the press. The hostility between the people of Watts and their so-called protectors was intense, their frustration over continued police harassment was escalating, and their tolerance for injustice was at the breaking point.

> The cops were part of the system of white supremacy, racism, and oppression that was unchecked in the early sixties. Black people felt they had no rights. They were fed up. It wasn't the poverty or unemployment that caused the riot—it was getting the monkey off their backs.
>
> Ronald Johnson, executive director, National Family Life and Education Center, Los Angeles

---

On that August evening in 1965, the mood of the community may have seemed lighthearted as neighbors stopped by to gossip, young mothers took their children for a walk, and teenagers eyed the passing cars for signs of action. But the underlying mood in Watts was one of frustration and anger over the black men who couldn't find jobs, over the schools that couldn't educate black children, over the merchants who exploited their black customers, over the crowded and dilapidated housing, over the poor transportation system, over the lack of medical facilities, over the police harassment and brutality. It was a time bomb waiting to explode, and the trigger was the incident at the corner of Avalon Boulevard and 118th Street shortly after 7:00 P.M. on the evening of August 11.

By the time the looting stopped and the flames subsided six days later, 34 people were dead, 1,032 had been injured, and property damage was estimated at over $182,565,000, making it the most costly urban riot in American history. In addition, 3,438 adults and 514 juveniles were arrested, over 70 percent for burglary and theft. It had taken 13,900 National Guardsmen, 934 officers from the LAPD, and 719 sheriff's deputies to bring the rioting under control.

The Watts riot was indeed a tragedy for the community, but it was also a comedy of errors by the Los Angeles Police Department. The police had misinterpreted the defensive behavior of the young black driver, had misunderstood the mood of the community, had misjudged the threat of a major riot, and had miscalculated the need for a swift and decisive response to control the situation. Ironically, a nearly identical scenario was destined to be played out twenty-seven years later, in the aftermath of the trial of four white police officers accused of beating a young black man named Rodney King.

Whatever happened to the dream and the promise of Los Angeles? Whatever caused so many people of all colors and cultures to vent their rage and strike out against this city and its institutions twice in twenty-seven years? Whatever moved so many young people to lose respect for their social institutions and for the police and to lose faith in the system of justice? Whatever is needed to repair the breach between whites and blacks, blacks and Koreans, rich and poor, and to revive the American dream for all Angelenos?

THE McCONE COMMISSION REPORT

On August 24, 1965, Governor Edmund G. Brown appointed a commission to "probe deeply the immediate and underlying causes of the riots . . . and develop recommendations for action designed to prevent a recurrence of these tragic disorders." John A. McCone, CIA director under President Eisenhower and former top executive of the Bechtel Engineering Company, was appointed to chair the commission, and Warren M. Christopher, a partner in a prominent law firm in Los Angeles, was appointed vice chair. The other six members represented a narrow band of the city's establishment—three white males, one white female, and two prominent black leaders.

After one hundred days, sixty-four meetings, and eighty witnesses, the McCone Commission submitted its report to the governor on December 2, 1965. The report identified seven major causes of the Watts riots: police misconduct and brutality, high unemployment and job discrimination, unequal educational facilities and de facto school segregation, substandard and segregated housing, inadequate and inferior health facilities and services, inadequate public transportation, and inferior consumer goods and services. Despite the overall moderate and cautious tone of the report, the unpaid citizens' commission had stripped the veil off the city's expensive illusions. But the commission, according to its many critics, did not face up to the serious charges of police misconduct and brutality against the black community, suggesting only cosmetic and minor changes in police practices.

Among the recommendations were the following: to strengthen the Board of Police Commissioners, to establish an independent inspector general to handle citizen complaints, and to expand police-community relations programs—all very safe and politically feasible suggestions. As expected, the commission also made a series of recommendations to expand job opportunities and job training, to improve school facilities and curriculum, to increase access to low-income housing, to expand health facilities, to improve access to public transportation, and to upgrade the quality of consumer goods and services in the targeted inner-city areas. The commission had discharged its solemn duties, and now the black community would wait for its long-heralded rehabilitation.

Only a few very astute critics realized that the McCone Commission had abdicated its responsibility to advocate the sweeping changes necessary to improve the socioeconomic status of the black community, and even fewer could have foreseen the tragic consequences of the commission's failure to expose and condemn the Los Angeles Police Department's use of excessive force and its officers' persistent violations of the basic civil rights of the black community.

SOUTH CENTRAL LOS ANGELES: A COMMUNITY IN CRISIS

South Central is the heart of black Los Angeles. Since it captivated W.E.B. Du Bois in 1913 with its pastel-colored bungalows and its palm tree–lined avenues, South Central has been the magnet for the black migrants from Texas and Louisiana who came to Southern California seeking a better life. As the black population rapidly expanded, so did the boundaries of South Central from Central Avenue (on the border of Watts) in the East to Crenshaw Boulevard in the west, to Slauson Avenue on the north, and to Century Boulevard on the south. By 1992, the mainstream media defined South Central as anywhere there was a critical mass of black people—everything south of the Santa Monica Freeway, from the Crenshaw district to Watts, from Compton to Inglewood, from Baldwin Hills to Culver City.

To blacks, South Central has always been more than an address—it is an invisible boundary, an ethnic identity, a white projection, a state of mind. It is also now home to nearly three million people, nearly half of whom are immigrants from Mexico and Latin America, gradually displacing the black community and threatening its sense of identity.

From 1965 to 1992, the black population in Los Angeles County grew from approximately 650,000 to 993,000, gradually accounting for 14 percent of the county's population. As the population increased and its boundaries expanded, the problems enumerated in the McCone Commission report grew exponentially over the next three decades.

After the Watts riots, middle-class blacks started a steady exodus from the South Central area, seeking better housing, better schools, and better urban amenities for their families. Immigrants from Mexico and Central America soon replaced the southern migrants, transforming the community with their own vibrant culture, their cantinas, and their mural-decorated buildings. Korean and Mexican "mom and pop" stores quickly replaced the Jewish- and black-owned shops destroyed in the 1965 riots. By 1992, South Central was no longer a homogeneous black neighborhood but had become a multiethnic and multicultural community, once again, with blacks, Latinos and Asians coexisting in an uneasy truce but with no sense of collective identity or common ground.

After the Watts riots, the recommendations of the McCone Commission were filed away in dusty archives and university libraries, useful to scholars but irrelevant to policy makers. The promises of the politicians were soon forgotten by a community that had long been politically disenfranchised. The eagerness of business leaders to develop the economic infrastructure of South Central soon dissipated in the absence of financial incentives and media attention. South Central was abandoned and left to its own inexorable fate, bereft of economic resources, social capital, and effective leadership.

Between 1965 and 1992, the unemployment rate in South Central increased as the availability of skilled and semiskilled jobs decreased. In just the five years from 1978 to 1982, South Central lost more than seventy thousand skilled and semiskilled jobs in defense and manufacturing industries, the very jobs that had enabled black men to support their families, black families to buy a home, and black children to grow up in a stable community.

Between 1965 and 1992, the public schools in South Central became more segregated, the facilities deteriorated, and achievement levels declined.

Between 1965 and 1992, housing in South Central became more segregated, public housing became more dilapidated, and home-owners had more and more difficulty obtaining financing from banks for home repairs, home equity loans, and mortgages in the area.

Between 1965 and 1992, health care facilities in South Central became increasingly inadequate as the population demand out-stripped the supply of health care services and providers, despite the building of a modern comprehensive hospital, named after Martin Luther King, Jr., on the edge of Watts in 1972, seven years after the city fathers vowed to build it.

THE QUESTION OF JUSTICE

> In the past climate of this city, the police have been exonerated for doing things that were grossly unjust. Eulia Love, Ron Settles, and so many others killed by policemen—then their murders were ruled justifiable homicide. In the early eighties, [the police] were choking black men to death every other day and it was [deemed] justifiable, so this has been the norm. So the actions that happen to African-Americans in this society, especially African-American men, have always been determined justifiable when done by law enforcement.
>
> Herbert A. Jones, director, Black Education Commission, Los Angeles Unified School District

---

Between 1965 and 1992, police misconduct and brutality continued unabated under the leadership of Chief Edward Davis (1969–1978) and Chief Daryl Gates, who was appointed in 1978. Gates had been a protégé of Chief Parker and a field commander during the Watts riots in 1965. For many blacks in South Central, this police abuse was the most blatant and egregious symbol of their second-class citizenship in Los Angeles. The fact that the LAPD could arrest them without provocation, enter their homes without a warrant, and harass or assault them with impunity provoked chronic anger and outrage in the community. The very presence of a police officer on his block or in a patrol car was sufficient to remind a black man of his vulnerability, his place at the bottom of the caste hierarchy, his powerlessness in a white society.

Between 1965 and 1992, long before the Rodney King incident, nearly every black family in Los Angeles knew some young black man who had been beaten or fatally injured in police custody. During the 1980s, at least sixteen blacks had died from police choke holds, many on the streets and in police patrol cars, arrested for "suspicious behavior," "loitering," or "resisting arrest." The coroner managed to rule that most of these cases were unfortunate "accidents," not really cases of excessive police force or misconduct. Chief Gates rationalized these "accidental deaths" by suggesting that the abnormal anatomy of black necks was responsible for the unusually high death rates from choke holds.

For blacks in South Central, there were two systems of justice—one for white folks and one for black folks. The black folks might not have all understood their civil rights guaranteed by the Constitution or the complexities of the legal process, but they fully understood that justice in Los Angeles was not colorblind—from the cop on the beat to the judge on the bench, justice in Los Angeles was colored white. And it was that visceral understanding that fueled their anger at the jury that exonerated the police assailants of Rodney King in April 1992 yet also aroused their empathy with the jury that acquitted O. J. Simpson of two brutal murders in October 1995.

2

Rodney King

Gentle Giant or Gorilla in the Mist?

Rodney King became a black everyman whose experiences with police came to symbolize African-American encounters with law enforcement.

Wade Henderson, national staff member, National Association for the Advancement of Colored People

---

Nobody wanted to address the issue or listen to young men on the street that they actually feel under siege by the police on the street. Young black men feel alienation and isolation from the system of law enforcement, the court system. . . . The issue is white supremacy, racism and oppression.

Ronald Johnson, executive director, National Family Life and Education Center, Los Angeles

The small city of Altadena, nestled in the foothills of the San Gabriel Mountains, looks like a Hollywood version of the Southern California suburb. Southern blacks began migrating there in the 1960s, drawn by its proximity to good jobs in Los Angeles, its climate, and its affordable housing. By 1990, the west side of Altadena had become an enclave for upwardly mobile working-class and middle-class blacks who owned small pastel-colored bungalows and lived their version of the American dream. The

King family was one of the largest families in the community, with at least twenty-five relatives living within two miles of one another. Rodney's father was a construction worker who, with his wife and children, had moved from Sacramento to Altadena in the early 1970s. The Kings, devout Jehovah's Witnesses, were a very close-knit family who prided themselves on the American virtues of hard work, thrift, and involvement in religious activities. One of their sons would challenge these values and cause his parents and law-abiding family considerable anguish. His name was Rodney Glenn King.

Born in Sacramento in 1965, Rodney was always large for his age, sometimes growing so fast that he was ungraceful and uncoordinated. By the time he was in elementary school, his family had moved to Altadena to join an ever widening circle of aunts, uncles, and cousins seeking a better life in Southern California.

Elementary school was not easy for Rodney, who had problems learning to read and spell. His teachers complained to his parents that he had a short attention span and was sometimes aggressive in class, but his family thought he was just a typical active boy, somewhat shy and usually quiet, except when he played in Little League baseball games. Perhaps his attention and learning problems might have been mitigated if he had received a proper diagnostic assessment in the early grades, but he entered high school just barely able to read at the fourth-grade level.

ADOLESCENT YEARS: NO PLACE TO BE SOMEBODY

> When you don't have the ability to read and write, you can't get the respect of your peers, and you begin to act up and act out just to get some respect. . . . So the ninth grade is the dumping ground, the dropout point. And these African-American children do not

drop out, they are *pushed out* of school, simply because they do not have the skills to compete past that grade level.

Herbert A. Jones, director of the Black Education Commission, Los Angeles Unified School District

---

Because of his learning problems, Rodney was slotted into special education classes at John Muir High School in Altadena. As a low-achieving black male in a suburban high school, Rodney's interest in academic pursuits was neither expected nor rewarded. Seeking some modicum of respect and recognition, Rodney joined the varsity baseball team, a familiar alternate route for mediocre black male students. He soon discovered that he didn't have the excellent coordination and competitive drive to make a first-rate baseball player, but he enjoyed the attention and the camaraderie of the team. With no place to be successful and no expectations of a professional sports career, Rodney began to lose interest in school and to skip classes. According to his teachers, Rodney dropped out of school six months before graduation. He had no diploma, no job, no skills, and no plans.

As dropouts do, Rodney began to drift aimlessly, spending his time hanging out with his friends in the nearby parks, playing pickup basketball games, looking at television for long hours, and drinking cheap beer.

Rodney was the kind of guy with an easygoing personality who made friends quickly and knew how to go along to get along. As a child, he had often been a target of teasing because of his large size and his slow mind, but by late adolescence, he had learned some street smarts and figured out a comfortable niche for himself in this tightly knit community of family and friends. The aggressive, learning-disabled child had matured into a soft-spoken, six-foot three-inch, 225-pound, well-built young man who avoided confrontation and enjoyed parties. Rodney's friends called him the "Gentle Giant." When he wasn't hanging out with his friends,

Rodney liked to watch animal shows on television and go to baseball games, activities that required little effort or concentration.

> These kids don't want a handout; they want a job. That's my roughest task—helping these kids find jobs. . . . They want to get out and work. They want to break the cycle.
>
> Dr. Gale L. Pauley, director, Youth Intervention Alternative School, Los Angeles Unified School District

---

Rodney worked briefly at McDonald's, one of the few jobs available in Altadena to a black male high school dropout. Even for a slow starter, it seemed like a dead-end job—long hours, low wages, and few benefits. When his job at McDonald's was abruptly terminated, Rodney worked intermittently with his father and grandfather on construction projects and odd jobs around the area. Most of the males in the King family worked in skilled, blue-collar, and semiskilled jobs—whatever it took to support their families, buy a house, and find a piece of the dream. But by the early 1990s, those kinds of jobs were becoming harder and harder to find in the Southern California economy, beset by severe cutbacks in the aerospace and defense industries and plagued by escalating unemployment rates as other manufacturing companies closed down their factories or moved away from Los Angeles County.

MARRIAGE AND MATURITY

Following his father's example, Rodney married his teenage girlfriend at age eighteen, not long after he dropped out of high school. Their marriage was doomed from the beginning for the usual reasons—they were both too young, too unskilled to find good jobs, and too immature to build a relationship. At the age of twenty-one, Rodney had not found success in school, in sports, or in marriage.

By twenty-three, Rodney had divorced his first wife and married Crystal Waters, another high school sweetheart, moving with her and her two young sons into a small house on Lincoln Avenue in Altadena, still surrounded by family and friends. The neighbors described him as always "polite" and the family as never causing any problems. But beneath the tranquil surface of this household festered problems that threatened to erupt. Because of his difficulties in finding steady employment, Rodney had trouble supporting his second wife and meeting the needs of their two growing sons. Inevitably, these pressures spilled over to create tension, multiplying the stresses on an already vulnerable marriage.

CRIME AND PUNISHMENT

Perhaps it was the need for money, perhaps it was the stress, perhaps it was the feeling of helplessness and hopelessness over his lack of options. No one really understands the reason why Rodney King entered a Monterey Park grocery store (the 99 Market) on an evening in November 1989, brandishing a two-foot-long tire iron and ordered Tae Suck Baik, the Korean owner, to open the cash register. After a brief struggle with Baik, who hit King with a three-foot-long rod, Rodney grabbed two hundred dollars from the register, hit the grocer with a metal pole, and quickly fled in his white Hyundai car—but not before the grocer ran outside and copied down his license plate. Luckless as usual, King was arrested ten days later and was sentenced to a two-year term at the California Correctional Center in Susanville. Even the Korean grocer saw the gentle side of Rodney King, testifying in court that he didn't believe that King would have struck him if he hadn't hit him first—a portrait of a very reluctant robber.

> I don't think the real problem of the community is crime. The real crime is the inability of these young people to extricate themselves

> from what they think is a hopeless situation. . . . The system now is not concerned with due process but with convictions, with locking people up, with being very tough. . . . But we're not doing anything to try to help them or rehabilitate them or keep them from getting into difficulty. All they're doing is trying to get rid of these kids.
>
> Hon. H. Randolph Moore, supervising judge,
> Kenyon Juvenile Justice Center, Los Angeles

Unhappy in prison and remorseful for his crime, Rodney wrote a letter to the judge requesting a reduction in sentence. The letter offers an insight into Rodney's life and thoughts while in prison. It is also a comment on his serious educational deficiencies, but it is as well a window on his vulnerability.

> I have all good time work time. I have seriously been thinking about what happen and I think if it is possible that you can give me another chance, your honor. I have a good job and I have two fine kid who wish me home. Have so much at stake to lose, if I don't get that chance. My job and family awaits me. So please reconsider your judgment, your honor. The sky my witness and God knows.

Despite this plaintive plea for help, the judge rejected Rodney's request, and he wasn't paroled until two days after Christmas, on December 27, 1990, after a year in prison. Rodney King had had his first serious brush with the criminal justice system, but it was not to be his last.

Soon after he was released from prison, Rodney found a temporary job as a laborer at Dodger Stadium, a place where he could indulge his lifelong love of baseball and perhaps fantasize about a career as a professional athlete, one of his early dreams that never materialized. His boss, Scott Dalgleish, praised him as a prompt, dependable worker, the kind of worker who puts in his time and doesn't expect much in return.

Secure in a steady job and reunited with his family, Rodney King, now twenty-five, was getting his life back on track. Like many working-class men, he maintained strong bonds with his male friends even after he married. So it was not unusual for him to hook up with some of his buddies, have a few drinks, and ride around town on spring evenings after work. On one of those Saturday evenings, March 2, 1991, he and two friends, Bryant "Pooh" Allen and Freddie Helms, headed north on the Foothill Freeway, looking for some action. Hearing a police siren behind him, Rodney panicked because he thought that he might be sent back to prison for a minor traffic violation. This misunderstanding of the parole laws would result in more action and reaction than Rodney King could ever have imagined in his most vivid fantasies.

ARREST AND ASSAULT

> When black people in Los Angeles see a police car approaching, they don't know whether justice will be meted out or whether judge, jury, and executioner is pulling up behind them.
>
> Curtis R. Tucker, Jr., California State Assembly representative from Compton

---

The undisputed facts of this case show that Rodney King tried to elude a California Highway Patrol car, leading the two officers on a high-speed chase up the freeway in the same white Hyundai that he had used to rob the grocery store sixteen months earlier. As the chase gained momentum, the CHP officers called for backup and were soon joined by a caravan of LAPD patrol cars from the Foothill Division, two security officers from a Los Angeles Unified School District patrol car, and a police helicopter hovering over the scene. By the time Rodney King was forced off the road near a complex of apartment houses in the Lake View Terrace area, a total of twenty-three Los Angeles police, two highway patrol officers, and two school security officers had stopped to investigate this speeding white car holding three black men.

After the car was forced to a halt, the facts are unclear, distorted through the multiple lenses of the various police officers, the onlookers, and the victims. Though the eyewitness accounts later varied, the presence of a police helicopter to illuminate the scene proved unwittingly to be a window to the truth. When two officers strode up to the car, one on each side, and ordered all the occupants out, Rodney King was frightened, unsure why he had been followed, and scared of being sent back to jail. All he knew for sure was that he was an unarmed black man surrounded by what appeared to be a battalion of white policemen. That reality alone was sufficient to make his heart pump faster, his palms sweat, and his knees feel weak. It was after midnight, exactly 12:50 A.M., early on the morning of March 3, when King finally pulled over to stop. What were these policemen planning to do to him and his friends when they stepped from the safety of the car onto the shoulder of the dark and uncrowded freeway?

Again, they were ordered to exit the car slowly, with their hands above their heads. Rodney King, his anxiety mounting, reached back into the recesses of his unconscious and came out of the car mugging and dancing a little jig. He had put on the blackface mask, the smiling and shuffling defense used by blacks since slavery days to distract and disarm the dangerous white folks. But it didn't seem to work this time—the officers were cursing and seemed very angry at him, but his brain was clouded by alcohol and paralyzed by fear, so he could only react by trying to defend himself as they began to use their nightsticks, raining blows on his body from every direction.

VIDEOTAPING THE VIOLENCE

As the confrontation got noisier and the helicopter lights seemed to get brighter, a crowd of people gathered near the fence separating the apartment buildings from the freeway. One of the people in this crowd was George Holliday, the thirty-three-year-old white manager of a plumbing company, who, awakened by loud sirens, had grabbed his new video camera and had quickly and eagerly begun taking pictures of the unfolding drama.

What Holliday saw through the lens of his video camera was a large black male, surrounded by a cordon of police officers who had pushed him down to the ground; while one officer shot darts from a taser gun to stun him, three others used their batons to beat him all over his body and their feet to kick him and stomp him. They shot him with an electronic harpoon and then dragged him around the ground by the long wires and hogtied him like a steer, all the while cursing him and shouting racial epithets.

In the eighty-one-second video, King can be seen getting up on his hands and knees at least twice, covering his face to ward off the blows, and trying to escape from the brutal assault. The unerring eye of the camera also records a group of police officers standing around the perimeter, watching the beating but not attempting to intervene to stop it, just as if they were spectators in the Roman amphitheater when they fed the Christians to the lions. This was just another blood sport.

What the camera could not see was the whereabouts of King's two companions, who had stepped out of the car on the passenger side. Helms and Allen were immobilized with fear; "Pooh" Allen really believed that the police were going to lynch them. They were both stretched out prone on the ground, lying there under the orders of two watchful policemen; they both listened in abject silence to the blows of the police and the painful cries of their friend. But George Holliday, the amateur videographer, had managed to capture for the first time on film an unprovoked assault on a defenseless black man—a virtual lynching in full view of a public crowd, an unprecedented record of violence and victimization in late-twentieth-century America. The police had been accused of unprovoked and unjustified assaults against black males since Africans first set foot on American soil in 1619, but an actual beating had never been documented on film. The charges of police brutality against blacks had nearly always been denied by the police, disbelieved by the public, and dismissed by the courts.

> It's nothing new to have a police officer beat up a black man, but this is just the first time they got caught beating on somebody on TV. It was very unethical, you know, a bunch of white policemen beating this one black guy. . . . And it was unjustified.
>
> H. R., focus group member, Youth Intervention Alternative School, Los Angeles

---

When the videotape is played in slow motion, one can count fifty-six blows and six kicks inflicted by the police on Rodney King's body in eighty-one seconds. But even after he was finally subdued, handcuffed, and unceremoniously dragged on his stomach to wait for the ambulance, the four officers stood around making jokes about their assault. En route to the Foothill Station, Sgt. Stacey Koon sent a cryptic message to the watch commander:

> "U [patrol unit] just had a big time use of force—tased and beat the suspect of CHP pursuit, Big Time." The commander responded in kind, "Oh well, I'm sure the lizard didn't deserve it—Ha, Ha—I'll let them know, OK."

Even when they finally took King to Pacifica Hospital of the Valley, as they deposited him at the emergency room, a nurse overheard one of the officers taunting King that they had really "hit a home run tonight"—apparently using his head as the ball.

When Rodney King was finally examined by a team of five doctors in the emergency room of the hospital, they found that he had sustained the following injuries: a fractured eye socket, a broken cheekbone, a broken leg, facial nerve damage, a severe concussion, bruises all over his body, and burns from the taser stun gun.

Dr. Edmund Chein, one of the examining physicians, said that the force of the blows had broken King's skull in eleven places and knocked out several fillings in his teeth. Dr. Chein and his colleagues, shocked by the ferocity of the attack, predicted that King would probably never fully recover. Despite the severity of his injuries, the emergency room doctors used only twenty stitches to patch up his most obvious wounds before he was transferred to the Los Angeles County–University of Southern California Medical Center jail ward.

About five hours after King's arrest, tests of his blood and urine samples indicated a blood alcohol level of 0.075 percent, suggesting that he had probably been legally intoxicated, defined in California as having a level of 0.08 percent or above, at the time of his arrest. However, drug tests revealed only slight traces of marijuana and no traces of PCP or any other illicit drug. The surgeons did not operate on Rodney King to repair his eye socket and his multiple broken bones until March 14, eleven days after the brutal beating.

The police had no compunction about booking King for evading arrest, even before he could receive adequate medical attention. He was held in jail for four days, but prosecutors finally released him on March 6, claiming that they did not have sufficient evidence to prosecute him but refusing to comment on the public uproar over his beating and subsequent arrest.

But through all his long ordeal, through all the blows, the kicks, the racial slurs, and the incarceration, Rodney King remembered what his late father had always told him: "Don't be weak. Never show pain. Take your punishment like a man."

AFTERMATH OF THE ASSAULT

On Monday, March 4, the day after the beating, George Holliday called the Foothill Police Station to make a report about the officers who had assaulted Rodney King. Holliday was politely informed that his call would be logged, but he soon realized that the desk officer did not seem very interested in or concerned about his eyewitness account of the police beating of a black man on the Foothill Freeway.

Paul King, Rodney's brother, had gone in person on Monday morning to the Foothill Station to lodge a formal complaint about the police brutality against his brother. After being treated in a rude and threatening manner by a police sergeant, Paul King left the station feeling intimidated and frustrated in his attempt to file a formal complaint on his brother's behalf.

In a true bureaucratic brush-off, the sergeant told Paul King that the police would contact him if they received or needed any further information, but he did not fill out any complaint form for further action—that was the standard operating procedure in such cases of a citizen's complaint. Fortunately for Rodney King, George Holliday, the amateur videographer, decided to pursue justice on his own and arranged to give his tape to KTLA, one of the largest television stations in Los Angeles.

Sensing a big story, the station manager decided to play the tape on the evening news that Monday night. It was picked up by CNN-TV later that evening and beamed by satellite to stations around the globe. By the next morning, March 5, people eating breakfast in homes all over America had their attention riveted on the television news; some suddenly lost their appetite as they watched the Los Angeles cops rain dozens of blows and kicks on a helpless Rodney King. The videotape lasted only eighty-one seconds, but it seemed like an eternity.

THE PUBLIC RESPONSE

> We cannot express to you—it is impossible to command the words—the outrage we feel. We believe this is a pattern, not an aberration, a pattern of brutality by some but not all police officers against African-American males in particular.
>
> John W. Mack, president, Los Angeles Urban League

> Just as we saw the missiles over Baghdad or the murders in Tiananmen Square, so we saw the four police officers beating Rodney King. It was clear-cut: fifty-six times in eighty-one seconds. That's what the American people saw on videotape.
>
> Sen. Bill Bradley, D.-N.J., United States Senate

People reacted viscerally to the beating—the outrage was immediate, intense, and implacable. Politicians from George Bush, the Republican president, to Jesse Jackson, the Democratic civil rights leader, decried the obvious police violence against an unarmed civilian. Black people felt overwhelmed by rage and disbelief that this beating could still happen in America in 1991, fully 128 years after Lincoln's Emancipation Proclamation freed the slaves. Whites felt anger and guilt that their own symbols of law and order could violate this black man's basic humanity. Women wept and hugged their children with an instinctive urge to shield them from this ugly sight. Old men turned away in shame from the painful exposure to the racism passed on by their generation to their children and grandchildren. It was a defining moment in the nation's consciousness—a moment of truth about race and class in America, a glimpse into the dark abyss of the human spirit, stunted by ignorance and diminished by hatred.

One of those who watched the video with a special intensity was Daryl Gates, chief of the Los Angeles Police Department. He initially reacted like the rest of the public by admitting that he had been shocked and felt "sick to his stomach" when he looked at it. Within days, after he realized the implications of this taped beating for him and his vaunted police force, he assumed a more defensive posture, disclaiming these officers as rogue cops and assuring the world, especially the citizens of Los Angeles, that the Los Angeles Police Department was still the most professional, best-trained, and best-behaved police force in America.

But even Daryl Gates, the master of media manipulation, could not quell the rising tide of protest and the insistent demand for an investigation into this police violence. The civil rights organizations and the public demanded accountability for the first time from Chief Gates, and he could not hide behind the mayor or the police commission or the city council. The ugly secret of the Los Angeles Police Department had finally been exposed for the world to see, and Daryl Gates knew his job was on the line. Even the *Los Angeles Times* and his conservative supporters were asking for answers and questioning his leadership of the LAPD.

Ira Reiner, the district attorney, sensing an opportunity to make political points from the continuing clamor for an investigation, quickly upstaged Chief Gates and announced that his office would investigate the beating. Less than two weeks after the incident, Reiner convened a grand jury, which determined on March 15, 1991, that there was sufficient evidence to bring an indictment against the four officers for unlawful assault and use of excessive force in the beating of Rodney King.

THE POLICE RESPONSE

By the time the grand jury had indicted the four officers, the Los Angeles Police Protective League, the department's police union, was mounting a counteroffensive to build support for the four officers who had been targeted for investigation—Sgt. Stacey Koon and Officers Laurence Powell, Ted Briseno, and Timothy Wind, a rookie still on probation. Naturally, the union insisted that Koon and his subordinates were merely doing their job to subdue an unruly suspect and, moreover, were entitled to due process and the presumption of innocence before the public judged them and before the chief imposed any disciplinary action on them. Union leaders issued the classic American appeal to justice for the accused, the moving mantra about "the presumption of innocence"—but where were these hallowed concepts when their fellow officers were battering Rodney King? Whatever happened to his right to be presumed innocent and to be treated with dignity and justice?

Less than two months after the four officers were indicted, the Los Angeles County grand jury, after hearing five days of testimony from only five of the police officers who witnessed the beating and two who were not even present, declined to indict any of the other seventeen officers who stood by and simply watched while Rodney King was assaulted by four of their colleagues in law enforcement. At a press conference on May 10, 1991, Reiner asserted: "However morally wrong their failure to intercede, in California law there is no criminal statute under which these officers can be indicted. . . . No matter how reprehensible their action or their inaction, no [persons] can be charged with a crime unless they have violated a statute."

Although Reiner refused to respond to any questions from the press, the community promptly responded to his announcement with outrage. Ramona Ripston, the executive director of the Southern California chapter of the American Civil Liberties Union, summed up the anger and dismay of many law-abiding citizens: "I think it sends a wrong message to law enforcement personnel throughout Los Angeles, that there is no obligation to turn in law enforcement officers who abuse people. If citizens stand by and see a crime being committed, they are expected to report it. How can we expect less of our police officers?"

The four officers hired lawyers to defend themselves even as the grand jury was still investigating the "Rodney King incident," as it came to be called in the press. After they were indicted, as expected by everyone except the LAPD, their lawyers launched a vigorous offensive to have the trial moved out of Los Angeles to another city, citing prejudicial pretrial publicity. On July 23, 1991, the Second District Court of Appeal sided with the defense and ordered a change of venue; Judge Stanley Weisberg of the Los Angeles Superior Court, just a week after being assigned to the case, made the inexplicable decision to transfer the trial to Simi Valley, a predominantly white suburb of Los Angeles.

> The California appellate court that ordered the change of venue in the King case, . . . in a passage both tragic and ironic, noted that riots had been predicted if venue were changed and the officers acquitted. But, as the court pointed out, it would be impermissible to abridge defendants' rights to a fair trial on the basis of predictions of violence.
>
> Barry Scheck, professor of law, Benjamin N. Cardozo School of Law, Yeshiva University, New York City

---

The lawyers for the defendants were absolutely delighted with the choice of Simi Valley as the site of the trial, but the district attorney and his team of prosecutors were not overly concerned. They were not even troubled by the prior decision of the same appellate court to remove Judge Bernard Kamins, the original jurist assigned to the case, because he had "created the appearance of bias" by engaging in ex parte communication with the district attorney's office over the change of venue. This time the prosecutors were very confident that the dramatic videotaped evidence, the severe injuries inflicted on the victim, and the numerous eyewitnesses to the assault would make an airtight case and bring them an easy conviction in any courtroom in the country.

The decision not to appeal the appellate court's decision was the prosecution team's first and most fateful mistake. How strongly they miscalculated the merits of their case and how seriously they underestimated the defense's strategic manipulation of the "evidence" turned out to be a strikeout for disaster—for the victim, Rodney King; for the morale of the black community; and for the future of the judicial system in Los Angeles.

3

The Color of Justice, I

The Trial, the Victim, the Verdict

> Our justice system has never been fair to the black community in an overall sense. . . . That's exactly the reason why the trial was moved out to Simi Valley, just to get a favorable verdict for those white officers. If they had taken the trial to Compton, it would have probably been a different story. So it does depend on where you are and who you are. Justice in this city is not blind.
>
> Rev. Eugene Marzette, interim pastor, Trinity Baptist Church, Los Angeles

Simi Valley is a bedroom community, located thirty-five miles northwest of downtown Los Angeles in Ventura County. A pretty suburban Southern California town, its 1990 population of 101,000 people is predominantly white, middle-class, and native-born. It is the home of the Ronald Reagan Presidential Library, situated on a hill overlooking the city.

What also makes Simi Valley unique in the area is its high proportion of citizens who are active or retired police officers, firefighters, and their relatives. Simi Valley has a well-earned local reputation as a bastion of law and order, family values, and conservative political views. And in February 1992, Simi Valley was on the brink of national and international fame as the site of *The People* v. *Powell et al.*, the trial in the matter of the beating of Rodney King, a black working-class male from Altadena, just on the other side of Los Angeles, but a world away from Simi Valley, with its suburban shopping malls and a population less than 2 percent black.

The first order of business in a trial, after the lawyers for opposing sides have disposed of all the legal preliminaries, is to select a jury. Despite valiant attempts to empanel a jury pool with a substantial percentage of nonwhites, the potential jurors represented the population of the surrounding communities in Ventura County, less than 33 percent nonwhite. Judge Weisberg chose to invoke Proposition 115, the California law that allows the judge the exclusive right to question all the prospective jurors in a trial. Thus neither the prosecution nor the defense was able to exclude any jurors on the basis of prejudice toward the defendant. This was the second major break for the defense. The twelve jurors—ten whites, one Filipina woman, and one Hispanic woman—were finally selected. The sex ratio was equal—six women and six men, prosperous-looking and comfortable in their suburban lifestyle, eager to fulfill their civic duty. This was a jury that fairly reflected the population of Simi Valley, but it was *not* a jury of Rodney King's peers.

Ira Reiner, the district attorney for Los Angeles County, felt confident that his office had an airtight case against the four police officers, particularly after the grand jury indicted them for the assault. So confident were the prosecution lawyers that they didn't even think it was necessary to put Rodney King on the stand. He was just the victim and not a particularly sympathetic figure to this Simi Valley jury. They did not think he would be a "good witness" and did not want to expose him to cross-examination. This one decision may have cost them their case.

The defendants chose their lawyers with care, clearly understanding that this case involved larger issues than the beating of one unremarkable black man. They understood that the Los Angeles Police Department would be on trial, not just for the beating of Rodney King, but for all the beatings that had preceded it.

The four police defendants looked like choirboys as the trial commenced in the first week of February. They could easily have reminded the jurors of their spouses, sons, brothers, nephews, and next-door neighbors. There was Stacey Koon, age forty, the sergeant who looked like a balding Marine drill instructor. There was Laurence Powell, age twenty-eight, the pudgy-faced baton wielder who resembled an overgrown teddy bear. There was Theodore Briseno, age thirty-eight, the tall, angular Mediterranean type with a dashing mustache. And there was Timothy Wind, age thirty, the baby-faced boy next door, a recent graduate of the police academy. It was easy for the jurors to identify with these four white policemen, but how would they find a common bond with Rodney King, the black victim in this case?

THE CASE FOR THE PROSECUTION

> Maybe the prosecutor overestimated the power of the videotape and underestimated the difficulties involved in convicting police officers generally. Whatever they were thinking, it was a mistake.
>
> Barry Scheck, professor of law, Benjamin N. Cardozo School of Law, Yeshiva University, New York City

---

> The pluses of putting Rodney King on the stand would be to try and humanize the case. . . . They could have made him like the victim that he is; those guys beat him up—and maybe there'll be a little sympathy for Rodney King.
>
> Johnnie Cochran, defense lawyer, Los Angeles

Terry White, the lead prosecutor, and Alan Yochelson, his co-prosecutor, presented their case carefully and made a compelling argument for sustaining the charge of excessive force against the police officers. After all, the prosecution had the Holliday videotape, which provided incontrovertible evidence that these four defendants had assaulted a defenseless man "under color of law," had wantonly abused the power of their positions, and had willfully betrayed the public trust. As far as the prosecutors were concerned, this was an open-and-shut case, and they expected a speedy verdict of conviction on all counts of use of excessive force.

The eighty-one-second videotape, which seemed so clear and so powerful the day after the beating, had lost some of its punch by the time the trial began. It had been played repeatedly on local and national television; the images were ingrained in the national consciousness, the afterimages imprinted in the dim recesses of human memory. But for many it had become too familiar, too ordinary—it had lost the power to shock, to sicken, to outrage. The brutality had become commonplace, codified, even comprehensible.

The prosecution's case was brief, straightforward, and streamlined. The prosecutors made a tactical decision not to place Rodney King on the stand but to let the videotape speak for him. In their calculations, King was a convicted felon, unemployed and not personally impressive. He had tested positive for alcohol and marijuana after his arrest, so he would be a vulnerable witness. They would clean him up, dress him up, and take him to court daily to bear silent witness to his horrific injuries. Of course the jury would feel sympathy for him and would redress the injustice against him! Clad in their mantle of righteousness, the prosecution proceeded on a collision course with the defense, which had a very different interpretation of the events in the early hours of March 3, 1991, on the Foothill Freeway northeast of Los Angeles.

It took the prosecutors only twenty-nine days of testimony and a total of six witnesses to present their case. They called the arresting officers from the California Highway Patrol, one of the passengers in King's car, and George Holliday, the amateur videographer. They did not put Rodney King on the stand, so the jury did not have any opportunity to see him as a human being who had been unjustly assaulted or to establish any empathy for him as the victim in this case. This was only one of several major miscalculations by the prosecution team, who also inexplicably did not present testimony from any of Holliday's thirty neighbors who had witnessed the beating that night. They were counting on the videotape to do their job for them; they didn't anticipate that the defense would take their strongest piece of evidence and turn it against the victim.

THE MISSING WITNESS

> It is always difficult to convict a cop, especially in the suburbs. . . . The prosecutor found out that in Simi Valley, at least, there is no such thing as a smoking gun.
>
> Marcia Chambers, legal columnist, May 1992

As the lead prosecutor, Terry White, young, ambitious, and black, must have made a tactical decision to downplay the race issue in his case, especially since he knew that white juries are generally reluctant to convict policemen and even more reluctant when the complainants are black. White was also aware that his race could be a liability, but he decided not to ask to be removed from the case. It was his first high-profile case, and he was determined to win it.

White had obtained one piece of very damning evidence in Laurence Powell's own words. Shortly before Powell wielded his baton on Rodney King, he was dispatched to investigate an incident of domestic violence in a black family, prompting him to send a computer message to colleagues in another patrol car that he had been dealing with "gorillas in the mist." Somehow the jury didn't seem either surprised or shocked by the obviously racist animal analogy. This jury believed in the integrity of the police and had faith that the police would do the right thing.

Without putting King on the stand, the prosecutors also failed to document his multiple physical injuries, to dramatize his vulnerability, and to capitalize on the sensibilities of the female jurors. The defense lawyers were quick to exploit this oversight by minimizing the injuries, attributing them to King's fall on the pavement, and flatly contradicting the medical evidence of severe traumas to

Rodney King's body, inflicted most certainly by the four police officer defendants.

Rodney King, the victim, had no voice in the trial of his victimizers. He was not allowed to describe his feelings as he lay on the ground, surrounded by a cordon of policemen, beaten into submission like an animal. Nor was King allowed to confront his tormentors, to express his anger, to achieve catharsis. To the police, he was a symbol of the aggressive black thug who had to be whipped, as in the days of slavery, for challenging the authority of the white police officers. To the prosecutors, he was a symbol of the feared black stud who had to be constrained from threatening the social order of the Simi Valley courtroom. To the black community, Rodney King was a symbol of over 350 years of mistreatment of black males in the criminal justice system, a system that stripped him of his dignity, violated his basic human rights, and then denied him a legitimate voice to protest his own treatment.

THE CASE FOR THE DEFENSE

> I thought it was clear from the tape that a reasonable person could surmise that officers used excessive force. It was clear in my judgment that the situation was out of control. . . . But I think one of the things that came out of this trial is the clear fact that there's a lot of misunderstanding between being inappropriate, out of policy, and illegal. And those are the lines that people dealt with. You may not have liked it, but was it illegal? It may not have been what we taught, but was it illegal?
>
> Bernard C. Parks, assistant chief,
> Los Angeles Police Department

The four police officers had each hired a defense lawyer, but by the time the trial began, their united front had cracked. Theodore Briseno, who had been suspended without pay five years previously for using excessive force, was highly motivated to separate himself from his three codefendants. He would be the only one to admit that they were "out of control," the very image the prosecution valiantly tried to establish and the defense vigorously denied.

The major strategy of the defense was to put Rodney King on trial, to portray him as an aggressive, dangerous drunk who was a threat to the arresting officers. Judge Weisberg, who was under intense scrutiny to conduct a fair trial, ruled that the defense attorneys could not introduce any evidence of King's prior conviction or imprisonment. His ruling did not deter the defense lawyers from creating a distorted and disturbing image of King as the archetypal animal-like black monster with superhuman strength, an unmanageable brute who was a danger to the (white) community and therefore needed to be forcibly subdued.

First, the defense described the California Highway Patrol's high-speed chase of Rodney King as the pursuit of a drunk, drugged, and dangerous driver. The CHP arresting officers claimed that King was driving his car at excessive speeds up to 110 to 115 miles per hour. This was patently untrue, inasmuch as the manufacturer later claimed that King's aging Hyundai could not exceed ninety-five at its optimum performance. But as in so many significant details in this case, the prosecutors failed to refute this exaggeration, one of many fabrications the jury was led to believe.

Next the defense lawyers put a very different spin on Rodney King's behavior as he stepped out of his car. What appears on the videotape to be a minstrel-type shuffle and comic gestures to placate the police was interpreted by the lawyers as aggressive, threatening gestures intended to intimidate the police. The officers testified, in turn, that they thought King was high on "angel dust" (PCP) because he was acting so strangely and erratically. Believing that he was "dusted," they felt justified in trying forcibly to restrain him for fear that the drug had made him superaggressive and violent. Despite the fact that a toxicology report, completed soon after King's admission to the hospital after the beating, did not show any PCP in his blood, the prosecutors allowed that inference to go unchallenged, and, as they would later learn, this testimony would convince the jurors that the police were dealing with a human time bomb.

PORTRAYAL OF VICTIM AS VICTIMIZER

> In Southern California, we have one of the most determined and focused criminal justice systems in the United States. It is determined to maintain white supremacy, the white power structure. . . . What was it Rodney King represented? Just this black guy who might have done something wrong. But in plain view of everyone, he is beaten down and beaten upon by a horde of police officers, who have the power to kill. . . . Law enforcement officials in Southern California kill an awful lot of people . . . and it's almost always somebody black or brown.
>
> Dennis Schatzman, reporter, *Los Angeles Sentinel*

The defense attorneys had set up the first two prongs of their three-pronged defense strategy: they had portrayed Rodney King as a dangerous drunk driver, and they had strongly suggested that his erratic behavior was due to the potent effects of PCP, reinforcing his image as a danger to the community and a threat to law and order. The pump of racial prejudice had been primed, and now they had only to make one more push before that prejudice would flood the minds of this jury, pushing aside all rational thoughts and uprooting all their unconscious fears and fantasies about black men.

That third prong of the defense strategy was the videotape itself, the prosecution's own prime piece of evidence. In what would prove to be a masterstroke of creative lawyering (and manipulation of evidence), the defense lawyers played the videotape in slow motion, then froze it frame by frame to present their version of the police beating of Rodney King. With this frame-by-frame analysis, they were able to isolate and disconnect the blows of the police officers as active agents of aggression from the responses of Rodney King as the passive recipient of the assault.

> The defense attorneys . . . had frame-by-frame stills made of each video, which were mounted on clean white illustration board, and then used as the basis for questions to "experts" on prisoner restraint. . . . Once the video was broken up like this, each still picture could then be reweaved into a different narrative about the restraint of King, one in which each blow to King represented, not beating one of the "gorillas in the mist," but a police-approved technique of restraint complete with technical names for each baton strike (or "stroke").
>
> Kimberlé Crenshaw and Gary Peller, writers, 1993

By viewing the sequence of events in single frames, the defense team effectively decontextualized the violence and deconstructed the entire encounter between King and the police. The defense lawyers had disconnected the actors from the assault just as coolly and as carefully as a zookeeper would defang a rattlesnake. They had taken the poisonous sting out of the videotape and successfully transformed it into a benign record of the police subduing an unruly drunk driver.

As several experts on moving images have noted, a series of still photographs cannot adequately convey the actual dynamics and kinesthetic relationships among people and objects in a moving film, which fully captures the speed, the intensity, and the ferocity of an assault. In this instance, the defense pointed out frame after frame where Rodney King appeared to rise after he had been hit, claiming that he was still a threat to the officers. Frame by frame, they showed the police, with their batons at rest, waiting for King to assume a "compliant posture." Frame by frame, they manipulated the video by selecting images that distorted King's jerky movements to escape from the repeated blows and made them appear to be aggressive gestures toward the police. In one frame, King appeared to be lunging at the officers, but on the videotape this same motion looked like he was trying to deflect the blows.

Of course, the defense did not play the audio part of the tape, where the police could be heard in the background shouting obscenities and racial epithets at King. Some of the words were inaudible and some garbled, but King reluctantly admitted later, under the prompting of his lawyer, that the officers had frequently called him "nigger" and referred to his sexual organs while they were viciously attacking him. King must have truly felt panicky when he heard those racial and sexual epithets accompanying the blows, because he would be dimly aware that white vigilantes in the South were always obsessed with a black man's sexual organs when they lynched him. Were these cops beating him because he was a drunk driver, or were they trying to castrate him because he was a black man? For some inexplicable reason, the prosecution did not feel it was necessary or judicious to focus on the racial and sexual slurs that accompanied the kicks and blows. And that was another miscalculation.

USE OF FORCE: POWER SWINGS AND POWER STROKES

> Our policy [on use of force] is restricted in that we don't want people on the ragged edge. We want them, when they do something, to be clearly legal and within policy. If they violate the policy, they could still be firmly legal, but outside of our policy. So there are really different levels of review.
>
> Bernard C. Parks, assistant chief,
> Los Angeles Police Department

Sergeant Charles Duke, an instructor at the Los Angeles Police Academy, was an excellent witness for the defense as he demonstrated the appropriate "use of force" techniques with a baton. He showed the jury "power swings," "chops," and "strokes" with the heavy batons, all within permissible departmental guidelines to subdue a violent suspect. Along with Sgt. Stacey Koon, the commanding officer on that fateful night, Duke convinced the jury that all of these officers were simply following the correct procedures to neutralize the resistant King "with managed and controlled use of force." Somehow it all seemed perfectly rational and perfectly justified to these suburban dwellers who had left the city to get away from violence and to avoid contact with people like the defendant, Rodney King. The prosecution never called an independent expert to challenge the defense's definition of "excessive force."

The defense lawyers used terms like *command* and *confront*, intended to foster an identification between the former military types on the jury and the police officers. They cleverly manipulated the video images to reinforce the notion that Rodney King actually *controlled* the action—controlled it by refusing to submit to police authority, by trying to defend himself against the kicks and baton blows, by not assuming a prone position so that the police would feel that he was ready to give up. This was a brilliant piece of logic for the defense—redefining the assaulted as the assailant, the pursued as the pursuer, the victim as the victimizer.

To buttress their version of events, the defense lawyers capped their argument with a scathing denunciation of the prosecution's claim that Rodney King had suffered severe injuries as a result of the beating. As supporting evidence, one of the lawyers presented the jury a photo of King taken shortly after the beating, showing only some bruises on his body. How they managed to locate such an innocuous photo remains a mystery, but it clearly was taken from an angle that obscured the lacerations and the evidence of broken bones and internal injuries that left King permanently disabled, physically and psychologically damaged for life. Again, the prosecution ceded this point to the defense by not calling King to the stand to bear witness to his multiple wounds and to put a human face on the monster created by the defense.

THE SIMI VALLEY JURY: A SUBURBAN PERSPECTIVE

> I tried to put the jurors in the shoes of the police officers. We got the jurors to look at the case not from the eye of the camera, but from the eyes of the officers.
>
> Michael Stone, attorney for Laurence Powell

The defense lawyers had done their homework, and they understood what they had to do to win over this jury. They knew not only that this jury was predominantly white and middle-class but also that the jurors shared some other attributes with the four defendants. The majority of this jury (nine of the twelve) had served in the military or been employed in the defense industry. Five men had served in the Navy, and two of the women had been in the armed forces. There were over two thousand police families living in the Simi Valley area, and one of the jurors was the brother of a retired police sergeant. Three members of the jury were members of the National Rifle Association. This was a jury who would resonate to the themes of law and order, to protect and serve, to support the local police.

The members of this Simi Valley jury were willing, if not eager, to accept the defense's dubious claim that the injuries were not really serious and, further, that some of the bruises were the result of falling on the hard pavement rather than from the kicks and blows of the policemen. What does this say about the ability to suspend belief in what one's eyes perceive when one's mind is predisposed to see something else? Perhaps this ability to compartmentalize the actual facts from the defense's version of the incident explains how this jury could look at Officer Ted Briseno's booted foot on Rodney King's neck and accept his explanation that he was simply trying to keep King in a prone position so the other officers would stop beating him. Perhaps this ability to overlook the stark reality of the evidence leaping out from the videotape accounts for the jury's willingness to accept Officer Laurence Powell's claim that he was just trying to subdue an uncooperative suspect. Perhaps this tendency to deny the shocking events unfolding on the screen explains this jury's uncritical acceptance of Paul De Pasquale's defense of rookie officer Timothy Wind: "He dealt with the situation as it unfolded in accordance with his experience and training. His situation was one of fear and frustration, and not pleasure in inflicting injuries."

CLOSING ARGUMENTS

> The jury wanted to acquit, despite the fact that the evidence was very clear. They could not see putting those nice white policemen in jail.
>
> Jerome Skolnick, professor of law,
> University of California, Berkeley

In their closing arguments, the prosecutors relied too heavily on the videotape evidence, assuming that the jury could see quite clearly that the four police officers had used excessive force on Rodney King. They had not called King to present his side of the story, nor had they called any of the thirty civilian witnesses to give their version of the incident. They did not emphasize the racial overtones of the officers' language and behavior toward Rodney King until the closing argument, but then it appeared to be anticlimactic. Terry White, the lead prosecutor, displayed a chart listing over twenty "lies" in Laurence Powell's testimony, described the use of "excessive force" by the four police officers, and appealed to the jury to punish these vigilante cops. It was a workmanlike performance, polished and professional, but observers noted that the jury seemed impassive and unmoved by White's appeal to their reason and sense of fairness. The black prosecutor was confident that this predominantly white jury would deliver a just verdict based on the overwhelming evidence in this case, a verdict that would send a message to the LAPD that excessive force against black males would no longer be tolerated.

In their closing arguments, the defense lawyers played the race card as blatantly as they could without ever mentioning race. They used all the rhetoric at their disposal to remind these mainly white jurors of the "thin blue line" that separates law-abiding citizens from criminals, that separates "civilization from chaos," and, by inference, that separates middle-class suburbs from the inner-city jungle. Without shame or sympathy, they appealed to the fears and anxieties of these jurors of the ever-present threat of blacks invading their neighborhoods and destroying their way of life. They manipulated the myths and stereotypes of this jury about aggressive, violent black males who could wreak havoc on their safe suburban havens. These defense lawyers casually but cynically referred to Rodney King as "charging like a bull," a "bear," and even "a gorilla," with calculated intent to evoke in the jurors' minds frightening images of a threatening, dangerous animal.

They played on the prejudices of privileged conservative whites toward disadvantaged ghetto blacks. By the end of this trial, the defense lawyers had succeeded in transforming Rodney King, the nonviolent unemployed father of four, into Bigger Thomas, Malcolm X, and Willie Horton, all rolled up into one Bad Black Bogeyman. They had turned the tables and put Rodney King on trial for being a black man in the wrong place at the wrong time.

It would soon become clear that these jurors had perceived the evidence in the context of their own experiences in the world. They had processed the infamous videotape according to their own interactions with the police, which is the only way that they were able to make sense of what they saw and what they heard. Just as Rodney King's thoughts, feelings, and actions had been irrevocably shaped by his experiences as a black man in America, so too had these jurors' thoughts, feelings, and actions been shaped by their very different sets of experiences. They were all—the victim, the defendants, the jurors, and the judge—captives of their past racial history in the American society.

> King just continued to fight, so the police department had no alternative. He was obviously a dangerous person, [of] massive size and threatening actions—Mr. King was controlling the whole show with his actions. . . . They're policemen; they're not angels. They're out there to do a low-down, dirty job.
>
> Female juror, Simi Valley

THE VERDICTS

Finally, on April 29, 1992, after six weeks of testimony and six hours of deliberation, Dorothy Bailey, the jury foreperson, a prim, middle-aged white woman, handed the judge the verdicts. In Los Angeles, Police Chief Daryl Gates had put his force on alert just in case there was a protest over the verdict. Rev. Cecil L. Murray had invited black and other community leaders to assemble at his First African Methodist Episcopal Church to await the verdict. The news media had assembled teams of reporters from all over the world to report the verdict. People throughout the United States and abroad turned on their radios and television sets to hear that justice had been meted out on Rodney King's behalf.

The twelve Simi Valley jurors found that Officers Briseno, Koon, and Wind were *not guilty* on all counts. Only Officer Powell was found guilty of one count of excessive force against Rodney King in the early morning of March 3, 1991. The jurors had bought the case for the defense, wholeheartedly and without reasonable doubt. The verdicts were met with stunned disbelief. Some people cried, others screamed, and still others cursed the judgments of this jury. Commentators and talk show hosts quickly went into action, interviewing the experts, gauging the public's response, trying to make sense of these senseless verdicts.

While all the pundits were pontificating, the preachers praying, and the politicians posturing, the pent-up anger and rage of the black community was slowly building up, gathering steam—in the projects and the playgrounds, the barber shops and the pool halls, in the hangouts of the homeboys and the gangbangers—until it exploded late that afternoon at the corner of Florence and Normandie in South Central Los Angeles.

4

Days of Rage

No Justice, No Peace

> It was really a smoldering volcano that had been building and building. It's a manifestation of a whole lot of things—injustice in the criminal justice system, reaction to the rampant police brutality that is so blatant in our community, particularly in relation to young African-American males. It was an expression, an acting-out of the have-nots.
>
> John W. Mack, president, Los Angeles Urban League

For many black residents, there are two eras in Los Angeles: before the Rodney King riots and after the Rodney King riots. For black Angelenos, those four days of rage were a transforming experience, a revelation, a time for judgment.

If you ask people in South Central about when they heard the not-guilty verdicts in the trial of the four policemen, they can vividly recall exactly where they were, what they were doing, and how they reacted to the news. Their memories are frozen in a frame of disbelief and shock, evoking memories of similar feelings when people first heard the news about the assassinations of John F. Kennedy and Martin Luther King, Jr.—visceral feelings of loss and pain, grief and depression, anger and anxiety.

Two weeks before the verdict was expected, Rev. Cecil L. ("Chip") Murray, charismatic senior pastor of the First African

Methodist Episcopal Church (appropriately called FAME, considering its high profile in the black community and its many prominent members), had worked out a plan with other community leaders for people to meet at his church when the verdict was announced and keep the community calm regardless of the outcome. He recalls that moment:

> When the verdicts were announced, I was downstairs in the church looking at television with about two hundred others. When they came, I just found the tears flowing—I guess I just cried out of sixty-four years of utter frustration and hope. The whole world had seen the video from the very beginning—surely now we can use this as a model for justice in America. When, in spite of the evidence, they shocked the world bringing in "not guilty" verdicts, I think several of our people wept. Then we stood in a circle and had a word of prayer.

John W. Mack, president of the Los Angeles Urban League, was in attendance:

> We had all gathered at First AME Church, waiting for the verdicts. I was sitting right next to Reverend Murray when the verdicts were first announced. When we first heard the verdicts, we were stunned—we couldn't believe it. And we knew that once again, a black man had not received justice. It wasn't long after that someone called the mayor, who was up there on the platform with us, and told him that there was some kind of demonstration at Florence and Normandie.

T. W., a former gang member who now works as a counselor in a gang prevention program, remembers:

> I was at home getting ready to go to work, so I wasn't looking at the TV. My mom called and left a message on the answering

> machine for me and my brother not to leave the house. Then Pops called and left the same message, so I knew something was up. I turned on the TV and saw black folks crying and the four officers walking away from the courthouse. My first response was to grab my mother's Bible; then I sat down in a chair and kept looking at the TV. I held the Bible real tight and I just cried.

Late that afternoon, Rev. Kenneth Flowers was sitting in his small office at Messiah Baptist Church at the corner of West Adams and Forty-Fifth Street, watching a small television set and waiting for the verdicts to be announced with a policeman who had been sent "to protect him" in case any violence erupted in his neighborhood. His voice rises and he punctuates each phrase as he remembers:

> When the verdicts started coming down, one by one, I jumped up and stood with my mouth open. And then as each verdict came—Not guilty! Not guilty! Not guilty!—I sat down in this chair and the first thing I said was, "They're gonna burn this city down!"

While Rev. Murray and a cross section of the community's most visible leaders were trying to make sense of these incomprehensible verdicts, the blacks and Latinos—the masses of people of color in Los Angeles—were beginning to understand the full impact of these "not guilty" verdicts for four white police officers who had assaulted one unarmed black man.

DAYS OF RAGE, APRIL 29–MAY 3, 1992

> So many things led to that uprising. It wasn't just the Rodney King verdict but so many things built up over so many years. Day in and day out, you look at the hopelessness and how bad the system has treated African-Americans. Our youth have basically

> been written off America's agenda. People just felt they had been put down so long that they had to stand up.
>
> Duane B. Bremond, director of community relations, AIDS Project of Los Angeles

---

> The Rodney King incident was just one thing. Lots of brothers get jumped on by the police. . . . There's a lot of people who don't have no jobs and some got fired because of their being black and the racism. And there's a lot of people that can't get the right education in school because we can't get the right books or the right information. . . . So all those issues built up over so many years, and when Rodney King got jumped on by the people that's supposed to protect and serve, you feel there ain't no more protection or serving. That was like a match in a matchbook, but the whole book lit up then.
>
> Former gang leader, Los Angeles

The crowd at Florence and Normandie mushroomed quickly as the people in South Central rushed out of their small homes and apartments, some bewildered, some angry, all in a state of shock over the verdicts. Black and Latino, young and old, men and women, workers and welfare recipients, dropouts and dope dealers, born-again Christians and lost sheep, they milled around in the street trying to connect with one another, hoping to share their frustrations, wanting to vent their anger.

The flashpoint came at about 4:00 P.M., after the crowd had thrown a few rocks and bottles, broken windows in the liquor store on the corner, and cursed helplessly at each other, at passing cars, at the heavens above. Drivers in passing cars, sensing the danger, ducked as they tried to drive through the intersection, hoping that they could navigate the narrow passageways, which expanded and contracted as the crowd surged forward and fell back in no predictable pattern or rhythm. Reginald Denny, a white truck driver en route to warn a black friend about the rumors of impending violence, was caught at a red light, pulled from his truck, and viciously attacked by three or four young black men simply because of his skin color.

As the television cameras recorded the assault, millions of Americans were transfixed in front of their television screens, repulsed by the violence yet somehow fascinated by this primeval scene of vengeance. Many blacks who had watched the tapes of the four policemen roping Rodney King like a bull and kicking him like a dog consciously condemned this unprovoked assault on Reginald Denny. Yet they too were able to empathize with the anger of those young black men whose lives, like Rodney King's, were unfocused and unfulfilled, who were themselves unwilling victims of police harassment, unable to articulate their frustrations or control their rage against the unfortunate symbol of a society that had blatantly denied justice to one of their brothers.

> The Reginald Denny beating caught my attention. I was very shocked and surprised at that. But everyone was so stunned when they heard the verdicts. It was easy for me to understand the protest, the sense of outrage.
>
> Gayle Pollard Terry, journalist, *Los Angeles Times*

> I only live four blocks away from Florence and Normandie, so when I saw them pulling that truck driver out and beating him, I started to run down there and try to save him. But my wife held me back because she didn't want me to get hurt. So we just held on to each other and looked at the terrible things on TV.
>
> D. N., salesman, Los Angeles

> Those guys were wrong to beat that truck driver like that. He just happened to be in the wrong place at the wrong time. I guess people were mad at all whites and they just took it out on Denny.

It's too bad they couldn't have grabbed those white cops and given them a taste of their own medicine.

C. C., youth member
Weingart Urban YMCA, Los Angeles

Reginald Denny was not the only victim at Florence and Normandie on the evening of April 29. The crowd vented its rage on several other whites, Latinos, and Asians who were unlucky enough to be walking or driving in that vicinity. This corner was the flashpoint, but it was only the beginning of the violence and conflagration that consumed South Central Los Angeles for four days and four nights until the National Guard finally reestablished order on the evening of May 3. It was only the beginning of the looting, the vandalism, and the burning that spread from South Central to East Los Angeles, from mid-Wilshire to West Los Angeles, from Koreatown to downtown, until few neighborhoods in the central parts of the city were completely spared. To some, it signaled the beginning of the end of the dream of Los Angeles; to others, it presaged the betrayal of the promise of the City of the Angels.

MOTIVES

It was the explosion of a dream. Langston Hughes asks, "What happens to a dream deferred? Does it dry up like a raisin in the sun? . . . Or does it explode?" That [riot] was the explosion of frustrated hopes. That was the explosion of delayed justice. That was the explosion of anxiety with no outlet."

Rev. Cecil L. Murray, senior pastor, First African
Methodist Episcopal Church, Los Angeles

Black Angelenos will quickly and emphatically tell you that the Rodney King verdict did not cause the riots—it was just the straw that broke the camel's back for the community. That straw topped an accumulation of bad debts, economic grievances, political injustices, and broken promises, festering through decades of neglect, swept under mounds of unrecycled garbage, and decomposing beneath the decaying projects, the drug-infested neighborhoods, the abandoned factories, and—most of all—the years of police brutality and unjust treatment in the criminal justice system.

People's voices are urgent and angry when they speak about the joblessness, the high rates of unemployment, and the "culture of dependency" in South Central.

> There's no resources in this community. No jobs for black youth. The white man is not going to create any jobs for us in the inner city. They create jobs for themselves. How are we going to tell young people to stop selling drugs if we ain't got no resources to offer them?
>
> N. D., former gang member

> There's so many underlying economic problems and so much extreme poverty, especially when you contrast the pool of affluent people in L.A. with people in minimum-wage jobs, caught in the trap of pervasive poverty. And the unemployment situation is complicated by legal and illegal immigration. Employers would rather hire Latinos.
>
> Joycelyn M. Crumpton, social worker,
> Center on Child Welfare, UCLA

Their voices are strident and passionate when they talk about the poor schools, the high rates of dropouts and failure, and the "culture of mediocrity" in South Central.

> There's a lack of education in the community—poor schools, poor teachers. Who wants to go to these schools? The schools have fences in South Central, but not out in the suburbs.
>
> L. F., high school teacher, Los Angeles

These schools ain't worth a damn. The teachers don't care about teachin' you nothin', so your classes are boring. There's never enough books or supplies, so you can't do your homework. You never know if somebody's going to pull a gun on you, so you feel scared all the time. It's a wonder more kids don't drop out.

V. O., high school dropout, Los Angeles

Their voices are full of pain and despair when they talk about the black-on-black crime and the drugs, the black teenagers carrying guns and killing each other, the police brutality, and the "culture of violence" in South Central.

You have black people being killed every day over little things—drive-by shootings and other things. Think about how many kids are killed every day and how many innocent people have lost their lives. But they don't put that on the news—they don't talk about that or make a big deal about it on TV. When a cat gets caught up in a tree and some fireman rescues it, that's news. But when a black child is killed, nobody cares. You don't see that on TV.

K. J., youth member, Weingart
Urban YMCA, Los Angeles

Gang violence has increased people's sense of danger and sense of feeling insecure. It keeps everyone on edge all the time. Random violence makes people afraid. There are so many pent-up emotions and so much hostility in and out of the community.

Joycelyn M. Crumpton, social worker,
Center on Child Welfare, UCLA

These young black males under thirty are those selling drugs, but it's a survival issue. Not that many use drugs, but they can't get jobs, so they get involved in the drug trade. Some of these gangs

> generate revenue through selling drugs, then use the profits from the drug sales to buy guns.
>
> L. B., probation officer, Los Angeles

Their voices are full of frustration and resignation when they speak about the lack of medical services, the unhealthy lifestyles of black youth, children having children, the AIDS epidemic, and the "culture of hopelessness" in South Central.

> The black community doesn't have adequate health care, not enough health services, no outreach services. People have to take the bus to get to Drew Medical Center.
>
> S. T., community college instructor, Los Angeles

> Nobody listens. Nobody is doing strategic planning for our communities. Because they didn't take care of it ten years ago, . . . ten years from now there's going to be a whole set of new problems. Yes, there's unemployment. Yes, there's police brutality. But you know, the bottom line is the sense of hopelessness, the stereotypes, and the prejudicial actions that have been going on since that first slave boat came across the ocean.
>
> Sandra Bankhead, community activist, Los Angeles

The anger, frustration, and hopelessness of blacks in South Central all seemed to coalesce in March 1991 when the wife of a Korean grocer shot a black teenager in the back after a brief struggle over a bottle of orange juice. The teenager's name was Latasha Harlins; her murder and her memory would unify the African-American community in its antipathy toward Korean shopkeepers and galvanize the community against the criminal justice system in Los Angeles.

THE LEGACY OF LATASHA

> Latasha Harlins was killed and nothing happened—they let the woman go free, community service. It was just a slap in the face of African-Americans in terms of devaluing the lives of our people. And it's a known fact that black people go to jail every day in Los Angeles for less. They get more time for less. And this woman got no time. It still is something that leaves a bad taste in everybody's mouth.
>
> Donzella P. Lee, vice president, administrator,
> Watts Health Foundation, Inc., Los Angeles

If there were one consistent and unanimous source of anger in the black community shortly after the beating of Rodney King, it was surely the killing of Latasha Harlins, a fifteen-year-old black high school student, fatally shot in the back by Soon Ja Du, who was tending the counter at the Empire Liquor Market, the family grocery store, on Saturday, March 16, 1991, a sunny spring morning.

The facts of the incident are not in dispute. A security videotape shows Latasha, a typical-looking teenager in casual clothes wearing a backpack, approaching the counter, presumably to purchase a bottle of orange juice visibly protruding from her backpack. There is some confusion as Latasha attempts to pay for the bottle of juice. Du confronts her and apparently accuses her of stealing the juice. They engage in a brief pushing match; then Latasha angrily turns around to return the juice. Du takes out a gun and shoots her in the back. In horror, we see this vital black girl on the brink of womanhood fall to the floor and slowly bleed to death over a $1.79 bottle of orange juice.

The killing of Latasha Harlins lit the spark of smoldering tensions in the black community toward Korean merchants and their treatment of black customers. But in November 1991, this spark grew into an unquenchable flame after the trial for Du, whose guilty verdict was vitiated by the lenient sentence of probation, meted out by Judge Joyce A. Karlin, a white female Superior Court jurist. Months of angry protest by aggrieved members and leaders of the black community brought no justice from the judicial system, no response from the business community, no empowerment from the political system. Over and over again, they complained, "No justice, no peace."

You can hear the legacy of Latasha's killing, considered by most blacks a cold-blooded murder, in the pained and angry voices of the community, both young and old.

> The media played the videotape of the Latasha Harlins killing hundreds of times, over and over again. It was like brainwashing. How much can you take of seeing a young child being shot in the back on TV? It was an atrocity. You start putting yourself in that person's place—being killed over some orange juice. Some Korean merchants come into our neighborhoods and don't show us any respect and then, on top of that, they're going to kill one of our babies?
>
> Sandra Bankhead, community activist, Los Angeles

> I personally felt that justice was not served in the Latasha Harlins case. You could see that Latasha was planning to pay for that juice, and she put it back on the counter when that Korean lady grabbed her. [That woman] had no right to just take a life that way. That was brutal. That was coldhearted. Then the woman got nothing more than a slap on the wrist. Just a few weeks before that, a white man who abused his dog was sentenced to six months in jail. That sent a message to the community that a dog's life was worth more than the life of a black girl.
>
> K. J., youth member, Weingart
> Urban YMCA, Los Angeles

The intense anger and frustration over the injustice in the Latasha Harlins killing exploded into violence after the virtual exoneration of the four white policemen in the brutal beating of Rodney King. But this was certainly not the first beating of a black man by the police in Southern California, and it was not the first time a video camera had captured apparent excessive force by police officers against an unarmed black male. Blacks in Los Angeles could still vividly recall Donald Jackson, the young handsome off-duty policeman who in 1989 had been thrown through a plate glass window by Long Beach police, enraged as he followed them around with his camera to document their harassment of black youth in that city.

Despite the videotape and eyewitnesses, the police officers convinced a predominantly white Long Beach jury that Jackson had thrown himself through the window simply to gain publicity and support for his campaign to discredit the Long Beach police force. The jury found those officers innocent of assaulting Jackson, even though most viewers of the widely publicized tape (in which the police were off-camera) did not share the jury's perception of the violent encounter.

The Los Angeles Police Department had a long and well-documented history of shooting unarmed blacks, but the officers involved were rarely indicted, tried, or punished in a court of law. Juries always seemed to accept their version of events, always seemed to find "reasonable cause" for these killings or assaults, always seemed to discount the testimony of eyewitnesses and the contradictory findings of coroners' reports, always supported the policies of deadly force by the boys in blue.

These random incidents of police brutality against blacks, the frequent humiliations and minor degradations of blacks by a myriad of merchants and gatekeepers in the community, the accelerating deterioration of the South Central area, and the growing tensions between blacks and the other ethnic minority groups—all of these factors exacerbated the tensions in the community and fueled the rapid spread of rage and violence after the verdicts were announced.

THE LABELING OF AN UPHEAVAL

Some people called what happened during those four days and four nights a riot. Some called it a rebellion. Some called it an uprising. By any label, it was a tremendous social upheaval, but the label applied to those events was like a Rorschach test, reflecting a person's political priorities, ideological beliefs, and personal values.

William Shearer, a prominent business leader and media executive who advocates a self-help philosophy and economic empowerment for blacks, called it a riot: "It was a riot, just a wanton destruction of property. We can't condone those actions by using a euphemism because it allows the victim mentality to continue in the black community."

For Dr. Kathy Sanders-Phillips, in the Department of Pediatrics at the Charles R. Drew Medical Center, faculty member at the U.C.L.A. School of Medicine, and committed community psychologist, it was a rebellion: "I'd call it a rebellion because 'riot' conveys a sense of chaos, but that wasn't what happened. I could predict which buildings would be burned down—the white-owned and Korean-owned businesses, the liquor stores, and the shops that had treated blacks badly."

John W. Mack, a prominent civil rights leader, agreed with this assessment: "It was initially a rebellion—an expression of rage, fury, anger, and shock over this grossly unjust and racist verdict. It was a spontaneous reaction. Expectations were so great and so high that I think it was a rebellion. It was a smoldering volcano that had been building up in reaction to rampant police brutality."

But for Professor Barbara Solomon, a noted black social work educator, it was not quite as clear-cut as using one unidimensional label. She suggests: "It was a riot or an uprising, not a rebellion. A rebellion is more organized with a clear target, but these riots reflected multiple agendas being expressed all over the city. They reflected enormous distress and depression in pockets of this city."

Those who called it an uprising eloquently defended their views, as articulated by Rev. Kenneth Flowers, pastor of Messiah

Baptist Church and one of the new generation of leaders in South Central:

> It was an uprising. . . . The term *riot* is defined as complete lawlessness and displaced anger for no apparent reason. What occurred in April and May . . . was triggered by the jury's verdict, but it was really built upon years and years of oppression. So just as there were slave revolts and slave uprisings when the slaves decided they couldn't take it any longer, I think African-Americans decided that we weren't gonna take it anymore.

Those who described it as "all of the above" offered the best analysis of what seemed to happen over that four-day period. The initial reaction seemed unplanned and unfocused, a primal scream of rage, erupting into dozens of scattered uprisings throughout South Central and downtown at Parker Center, the headquarters of the Los Angeles Police Department. Gangs began looting weapons stores, and by the second day, according to many observers, the predominantly black and Latino crowds in South Central appeared to be more organized and targeted grocery and discount stores. There was a general sense of the poor and dispossessed rebelling against those who had some wealth and visible possessions.

While the television cameras were zeroing in on the young men looting the liquor stores and stealing the television sets, low-income mothers were taking diapers and food for their children, teenagers were taking sneakers to wear to school, and couples were taking furniture for their apartments—items that they really needed but, on their limited incomes, were always beyond reach. By the third day, the media had spread the news and pinpointed the exact locations of all the areas that the police had essentially abandoned to the looters, so it became an equal-opportunity riot, joined in by whites and Asians, college students and yuppies, workers and welfare recipients, all hoping to get a piece of the action before the police restored order.

The mood of the crowds had rapidly shifted from rage to revenge to larceny. Watching the television images on the third day, I was struck by the carnival-like atmosphere, the camaraderie of the crowds as they ran in and out of stores, the casual comparison shopping of the looters as they flagrantly and—without a trace of remorse—broke the law.

THE PEOPLE QUAKE

By May 3, when the National Guard had been deployed and the riots were finally under control, Los Angeles had become a nightmare, a city in shambles, a city with no visible leadership, a city in shock. The riots had produced a "people quake," in the words of Dr. Alice Walker Duff, cofounder and executive director of Crystal Stairs, a resource center for low-income mothers and their children:

> It was a "people quake" because the decision in the King case was like a 7.0 shake of the foundation of this city—it revealed the underlying faults and the pressure building up in the system, which finally erupted in destruction and shaking the foundations. Very much like the earthquake—it shook our basic belief in our rights. It was a shock when we again realized that black people basically don't have rights that white people are bound to respect.

"People quake" probably best captures the essence of those four days and nights of rage in South Central Los Angeles. When the fires turned to ashes and the rage turned to resignation, South Central Los Angeles looked like the aftermath of a natural disaster. Large pockets of the community were destroyed, particularly in the commercial areas on Crenshaw Boulevard, Western Avenue, and Slauson Avenue, where one could see whole blocks of burned-out stores, offices, and markets.

It is easy to feel sympathy for the owner of the small corner grocery store that was looted and vandalized, simple to understand the anger of the restaurant owner whose newly renovated diner was gutted by fire, uncomplicated to relate to the people who lost their jobs when their grocery store chain closed its doors after looters cleaned out the shelves while the police stood by. But these individual tragedies were dwarfed by the magnitude of the community destruction, figures and facts that are much harder to conceptualize and to comprehend.

The insurance industry estimated that the riots caused nearly $1 billion in property damage and looting. Nearly 1,100 businesses were burned or destroyed, and 52 people were killed and over 2,500 injured as a direct result of the four days of violence. It was the fifth most costly disaster, natural or otherwise, in U.S. history. It was also a multiethnic equal-opportunity riot: 37 percent of those arrested for looting or vandalism were Latinos, 30 percent were black, and 33 percent were whites, Asians, and "others" who had joined in the mayhem.

In addition to the deaths and injuries of many innocent bystanders and the destruction of a significant number of the area's small businesses, hundreds of people were treated for physical injuries and psychological trauma for weeks and months after the riots. According to mental health professionals, scores of adults and children experienced the classic symptoms of posttraumatic stress: nightmares, frequent crying, headaches, anxiety, fearfulness, and loss of appetite. What could not be measured was the cost of human suffering, the cost of broken dreams, and—buried beneath all the devastation and destruction—the incalculable cost of racism.

Like the unpredictable earthquakes that wreak havoc in Southern California, this disaster exposed the raw tensions and frustrations that lie just below the surface of the community. It revealed the vulnerability of the city's poor and powerless. It uncovered the simmering conflicts among the people of color, all struggling and competing downstairs for the leftover crumbs from the kitchens upstairs. And it shattered the social contract between the people and their political leaders, between the people and the police, between the police and their powerful patrons in the white community.

CONSPIRACY THEORIES

> I was surprised to see how fast those fires spread. It seemed like an organized response because of the way certain businesses were hit—especially those owned by Koreans and Asians.
>
> Gayle Pollard Terry, journalist, *Los Angeles Times*

Black Angelenos were not surprised when the disturbances broke out at the corner of Florence and Normandie, nor were they surprised when the unrest escalated so quickly and spread throughout the black and Latino areas of the city. There had been rumors circulating for weeks that some of the gangs were going to organize a protest if the cops were acquitted, but most of the community leaders had discounted those rumors.

Still, months later, the rumors had achieved the status of an urban myth. Dozens of people, young and old, repeated their favorite version, unaware of the many inconsistencies and unmindful of their implications for the conspiracy theorists who feed on such rumors to fuel the endemic paranoia and volatile anger in the black community.

Versions of the conspiracy to incite the riots were creative and varied, ranging from blaming gang members, who wanted to create chaos for criminal gain, to community leaders, who wanted to inflame the community for political gain.

> There had been rumors around town that some of the gang leaders wanted to start a riot so they could use it for cover to steal some big-ticket items. A lot of people suspected that white jury in Simi Valley was going to let those cops walk, so the gang leaders were one step ahead of everyone else, figuring a way to make some profit out of the situation.
>
> H. M., junior college student, Los Angeles

> Some of these leaders in this town are paranoid about power. It's easy to believe the rumor that some of them actually got together and decided to fuel the anger of some of these street youth, just so they could then step in when things got out of hand and act like they were in control of the community. Unfortunately, once things got started, no one could stop them.
>
> W. A., small business owner, Los Angeles

No conspiracy to incite the rioting has ever been proved or even weakly substantiated, but there are nearly as many alternative explanations of the riots as there are blacks in South Central. Some who had survived the Watts riots in 1965 had the uncanny feeling of déjà vu. All felt the inevitability of these riots, all understood the rage of this community, and all shared the sense of anger and despair at justice denied.

THE COSTS OF RACISM

> There are the institutional forms of discrimination, racism and violence. One example would be the long-standing practice of redlining. Inferior quality of education for our youngsters is all too commonplace, but lack of jobs is also a severe problem. There's also the issue of substandard housing—all the things that make a community less desirable, such as the lack of recreational options, the lack of supermarkets, the proliferation of liquor stores. It is not merely coincidental that the backdrop of Florence Avenue and Normandie Avenue was a liquor store operating on April 29, 1992.
>
> Mark Ridley-Thomas, member,
> Los Angeles City Council

For many in the black community, youth and leaders alike, the underlying cause of the riots was racism. Whether they couched it in the precise language of academia or the slang of the streets, the youth and their elders were in striking agreement that the riots were an inevitable response to the decades of discrimination, poverty, joblessness, inadequate housing, lack of health care, and police brutality experienced by blacks in inner-city Los Angeles.

Racism was described in its many guises, but the chief complaints were a sense of powerlessness and hopelessness that had developed in response to the chronic economic deprivation, the persistent social and legal inequities, and the overwhelming sense of isolation of the black community, which was denied access to the benefits, resources, and privileges shared by white Americans as their birthright.

> We all felt fed up with the system. It was one of those things where the system ain't no good. It's like an old car—you give it a tune-up and a brake job and you do all you can, but some cars you just can't fix—you just gotta junk them. That's how I feel about this system—it needs to be junked. It was set up a long time ago by people who were racist. It's not set up to help minorities—it's set up to hurt minorities.
>
> B. B., former gang member

Sandra Bankhead, community activist and coordinator of a program for teenage parents, speaks forcefully on racism in Los Angeles:

> Black people are acutely aware of the mistreatment they receive. They can't hide who they are, and they don't want to, but they continue to suffer injustice—the painful reminder of slavery. Some [people] still want us to look down and shuffle our feet. No one can stand that anymore. No one's gonna let that happen anymore.

Dr. Reed Tuckson, president of Charles R. Drew University of Medicine and Science, articulates this view as a physician overwhelmed by the health needs of the black community:

> The chronic root of the riots was the pervasive sense of hopelessness, the sense that there was no possibility of a meaningful future. We're trying to deal with issues of poverty, unemployment, and an education that doesn't prepare folks to live in the twenty-first century; so they feel irrelevant to the future of this country. The issues of racism, the denigration of people, the self-hatred, as well as the hatred of others. And then, of course, the enormous tensions between the police department and young African-American men and the degree to which their perception of being stalked and harassed and singled out makes them view the police department as *just another gang that wears colors*.

BOULEVARD OF BROKEN DREAMS

A year after the upheaval in Los Angeles, on a sunny afternoon in August, I was driving through South Central to experience the mystique of the community and to view the ravages left by the rioters. After I had driven up and down the broad avenues named Vermont, Slauson, and Figueroa, I turned south on Crenshaw Boulevard. Crenshaw is one of the major arteries through South Central Los Angeles, a commercial strip that caters to the stable working- and middle-class community that surrounds it on the east and west. As one drives south on Crenshaw, the comfortable, well-kept homes of Leimert Park, one of the older black middle-class neighborhoods on its eastern boundary, are gradually supplanted by the more spacious and elegant homes of Baldwin Hills and View Park, preferred addresses of the upwardly mobile black professionals, the business executives, the show business celebrities, the star athletes, and the wanna-bes.

Turning around to return to my hotel and driving north on Crenshaw, I passed a virtual emporium of shops, churches, beauty parlors, boutiques, fast-food restaurants, and small businesses. Brightly painted shops with names like African Bazaar and Soul Sister's Boutique; churches called the Sweet Hour of Prayer Center, the King David Missionary Baptist Church, and the Bible Way Community Church; the Crenshaw Tot Academy and the Community Youth Sports and Arts Foundation—places that specialize in making the body beautiful, the mind enriched, and the soul satisfied. A mural farther down the street speaks in its own voice, depicting heroic scenes of the black struggle with slogans like "Knowledge is power," "Hope, not hate, will triumph," and "Dare to dream."

Then I noticed further down on Crenshaw, the graffiti-scarred, boarded-up buildings and the taped, shuttered windows, silent witnesses to the rage of the righteous. But life goes on around these mute buildings: people go in and out of the stores, and two women are hosing down the sidewalk in front of the Bible Way Community Church, preparing for Sunday service. Mothers push their babies in strollers, teenagers wait for the bus, and young men in baggy pants hang out with studied coolness in front of Church's Chicken fast-food restaurant.

Some people on Crenshaw Boulevard lost their businesses and put their dreams on hold. Others on the street are still struggling to turn their dreams into dollars. But what of those who never really learned to dream at all? Were they the ones who threw the rocks, looted the shelves, and lit the fires? Without dreams, were they also without voices to express their anger, their frustration, and their despair? Without dreams, were they also without hope, with no interest in the dreary present and no stake in the uncertain future?

Just after I passed the Crenshaw Faith Temple, the sun glinted on something white on the hills in the distance. It was the Hollywood sign, large white letters nestled in the distant olive-green hills overlooking South Central and Crenshaw Boulevard. As the sign came closer into focus, it seemed like a dramatic sentinel guarding the gates of the privileged. I thought about the irony of the black youth in South Central with their tattered and tarnished dreams, looking up daily at that sign, the ultimate symbol of the fantasies and dreams of millions of white Americans, those who believe in the myth that every American can become successful, make a million dollars, grow up to be a star.

But blacks in Los Angeles were still trying to realize their own American dream, still trying to connect to Martin Luther King's vision of that dream, still struggling to hold on to the promise.

As the sun vanished in the late-afternoon sky and the sign receded in the distance, I couldn't help but remember the lines from one of my favorite poems by the poet Langston Hughes:

> What happens to a dream deferred?
>   Does it dry up
>   like a raisin in the sun?
>   Or fester like a sore—
>   And then run?
>   Does it stink like rotten meat?
>   Or crust and sugar over—
>   like a syrupy sweet?
>   Maybe it just sags
>   like a heavy load,
>   Or does it explode?

5

Two Commissions and Three Trials

Community Conflict and Concepts of Justice

> The problem of excessive force is aggravated by racism and bias within the LAPD. . . . Witnesses repeatedly told of LAPD officers verbally harassing minorities, detaining African-American and Latino men who fit certain generalized descriptions of suspects, employing unnecessarily invasive or humiliating tactics in minority neighborhoods, and using excessive force.
>
> Report of the Independent Commission on the Los Angeles Police Department, 1991

On April 1, 1991, a month after the King beating and a year before the police officers' trial and the subsequent riots, in response to the public outrage, Mayor Tom Bradley established an independent commission to investigate the Los Angeles Police Department. Warren Christopher, the chairman of O'Melveny and Myers, one of the city's oldest and most prestigious law firms, was selected to head the commission, which included nine other respected and respectable members of the Los Angeles establishment. Christopher, who had been vice chair of the McCone Commission investigating the Watts riots in 1965, had also served in the Carter administration and had a reputation as a political moderate and a skillful negotiator. The mayor's commission was merged with the investigatory committee set up by Daryl Gates, the chief of police, and its charge was to investigate the use of excessive force in the Los Angeles Police Department.

While most white community leaders enthusiastically hailed this new commission as the first step toward healing the community's shock and anger over the police assault on Rodney King, black community leaders were cautious and expressed cynicism about the "blue ribbon panel" that included only two blacks (both males, one a college president new to the area) and no local leaders affiliated with African-American organizations. Would this be just another race relations commission to "whitewash" the real problems of police misconduct, just another report to be put on the shelf until another beating or another killing of a black man?

THE CHRISTOPHER COMMISSION

The commission held five public hearings in different neighborhoods to allow a broad cross section of Angelenos to air their opinions and grievances against the LAPD. People of all colors, classes, cultures, and ages packed these hearings, eager and anxious to express their feelings and to document their experiences with the police. As the commission members listened attentively but impassively, the witnesses spoke passionately, angrily, and forcefully about the insults, the injuries, the intemperance they had suffered in their contacts with police officers throughout the black ghettos and Latino barrios of the city. Despite the valiant efforts of the chair, the hearings often became raucous, unruly, and unmanageable. People made it crystal clear that they viewed the Los Angeles Police Department as an occupying paramilitary force with a siege mentality, a department full of racist officers who perversely enjoyed harassing minority females, brutalizing minority males, and violating the rights of minority families.

Bearing Witness to Police Misconduct

These witnesses provided the commission with a litany of police abuses, describing the misconduct in graphic and sometimes gruesome detail. Young black and Chicano men described frequent police "stop and search" forays in which they were stopped for no apparent cause in late-model cars or on street corners, ordered to lie on the ground to be searched for drugs or stolen goods, and then laughingly dismissed without any explanation or apology. They knew better than to object to this harassing behavior because if they did, the police would rough them up and accuse them of "resisting arrest," an excuse to book them and enter yet another minority male's name in the computer as a suspected "gang member."

Black adults, with barely restrained emotion, described the invasion of their privacy when police officers forcibly entered their homes to search for illegal drugs or weapons, rarely arriving with a search warrant. Heads of minority households complained bitterly about renegade cops who broke down their doors, destroyed their property, intimidated members of their families, and then left them to clean up the mess and spill out their rage on the nearest target. Even black and Latino children could have told the commission about the many times police cars would cruise through the projects and point guns out of their car windows, miming a drive-by shooting, then laugh as they drove away yelling out racial slurs at the bewildered but frightened youth.

The hearings allowed these people of color to vent their feelings and avenge some of their mistreatment at the hands of the Los Angeles Police Department. They had painted a disturbing and chilling picture of the police that portrayed them as insensitive, impulsive, and even psychopathic. It was not a pretty picture, but it was also not the major issue that the commission would have to confront.

Chief Daryl Gates: Enemy of the People

The major issue for many blacks and Latinos was getting rid of Daryl Gates, the arrogant and unrepentant chief of the LAPD. When the riots broke out, Chief Gates, who had refused to offer Rodney King a gracious apology for his assault by four uniformed police officers, was actually in the San Fernando Valley attending a fundraiser to defeat an upcoming ballot initiative limiting the powers of the police chief and providing more oversight to the Los Angeles Police Department. In the months following the beating, Gates had become the lightning rod for all those dissatisfied individuals and groups who strongly believed that his style of leadership and his attitudes toward minorities had both tolerated and encouraged widespread police misconduct and brutality. The embattled protesters were aiming to destroy the messenger as well as his message.

The Los Angeles City Council had demonstrated a severe crisis of leadership, as the majority expressed support for Chief Gates and the minority bemoaned their lack of power to fire him under the terms of the city charter. It took Geoffrey Gibbs, a young black lawyer who was new to the city and not indebted to the vested interests of any local political camp, to go down to the city hall and read the actual charter, which clearly spelled out situations in which the chief of police could be relieved of his duties "for cause."

When these charter provisions were read at the first hearing of the commission, jam-packed with an angry and volatile crowd, the news was greeted with cheers and wild applause. The commissioners did not seem pleased by the outburst, as the television cameras scanned their somber and slightly disapproving faces, but they may have been secretly relieved to learn that the chief was indeed vulnerable and not above the law. Chief Gates would prove to be a very stubborn adversary, but the commission now held the trump card, and he would play the rest of the waiting game with a losing hand.

The Culture of the LAPD

As the staff of the commission worked for more than three months to interview witnesses, police officers, community leaders, and concerned citizens, they accumulated a mountain of evidence against the police department in its treatment of minorities. They began to document a pattern of police misconduct, harassment, and brutality that was extensive and pervasive, permeating all levels of the department. The investigators identified forty-four police officers who had sustained frequent complaints of excessive force but had not been severely disciplined, suspended, or terminated from the department. The problem of misconduct was not an exception or an aberration; it was systemic, an old "family secret" in the LAPD.

The report documents several of the most egregious cases of excessive force against minority persons and groups, including the particularly poignant killing of Eulia Love on January 3, 1979. Love, a thirty-nine-year-old African-American widow, had been unable or unwilling to pay the gas company $20 on an overdue bill. After an unsuccessful attempt by a collection agent, the company sent two LAPD officers to her home to collect the money. Obviously distraught, Love refused to admit the officers into her home and, according to their version, came out into the yard and threatened them with a kitchen knife. The two policemen shot her pointblank twelve times, killing her instantly. Chief Gates refused to discipline the officers, but the public outcry over the killing resulted in some reforms in the LAPD's procedures involving the use of force.

Despite the fact that nearly six thousand officers had been involved in "use of force" reports between 1987 and 1991, the commission found that performance evaluations rarely reflected all of their infractions, complaints, or disciplinary actions. Even more surprising was the volume of improper and offensive police communications over the mobile digital terminals (MDTs), transmitting messages about using excessive force against suspects and expressing enthusiasm over opportunities for violent confrontations with them. Failure to monitor or censor these comments indicated a major problem of lax supervision as well as a culture of intolerance and insensitivity.

Still more shocking was the department's reluctance or refusal to discipline police officers who were involved in serious incidents of misconduct or excessive brutality, such as the eighty-three cases resulting in civil damage awards of more than $15,000 between 1986 and 1990. According to the commission's report:

> The LAPD disciplined only 21 percent of the officers investigated in the 83 incidents. . . . Only three officers, 6 percent of those investigated, were terminated. The majority of the officers (84 percent) received overall positive ratings in their personnel performance evaluations . . . and 42 percent of the officers have been promoted since the date of the incident.

The majority of the officers involved in these cases received no punishment for causing severe or fatal injuries to innocent victims.

Racism, Code Words, and MDTs

The commission also documented the pervasive attitudes of racial bias within the Los Angeles Police Department in a survey showing that one out of four police officers admitted both the existence of racial prejudice within the department and its relationship to the use of force against minorities. Police messages on the MDTs were full of racial epithets, negative characterizations of minorities with derogatory and dehumanizing stereotypes, and offensive jokes and threats about killing them or burning and destroying their communities. If the messages could have been dismissed as the rowdy comments and rhetoric of bored and frustrated "good old boys," the testimony of numerous witnesses about the reality of these views could not.

Certainly Chief Daryl Gates had not provided any leadership in this area, with his record of intemperate and injudicious comments about minorities, but neither had the station commanders or field supervisors set even minimal standards of tolerance and respect in dealing with the minority communities.

The Commission's Recommendations: Mediating Conflict

After twenty-six executive sessions, five public hearings, and one hundred days of meetings and consultations, the commission submitted its report to Mayor Tom Bradley on July 9, 1991. They made a number of forthright and unanimous recommendations about the Los Angeles Police Department, poised on the brink of an unwelcome yet inevitable assault.

The commission did not try to mince words or mollify egos. It placed responsibility squarely on the shoulders of the chief of police to root out racism and to promote equal opportunity within the Los Angeles Police Department. The commission also recommended major changes in the following strategies, methods, and procedures of the LAPD:

- To institute community policing in order to be "accountable to all segments of the community"
- To revise recruitment strategies through improved screening and psychological evaluation of applicants
- To revise training programs and procedures to include more training in cultural awareness, communication skills, community relations, nondiscrimination, and appropriate use of force
- To evaluate officers' records of unsustained complaints in personnel decisions and to "increase rewards and incentives for patrol officers"
- To revamp the disciplinary system by creating an office of inspector general within the police commission "to oversee the disciplinary process and to participate in the adjudication and punishment of the most serious cases"
- To restructure the existing balance of power between the chief of police and the police commission by limiting the chief to two five-year terms of office and strengthening the power of the police commission to monitor the department and make the chief accountable for his leadership of the Los Angeles Police Department

In the final section of the report, on implementation, the commission delivered a *coup de grace* to Chief Gates by strongly suggesting that it was time for him to retire and turn over the leadership of the department to a new chief who would be responsible for implementing the group's recommendations for radical reformation of the LAPD.

It took Gates nearly one year of intractable and undignified resistance to turn over the reins of leadership of the LAPD to Willie Williams, a police chief from Philadelphia, in June 1992. There was more than a little irony that Daryl Gates, a white, self-styled commander of a paramilitary force in the City of Angels, was replaced by Willie Williams, a black advocate of community policing from the City of Brotherly Love.

THE CALIFORNIA STATE ASSEMBLY: INVESTIGATING URBAN CRISIS

May 1992 to May 1993, the year following the civil disturbances in Los Angeles, was a very tense and turbulent time in the city. In the summer of 1992, the California State Assembly had established its own committee to investigate the causes of the riots and to propose remedies for change. The city's business and political establishment had formed a nonprofit corporation called Rebuild L.A. to develop economic resources and strategies for rehabilitating the riot-scarred areas of South Central. Leaders of the African-American community were alternately angry and optimistic about the city's pledge to address the chronic problems of unemployment and poverty and to redress the social and political grievances in South Central.

In June 1992, only a month after the riots had cut a destructive swath through South Central Los Angeles and parts of the adjoining predominantly black communities of Compton and Inglewood, Walter Tucker, Jr., the Democrat who represented the constituents of the Fifty-First District in the California State Assembly, spearheaded the formation of a special committee on the Los Angeles crisis. Adopting the format of the Christopher Commission, the eighteen-member legislative committee hired two young minority lawyers (a black male and an Asian female) to staff the committee, which set up hearings and conducted background research on the causes and consequences of the civil disturbances in Los Angeles. Propelled by the urgency of the situation and the devastation of the community, the committee completed its investigation and issued its report in late September, less than five months after the initial upheaval.

Whereas the Christopher Commission report had focused almost exclusively on ways to reform the Los Angeles Police Department, the Assembly committee report acknowledged the chronic and endemic problems in the community and proposed a much broader agenda to address the multiple social and economic inequities in the affected inner-city areas. Its report clearly recognized the complex relationship between social problems and social stigma, between economic impoverishment and political powerlessness, between racial isolation and racial exclusion. Police brutality was, in the committee's view, symptomatic of a much deeper, more pervasive, and more intractable pattern of racial discrimination, persistent poverty, and urban decay in Los Angeles.

The special committee made ten major recommendations in its final report on the Los Angeles crisis:

1. To end the economic isolation of the inner city
2. To support economic development
3. To support community self-determination
4. To develop a long-term economic strategy for future economic growth
5. To address the concerns about the criminal justice system
6. To address the need for low-income housing
7. To address the need for an improved educational system, including school-linked service programs

8. To address the lack of adequate public transportation facilities
9. To improve human relations among all ethnic groups
10. To improve the media coverage of ethnic communities to reflect the city's diversity.

It was an ambitious plan for the City of Los Angeles, but the ideas were neither new nor unfamiliar. The report of the special committee on the Los Angeles riots in May 1992, stripped of its cover page and committee membership, bore a striking similarity to the report of the McCone Commission on the Watts riots in the summer of 1965. As Yogi Berra, the legendary baseball player, would say, it was "déjà vu all over again."

Despite the rhetoric of change and empowerment, there were few obvious signs of progress in South Central by spring 1993, nearly a year after the riots. The community seemed in a state of suspended animation, waiting for the resolution of three other trials, all related to the Rodney King assault and the subsequent South Central riots. It seemed as if the City of Angels could not reshape its image and restore its luster until it had rubbed off the tarnish of the pending prosecution of the four police officers in the federal civil rights trial, the prosecution of the four suspected assailants of Reginald Denny, and the Rodney King civil suit against Los Angeles for the violation of his civil rights.

TRIAL ONE: THE FEDERAL CASE AGAINST THE LOS ANGELES POLICE DEPARTMENT

> A *Los Angeles Times* poll conducted on March 7–8, 1991, found that nearly two-thirds (63 percent) of the respondents in the City of Los Angeles, including a majority of whites, said that they believed incidents of police brutality involving the LAPD are common.
>
> Report of the Independent Commission on the Los Angeles Police Department, 1991

The Department of Justice in Washington, D.C., could no longer ignore the beating of Rodney King by four police officers. The verdict had shocked many local and state law enforcement officials, but the riots had shocked the nation. Now the federal government found itself on the defensive as the president and the politicians tried to explain the verdict and its explosive aftermath to their constituents at home and their allies and enemies abroad. If the pressures from the black community leaders and civil rights organizations had not been sufficient, the national and international revulsion at the beating and rejection of the verdict were more than enough to spur the Justice Department to action. Following a brief investigation of the case, the department brought federal charges against the four police officers for violating Rodney King's civil rights.

Blacks were elated that King would get another chance to confront his assailants and seek some redress for his pain and suffering. Most whites were relieved that the system could still protect minorities who had been wronged. But there was a curious coalition between the civil libertarians and the right-wing conservatives who strongly asserted that a second trial created a situation of double jeopardy and violated the Fifth Amendment, which prohibits a person from being prosecuted twice for the same crime. Then there was the small band of black conservatives who always managed to alienate the larger black community through their blatant attempts to placate the white community by decrying the need for another trial and appealing for blacks to accept the status quo—in other words, the initial verdict, which they seemed to view as predictable and reasonable.

Nevertheless, on February 3, 1993, jury selection began in the federal civil rights trial of the four police officers accused of assaulting Rodney King. The trial was held in Courtroom 890 of the U.S. Federal Building in Los Angeles with Judge John G. Davies of the U.S. District Court presiding. Rodney King's civil suit against the City of Los Angeles, filed in May 1991, was still pending and seemed no closer to settlement. Lawyers for Reginald Denny's assailants were still negotiating with the district attorney's office, so no trial date had yet been set. Spring had arrived early in Los Angeles, and along with the anticipation of longer days and leisure-filled weekends came the anxiety of continuing conflict, confrontation, and community discord over the uncomfortable issues of race relations, police power, and social justice.

The Prosecution Case: A Change in Tactics

> The intent I had was to cripple him, to make him unable to push off the ground. You can't push off the ground if your elbows are broken. You can't push off the ground if your knees are broken.
>
> Sgt. Stacey Koon, LAPD

This time the federal prosecutors were Steven Clymer and Barry Kowalski, experienced litigators who had carefully analyzed the first trial in Simi Valley. This time the jury consisted of nine whites, two blacks, and one Hispanic, not much more racially heterogeneous than the Simi Valley jury, especially in a city with a population more than 60 percent minority.

With chief prosecutor Steven Clymer making the major calls, the prosecution planned its overall strategy very carefully. First, the prosecutors decided to dissect the videotape to emphasize the brutality of the beating and to play it in real time, not in slow motion, thus showing the frequency and ferocity of the sixty-two baton blows and kicks. This time, they would not depend solely on the visual evidence, which the defense lawyers had previously manipulated to their advantage, but would call additional witnesses, both police and civilian, who had seen the beating. And this time, they would call their own police expert on the use of force to testify that these officers had far exceeded any reasonable definition of permissible force in subduing Rodney King.

This time, the prosecutors planned to put Rodney King on the stand in order to humanize him and to show that he was not the monster depicted by the defense in the state's case. In fact, King proved to be an excellent witness, one reporter noting that he "spoke softly and dressed meticulously."

Further, they intended to prove that these police officers showed malicious intent in assaulting King, thus depriving him of his civil rights. They were able to accomplish this by playing the videotaped testimony of officer Theodore Briseno asserting in the first trial that his fellow officers were "out of control." But they were able to elicit an even more damning statement from Sgt. Stacey Koon in this trial when he unwittingly admitted that King had been "beaten into submission" by the officers.

Finally, although the evidence against Briseno and against Timothy Wind was weak, they decided to include them as defendants so that the jury would have some choices about convictions and acquittals.

The Defense Case: Hoisted by Their Own Petard

By the time the prosecution had methodically followed its game plan and completed its presentation to the jury, the attorneys for the accused were unsettled and on the defensive. They had presumably planned to employ the same strategies and tactics that had been so successful in the state's case, but they had to regroup quickly and respond to the prosecution's aggressive attacks on their clients. Ira Salzman and Michael Stone, representing Stacey Koon and Laurence Powell, respectively, were most concerned about crafting a new defense for their clients, who were facing the most serious charges.

Defense Attorney Stone decided not to put Powell on the stand; Powell was accused of striking King with the most blows and had the most to lose on cross-examination. Perhaps this decision was a miscalculation and backfired, as the jury was never given any explanation for Powell's aggressive behavior. However, Stone also miscalculated in attacking the credibility of two other witnesses when he examined Melanie Singer and cross-examined Rodney King.

Though she was called as a defense witness in this trial, Singer, the California Highway Patrol officer who had initially chased King on the Foothill Freeway, had been helpful to the prosecution in describing her version of the arrest and assault. Singer graphically described seeing the defendants hit King in the head with six baton blows, recalling, "There was blood dripping literally from his mouth, and there was a pool of blood beneath his chin." She said that her fellow officers were just "standing around and joking" while they observed the beating. She also denied the defense claim that King was high on PCP, pointing out that he displayed none of the usual symptoms associated with PCP intoxication and thus did not appear to be dangerous.

When Singer broke down and cried in response to Stone's harsh questioning, her expression of remorse and her wrenching sobs clearly conveyed her feelings of pain and guilt over her role in the arrest and her inability to prevent the assault. Singer's testimony was a crucial blow to the defense's case; she had violated the code of silence and crossed over the thin blue line.

Rodney King: Reluctant Witness

Perhaps the most ironic twist in a trial full of unexpected turns was Stone's cross-examination of Rodney King. In a blistering assault, Stone literally bullied and browbeat the slow-thinking and slow-responding King. When he tried to get King to read some testimony from the grand jury transcript, King was forced to admit, with great reluctance, that he could not read. For King, it was a moment of painful embarrassment, his fragile self-esteem shattered and his frayed dignity stripped away in front of the entire courtroom. For everyone else in that courtroom, including the members of the jury, it was a shared moment of shame and a painful recognition of the power of the law to demean and destroy a human being. Perhaps this was the defining moment of the entire trial, when the jurors began to empathize with Rodney King, the human being, and began to understand the enormity of the injustice perpetrated against him by a criminal justice system that had allowed him to be victimized over and over again.

In closing arguments, the prosecution had the burden of proof to show that the four police officers had intended to inflict physical injury on Rodney King and to deprive him of his civil rights. Prosecutors hammered away at the insensitive testimony of Stacey Koon, the emotional testimony of Melanie Singer, and the use-of-force expert witness that flatly contradicted the officers' denials of violating departmental policy. This time the federal prosecutors did not overly rely on the videotape of the beating; they simply let the officers' own arrogance incriminate them.

The Verdict

On April 10, six weeks after the beginning of the trial, Judge Davies sent the case to the jury. The trial had included sixty-one witnesses and more than one hundred exhibits, and the jury had been sequestered for fifty-one days. It was now the day before Easter, the most sacred holiday on the Christian calendar, a time of hope, faith, and redemption. The people of Los Angeles were truly hoping for a just resolution to this case and had faith that the city could rise again from the ashes of the riots.

The jury deliberated for thirty hours while the defendants, the victim, the officers of the court, and the community waited impatiently for the verdicts. When a verdict was imminent, the judge notified the LAPD, and Chief Williams placed the department on tactical alert, ready to respond with massive force to prevent a replay of the 1992 riots. Pete Wilson, the governor of California, authorized the call-up of 600 members of the National Guard to assist the 7,755 members of the LAPD in maintaining order in case of a violent demonstration in response to the verdicts.

On April 17, the jury returned its verdicts: Stacey Koon and Laurence Powell were found guilty of violating Rodney King's civil rights, with an additional count of "causing injury" against Powell. Theodore Briseno and Timothy Wind were found not guilty of violating King's rights. It was a Solomonic decision—two for the prosecution and two for the defense. It was also a decision that was bound to offend the extremists on both sides of the racial divide and to provoke more controversy in legal and political circles.

Rodney King had finally found a measure of justice and a moment of vindication. It would prove, however, to be a Pyrrhic victory. But on that spring day in that turbulent city, a jury of King's peers had finally found the courage to punish two of the four police officers who had caused him so much pain and grief.

The lawyers for Koon and Powell were just as vindictive in defeat as they had been boastful in victory. Ira Salzman, Koon's defense lawyer, angrily declared, "Justice is not a circus. . . . Stacey Koon is not some kind of sacrificial animal to be cast aside for peace and order in L.A."

The Response and the Aftermath

Predictably, the split verdicts evoked mixed emotions from the multiple constituencies concerned with the case. Rev. Cecil Murray, gathered with his parishioners and black community leaders at the First African Methodist Episcopal Church, led a rousing cheer when the guilty verdicts were announced. Blacks and whites in neighborhoods around the city and communities around California and the rest of the country seemed satisfied, if not totally pleased, with the verdicts. The two officers perceived to be the most responsible for the beating had been convicted, so the system had ultimately worked. But there was an unspoken sense that the verdicts represented some kind of compromise, a tacit acknowledgment that both sides needed to be appeased. There was, yet again, the lingering suspicion that factors beyond the evidence and outside of the law had influenced the jury's deliberations—factors of race, of riots, of reconciliation.

In response to vocal critics of the jury's "politically correct" verdicts, several jurors simply stated that the videotaped evidence of the beating was sufficient to convict Koon and Powell but not sufficient to convict Briseno and Wind. One of the white male jurors, who was particularly troubled by Koon's frank admission about the brutality of the assault on King, explained his vote for the two guilty verdicts: "Just because a man was driving drunk—he should be punished—but you don't beat him into submission."

The LAPD may have been the only segment of Los Angeles society that was not pleased with the verdict. The federal prosecutors, unlike the state prosecutors, had shown the department no mercy and had exposed its culture of racism, its toleration of misconduct, and its code of silence to the world. This jury had not been hoodwinked by the obfuscations and outrageous tactics of the defense lawyers, nor was the public fooled by the denials and the deceptions of the department's leaders. What had become crystal clear to the people of Los Angeles in these two high-profile trials was that police misconduct and brutality were not rare occurrences of "aberrant behavior," as Chief Daryl Gates had insisted, but standard operating procedures and, even more troubling, something of a spectator sport in the LAPD.

The Controversial Sentence

Judge Davies had postponed sentencing Koon and Powell until August 1993, giving both the prosecution and the defense time to submit recommendations. On August 4, in another stunning development in this case, Judge Davies sentenced the two defendants to terms of thirty months each in federal prison. The prosecution had recommended the minimum sentence of ten years under the federal sentencing guidelines, but Judge Davies actually reduced the mandatory sentences by eight levels and wrote a fifty-four-page sentencing memorandum to explain his unusually lenient sentences. He spelled out four "mitigating circumstances" to justify reducing the sentences for these two police officers: "First, Mr. King's wrongful conduct contributed significantly to provoking the offense behavior"; "second, defendants Koon and Powell have already sustained, and will continue to incur, punishment in addition to the sentence of this court"; "third, . . . there is no evidence that Koon and Powell are dangerous or likely to commit crimes in the future"; and "fourth, . . . the successive state and federal prosecutions, though legal, raise a specter of unfairness."

Further, Judge Davies asserted that the defense's description of King's behavior on the night of the beating "supports a finding that Mr. King engaged in illegal conduct prior to and during his arrest. . . . He attempted to escape from police custody." However, these assertions were challenged by prosecution lawyers and were never substantiated or upheld as factual evidence in either trial of the police officers.

Judge Davies had revealed where his basic sympathies lay and had shown an utter disregard for the laws he had sworn to uphold. Joining in the universal disbelief and disgust over this blatant manipulation of judicial discretion, the federal prosecutors appealed the sentences in the hope that a higher court would prove to be faithful to the letter and the spirit of the sentencing guidelines.

The judge who symbolized the power of the federal government, which was pledged to protect King's civil rights and to redress the wrongs committed against him, had delivered the final *coup de grace* to King's human dignity. Without having been convicted of any crime in this case, the man had been brutalized by the police, betrayed by a Simi Valley jury, and now branded by a federal judge as a dangerous felon! When these sentences were pronounced, Rodney King might well have felt like Dred Scott, standing before a racist southern judge who not only denied him his basic human rights but also championed the very law enforcement officials who had blatantly violated his civil rights.

TRIAL TWO: REGINALD DENNY AND COMMUNITY JUSTICE

> The media really played up the Reginald Denny beating—every time you turned on the TV, that's all you could see. They made it look like only the blacks were rioting and burning and looting,

> but everyone was out there—the Hispanics and every other race. Everyone is angry. People are tired of the injustice, tired of being beat up by the cops, tired of seeing all these foreigners get ahead. The media showed all the negative things, but they didn't show the whole story.
>
> L. T., female youth member, Weingart Urban YMCA, Los Angeles

---

On April 29, 1992, the first night of the riots at the corner of Florence and Normandie Avenues, the media had taped the vicious assault of Reginald Denny, a thirty-six-year-old white truck driver, in living color. The pundits had analyzed it ad nauseam. The black community had agonized over it, prayed over it, and rationalized it. On May 12, as one of his last official acts, Chief Daryl Gates had spearheaded a predawn raid in South Central to arrest three suspects who had been recognized among the two thousand felony suspects identified in videotapes of the riots. Leading a force of more than two hundred police officers and FBI agents, with the media trailing close behind, Chief Gates personally arrested Damian Williams, the primary suspect in Denny's assault, while other officers took Henry Watson and Antoine Miller into custody. Later Gary Williams, another suspect in the assault, surrendered to police. All four suspects were presumed to be members of the notorious 8-Trey Gangster Crips, the gang that controlled the neighborhood where the riots broke out. These four young black men soon were christened the "L.A. Four" and became potent symbols of the racial schism polarizing the city.

The L.A. Four

To many Angelenos, the four young black defendants were violent thugs who took advantage of the riots to attack an innocent white man. To some community activists, these young men, overcome by anger and rage at the unjust verdict in the police beating of Rodney King, had lost control and vented their frustrations on the nearest white person. To a few hard-core black nationalists, Damian Monroe ("Football") Williams, nineteen; Antoine ("Twan") Miller, twenty; Henry Keith ("Kiki") Watson, twenty-seven; and Gary Williams, thirty-three, were folk heroes, martyrs of the revolution against white supremacy. In the projects and pool halls of South Central, they were all of the above to their shifting coterie of supporters, detractors, and apologists.

At one of the community rallies held for the L.A. Four during the 1992 Christmas holiday season, the demonstrators became violent at the intersection of Florence and Normandie, the site of the original riots. Although twelve people were injured, Willie Williams, the new Los Angeles police chief, immediately responded with a force of three hundred officers, who made fifty-five arrests and quelled the disturbance almost immediately, before any serious injuries or significant property damage could occur. Chief Williams was sending his own signal to the community that random violence and wanton destruction would not be tolerated under his watch, no matter what the cause or the color of the protesters.

Pretrial Strategies and Developments

Again the district attorney had to make a difficult decision about the best venue for this trial, just as the community was beginning to cool down after the heat of the riots. Again the prosecutors had the difficult task of selecting a jury that would be objective and unbiased by all the public outrage and public debate about the assault. Again the defense had to protect the rights of the defendants to ensure that they had a jury of their peers in a venue that would not be automatically hostile to them. All parties in this case were keenly aware that the media interest was intense, but they were also aware that the public interest must be served to conduct a fair trial both for the black defendants and for the white victim, the mirror opposite of the defendants and the victim in the Rodney King case.

In the spring of 1993, Gary Williams, now thirty-four, had decided to plead guilty to charges of robbery and assault in a separate trial and had been sentenced to three years in prison. On July 12, Judge John W. Ouderkirk granted Antoine Miller, twenty-one, a separate trial on the grounds that the stronger evidence against Williams and Watson might be prejudicial to his case. That left just two of the original defendants to stand trial for multiple felony assault charges against Reginald Denny and seven other victims. But the judge ruled against a defense motion to dismiss the charges against the remaining two defendants because of racial bias in the prosecution's charges against them. This was one of many rulings that favored the prosecution but would ultimately benefit the defense. The original L.A. Four were now reduced to the L. A. Two, without all the supporters, without the rallies, and without the media frenzy.

Damian Williams and Henry Watson had been charged originally with attempted murder, but Williams, allegedly seen on the video striking Denny in the head with a brick, was additionally charged with "aggravated mayhem." These charges were far more serious than the assault charges filed by the Los Angeles District Attorney's office in 1992 against the four policemen arrested for the Rodney King beating; even in their subsequent federal trial, these police officers were charged only with violations of King's civil rights. This was duly noted by the black community, as was the glaring disparity in the bail hearings for these two sets of defendants. While the police officers had been granted relatively low bail in both the state and federal trials on the assumption that they were unlikely to flee and were not a threat to the community, bail for the three young black men ranged from $500,000 to $580,000, amounts so high that their families were unable to post bond to release them from jail until the trial began; the high bail was justified on the grounds that these suspects did pose a flight risk and were indeed a threat to the community. Edi Faal, the defense attorney for Damian Williams, accused the district attorney's office of racially discriminatory prosecution policies.

Before the trial date was set, the prosecutors made a number of strategic decisions. First, they approached the defense lawyers about a plea bargain for their clients, but they could not agree on terms. Second, they threatened to charge the defendants with membership in a gang, which would have resulted in longer prison sentences if they were convicted. But these charges were quickly dropped after the Los Angeles Police Department revealed that one of the investigating officers in the case was himself a target of disciplinary action. To neutralize any potential empathy for the defendants from the bench, the prosecutors played their trump card and successfully requested the removal of a black judge randomly assigned to the case. He was replaced by a white judge with a reputation as a "law and order" jurist. The district attorney's office was determined to win this battle, even at the cost of losing the war for the hearts and minds of the disgruntled black community.

The Trial Begins

On Wednesday, July 28, 1993, the trial of Damian Monroe Williams and Henry Keith Watson began in Los Angeles Superior Court with Judge Ouderkirk presiding. These two defendants were charged with the assault of Reginald Denny, five other motorists, and two firefighters who were driving past the intersection of Florence and Normandie shortly after the outbreak of the riots on April 29, 1992. Fifteen months after he was nearly beaten to death in South Central Los Angeles, Reginald Denny faced his assailants in court for the first time. His beating had also become a cause célèbre in the media, and the world was watching yet another traumatic trial in the annals of Los Angeles race relations.

In this case, the court called a large, racially mixed pool of potential jurors to be questioned. Strangely, no attempt had been made by the prosecution for a change of venue. On August 12, 1993, the panel of twelve jurors was selected, an eclectic group of typical Angelenos: five whites, three blacks, three Latinos, and one Asian. Both sides seemed relieved and pleased. Ever mindful of the shadow of Rodney King, Judge Ouderkirk had earlier lectured the prospective jurors that they would be "listening to the evidence in this case and not concerned about outside issues" and that their verdicts should not be reached "because you think that events in another case were fair or unfair and that this is some way to even the score."

The Case for the Prosecution

The prosecution's case was straightforward and, for the second time in fifteen months, relied heavily on the videotaped beating as incontrovertible evidence. One would never lightly accuse the Los Angeles District Attorney's office of naïveté or incompetence, but it clearly did not learn from its earlier miscalculation about the significance of videotape evidence. With a multiracial jury to hear the case, the prosecutors seemed completely unaware of the irony of using visual evidence to convict two black defendants of assaulting a white man just over a year after a nearly all-white jury had rejected similar evidence to convict four white police officers of beating a black man.

To strengthen the case against Damian Williams and his codefendant, the prosecutors built up portraits of these young men as unsavory and unworthy inner-city thugs, gangbangers, and petty criminals. They wanted the jury to view these defendants as antisocial and alienated from community norms. They hoped to convince the jurors that these defendants were not only guilty of the assault but also beyond rehabilitation and redemption. After failing so badly to obtain a conviction of Rodney King's attackers, the prosecutors were hungry for a victory and vindication in Denny's assault.

This time, the videotape evidence came from a freelance news photographer who had been hovering over the scene of the beating at the intersection of Florence and Normandie in a helicopter. The picture, fed live to KCOP, an independent television station in Los Angeles, is clear and unambiguous as three young black men drag Reginald Denny, a well-built young white man, from the cab of his truck and proceed to punch, pummel, and kick him with such ferocity that the viewer flinches. They throw him down on the ground, and as he tries to cover his head, one of the attackers strikes his head with a brick; then they kick him some more, cursing and yelling as they plant the blows all over his body. The beating seems to go on forever until suddenly two older black males emerge from the crowd of onlookers and try to extricate him from his attackers.

After a brief struggle, they push Denny back into his truck, and one very courageous man drives through the crowd and takes him to the hospital. Denny would later credit this man, Bobby Green, with saving his life and, with an amazing lack of bitterness, publicly thank the black people who had come to his rescue.

On Thursday, August 19, Lawrence Morrison, a deputy district attorney, delivered the opening statement for the prosecution, showing color slides that dramatically documented the assault on Denny and the other victims, including Gabriel Quintana, a service station attendant who also claimed he was beaten and robbed by Damian Williams. A week later, in the dramatic highlight of the trial, he would play the videotape showing the shocking sequence of Denny being dragged from his truck, kicked, beaten with a claw hammer and an oxygen tank, and then left lying prone on the ground with his face covered in blood.

The prosecution dwelled on Denny's severe injuries, calling doctors to describe his broken jaw, shattered eye socket, fractured skull, and blood clots in his legs and lungs. Dr. Leslie Geiger, the neurosurgeon whose surgical skills probably saved Denny's life, was a most effective witness. Jurors winced and spectators cried as he described his efforts to repair Denny's skull and restore his left eye.

Witnesses for the Prosecution

As in the two trials of the police officers charged with assaulting Rodney King, the videotape was the centerpiece of evidence against the two defendants. But Morrison and his coprosecutor, Janet Moore, recognized the need to call a parade of eyewitnesses to the assault on Denny, as well as the other victims, who could corroborate their version of events. However, prosecutors were not eager to reveal their witnesses to defense lawyers, who complained to the judge that they needed to have access to the witnesses in order to prepare their case.

In a highly unusual ruling, Judge Ouderkirk refused to allow defense lawyers direct contact with the prosecution witnesses because he expressed "concerns about their safety." He ordered the defense to contact those witnesses through the prosecutor's office, which was directed to send the written witnesses' responses directly to the judge. With this ruling, Judge Ouderkirk sent a clear signal that he needed to protect the prosecution witnesses against potential harassment or intimidation from the friends and associates of the defendants.

Despite these instructions, Donald Jones, a Los Angeles firefighter who had rescued one of the victims at the scene of the attack, testified on August 25 that prosecutors had never contacted him about talking to any defense lawyer. Following his testimony, Edi Faal, Damian's lawyer, requested a mistrial on the grounds that prosecutors had unfairly hampered the defense by denying them access to material witnesses. Although Judge Ouderkirk denied the defense's request, Faal succeeded in sending a strong signal to the black community that his clients, unlike the four white police officers, did not have any guarantee of getting a fair trial in the Los Angeles criminal court system.

In late August, the prosecutor called as witnesses the four black "Good Samaritans" who had rescued Denny and driven him to the hospital as he lay bleeding and semiconscious in the cab of his truck. Bobby Green, Lei Yuille, Titus Murphy, and Terri Barnett had all been watching the riots on television when they saw the angry young men pull Denny out of his truck. Each of them, for reasons of conscience and concern, rushed out to go to Denny's aid. The prosecution rightfully portrayed these four as heroes, hoping to contrast these "good black citizens" against the "bad black thugs" like Williams and Watson.

But this strategy backfired on cross-examination when two of the rescuers noted that if there had been any police at the intersection, they would not have gotten involved. So these "good citizens" were reluctant heroes, in contrast to the absent Los Angeles police officers, who were widely seen beating a hasty retreat from the flashpoints of the riots. The rescuers also testified that they had encountered at least one LAPD patrol car on their way to the hospital, but the officers did not stop when they tried to flag the police down for assistance. It must have been difficult for the jurors to understand how an LAPD police car could ignore a white truck carrying an eighty-thousand-pound rig of two trailers filled with gravel, traveling over fifty-five miles per hour behind a small Honda Civic driven by a black woman (Terri Barnett) with her emergency flashers on, honking her horn to clear a path to get this wounded white truck driver to the nearest hospital, Daniel Freeman Memorial Hospital in Inglewood. Defense Attorney Faal had scored an important point and had reminded the jury that on the evening of April 29, 1992, the Los Angeles police had abandoned the "good citizens" of South Central to the looters, the gangbangers, and the thugs.

In early September, the prosecution produced an impressive battery of witnesses who placed Williams and Watson at the scene and identified them as Denny's attackers. Among these witnesses was mob victim Quintana, who testified that he saw Damian Williams throw a brick at Denny, and three television cameramen who had videotaped the violent scene. In the final week of their case, the prosecution introduced its *pièce de résistance*, an expert who showed the jury an enhancement of the video and traced the minute-by-minute actions, leading clearly and directly to Williams. Confident that they had proved their case and had convinced the jury of the defendants' culpability, the prosecutors rested their case on September 17, 1993.

The Case for the Defense

> The defense strategy is "We weren't there. If we were there, that wasn't us on the videotape. If that was us, we didn't do anything. If we did anything, we didn't intend it."
>
> Trial observer, Los Angeles

On September 20, lawyers for the defendants began to argue their case. Edi O. M. Faal, born in Gabon, West Africa, and educated in England, mounted an aggressive and energetic defense for his client, Damian Williams. With carefully controlled passion, Faal set out to challenge the main pillar of the prosecution's case, the videotaped evidence, and to undermine the prosecution's charge of attempted murder against his client. On cross-examination of the prosecution witnesses, in his lilting British colonial accent, Faal proved to be a tenacious and tough adversary.

Profiting from the lessons of the Simi Valley trial of the police officers, Faal was able to manipulate the videotaped account of the assaults and minimize its impact on the jury. He emphasized the notorious unreliability of eyewitness evidence, particularly in a scene of mob violence, and hammered away at the conflicting testimony of the witnesses. When the prosecution claimed that a menacing gap-toothed figure on the tape was Damian Williams, Faal paraded a smiling Williams before the jury, who could clearly see his even set of teeth. Unlike the prosecutors in the Simi Valley trial, Faal humanized Williams for the jury by portraying him as a misguided victim of poverty and racism, not the monster described by the prosecution.

As Faal played the forty minutes of videotaped evidence over and over again to challenge the prosecution's claims against his client, he successfully raised doubts in the jurors' minds about Williams's identity and involvement in the attack. And as he had hoped it would, the repetitive playing of the videotape anesthetized the jurors and distanced them from the actual violence and vicious behaviors perpetrated by the defendants.

Faal was also able to counter the prosecution's charge that Williams had demonstrated willful intent to engage in the two most serious felony charges, mayhem and attempted murder. Again, through clever use of the videotaped scenes, Faal was able to make a credible case for unpremeditated assault, arising from the explosive anger and the rampant rage of the mob venting its frustrations over the acquittals of the white police officers. Despite numerous objections of the judge, Faal managed to make a number of subtle and not-so-subtle linkages between the riotous behavior of the two young black defendants and the miscarriage of justice in the trial of Rodney King's assailants. It had been only fifteen months since those police officers were acquitted, and every member of this jury would remember those verdicts and their traumatic consequences. It was a gamble Faal had to take.

Faal also joined forces with Earl C. Broady, Jr., Watson's defense lawyer, not only to humanize their clients but also to contextualize their miserable and meaningless lives. Williams and Watson were portrayed as archetypal young black males, school dropouts, chronically unemployed, with juvenile records, troubled families, and few wins in a lifetime of losses. He effectively ratcheted up the "misery quotient" to paint these defendants as trapped in a cycle of poverty, deprivation, and despair that inexorably propelled them into a situation that escalated into violence and in which they were acting out the uncontrollable fury of the mob, enraged by yet another miscarriage of justice for a black man in Los Angeles.

Closing Arguments: Diametrically Opposing Views

In their closing arguments, the defense lawyers did not talk about family values or personal responsibility or the Golden Rule to counteract the prosecution's characterizations of the defendants and their actions; they wanted this jury to empathize with their clients, who were products of broken families, failed social institutions, and a rejected social contract. In fact, the defense fully intended to switch the focus and the blame for these assaults onto the society that spawned Damian Williams and Henry Watson, not on the individual pathology and paranoia that lay just beneath the surface of their antisocial aggression.

In a surprise move, Faal even disputed the cause of Denny's severe head injuries, suggesting that someone else had thrown a piece of concrete that had shattered the window and dazed Denny before the brick was thrown and, further, that the videotape did not clearly establish that his client had thrown anything. On September 23, the defense lawyers rested their case.

While the defense depicted Williams and Watson as "scapegoats" and sacrificial lambs to appease the community for the riots, the prosecutors used their closing argument to portray the defendants as willful and wanton attackers who fully intended to kill Denny. On the last day of September, after two days of closing arguments, Judge Ouderkirk submitted the case to the jury.

The Verdict

On October 5, Judge Ouderkirk announced that he had sequestered the jurors as soon as they began their deliberations. By October 8, it was clear that the multiracial jury was experiencing great conflict and tension over the case, so the judge ordered a brief hiatus in jury deliberations. Before the end of the first week, Judge Ouderkirk had dismissed two jurors and nullified two of their initial verdicts. One juror was dismissed for mental incompetence, another for "good cause." Lawyers on both sides were concerned about a mistrial or a hung jury, and legal experts hotly debated the judge's rulings, but the black community was more concerned about another miscarriage of justice due to what appeared to be an unprecedented use of judicial discretion to remove two jurors on questionable grounds and to force the jurors to continue their deliberations until they reached a verdict.

On October 13, the defense requested the removal of a third juror, but Judge Ouderkirk refused the request. However, by the end of the trial, the judge had replaced five of the original twelve jurors, some on questionable grounds in the view of the defense team. Legal experts were weighing in to debate the judge's actions, but the black community was rallying around the defendants and growing increasingly suspicious of the judge's intentions. Again on October 16, when the jurors announced that they had reached consensus on some counts but were deadlocked on other counts, Judge Ouderkirk firmly and sternly ordered them to resume their deliberations on the unresolved counts.

On Monday, October 18, after the judge had advised the LAPD to prepare for a tactical alert, the verdicts were announced to an anxious public and press. Out of twelve possible felony counts charged against them by the prosecution, the jury found Damian Williams guilty of only one felony count of simple mayhem and one misdemeanor assault charge. Henry Watson, his codefendant, was found guilty of only one misdemeanor assault, a charge carrying a maximum prison term of six months. Since Watson had already spent seventeen months in jail before the trial, he was given credit for time served and was immediately released.

The defense was ecstatic, for their clients were acquitted of the two most serious charges against them, attempted murder and aggravated mayhem, which would have resulted in long prison sentences. The prosecutors were stunned, unable to comprehend how they could have crafted a more convincing case or how they could have failed to communicate better with the jury. Meanwhile, the families of the defendants were celebrating, crying and hugging each other; the defendants themselves seemed immensely surprised and relieved by the unexpected good news. But the most astonishing response came from Reginald Denny himself, the beleaguered and bewildered victim of the brutal assault. In a totally spontaneous gesture, Denny walked over to Georgina Williams, Damian's mother, and hugged her. Other family members surrounded him, and they all exchanged warm embraces and words of reconciliation. And Reginald Denny, like Rodney King before him, offered an olive branch to the families and to the Los Angeles community when he spoke to the waiting press: "The trial is over. . . . Let's get on with life."

The Response and the Aftermath

Reaction to the verdicts was swift, strong, and severely critical. Press pundits wasted no time in describing the outcome in the Denny beating trial as a "payback" for the acquittals of the police officers in the King beating trial. The white community in Los Angeles and throughout the country expressed outrage that the jury ignored the videotaped evidence and had acquitted these two attackers in such an obvious travesty of justice.

For weeks afterward, newspapers, television programs, and radio talk shows featured stories, editorials, and public forums about the verdict, generating heated discussion and rancorous debates about the racism of the jurors, their nullification of the evidence, and their apparent fear that guilty verdicts on the more serious felony charges would have provoked riots in the community. Judge Ouderkirk was subjected to his share of criticism for his conduct of the case, for bullying the jury, and for appearing to favor the prosecution.

Much of the extreme criticism seemed to come from conservative critics, who quickly indicted the entire African-American community of Los Angeles, particularly those who lived in South Central, accusing blacks of condoning the mob violence, fostering a climate of lawlessness, and making martyrs of Williams and Watson and their coconspirators. As in the King case, the black community was by no means united in support of these defendants. In fact, Joseph Duff, the president of the Los Angeles chapter of the NAACP, had been publicly chastised during the trial by some community members when he described Denny's attackers as a "lynch mob." Duff was one of the few leaders courageous enough to express the opinions of perhaps the majority of the community, who were actually repelled by the extreme behavior of the rioters and rejected violence as a solution to the community's problems.

Concepts of Justice: Blacks Versus Whites

The visceral responses to the verdicts in the Denny assault trial again revealed the deep schisms among blacks and whites in their views of the American criminal justice system. Some blacks believed that whites were overreacting because this time the victim was white and the system was not expected to fail him. Moreover, for the first time in memory, whites were feeling frustrated and helpless in a system that systematically stripped blacks of their rights and generated chronic feelings of frustration and powerlessness in the black community. This lesson was not lost on some of the more liberal commentators, who even suggested that whites might gain some much-needed insight and empathy with blacks from the experience of being doubly victimized by the crime and then by the criminal justice system.

Within three days, some of the jurors began to defend themselves against the chorus of critics. Jurors insisted that their verdicts were based on the evidence and not on any racial bias or fears of a potential riot. Within the next three months, when cooler heads had time to evaluate the case, legal scholars and dispassionate intellectuals laid out careful analyses to support the jury's verdicts.

In a well-constructed article in *Time*, Richard Lacayo succinctly summarized the weaknesses in the prosecutors' case: they overcharged the defendants and could not prove intent on the charges of attempted murder and aggravated mayhem, they undercharged by failing to charge Williams with one count of assaulting Denny with a deadly weapon, and they relied too heavily on the videotape, which loses its impact on a jury after repeated exposures. According to several experts, the jury had dutifully followed the judge's instructions, had studied all the evidence carefully, and had concluded that the prosecution had not proved its case on the two most serious felony counts "beyond a reasonable doubt." As Jerome Skolnick said in an op-ed piece for the *Los Angeles Times*, "The people's jury just did its job."

The debate continued to divide the community throughout the fall and into the holiday season as Damian Williams was denied bail while awaiting his sentence and two other members of the L.A. Four were reunited with their families. On December 7, 1993, Judge Ouderkirk sentenced Williams to ten years in prison, the maximum term possible for his guilty charges and "lack of remorse." Williams could expect to be released in four years if he could manage to get time off for good behavior.

Another traumatic trial had come to a conclusion that would please some and offend others; some would argue that it was a just verdict for an unsocialized black assailant, and others would compare it unfavorably to the sentence of thirty months meted out to the two white police officers who had assaulted Rodney King "under color of authority." Now it was time for healing, for racial reconciliation, and for the City of Angels to enjoy the holidays.

TRIAL THREE: RODNEY KING'S CIVIL TRIAL

On May 9, 1991, Rodney King filed a civil suit against the City of Los Angeles for damages stemming from the violation of his civil rights by the Los Angeles Police Department. Untutored in the intricacies of the legal system and the entitlements of lawyers, King had hired to pursue his claim Steven Lerman, a white lawyer specializing in personal injury cases with little, if any, previous experience with or exposure to police misconduct in the black community. Black lawyers in Los Angeles and the San Francisco Bay Area who had been assiduously trying to gain his confidence and his contract were both disappointed and disturbed by his choice, privately complaining that a white lawyer without civil rights experience could not possibly represent him effectively.

At first, the city council seemed to take a conciliatory stance toward the suit, suggesting that it would propose a generous out-of-court settlement to compensate King for his brutal beating by four LAPD police officers. But several funny things happened on the way to a negotiated settlement, and the city council's stance gradually changed from conciliatory to confrontational. In the battle to obtain just compensation for his physical injuries and to restore his wounded psyche, Rodney King was his own worst warrior.

Public Woes and Private Devils

Whether the beating had damaged his brain or simply exacerbated his already impaired judgment, King found himself involved in a series of embarrassing incidents during the months following the assault. He had been arrested for drunken driving, but the police cited him and released him, treating him with uncharacteristic courtesy. A few months later, he was arrested again after an altercation with a prostitute, who turned out to be a transvestite in drag. On this occasion, he was parked in an alley in Los Angeles, and critics suggested that the police were targeting King and harassing him to find an excuse to arrest him as payback for his role in embarrassing the department. But public sympathy for King had eroded substantially when he was arrested the third time within two years for assaulting his wife, Crystal.

With each arrest, King's image underwent a subtle transformation in the media from an aggrieved victim of police brutality to an antisocial violator of public morals. The gentle giant had, in fact as well as in myth, been revealed as just another Bigger Thomas, the tragically flawed protagonist of *Native Son*.

On August 9, 1993, twenty-seven months after King's claim was filed, the lawyers on both sides were given thirty days to settle the civil suit. After much public posturing and private bargaining, they failed to reach a settlement, and a trial date was set for March 1994. Jury selection began on March 22, 1994, and the trial began one week later. After the 1992 civil disturbances, Milton Grimes, a black attorney from Orange County, had been hired as the lead counsel in Rodney King's civil case against the City of Los Angeles. While he coordinated the overall case, he hired John Burris, an Oakland civil rights attorney with extensive experience in police misconduct cases, to plan the courtroom strategy for the trial.

The Plaintiff's Case

This time, King's lawyers did not hesitate to make race a central issue in their case. They reenacted the beating in real time, not in slow motion. They isolated the racial epithets on the tape and solemnly played them for the jury. They dramatized his physical injuries. Most important of all, they put King on the witness stand to let the jury see that he was a simple man, big but not Bigger, the victim, not the victimizer.

> Rodney King was a handsome and gentle young man, but his intelligence was rather limited. He had a street sense of life, but like many young black men, he had been in trouble with the law. . . . Everyone knew King had been wronged, and his case was symbolic. Rodney King got some justice, but he didn't get full justice. There is still much work to be done.
>
> John Burris, civil rights attorney, Oakland

On April 13, 1994, three years and six weeks after the videotaped assault, the judge sent the case to the jury. Rodney King sought $15 million from the City of Los Angeles for the beating he sustained at the hands of the Los Angeles Police Department. After a week of deliberating, the jury returned its verdict on April 21, 1994. The jury found that the City of Los Angeles was indeed culpable for the illegal acts of its police officers and awarded King $3.8 million in compensatory damages for his injuries. The award was just over one-fourth of the amount sought by the victim but triple the $1.25 million the city had originally offered to settle out of court. The city anxiously awaited the second phase of the trial, the jury's decision about punitive damages against the police officers.

But the agony of this assault on the body politic was not yet over. King's lawyers pursued a scorched-earth policy to make an example of the LAPD and to vindicate their client completely in the eyes of the public. In the second phase of the trial, they called Laurence Powell, the only officer convicted in the state's trial, as a witness, but he invoked the Fifth Amendment on April 21 and refused to testify. On May 6, confident that they had convinced the jury of King's right to generous punitive damages, the lawyers for the plaintiff rested their case.

The Defendants' Case

On May 12, after four more days of testimony challenging King's claims that excessive force by the police had resulted in severe injuries and permanent damage to his health, the defense lawyers for the city also rested their case. On June 1, 1994, just over two years after the South Central riots had erupted, the jurors returned the final verdict in the case of *Rodney King* v. *City of Los Angeles:* they refused to award him any punitive damages against the Los Angeles Police Department for their violation of his civil rights. Rodney King had been beaten by the criminal justice system yet again: twice as a victim and twice as a loser.

When the jury refused to grant him punitive damages, King might have found himself identifying with Sethe, the tragic heroine of Toni Morrison's novel *Beloved,* raped again and again by the respected law-abiding members of the community.

The black community was outraged by this callous insensitivity to King's rights and this double message to the police. To them, it was another classic case of injustice to a black man who was without power, wealth, or influence. The media were not very surprised; after all, they had contributed much to the trashing of King's image and the erosion of any empathy for him as a tragic victim. The city's political establishment and law enforcement officials were relieved that the painful public scrutiny of their racist police practices was finally over. The people of Los Angeles just wanted to put the King case behind them and to move on to heal the racial divisions and rebuild the ravaged community.

Part II

O. J. Simpson

6

O. J. Simpson

The Man, the Myth, the Marriage

> O. J. did not evolve out of Orenthal James, but parallel to and distinct from him. The realities of Orenthal James—not least among them the challenges, the absurdities, the ongoing and often unresolved contradictions of starting out poor and growing up black and male in America—appear to have been denied, ignored, sublimated or perhaps simply repressed.
>
> Harry Edwards, *Sport*, February 1995

Potrero Hill is one of San Francisco's funkiest neighborhoods, isolated from the rest of the city by the James Lick Freeway on the west and ringed by a sprawling maze of light and heavy industries on its three other sides. To a visitor, it has the ambience of a small town, where you slow down your pace and enjoy the spectacular views of the San Francisco Bay to the east and the skyline of the city to the north. It is a neighborhood of neat cottages lining the steep hills, populated by a mélange of artists, community activists, and working-class artisans.

Inspired by its original Spanish name of Potrero Nuevo ("new grazing ground"), Potrero Hill has welcomed successive waves of immigrants, from the Russian Molokani sect seeking freedom of worship to the blacks who sought housing when they came to work in the shipyards and factories in World War II to the more recent Asian immigrants seeking political refuge. This colorful neighborhood, claimed as home by beat poet Lawrence Ferlinghetti and some of San Francisco's other noted artists and writers, also claims O. J. Simpson as its native son.

O. J. SIMPSON, THE MAN

> If there is an obvious racial story in the Simpson case . . . [it is] what it reveals about our own stereotypes and anxieties—many of them unacknowledged—about violent black men, about interracial sex, about the price of admission to the mainstream world.
>
> Ellis Cose, *Newsweek*, July 11, 1994

Orenthal James Simpson, born in 1947, was the third child and second son of Jimmy and Eunice Simpson. O. J.'s parents were originally from rural Texas and joined the great migration to the west in the early 1940s, seeking better jobs and better opportunities for their family, just as Rodney King's family and millions of other blacks would do. His father worked as a custodian, and his mother worked as a hospital orderly on the night shift so that she could be with her children during the day.

A sickly child, O. J. suffered from rickets as a result of early nutritional deficiencies. Because the family could not afford corrective braces for his badly bowed legs, his mother devised the creative remedy of putting the wrong shoe on each foot to straighten his legs. O. J. grew up in a volatile household. His father battered his mother, abused his children, and made life a living hell for his family. The turmoil was constant, and family conflict was the norm. O. J. learned early that a man's most dangerous weapon was his fist, a symbol of power and domination over his wife and children. It was a painful, bitter lesson but one forever imprinted on his impressionable mind. Another early lesson was the importance of keeping up a front for the outside world, protecting the family's image from ugly rumors that his father was not only a wife beater but also an alcoholic, drinking and fighting perhaps to prove his masculinity and deny his confusion about his sexual identity.

When O. J.'s father left the home and became openly homosexual, it was a terrible blow to all the family, but especially to his son O. J. Many families in the projects were headed by single mothers, but at least the sons in these families had fathers who were "normal" and were not ridiculed by their friends and neighbors. Well before San Francisco became a mecca for the gay community and a haven for that lifestyle, O. J. had to cope with the blatant homophobia of the black community and the derision and contempt of his peers toward "queers" and "faggots." O. J.'s father's unconventional lifestyle, flamboyant behavior, and effeminate male friends embarrassed him and made him feel ashamed. His father's homosexuality also confused him because, after all, hadn't the man fathered four children, all of whom were healthy heterosexuals? Perhaps he was fearful about growing up and turning into a homosexual like his father. Perhaps he felt he had to prove his own virility and masculinity so that his friends would not reject him as the son of a "queer." Perhaps his early sexual interest in girls and later promiscuity can be traced to deep fears about his sexual orientation and deep anxieties about his sexual performance. Even his friends wondered if O. J.'s obsession with sex and his own virility may have had its roots in his conflicted feelings about his father's homosexuality.

Growing Up in the Projects

O. J. and his three siblings grew up in the projects on Potrero Hill. As a frisky young boy, he and his peers would dart in and out of the tunnel under the hill at Sierra Street, dodging the trains as they rumbled through to Nineteenth and Arkansas. Agile and quick, he seemed to enjoy high-risk games where he could display his bravado and simultaneously outwit his opponents. According to one of his childhood buddies, when O. J. got too frisky, Eunice Simpson quickly and forcefully brought him back into line, "whipping him with anything she could find—a belt, a bottle . . ." O. J. grew to be very close to his mother, but he never forgot those whippings.

Staff members at the Potrero Hill Neighborhood Center who can still recall his escapades remember him as a lanky youth with an infectious grin and a mischievous twinkle in his eye, always in motion and frequently in trouble. In fact, his nickname, "Juice," was bestowed by his family because he was so hyperactive, always "juiced up." Most of the time he went to school, but he could often be glimpsed on the streets just hanging out or shooting baskets with his buddies.

On the weekend, O. J. and his boys, who called themselves the "Persian Warriors," looked for excitement in the projects around Potrero Hill and in the nearby Hunter's Point area. Their idea of fun was to crash parties, make out with the cute girls, and vandalize fancy cars. Sometimes they got into fights with gangs from other neighborhoods, sometimes they got involved in petty crime, and sometimes they just drove around the city talking aimlessly about their dreams and aspirations to get out of the ghetto, to have a better life.

Like Rodney King, O. J. got in trouble with the law when he was almost fifteen. He was caught robbing a liquor store and landed in juvenile hall for the weekend. But he was luckier than Rodney. A black social worker—one of the many women who would be captivated by his charm—recognized O. J.'s potential and asked Willie Mays to give him a pep talk. O. J. spent an afternoon with Willie, visiting his mansion on the San Francisco peninsula and watching him sign autographs for his adoring fans. O. J. recalled that he was awestruck by Willie's success and celebrity status, thinking, "Wouldn't it be great for people to know me and love me and want to come up to me?" For the first time in his young life, O. J. realized that there was a world worth aspiring to beyond the ghetto, a world that offered fortune and fame to those with talent and ambition. This may have been the moment when O. J. resolved to find out what lay beyond Potrero Hill, to see if there were other mountains to climb.

One of O. J.'s main buddies was Al Cowlings, who shared many of his dreams. They were both boys from the Hill, both hell-raisers who were in and out of trouble with the cops, both good athletes, and both attracted to the same girl. In fact, Al Cowlings was going out with Marguerite Whitley when O. J. first met her. Despite their close friendship, O. J. wasted no time in wooing this pretty, lively, and intelligent young woman from his best friend. He thought Marguerite fit the profile and the program he had begun to lay out for his life. He could envision her as a companion to be by his side as he made the great leap from the ghetto to the world outside. He had no inkling at that time how quickly he would outgrow Marguerite and how troubled their relationship would become.

Growing Out of the Ghetto

> The ghetto makes you want to hide your real identity—from cops, from teachers, and even from yourself. It forces you to build up false images.
>
> O. J. Simpson, 1974

Football was O. J.'s ticket to leave the ghetto behind. He and Al Cowlings were stars on the Galileo High School football team, hailed by the local coaches and sportswriters for their physical grace, athletic prowess, and down-to-earth personalities. In contrast to Rodney King, the would-be baseball player, O. J. had the skills, the motivation, and the media attention to ride right to the top.

Growing up poor and black in a city noted for its wealth, O. J. was not even on the periphery of the mainstream white establishment, nor was he touched by the bohemian ferment and eclectic rhythms of the counterculture emerging in San Francisco in the mid 1960s. Yet he sensed that there were worlds unseen and challenges unmet. Though his grades were too poor to gain admission to any four-year college, he was recruited by San Francisco City College after managing to obtain a draft deferment to avoid the war in Vietnam. City College was not that far geographically from Potrero Hill, but it was light-years away culturally from the mundane interests and limited views of the projects. For the second time in his life,

O. J. had a glimpse of the white world and the privileges it offered to a promising athlete. He set his sights on succeeding in that world and never turned back.

It was a pivotal decision. Still skinny and bowlegged, O. J. exploded as a running back for the City College football team and quickly attracted the attention of coaches up and down the West Coast. After breaking records and dazzling local fans with his flashy running style, O. J. was recruited by an assistant coach from the University of Southern California. He convinced O. J. that USC—known as the finishing school for the scions of the Southern California elite who couldn't get into Berkeley or Stanford—was the right school with the right team and the right contacts for him. For the ambitious jock from the wrong side of the hill, this was what he had been waiting for. But for the poor black boy from the projects, this was also the beginning of a lifelong struggle with his black identity.

The USC Experience

> Think of how much a black person has to sell of himself to try to get race not to matter. . . . You have to ignore the insults. You have to ignore the natural loyalties. You have to ignore your past. In a sense you have to just about deny yourself.
>
> Sharon Collins, sociologist, University of Illinois

From the day O. J. reported for football practice in the summer of 1967 until the day he left USC two years later, he would be painfully reminded of the distance he had traveled to achieve that goal. He was a black male from the inner city on a campus of white fraternity boys and sorority girls from the affluent suburbs. The only other visible blacks were athletes and unskilled service workers. His speech, dress, and manners betrayed his ghetto roots in a social environment where money and breeding were taken for granted. He was keenly aware of his limitations and deprivations, making him even more resolute to master the social graces as well as he had mastered the playing fields.

In a preview of his later ambivalent attachment to the black community, O. J. even refused to join the small Black Students Union, ostensibly for fear of losing his financial aid but perhaps also to avoid being labeled a militant black on that conservative campus. O. J. was a quick study, so he made good use of his years at USC to prepare himself for life in the mainstream, to make himself acceptable to white people, and to rid himself of the vestiges of blackness. Ever the optimist, O. J. was confident that he could transform himself from a dude from the projects to an American football hero, brown on the outside and neutral on the inside. He could never have imagined the cost or have predicted the consequences of this transformation.

> "Hertz told me in all their surveys that I was colorless," Simpson once said. ". . . The risk we take by embracing that role in white society is swapping identities. In wanting to be invited to white society's ball, we often put on so many layers of clothing that we forget what we wore to the party in the first place."
>
> W. C. Rhoden, *Emerge*, September 1994

After two years of football glory at USC, O. J. established himself as one of the greatest running backs in college football history. He set a national rushing record with his flashy zigzag style of running, was twice named to all-American teams, and won the coveted Heisman Trophy in 1968 at the end of his final college football season. O. J. was celebrating his first taste of celebrityhood at the Heisman award banquet when Marguerite, now his wife, sent a message that his first child, Arnelle, had arrived. It seemed as if the gods were truly smiling on him.

O. J.'s official statistics told only a part of the story, for he had picked up much more than record yardage and numerous trophies in his college football career. He had also picked up some skills that were less tangible but much more valuable for his future aspirations. He had learned how to manipulate people with his natural charm, magnetic personality, and self-deprecating sense of humor. He had learned to control his temper and channel his underlying anger and aggression. He had improved his diction and expanded his conversational repertoire. Most of all, he had learned some important social skills from the affluent and ambitious white boys who were only too pleased to bask in his reflected glory.

So with his rough edges smoothed out; his physical, mental, and social skills sharpened; and his personal horizons expanded, O. J. Simpson was drafted by the Buffalo Bills professional football team as their top choice in the spring of 1969—but only after holding out for a higher salary in his first contract negotiations. Clearly, he had learned something besides football plays at USC.

The year 1969 was a banner year for O. J.—he got his dream contract, he signed his first product endorsement with Chevrolet, and he bought a fifteen-room home in Woodstream Farms, an affluent area of Buffalo. By 1970, when his son Jason arrived, he and Marguerite truly epitomized a couple who were young, gifted, and black: parents of two beautiful children, poised on the brink of fame and fortune. Photos of the family in the mid 1970s show a handsome, healthy group enjoying a comfortable lifestyle and privileged status in America's race-conscious society.

It was a heady time for two kids from the wrong side of the Hill, two kids who were living the fantasy that most of their friends had never even dared to dream. But O. J. had also learned to enjoy the less public privileges of a good-looking star athlete, especially the access to wine, women, and the fast-track nightlife. He loved the spotlight, the glamour, and the excitement, but having a wife and children put a crimp in his style. By 1975, O. J. had decided to leave Marguerite and their kids in Los Angeles while he pursued the privileged and protected life of the professional athlete as a Buffalo Bills "bachelor."

THE MYTH

> Before Magic Johnson, Michael Jordan, Charles Barkley or Shaquille O'Neal, there was O. J.—superstar pitchman, actor, sportscaster and all-around celebrity. With unrivaled crossover appeal, he was living out the American dream, living proof of the vitality and viability of America's promise to all its people.
>
> Harry Edwards, *Sport*, February 1995

Buffalo, a cold, gray, working-class city, welcomed O. J. with less warmth and enthusiasm than he had anticipated. The leaders of the black community criticized him for buying a home in a predominantly white neighborhood, the first of many such conflicted interactions he would have with prominent blacks as his career exploded. But as he sparked the team to more exciting games with his record-breaking performances season after season, the Poles, the Germans, and even the blacks of Buffalo embraced this all-American football hero like a long-lost native son, quickly elevating him to the status of community legend. O. J. wasted no time in justifying their faith in him and rewarding their adulation.

From his first game in Buffalo's Rich Stadium in the fall of 1969 until his last game in 1978, O. J. broke all the team's records as a running back, won four rushing titles, and dominated the game as his hero Jim Brown had done before him. O. J. earned his place in sports history as one of the legendary football players of the 1970s, if not of all time, rushing for a record of 2,003 yards in the 1973 season. He got his chance at the brass ring and worked his tail off to catch it, understanding at some elemental level that this particular brass ring could also catapult him into the charmed circle of sports celebrities, if only he could hold on to it long enough.

O. J., the Playboy

> Our society's sports worship creates its own royalty for American men, demolishing every rule of status, birthright, entitlement.

> There is really no other hierarchy quite like it, enabling once poor men to socially vault so far, so fast.
>
> Sheila Weller, *Raging Heart*, 1995

Rumors began to surface that O. J.'s playing and running were not confined to the football field. He was seen frequently at Mulligan's Café, a popular sports bar, and other hot spots around town, usually surrounded by pretty girls and adoring fans. There were also unconfirmed rumors that O. J. was no stranger to drugs, especially cocaine, which was easily available and affordable in this crowd. Enjoying a bachelor existence in his rambling house for nearly half of every year, O. J. learned a whole new set of survival skills. He also proved himself to be an eager pupil in adapting to the perks and privileges of the superhero—the complimentary gifts, the clandestine sex, the casual drug use.

When O. J. was ostensibly spending time with Marguerite and his kids in the off-season, he was also busy filming commercials for companies like Hertz, which hired him in 1975 as the first black celebrity spokesman for a major corporation. The popular commercials showed him running through airports to catch a plane and soon led to other lucrative contracts with companies such as Tree Sweet orange juice, Foster Grant sunglasses, RC Cola, and Nabisco. Soon he was learning how to play golf and showing up at celebrity tournaments, schmoozing with corporate executives and politicians who wanted to rub shoulders with their sports heroes.

But while O. J. was learning to parlay the fringe benefits of being a sports hero, Marguerite was learning the pitfalls of being the hero's wife. In their rare times alone as a family, O. J. seemed increasingly restive, distracted, and disengaged. When she complained of his inattention and frequent absences, she told a few of her friends that he became enraged and abusive. Perhaps it was her loyalty to her childhood sweetheart or perhaps the rumors were exaggerated, but Marguerite apparently never made any official complaints about

O. J. to the police for any physical abuse. If the allegations were true and if she had reported them, perhaps this story would never have been written. What is fairly certain about the Simpson marriage in the 1970s is that it was in trouble, with O. J. the villain and Marguerite the victim.

> O. J. Simpson has been a narcissist for as long as any of us can remember him. . . . In the early years, we saw only the charming side of the condition. The extroversion, the cheerful response to adulation. Part and parcel of that same package, however, is a pathological self-absorption, an inflated sense of one's own entitlements, feelings of shame and humiliation capable of exploding into rage.
>
> Teresa Carpenter, *Esquire*, November 1994

In hindsight, O. J. was establishing a significant pattern in his adult life—the public persona of a respectable and responsible family man versus the private persona of a promiscuous and abusive Don Juan. The seeds were sown for what would later emerge as O. J.'s split personality—the Jekyll-and-Hyde of the all-American hero.

The Brentwood Dream House

While O. J. rocketed to fame with his exploits on the football field, Marguerite settled into a life of domesticity and motherhood. While he basked in the limelight of fans and fun-filled times in Buffalo, she retreated to the routine of child rearing and carpooling in Los Angeles.

In 1977, O. J. purchased a $5 million estate on North Rockingham Drive in Brentwood Park from celebrity real estate agent Elaine Young, the wife of actor Gig Young. It was his ultimate fantasy fulfilled—a luxurious Tudor-style mansion with a guest house, tennis courts, and a swimming pool. He boasted that his neighbors included Michael Ovitz, one of Hollywood's most powerful agents, and a number of movie executives and prominent politicians. Ironically, by the time of the murders, Simpson's neighbors would also include Richard Riordan, the recently elected mayor of Los Angeles, and Gil Garcetti, the Los Angeles County district attorney who would be directing the prosecution's case against him. Surely O. J. had broken the race barrier—he had finally made it into one of white America's most prestigious neighborhoods, played golf at one of its poshest country clubs (the Riviera Country Club in Pacific Palisades), and hobnobbed with some of its most powerful patriarchs.

O. J. Meets Nicole

> As a black woman, I have some problems with O. J. leaving his black wife, his black family, and the black community to go and marry a white woman. I think O. J. Simpson has racial identity problems himself. Why is it that every time some black man gets into trouble in the white world, he looks for the support of the black community that he has abandoned in the first place?
>
> Monique Jones, cosmetologist, Oakland

Along with O. J.'s ability to live in the white world came his license to claim one of its beauty queens as his own. While still married to Marguerite, O. J. was openly playing around, making the scene at the current "in" places in West Los Angeles. In June 1977, a pretty blonde waitress with a carefree air and a quick wit caught his attention at the Daisy Nightclub, a chic disco in Beverly Hills. Just out of high school in Orange County, Nicole Brown was only eighteen and very unsophisticated when she was drawn into the orbit of O. J.'s world. O. J. saw Nicole, with her long blonde hair, smoky amber eyes, and model's figure, as the ultimate trophy, a tangible prize for his hard-won success and a visible symbol of his complete assimilation into the white world. O. J. didn't waste any time or money wooing Nicole, nor did she fail to live up to her part of the bargain as his "trophy" lover.

The former homecoming princess at Dana Hills High School in Monarch Point knew a good thing when she saw it. She was, of course, too young to recognize O. J. Simpson as the runner in the Hertz TV ads, the famous USC football legend, the celebrity sportscaster. But she soon learned that O. J. really had "juice" in a town where image was everything. She was impressed by his glamorous lifestyle, his wealthy friends, his adoring fans. She also knew he liked to party and liked pretty women, squiring them around town in his fancy sports cars, flashing his famous smile, and enjoying the attention of the crowd. But Nicole wanted more than a one-night stand and a few trinkets from this charismatic man—she wanted the whole package and planned her strategy to have him signed, sealed, and delivered for a long-term relationship.

Soon after they began dating, O. J. set Nicole up in an apartment, and they became one of L.A.'s high-profile couples, making cameo appearances in all the trendy bars and restaurants, showing up at the glamorous parties and shows, participating in the charity golf tournaments and benefits. For a laid-back beach beauty from a middle-class family, Nicole quickly eased into the fast-paced life of West Los Angeles, where a woman's worth is measured by her cars, her clothes, and her credit cards. When she wasn't catering to O. J.'s whims or being exhibited as his newest prize, Nicole discovered that she really got a rush shopping on Rodeo Drive, going to lunch at chic restaurants, and hanging out with the pretty and pampered wives and girlfriends of O. J.'s celebrity friends, like Chris Kardashian Jenner and Cynthia Garvey. Meanwhile, Marguerite and her children remained in the Brentwood mansion, still maintaining the fiction that they were a family but resigned to the fact that O. J. had a very public and very pretty mistress.

Rebuilding a Life

In 1979, the year after he was traded to the San Francisco 49ers and returned to his hometown as a hero, O. J.'s grasp on the brass ring slipped and he came crashing down to the real world again. Like so many of his fellow athletes, he had played for years with bruised bones, torn cartilage, sore muscles, and constant pain. He prided himself on pushing himself to the limits of his physical endurance, then punishing his body to go beyond it. But his knee had for several years been a chronic source of irritation and pain, and he finally had to have surgery to repair it. The operation repaired the knee but ended O. J.'s football career. At the age of thirty-two, O. J. Simpson's running days were over. What was he going to do for the rest of his life?

> He wanted to be accepted. . . . They hailed him as "the Juice," the black superjock. That was a safe and flattering way to go for him. Because when it came to doing something beyond parading his image, when it came to acting and doing commentary, he wasn't very good, and he knew it. . . . He really tried, but he just couldn't make it.
>
> A white friend of O. J.'s

Two other events in 1978 and 1979 also changed the course of O. J.'s life. In September 1978, after eleven years of an ever stormier marriage, he and Marguerite had separated but kept in touch because of the kids. One day, in the summer of 1979, O. J. got a frantic call from the hospital that his youngest daughter, twenty-three-month-old Aaren, had drowned in the family's swimming pool. It was a tragic accident, but O. J. was distraught, accusing his estranged wife of "murdering his child."

But not even the death of his baby daughter could change his feelings about his Rockingham house, the symbol of his successful assimilation. In March 1980, he and Marguerite finalized their divorce, and he faced a new decade with the loss of his career, the loss of his wife, and the loss of his remaining children. But O. J. played hardball in the divorce negotiations and kept his dream house in Brentwood. Marguerite and their children moved to a more modest house in a far more modest neighborhood.

Not to worry. O. J. was one of those rare black athletes fortunate enough to have selected good lawyers and a good agent who were building his financial interests while he was building his football career. Long before he was traded by the Buffalo Bills and forcibly retired from the San Francisco 49ers, he had diversified his interests and laid the groundwork for a long-anticipated career in the media as a sports celebrity. O. J. had his own production company (Orenthal Productions), a long-term contract with Hertz Rent-a-Car, investments in a fried-chicken franchise (Pioneer Chicken), several Honey-Baked ham stores, and other business ventures. He was in great demand on the endless circuit of convention banquets, celebrity golf tournaments, motivational workshops, and personal "cameo" appearances—a true American hero, a rags-to-riches story in living color.

O. J., the Crossover Celebrity

> Simpson has been a player in the American celebrity scene for close to 30 years. In addition to other issues it raises, the road that has taken Simpson to this point raises deeply rooted issues of escaping, or being delivered from Blackness.
>
> W. C. Rhoden, *Emerge*, September 1994

O. J. wore the mantle of his celebrity status with charm, grace, boundless enthusiasm, and that self-effacing humor and humility that had so endeared him to the press and the public. He always seemed to have the right word, the right smile, and the right style for all occasions. He seemed the embodiment of self-confidence, self-control, and self-discipline, the very antithesis to the usual stereotype of the inferior, aggressive, and unmotivated black man in our society. In fact, O. J. often commented to his friends that he was treated "as well as a white man" wherever he went. He truly believed the public relations propaganda that he was "colorless." Thus O. J. Simpson became the first black athlete or entertainer—before Magic Johnson, before Michael Jordan—to "cross over" to become a celebrity endorser on TV. O. J. had finally run down the hill and crossed the freeway to the other side—he could confidently walk the walk, talk the talk, and even live the life of a white man in America. The USC lessons were beginning to pay off in gold.

Most of all, O. J. enjoyed his newfound freedom to "play the field" when Nicole wasn't around to rein him in. As his fame and fortune grew, so did his reputation as a Don Juan, a man with a voracious sexual appetite who seemed to have to prove his manhood with every attractive woman he encountered.

THE MARRIAGE

> The marriage has driven some blacks to fury: "Why do so many successful black men have to marry white women? . . . If he had stayed with that black woman, he wouldn't be in all this trouble."
>
> W. C. Rhoden, *Emerge*, September 1994

After O. J.'s divorce, Nicole was not satisfied with just being a live-in lover, so she cajoled him and nagged him until he finally capitulated and conceded to her wish for a lavish wedding with a cast of hundreds, a catered dinner, and enough flowers to fill a ballroom. Guests at the wedding noted with some surprise that O. J. had chosen friends from his pro football years (Marcus Allen, Al Cowlings, Lynn Swann) as his ushers, all but one of them handsome African-Americans. For a man who had compulsively surrounded himself with white friends, business associates, and hired help—his secretary, his lawyer, his business manager, his accountant, and his doctor were all white—there was something very revealing about his choice of ushers. The man who wanted so much to be seen as "colorless" had reached out to his "homeboys" to stand by his side at the very ceremony that would tie him unequivocally to the white world.

Nicole also got pregnant, perhaps as an insurance policy against O. J.'s indecision and lack of enthusiasm. Apparently O. J. was not pleased and, according to several close friends, vehemently told her to get an abortion. She had seen his temper on many occasions, always giving in to placate him. This time she stood her ground and played her cards just right, and this time O. J. capitulated. They married on February 2, 1985, when Nicole was twenty-six and O. J. was thirty-eight; eight months later, they had a beautiful baby girl, whom they named Sydney. Now the homecoming princess and her black knight were a real family, ensconced in their Rockingham castle and eager to establish their own circle of friends and family traditions.

Media and Movie Star

While Nicole was settling in to a more sedate role as wife and new mother, O. J. was blossoming in his career as a TV sports commentator and character actor. In 1985, O. J. was inducted into the Football Hall of Fame. He was also able to transfer his fame as a superathlete to his new roles as genial sports commentator and macho movie star. His image was unblemished, his reputation untarnished, his lifestyle enviable. From the late 1970s to the early 1990s, O. J. was a supporting actor in several "B" adventure movies with titles like *The Klansman*, *Firepower*, *The Cassandra Crossing*, and a series of *Naked Gun* movies, most long on action and violence but short on plot and character development. O. J.'s roles rarely had much dialogue or psychological complexity, but they always managed to show off his impressive physique and athletic skills. For O. J., the movie career, though modest, was just another venue for his success, another testament to his versatility, another proof of how far he had traveled from Potrero Hill.

> Here was a man, in his prime a remarkable athlete, whose remaining talents were minor except for the ability to make people like him. He had distilled the essence of affability and somehow marketed it.
>
> Richard Hoffer, *Sports Illustrated*, June 27, 1994

But by the late 1980s, a decade after his retirement from pro football, O. J. was beginning to realize that he would never be a polished actor or a romantic leading man. His dream of a full-time acting career began to fade, and he even joked to his friends that his roles were pretty limited. In 1978, he set up Orenthal Productions. He had sold some successful films to NBC, but the network abruptly canceled its contract with him after five years. He had a brief but unsuccessful trial as a commentator for ABC's *Monday Night Football*. He was still promoting rental cars for Hertz and products for a few other companies, but he knew it was only a matter of time before he was replaced by a younger celebrity who had captured the public's imagination. His father, Jimmy, stricken with AIDS, had died in 1986, just a month before O. J.'s thirty-ninth birthday. O. J. was facing a midlife crisis just in time for his fortieth birthday.

Marital Problems: The Moth and the Flame

> She was as locked in to him as he was to her. There was nothing they didn't know about each other. Whether they were together or apart, they knew there would never be a relationship like the one they had with each other. They just couldn't finish this thing between them. They were totally in love.
>
> Cici Shahian, a good friend of Nicole's

From the very first day of their celebrity-studded wedding, the Simpson marriage, like so many other relationships in West Los Angeles, was more show than substance. O. J. expected Nicole to blend in with his buddies and their wives, a group of middle-aged nouveau riche businessmen, lawyers, and sports celebrities. For naive and nonchalant Nicole, the glamour and high visibility of their constant parties, club-hopping, and vacations was a fantasy come true, a world where her every impulse and desire could be fulfilled. But their glamorous public profile masked their growing tensions and conflicts over O. J.'s dominating behavior, his jealous rages, and his continuing affinity for pretty girls, especially blondes.

Their public profile also masked something even more troubling—O. J.'s psychological and physical abuse of Nicole. Even before they were married, O. J. had roughed up Nicole and had on several occasions thrown her clothes down the stairs and swept all her family pictures off the staircase wall. Whenever Nicole mentioned these rages and physical intimidation to her mother, Juditha always minimized them and urged her to work things out with O. J. According to one writer who interviewed the Brown family members, Nicole's mother warned her not to provoke O. J.'s violent temper. Did her mother's conciliatory attitude reflect her own traditional European upbringing, or did it reflect her family's reluctance to cut itself off from O. J.'s beneficence?

O. J., the Benefactor

O. J. had been very generous to the whole Brown family ever since he and Nicole started going out together. He had paid for family vacations to Aspen, Hawaii, and Mexico, footing the bill for Nicole's parents, her sisters, and their children. He also subsidized Nicole's mother's travel agency business. He had helped Nicole's father get a Hertz dealership in Laguna Niguel, which was very profitable. He had paid college tuition for one of Nicole's younger sisters. O. J. Simpson was both shining knight and fairy godfather to the Brown family. After the murders, there were some friends who accused Juditha and Lou Brown of collusion in Nicole's battering in exchange for O. J.'s continued generosity. What price were they willing to pay to sacrifice their own beautiful daughter?

Then there were other friends who pointed to Juditha's background to explain her apparent acquiescence with Nicole's batterer. After all, Nicole had followed in her mother's footsteps. Juditha, a handsome brunette version of Nicole, had met Lou in 1954 in her native Germany, where he was a circulation manager for the U.S. Army newspaper *Stars and Stripes* and she was working as a secretary on the American base. It must have been a powerful attraction because Lou left his wife and three children to move in with Juditha, and shortly afterward, they started their own family. Nicole and her older sister, Denise, also a striking brunette, were born in Germany before their parents were legally married; later the family moved to California to begin a new life together.

Juditha described herself as a "typical German *Hausfrau*," completely dedicated to her husband and family. A good German girl, Juditha had been reared to respect her husband as the head of the household and to keep her family together for better or worse. So she minimized Nicole's complaints about O. J.'s abuse and counseled her to be more loving and patient with him. Hoping to shore up their shaky marriage, Juditha did not really seem to understand that the abuse was escalating as O. J.'s private persona was getting more and more out of control.

As Nicole matured and increasingly asserted her autonomy, O. J. become more and more controlling and abusive. She confided to close friends that he resented her pregnancies, so much so that he forced her to have several abortions in the seventeen years they were together. When she insisted on carrying two pregnancies to term, he expressed his anger by ridiculing her weight gain, embarrassing her in front of their friends, and flirting openly with other women. Was this, perhaps, a classic example of the immature man-child who could not endure the thought of being displaced as his wife's primary love object, not even by his own child?

Becoming a Family

When Justin was born on August 6, 1988, O. J. welcomed his second son enthusiastically. Observers noted that he had always shown a preference for his son Jason over his two daughters. He liked to think of himself as a man's man, so another male child would be a guy with whom he could engage in roughhousing, play games of touch football, and shape in his own macho image. As Justin and Sydney developed into two beautiful children with bronze skin and dark blonde hair, O. J. treated them, too, like trophies, taking them along to charity fairs and celebrity events and showing them off to his neighbors and friends. He seemed particularly delighted that they looked "white" like their mother, although to an unbiased observer they were obviously racially mixed, indistinguishable from the thousands of biracial and multiracial children in Los Angeles. The "colorless" celebrity became annoyed with Sydney when she would ask if she was black; he felt that they lived in a rarified social sphere where race was irrelevant and people were colorblind. O. J. could live in a white world and could marry a white woman, but despite his private fantasies, his children would always be black in America.

ESCALATING CONFLICTS AND CONFRONTATIONS

By the Christmas holidays of 1988, the Simpsons' marital problems were well known among close friends and family members. Nicole had called the police on at least eight occasions when O. J. had beaten her, but the police had always mediated the disputes without filing charges. On New Year's Eve, the escalating tensions in their marriage, fueled by a disastrous Christmas holiday visit to their apartment in New York City, erupted into a bruising fight that culminated in a frantic call to the police in the early morning hours of January 1, 1989. Nicole, badly beaten and humiliated, finally filed assault charges against O. J. and, for the first time in their rocky relationship, followed through with a court hearing.

Although the police had seen her frantically running from the house screaming, "He's going to kill me! He's going to kill me!" and had seen her badly bruised face, the charge against O. J. was reduced to a misdemeanor count of spousal battery, to which he reluctantly pleaded "no contest." As she had predicted to friends, O. J. received a light sentence: a $470 fine, 120 hours of community service, and mandated counseling of two sessions per week. Even the judge had succumbed to O. J.'s charm and his celebrity status. Again, Nicole must have felt discouraged and abandoned by all those who professed to love and care about her welfare—her family, her friends, and now the judicial system.

The Discreet Arrest

The arrest was handled discreetly in the press, with the Simpsons issuing a statement that they loved each other and that their marriage was "stronger than ever." O. J. was most concerned about losing his lucrative contracts with Hertz and NBC Sports. But these giants of corporate responsibility and community involvement treated the incident as if it were a private family matter, of no concern to the public or to their stockholders. This was the critical opportunity, the "teachable moment," when a few words of warning or advice from his executive role models might have helped O. J. acknowledge his violent proclivities and led him to seek professional help. As it was, he was able to count nearly all of his celebrity appearances as part of his "community service" and even convinced the court that he could substitute telephone counseling sessions for fifty-minute office visits. Over the next two years, Nicole became more and more angry at O. J.'s blatant infidelities, more and more intolerant of his daily golf outings, and more and more disenchanted with their public and private lives.

Separation and Divorce

In March 1992, Nicole finally resolved to leave O. J. and to live her own life, away from the glare of publicity and the glamour of the spotlight. Despite his strong objections and promises to change his ways, Nicole filed for divorce, citing "irreconcilable differences," and moved into a nearby town house complex on Gretna Green with their two children. Nicole was free for the first time since she had graduated from high school.

She relished this newly minted freedom. She found new friends, bought new clothes, and discovered new clubs, restaurants, and gyms in the expanding "Lower Brentwood" yuppie scene on San Vicente. Her new friends included Faye Resnick and Kato Kaelin, who would become willing partners in her search for the carefree single young adulthood she had never experienced. One of her favorite restaurants was the Mezzaluna (Italian for "half-moon"), with its young hip waiters like Ron Goldman, a twenty-five-year-old aspiring actor.

O. J.'s friends report that he was obsessed with Nicole's leaving, calling them at all hours to talk about her, pleading with her to return, appealing to her family for support. They also noted a troubling change in O. J.'s moods and behavior—he began to follow Nicole around, to show up at restaurants that she frequented, and to try to embarrass or humiliate her dates. One evening, O. J. followed her home and spied on her while she was having sex with an attractive new beau, the manager of the Mezzaluna. A few weeks later, on October 25, 1993, she had to call 911 again after he tried to break her back door down. The operator could hear him in the background, shouting and cursing in his rage at her sexual encounter.

As O. J.'s private devils were becoming more and more public, Nicole was growing more and more fearful of his violent temper. In early 1993, she joined a therapy group for battered women but quit after a dozen sessions. This was her second attempt to get help for their abusive relationship. In 1992, she had rejected the warning of Susan Forward, a therapist who had urgently advised her to leave O. J. and cut off all contact with him. Even in the face of expert advice and her own inner feelings of dread that O. J. would someday try to kill her, Nicole still had a strong attachment to him and was ambivalent about the divorce up until the moment she signed the final papers.

Their divorce was bittersweet, for Nicole had signed a prenuptial agreement and O. J.'s lawyer fiercely protected his financial assets. She had to leave their beautiful house on Rockingham and give up the perks and the privileges of a celebrity's spouse. With her lump-sum financial settlement of $433,750 plus $10,000 in monthly child support, she bought a town house on South Bundy Drive in Brentwood, within walking distance of O. J.'s home, so the children would not be totally uprooted from their neighborhood, their friends, and even their dogs, who liked to have the run of both houses. But Nicole had finally escaped from O. J.'s smothering embrace, and now she would plan her own plans and dream her own dreams.

Starting Over

> Nicole's [friends] could see the difference in her: there was about her now a finally grounded sense of freedom, an understanding that O. J. would never change—not his womanizing, not his obsession with her, not his stalking, and not his violence.
>
> Sheila Weller, *Raging Heart*, 1995

But O. J. could not give up his blonde princess so easily. When Nicole made some overtures to him, his pride nearly got in the way of his passion for her. After playing cat and mouse for several months, they tried a reconciliation in early 1994, but Nicole soon realized that old dogs cannot learn new tricks. O. J., the inveterate womanizer, had not changed, nor had he learned to control his volatile temper. In May 1994, Nicole finally terminated her relationship with O. J. She also resolved to leave her house on South Bundy Drive and move to a rental home in Malibu overlooking the Pacific Ocean, away from O. J. and closer to her family, back to the beach where she felt most at peace.

O. J. may have sensed that this time Nicole's decision was irrevocable. He may have felt that he was losing control of his life, a déjà vu experience that brought back unhappy memories of his first divorce and the end of his football career in 1979. Facing the loss of his trophy wife, his two beautiful children, and his image as a family man, he also may have felt himself sliding back down the mountain, slipping ever so gradually in his work, slowly losing his youth, feeling new aches and pains daily in his arthritic body. He had reluctantly given up his dream of Hollywood stardom and was dimly aware that he was still just barely on the periphery of the A list, the true movers and shakers of Los Angeles society. He had climbed nearly to the top of the mountain, but now he was afraid it was all going to come crashing down.

Nicole may perhaps have unwittingly delivered the final blow to O. J.'s fragile ego on Sunday, June 12, when she and her whole family attended Sydney's dance recital at the Paul Revere Middle School in Brentwood. O. J. was also there—on his own, as Kato Kaelin had declined to accompany him. (Kaelin had moved into the Rockingham guest house after O. J. objected to his staying as an unpaid guest at Nicole's town house.) Both of her parents proudly watched nine-year-old Sydney Simpson dance in a number called "Footloose," but they had very little to say to each other. When the recital was over about 6:00 P.M., O. J. genially greeted many of his neighbors in the audience and then asked Nicole if he could join them all for dinner at the Mezzaluna. Nicole said no and quickly left with her parents, her two sisters, her three nephews, and Justin and Sydney. They left O. J. standing there alone, publicly rejected by his former wife and humiliated in front of his friends and neighbors.

7

The Crime, the Chase, the Arrest

The evening of June 12, 1994, was a typical summer Sunday evening in Los Angeles. It was warm, slightly humid, with a crescent moon partially obscured by seasonal fog. In the early evening, the streets in the Brentwood neighborhood were full of couples strolling, children riding bicycles, and singles walking dogs. Diners at the Mezzaluna restaurant remember seeing Nicole Brown Simpson and her family enjoying their dinner and one another, leaving the restaurant about 8:30 P.M.

About 9:40 P.M., Juditha Brown called Nicole to say that she had left her prescription sunglasses at the restaurant and asked her daughter to retrieve them. When Nicole called the restaurant, her new friend, waiter Ron Goldman, offered to drop the glasses off on his way home from work. Ron left the Mezzaluna on foot around 9:45 P.M. By the time Ron was approaching Bundy, Nicole had put her two tired children to bed, perhaps after reviewing the day's exciting events with them. About an hour later, at 10:45 P.M., a limousine driver arrived at O. J. Simpson's Rockingham estate to take him to the Los Angeles Airport, but the driver had to wait nearly fifteen minutes before O. J. answered the door. The limo left the Simpson driveway at 11:15 P.M., and by 11:45, O. J. was comfortably settled in the first-class cabin of a United Airlines plane on a "red-eye" flight to Chicago.

THE CRIME

> O. J. Simpson is a creation of Hollywood and Madison Avenue where image is everything. The image, regardless of the finding of guilt or innocence, has been shattered. Simpson will spend the rest of his life picking up the pieces.
>
> W. C. Rhoden, *Emerge*, September 1994

Shortly after midnight, a couple walking their dog encountered a white Akita with bloody paws, barking furiously and aimlessly wandering around the neighborhood. They followed the dog until he led them to a town house at 875 South Bundy Drive, where they discovered the bodies of Nicole Brown Simpson and Ronald Goldman, lying grotesquely in pools of blood. The front door was open and candles from the living room windows cast flickers of light on the two prone figures, the woman curled up in the fetal position and the man leaning against a palm with his eyes open.

By the time the police arrived at the scene, a small crowd had gathered to stare at the grisly scene, partly hidden by the shrubbery framing the entryway. Neighbors spoke in hushed tones about hearing a dog's persistent barking and plaintive wailing earlier in the evening, but no one remembered hearing or seeing anything that would have prepared them for this horrible crime.

Someone informed Ron Phillips, the first police detective to arrive at the crime scene, that Nicole was the wife of O. J. Simpson, who lived only a few blocks away. Phillips and three other detectives—Tom Lange, Phillip Vannatter, and Mark Fuhrman—drove to the Simpson home but were unable to rouse anyone. Fuhrman offered to jump over the high fence, then went around to the guest house and woke up Kato Kaelin, who took them find Arnelle, O. J.'s oldest daughter, who was asleep in another part of the house. It was Arnelle who would call O. J. at his Chicago hotel so that the police could break the news to him about the murders of his ex-wife and her friend. It was Arnelle who would go down to police headquarters to pick up her younger siblings, Sydney and Justin, to take them back home to their father's Rockingham estate. It was also Arnelle who would later contradict some crucial police testimony about how they entered the house, how her father responded to the news of the murders, and how they searched the house without a warrant.

The next few days were confusing and chaotic, with frazzled police investigators, frantic media reports, and frustrated family members and friends all trying to obtain credible information to form a coherent picture of this double tragedy. The rumor mill immediately churned out lurid tales of drug deals gone awry, Mafia hit men, and even a murder-suicide pact. And one persistent but preposterous rumor was gaining ground—that O. J. was the perpetrator of these crimes. After returning from Chicago, O. J. had been taken down in handcuffs to the Los Angeles Police Department for a "friendly and informal interrogation" and had talked to the police for three hours without his lawyer present. His lawyer and close friend, Howard Weitzman, was said to be highly disturbed by O. J.'s voluntary offer of an alibi to the police, who had manipulated his client. On Wednesday, June 15, Weitzman resigned from the case, and Robert Shapiro, a well-known Los Angeles "celebrity" lawyer, took it over.

By June 16, the day of Nicole's funeral, the papers were reporting that Simpson was the major suspect and that he had assaulted Nicole in several previous incidents of domestic violence. Unofficial reports leaked from the medical examiner's office indicated that Nicole and Ron had both been repeatedly stabbed with a sharp knife by an assailant powerful enough to sever her head almost completely and fast enough to kill them both in a matter of minutes. At 8:30 that evening, police said their preliminary laboratory tests revealed a match between blood at the crime scene and O. J. Simpson's blood, drawn with his permission three days earlier.

THE CHASE AND THE ARREST

> A CNN-Gallup Poll, conducted on June 22, 1994, found that 43 percent of whites and 23 percent of blacks felt that the police had treated O. J. Simpson "too leniently" on the day he was arrested.
>
> *Gallup Poll Monthly*, June 1994

By Friday, June 17, the case was being called "the crime of the decade," but the victims had taken a back seat to the suspect. The police were negotiating with Shapiro for O. J. to give himself up, the media were in a frenzy, and O. J. was surrounded by his entourage of lawyers, four doctors, and several close friends. When O. J. did not surrender voluntarily by noon, the police arrived at the San Fernando Valley home where he had been staying, only to find that he and his buddy Al Cowlings had fled in Simpson's white Ford Bronco. The next few hours resembled both soap opera and circus, with the police declaring O. J. a fugitive, Simpson's lawyer declaring him "suicidal," Simpson's friend Robert Kardashian reading a letter O. J. wrote proclaiming his innocence, and dozens of anonymous callers "revealing" his whereabouts. The police located the Bronco just before 6:00 P.M. by tracking O. J.'s cellular phone calls. Cowlings had driven his friend to Orange County, very near Nicole's burial site; they were spotted at a freeway interchange called the El Toro Y, headed toward the San Diego Freeway.

The chase began with dozens of highway patrol cars, police helicopters, and television crews following the slow progress of the Bronco as it wandered aimlessly through Los Angeles County. This may have been the most widely publicized event in television history, as 95 million Americans (two-thirds of the country's households) were riveted for nearly two hours in front of their TV sets, watching with a mixture of fascination and fear as Al Cowlings drove his lifelong friend to an uncertain fate. O. J. had dialed 911 on his car phone, told the police that he was armed, and threatened to kill himself unless he could talk to his mother in San Francisco. Were they headed to the cemetery where O. J. would say farewell to Nicole for one last time? Was O. J. planning to kill himself with the .357 magnum that Cowlings had warned the police he was cradling in his arms, along with a picture of his children? Would the police close in on the Bronco and force it into a ditch or cause a fatal crash?

The suspense finally came to an end when Cowlings drove the Bronco into the driveway of Simpson's dream home just before 8:00 P.M., passing hundreds of well-wishers with signs supporting O. J. The nation breathed a collective sigh of relief as police finally convinced O. J. to relinquish his gun and give himself up. When he walked into his home, he submitted to a search and then asked to call his mother in San Francisco. Before he was handcuffed and put into the police car to go down to LAPD headquarters, he asked for a glass of orange juice. O. J. Simpson, American hero, seemed for a few moments like the little boy from Potrero Hill, seeking the familiar comforts of home. The football star whose number 32 jersey hung in the Football Hall of Fame was booked at 10:00 P.M. as number BK4013970–061794 at the Los Angeles jail.

The Grand Jury Fiasco

Public opinion polls conducted nationally and locally by newspapers, weekly magazines, and radio and television talk shows revealed a wide discrepancy between the views of blacks and whites on O. J.'s arrest and possible indictment. In a *Los Angeles Times* poll reported on June 28, 1994, three out of four blacks (74 percent) sympathized with Simpson, compared to 50 percent of Latinos and only 38 percent of whites. A *Newsweek* poll taken in late July showed that 60 percent of blacks in the United States believed that O. J. was a victim of a setup, but the majority of whites thought his arrest was warranted. In the July Gallup poll, 64 percent of blacks believed that O. J. would not receive a fair trial, but only 41 percent of whites had that opinion.

The drama of the trial was foreshadowed by the aborted grand jury hearing and the preliminary hearing, both of which whetted the public appetite for more details about the crime, the victims, and O. J. himself. Only three days after Simpson's arrest, Gil Garcetti, the Los Angeles County district attorney, elected to office in 1992, convened a grand jury to consider whether the evidence in the case justified an indictment of O. J. Simpson as the presumed assailant of his former wife Nicole and Ron Goldman.

By the time the grand jury had been convened, O. J. Simpson had hired a cadre of defense lawyers from across the nation, all celebrities in their own right. Shapiro, the head lawyer, was a suntanned, sophisticated, slick operator from Los Angeles, the quintessential Hollywood attorney. Shapiro contacted his old friend F. Lee Bailey, the bombastic battering ram from Boston, and assembled a stable of legal experts from New York, San Francisco, and Los Angeles—all of them successful and highly visible white males. They were quickly dubbed the Dream Team by the press, described as the best team money could buy, clear testimony to the resources available to the millionaire defendant. It was still unclear why his personal attorney, Howard Weitzman, had resigned abruptly after his interrogation at police headquarters. Only the tabloid press dared ask the obvious question: Were these legal developments signs that O. J. was really guilty as charged? If not, why would his good friend decline to represent him, and why would he be willing to risk bankruptcy from massive legal fees sure to be submitted by the Dream Team?

Garcetti, wounded politically from a series of badly botched trials (the Rodney King police brutality case, the Menendez brothers' first trial for killing their parents), was obsessed with a victory in this high-profile murder case. But he immediately got off to a bad start with the grand jury, which, despite its presumed secret proceedings, was compromised early in the hearings. Defense lawyers objected strenuously to the media accounts of the murder and the portrayal of O. J. Simpson as the perpetrator, claiming that the grand jury proceedings were inevitably biased and could not lead to an objective finding in the case. Surprisingly, their charges struck a sensitive nerve in the district attorney's office; on June 24, he disbanded the grand jury, an unprecedented move, but only the first in a series of unusual precedents in this unconventional case.

The Preliminary Hearing

The defense team was ecstatic about this development. Eager to publicize their side of the case, the defense lawyers agreed to a preliminary hearing to determine if there was sufficient evidence against their client to warrant an indictment. They also hoped to elicit sympathy for their client from his many fans and supporters, not to mention the unstated but not unsubtle goal of convincing the potential jury pool of their client's innocence. The preliminary hearing began on June 30, 1994, in the Los Angeles Municipal Court with Judge Kathleen Kennedy-Powell presiding.

The preliminary hearing proceeded at a glacial pace while counsel for the opposing sides invoked every legal technicality to win an advantage and to shape the direction of the widely anticipated trial. Much like boxers in preliminary matches, the prosecution and defense lawyers circled around each other, testing for weak points and trying out their strategies as they prepared for the main event. But after six days of testimony, Judge Kennedy-Powell found that there was sufficient evidence to justify bringing O. J. Simpson to trial on a charge of double murder.

THE MEDIA RESPONSE

From the moment O. J. Simpson was arrested, the media went into a frenzy. Television commentators, newspaper columnists, and radio talk show hosts quickly discovered that O. J. generated even more excitement as an accused killer than he did as a football player. The public appetite for information about the murders was insatiable from the very beginning, so the media found ever more creative ways of filling that need. Within days, they had abandoned any pretense at objectivity and were slanting stories to portray O. J. as a callous husband and a cold-blooded killer. The media had found another celebrity with clay feet, and they were eager to shatter the myth, delighted to destroy the image of O. J. Simpson, American hero.

By the end of June, the weekly magazines had rushed to expose all of O. J.'s dirty laundry, information that sportswriters, his friends, and the Los Angeles Police Department had carefully screened from the public in his glory days. *Time,* in its June 27, 1994, issue, ran O. J.'s police mug shot on its cover with the caption "An American Tragedy." The photograph had been altered to make him look darker and more menacing, the epitome of white America's stereotype of the violent and sexually aggressive black male. It created a firestorm of controversy about journalistic ethics (much of it blatantly hypocritical), but it set the tone for the media coverage to follow. Articles in *Newsweek*, *Sports Illustrated*, and *U.S. News and World Report* all reflected an undertone of race, the subtext that would dominate the analysis of the case and the dynamics of the trial; ultimately, the race issue would permeate even the deliberations of the jury.

After the preliminary hearing in late June, the media coverage took on an even more aggressive posture toward O. J., exposing his physical abuse of Nicole, his obsessive behaviors, his alleged drug use, and his promiscuous sexual history. Op-ed pieces in the *New York Times*, the *Washington Post*, and the *Los Angeles Times* portrayed him as the "poster boy for domestic violence." By September, monthly magazine articles began to appear that further demonized and discredited O. J. as an abusive husband, a neglectful father, and a failed sportscaster. Profiles in upscale magazines like *Vanity Fair* and *Esquire* focused on O. J.'s ghetto roots, his racial identity problems, and his career frustrations. Again, the presumption of guilt precluded any dispassionate analysis of the case, even the possibility that there had been a "rush to judgment" to arrest an innocent man. After all, as many of these writers implied, O. J. had had the audacity to succeed at the white man's game, to marry the white man's woman, and to live in the white man's world, but underneath all his veneer of upper-middle-class success and sophistication, O. J. Simpson was just another black man who had stepped out of his place.

During the seven months that elapsed between O. J. Simpson's arrest in mid June and the beginning of his trial in late January, O. J. had been subjected to his first trial by the media, in the court of public opinion. He was "convicted" solely on the basis of circumstantial evidence, frequently misidentified by "reliable informants" and misconstrued by the media. The same reporters who had created and nurtured the myth of O. J. Simpson the superstar, excused his dissolute lifestyle, and covered up his spousal abuse were now competing to tarnish and destroy his dignity and his reputation. His positive image as a sports legend, a celebrity businessman, and an assimilated black role model was irreparably damaged, presumably beyond any possibility of future rehabilitation.

The American media machine, in all of its power and persuasiveness, had succeeded in transforming O. J. Simpson, all-American hero, into O. J. Simpson, African-American villain. The media, which had once merchandised O. J. Simpson as the quintessential Oreo, had now repackaged and relabeled him as the pathological Othello, a brutish black man, just another Rodney King.

8

The People v. *O. J. Simpson*

The Trial Begins

> Simpson has been depicted as Othello, Richard Wright's Bigger Thomas, William Faulkner's Joe Christmas, and above all, as Emmett Till, the 14-year-old Chicago boy lynched in Money, Mississippi, after he flirted with a white woman in the summer of 1955.
>
> E. R. Shipp, *Columbia Journalism Review*, November-December 1994

It was called the trial of the century from the moment Judge Lance Ito took his seat on the bench in Courtroom 9–307 of the Los Angeles County courthouse on September 26, 1994, to the final rendering of the verdict on October 3, 1995, just over a year later. It could have also been called the ultimate media event, the first major trial in American history given gavel-to-gavel media coverage, seen on millions of television screens, and heard on thousands of radio stations around the world. Like Romans enjoying the spectacle of lions mauling Christians in the arena, the public was fascinated by the spectacle of lawyers attacking witnesses in the courtroom. Ironically, few of the many commentators and instant experts could have predicted that the trial itself, irrespective of the crime and the defendant, would extend its tentacles throughout the community like an octopus, crushing its own unintended victims in a series of bizarre encounters and bruising confrontations.

PRETRIAL POSITIONING

As the Simpson trial unfolded, the public was treated to a crash course in American jurisprudence and an intimate view of the criminal justice system. The trial demonstrated the extraordinary measures the system provides to safeguard the rights of the accused and the somewhat arcane legal strategies employed by the judge and the defense lawyers to guarantee the protection of these rights. But the trial also exposed the weaknesses inherent in the system, from the relatively minor errors in recording and storing evidence to the egregious mistakes of the police, the coroner, and the criminalists in collecting and analyzing the crime scene evidence.

Viewers of this trial, not unlike soap opera fans, quickly became addicted to the continuing drama, grading the prosecution and defense lawyers for their attacks (direct examination) and counterattacks (cross-examination) and wagering bets on which witnesses would falter under their assaults. This was a trial in which lawyers on both sides would be fined and threatened with contempt, witnesses would be embarrassed and impeached, and experts would be discounted and discredited. A mini-industry of legal analysts and "talking heads" on the O. J. Simpson trial burst forth on the talk shows. Americans would learn a whole new vocabulary of legalisms, quickly incorporating terms such as *sidebar*, *discovery violations*, and *hostile witness*.

The Judge

Lance Ito, a forty-four-year-old Japanese-American, had worked his way up through the Los Angeles legal system from the prosecutor's office to the Superior Court. He had a reputation as a jurist who was well informed, balanced, and fair. He was a "judge's judge," knowledgeable about the law, cautious about its interpretation, and evenhanded in its application. As a victim of discrimination whose parents had been interned during World War II in a relocation camp for Japanese aliens, Judge Ito was acceptable to the defense, who perhaps assumed that he would be empathic with the plight of the black male defendant. As a former assistant district attorney with extensive trial experience, he was also acceptable to the prosecution. As the trial unfolded, both the prosecution and the defense would have ample cause to revise their assumptions and expectations about this judge, who would swing rather dramatically from patience to impatience, from civility to incivility, and from judicial restraint to judicial tyranny.

Two other facts about Judge Ito would assume increasing importance in the case, raising fundamental issues of his objectivity and fairness. As a young prosecutor in the district attorney's office, he had once been supervised by Johnnie Cochran, who would become the lead defense lawyer in the case after a major rift between Robert Shapiro and F. Lee Bailey.

Observers noted that Judge Ito seemed unusually friendly and somewhat deferential to Cochran, who excelled at massaging his ego and soothing his frayed temper, but was this prior relationship influencing his treatment of the defense? Even more intriguing was the fact that the judge was married to Captain Margaret York, the head of the Internal Affairs Division of the Los Angeles Police Department. Was this a mere coincidence, or was he part of a grand conspiracy against O. J. Simpson outlined by the defense in its opening argument?

The Jury

> Race plays a vital role in this case and has from the beginning. The black jurors are not as likely to believe the testimony of the police as much as the white jurors. Race will be an issue with any jury and the way they look at this case.
>
> William Kunstler, criminal defense lawyer,
> July 10, 1995

Jury selection proved to be the first major battleground in the war between the prosecution and the defense. Ordinarily, the defense in such a high-profile murder case could be expected to ask for a change of venue on the grounds of excessive and prejudicial pretrial publicity. In this case, the defense team actually relished the prospect of empaneling a jury of O. J. Simpson's peers. After all, O. J. had been a beloved local hero and celebrity ever since his days of football glory at USC, so the defense firmly believed that it would be impossible to find a jury in Los Angeles that would convict O. J. of any crime. After all, O. J. was an authentic black hero in a city with a substantial population of people of color, for whom he was a unique symbol of hope who represented their own fantasies of fame and fortune. The defense was confident that his dream was their dream, his nightmare their nightmare.

Understanding their disadvantage in jury selection, the prosecution insisted on casting a wide net in Los Angeles County, hoping to achieve a well-balanced jury with reasonable expectations of objectivity without sacrificing diversity. Over one thousand prospective jurors had been contacted, representing a racial and economic cross section of Los Angeles; 219 reported for jury selection on the first day of one of the most celebrated trials in the city's colorful history.

After completing a seventy-nine-page questionnaire, most of the potential jurors were eliminated from an ever shrinking pool by an exhaustive process of examination about their marital relationships, their attitudes toward domestic violence, their previous contacts with police and the criminal justice system, and their personal and professional lives. The two sides finally agreed on twelve jurors and the same number of alternates; they anticipated a lengthy trial ahead.

On November 3, all parties were pleased with the jury that had been sworn in: eight women, four men; eight blacks, two Hispanics, one white person, and one of mixed race (Native American and white). Surely they had winnowed out the O. J. groupies, the police haters, the sociopaths, and the legal eagles—both sides felt that this jury had the stamina to survive a long trial, the intelligence to evaluate the evidence, and the wisdom to render a just verdict.

However, due to a high attrition rate of people with hardship excuses, problematic backgrounds, or possible biases, the final group of twelve jurors were disproportionately black, female, and working-class. It was not until December 8 that the prosecution and defense could agree on another group of twelve alternate jurors, consisting of seven blacks, four whites, and one Hispanic, completing the challenging process of jury selection. The race issue, which increasingly came to dominate the case, was to play itself out in the frustrations of this jury's lengthy sequestration. Thus from the outset of the trial, jury selection and retention were major problems.

In fact, despite the fact that they were disproportionately people of color, this jury was not a group of O. J.'s peers in education, income, or social status; only six had more than a high school diploma, and they reflected the working-class and middle-class residents of Los Angeles: flight attendant, telephone company worker, rental-car company employee, legal secretary, real estate appraiser, sales clerk.

As the days turned into weeks and the weeks lengthened into months, the very diversity of this jury was to become the root of its tensions. Its surface harmony in the courtroom came to mask its emerging conflicts over racial differences, personality differences, and differences of opinion over the conduct of the trial and the defendant's guilt or innocence. Most important, this jury came to play an active rather than a passive role in the trial and in the process created a major subtext to the ongoing drama of the trial itself. The jury reflected not just the diversity of Los Angeles but also the simmering hostilities between the ethnic groups that had exploded over the Rodney King verdict.

For the next six weeks, after the jurors and the alternates were seated, the lawyers for the prosecution and defense jousted politely but furiously to gain an advantage in the pretrial rulings about evidence, witnesses, and the legal minutiae that would threaten to derail the trial at several crucial junctures.

By the time testimony in the trial finally began on Monday, January 23, 1995, O. J. Simpson had been languishing in jail for seven months.

THE CASE FOR THE PROSECUTION

> I'm getting sick of the media. You see what's happening with O. J.? All of this started with Rodney King. King's case was tried before it ever got to court. The same thing is going to happen with O. J. There isn't any way in the world he's going to have a fair trial.
>
> S. R., black male lawyer, Los Angeles, June 1994

On the first morning of the actual trial, the media went into overdrive, with hundreds of reporters from all over the world jockeying for seats in the courtroom, positioning themselves in strategic locations inside and outside the courthouse, darting wildly after every celebrity or wanna-be who passed by to get a "sound bite" on the case. In the parking lot across from the courthouse were more than forty satellite trucks and air-conditioned trailers for television and print journalists to file their stories on this most phenomenal event; it would soon be dubbed "Camp O. J."

The Cable News Network (CNN), as well as several local TV stations in California, had announced that it would televise the entire trial daily, and most major radio stations on the West Coast promised hourly updates. Viewers on day one of the trial were treated to the impressive sight of a handsome O. J. Simpson, dressed in his usual stylish attire, surrounded by his Dream Team of lawyers at the defense table, and an attractive, petite brunette Marcia Clark, deputy district attorney, surrounded by her team of colleagues at the prosecution table: William Hodgman, Christopher Darden, Brian Kelberg, and Hank Goldberg. Darden, a thirty-eight-year-old deputy district attorney, had joined the team the previous October and was highly visible as the only African-American prosecutor. As the trial wore on, these lawyers would be reinforced by colleagues who specialized in technical evidence, but they would be the "first teams" who would compete for the ultimate victory.

> The most important thing about O. J. in this case is not that he's a sports celebrity, not that he's a black man, but that he's a multimillionaire and can afford the Dream Team of lawyers to defend him, so he'll probably get off.
>
> Black male radio caller, San Francisco, July 6, 1995

Over the course of the lengthy trial, the cast of characters on both sides of the aisle would change as in a game of musical chairs, with an impressive array of lawyers specializing in arcane branches of evidentiary law such as forensics, DNA, and hair and fiber trace evidence. But it was clear from the outset that the prosecution lawyers, most of them underpaid and unglamorous alumni of second-tier local law schools, would be outmaneuvered and outshone by the defense lawyers, successful and sophisticated alumni of elite national law schools—the Keystone Kops facing the Dream Team. The defense challenged the credibility of every witness and the validity of every damaging piece of testimony, vigorously undermining the state's case and trying to raise reasonable doubt about O. J.'s involvement in the crime at every possible opportunity.

The Opening Statement for the Prosecution

The high point of the state's case came with Deputy District Attorney Clark's masterful opening statement on the first day. With an impressive catalogue of evidence, a graphic reconstruction of the brutal crime, and a plausible motive, Clark presented a compelling case against O. J. Simpson. Observers noted that Simpson sat rather stiffly throughout her speech but was clearly attentive and frequently took notes while she talked. Again and again she referred to the "mountain of evidence" implicating O. J. as the murderer, but she carefully failed to mention that all of the evidence was circumstantial—there was no weapon, no eyewitness, no "smoking gun" to tie Simpson directly to the crime.

Christopher Darden, embarking on what would prove to be a pivotal role and a painful personal odyssey as the prosecutor of a black superstar, presented a graphic portrait of O. J. Simpson to leave with the jury before the defense got its turn. He described O. J. as "a jealous, abusive, and controlling man who viewed his wife as his own personal Barbie doll. During their seventeen-year relationship, Mr. Simpson dominated, intimidated, ridiculed, struck, stalked, and terrorized his wife."

The Defense Response

Johnnie Cochran, now the lead lawyer for the defense, was not intimidated by Clark's dramatic opening. By contrast, he established a warm, friendly tone with the jury, projecting his legendary charm to paint a portrait of his famous client as a much maligned but innocent client and implied that he may have been the target of a police conspiracy or, at the very least, a victim of a "rush to judgment." He also raised the possibility that Nicole Brown Simpson and Ron Goldman might have been the mistaken victims of a drug killing by unknown Colombian assassins who were really looking for Faye Resnick, Nicole's friend and former houseguest. The defense team returned again and again throughout the trial to these two alternative scenarios. But Cochran also predicted a third possible line of attack on the evidence itself—the fail-safe strategy of documenting the innumerable errors and inadequacies in the police investigation, the forensic examination, and the criminalists' handling of the evidence in the case.

By the time Cochran sat down, he had managed to make the prosecution's case look like Swiss cheese, and even more impressive, he had raised doubts in the minds of millions of interested observers about the case against O. J. Simpson. He had articulated the suspicions of so many blacks that O. J. was another victim of white racism and, like Rodney King, was just another black male targeted for destruction by the police and the criminal justice system. As a black clergyman said shortly after Simpson's arrest, "We're keeping a close watch on this situation. We haven't seen the evidence yet, but we wouldn't be surprised if the LAPD were trying to frame O. J. After all, it wouldn't be the first time in this city." To blacks all over America, it was a familiar and frustrating story.

By the end of the first week of the trial, Cochran's aggressive tactics and attacks on the credibility of the state's initial witnesses were so unrelenting and so effective that William Hodgman, the dignified and soft-spoken second-in-command of the prosecution team, became so agitated and angry that he had to be rushed to the hospital for treatment. This unfortunate incident foreshadowed the many bitter exchanges and bizarre moments that were to characterize the interactions between the prosecution and defense lawyers throughout the trial.

The Motive

During the weeks following the opening statement, the prosecution attempted to establish a motive for the crime by portraying Simpson as an insanely jealous husband who battered his wife and could not bear to lose her after their divorce. Despite the prosecution's use of photos of a bruised Nicole and tapes of her calls to the police to report O. J.'s abuse, the defense portrayed him as a loving husband who occasionally lost his temper and "was not proud of his behavior on those occasions."

The testimony of Denise Brown, Nicole's sister, was considerably compromised by her own admission that these incidents frequently happened when they had both been drinking heavily and that her sister had remained in the marriage after several such incidents. As Denise Brown testified, Cochran was able to transform her image from a sympathetic grieving sister to a fast-living, hard-drinking woman of the world who was somehow implicated in her sister's willingness to continue in an abusive relationship. Through subtle but pointed questioning, he elaborated on his opening statement that O. J. was a generous and loving husband, extremely generous to his wife's family, implying that there was an implicit quid pro quo between O. J.'s generosity and the Brown family's tacit tolerance of Nicole's abuse.

This theme resonated in the black community, especially among middle-class black women, who often greatly resent black celebrities who marry white women—they see this as a rejection of black women and another weapon in the society's effort to undermine the black family.

> As I see it, O. J. was supporting the entire Brown family. As far as I am concerned, the parents of Nicole tolerated the alleged abuse of their daughter in order to remain employed as franchise dealers for Hertz car rental services. This franchise afforded them a very high level of living that had not been their standard before. The situation was not healthy for any of them.
>
> Sara McNeil Boyd, former school administrator, Palo Alto

> Well, I heard O. J. took good care of Nicole's family and now they are all turning on him. He set her father up in a car dealership, set her mother up with a travel agency, and sent her younger sisters to college. I bet he never did all that for his first wife's family, but you know how these black male celebrities go after these blonde bimbos.
>
> P. H., secretary, Los Angeles

The Fickleness of Friends

Then there was Brian "Kato" Kaelin, O. J.'s live-in houseguest, who looked like a caricature of the Southern California surfer with his shaggy blond hair, suntan, and wrinkled blue jeans. A would-be actor, Kaelin was a reluctant witness, testifying in fits and starts about going with O. J. to a nearby McDonald's for a hamburger on Sunday evening, just about 9:15 P.M. Establishing the time of this outing was crucial for the prosecution in order to demonstrate that O. J. had sufficient time to commit the crime before the limousine driver picked him up about 11:00 P.M. for a trip to the airport. Kaelin was also the person who heard "thumps" against his bedroom wall, where the bloody glove was later discovered. That glove, its location, and its discoverer were to become one of the central issues in the police "conspiracy" theory of the defense.

But Kaelin came across as a vague and spacy witness with his own agenda to protect O. J. After all, as a beneficiary of the Simpson largesse, he lived rent-free in a Brentwood mansion, had access to the celebrities who always surrounded O. J., and led the lifestyle of a West Side wanna-be. Kaelin knew that there is no free lunch, but how much was he willing to sing for his supper? Out of the courtroom and away from the jury, Kaelin sang a very different tune on the talk show circuit. He was to prove the first but not the last of O. J.'s buddies to raise questions about O. J.'s feelings about Nicole and his actions on the night she was murdered.

It was more than a little ironic that the Simpsons' two young children had named their dog after Kaelin, one of their favorite babysitters. So lawyers on both sides would frequently have to distinguish between Kato the loyal dog, whose barking alerted the neighborhood about the murders, and Kato the not-so-loyal houseguest, whose tattling entertained the world on the talk show circuit.

Ron Shipp, a retired Los Angeles policeman, proved to be another ambivalent witness for the prosecution. Handsome and well built, Shipp was one of the few black men in O. J.'s wide circle of friends intimate enough to join the Simpson family and close friends who gathered at his Rockingham home on the evening of June 13 to offer support and sympathy. Initially, he seemed reluctant to reveal his conversation with O. J. when he claimed they were alone in O. J.'s bedroom later that night. In direct testimony, Shipp made two statements very damaging to O. J. According to Shipp, O. J. jokingly said: "You know, Ron, I have dreamed about killing Nicole." O. J. also seemed concerned about giving his blood to the police and asked Shipp if, as a former police officer, he knew how long it usually took to obtain DNA results. Defense lawyer Carl Douglas, resembling a cross between a bantamweight fighter and a bulldog, attacked Shipp with surprising ferocity, impugning his motives, questioning his credibility, and accusing him of being an O. J. groupie and a freeloader.

With his reputation tarnished, his marital infidelity revealed, and his dignity in shreds, Ron Shipp fought back and gained some observers' sympathy when he looked over at the defendant and said, "This is sad, O. J.," implying that Simpson would destroy a friend to save himself. But his appearance as a witness for the prosecution raised a nagging question in the minds of many black trial observers: Could Ron Shipp, a former police officer, be part of the conspiracy against O. J. Simpson, or was he slanting his testimony in the hope that the media exposure would jump-start his dormant acting career?

Then came Rosa Lopez, the most elusive and reluctant witness of all. Lopez, who had been employed as a maid by the Simpsons' next-door neighbors, was an admitted admirer of O. J. and occasionally dropped by to visit his maid, Josephine "Gigi" Guarin. According to the defense, her testimony was crucial to establish the presence of the Bronco parked near the house at the approximate time the murders were committed. Since Lopez was threatening to return to El Salvador to escape the scrutiny of the media, the defense asked for a special hearing to allow her testimony to be videotaped out of sequence and introduced later during the defense phase of the trial.

Lopez was a minor disaster for the defense, who claimed she had been interviewed the day after the murders by Detective Mark Fuhrman of the Los Angeles Police Department and that she had told him about seeing the Bronco when she walked her employer's dog shortly after 10:00 P.M. on Sunday evening. Noting that Fuhrman had never followed up on this lead, the defense implied that he had deliberately ignored evidence that corroborated O. J.'s alibi—more proof of the rush to judgment to arrest Simpson for the crime.

This time it was the prosecution's turn to savage a witness, as Chris Darden proceeded to do. Darden exposed the apparent lies, numerous inconsistencies, and frequent and convenient *no me recuerdo* ("I don't remember") responses of Rosa Lopez, who became increasingly defensive, resistant, and hostile on the stand. Darden effectively discredited Lopez, generating considerable skepticism about her story and providing instant fodder for late-night comedians.

But among the people watching the trial were minorities, especially blacks and Hispanics, who could empathize with the Rosa Lopezes of this world, the invisible maids and unskilled workers who serve the privileged class, sentenced to a lifetime of long hours, low wages, and little glory. They could easily understand that she had difficulties explaining herself in English, that she might feel intimidated by the lawyers, and that her testimony sometimes seemed confused and contradictory. To them, she seemed very vulnerable, a humble servant pitted against the might and majesty of the most publicized criminal justice system in America. Was Rosa Lopez just seeking her own moment in the sun, or was she, too, an innocent victim of the police conspiracy to ignore or discredit any evidence that supported O. J.'s innocence? Ironically, the defense decided not to introduce her taped testimony, so the jury never had a chance to decide if she was a credible witness.

Fuhrman: Choirboy or Rogue Cop?

Mark Fuhrman's name came to dominate the early phase of the trial, as the defense lawyers frequently invoked it to support their conspiracy theory. Fuhrman was one of the four LAPD detectives who first went to notify O. J. of his ex-wife's murder. Fuhrman was the one who jumped over the wall to open the gate so that his colleagues could enter the estate. He was also the one who prowled around the house and the grounds, without a search warrant, rousing a sleeping Kato Kaelin in the guest house. Unfortunately for the prosecution, Fuhrman was also a rogue police officer with a history of racially tinged encounters. He was a problematic witness for the prosecution and a perfect foil for the defense.

In the face of F. Lee Bailey's aggressive cross-examination, Fuhrman seemed unflappable, denying allegations of past racial prejudice and harassment. In response to a pointed question from Bailey, he specifically denied using the word *nigger* at any time in the past ten years. He seemed almost incredulous at the insinuation that he might have planted the bloody glove and other damaging evidence at the Rockingham estate to implicate O. J. Simpson in the murders. When he was excused from the witness stand, he had withstood two days of withering scrutiny from both sides and walked out of the courtroom leaving a number of tantalizing questions still unanswered. For those leaning toward the prosecution's case, Fuhrman was a symbol of a rehabilitated police officer who exuded confidence, competence, and professionalism. They were visibly relieved that he had proved to be a good witness.

For those leaning toward the defense's theory, Fuhrman was a symbol of a racist cop who was capable of planting evidence and manipulating witnesses in order to destroy O. J. Simpson out of his extreme antipathy to interracial marriage. Again, blacks recognized this familiar obsession of white males, which had its twisted roots in slavery and laws against miscegenation, its growth in the post–World War II social revolution, and its full flowering in the celebrity culture of Los Angeles. How many could relate stories of cops stopping black men with white women, harassing them for no obvious reason? How many could imagine the countless hostile stares and subtle insults that O. J. and Nicole must have experienced in their years together? How many could instinctively believe that this unstable, unpredictable cop had tried to frame an authentic black superhero?

Fung Fumbles

Fuhrman looked like a choirboy on the witness stand compared to Dennis Fung, the criminalist from the Los Angeles police laboratory who was in charge of collecting the evidence from the crime scene at Bundy Drive and the Simpson house on Rockingham Avenue. When he took the stand in early April, Fung was a nervous witness, alternately seeming stubborn and defensive. Despite the prosecution's attempt to minimize the innumerable procedural and processing errors in the collection of evidence, Fung haltingly recounted a catalogue of mistakes and grudgingly admitted that some of these mistakes could have compromised the integrity of the evidence. From the initial chaotic condition of the crime scene, where police and other personnel trampled all over the entryway for hours before the bodies were removed to the coroner's morgue, through the physical collection, recording, booking, and storage of the multiple items of evidence, Fung's testimony revealed a clear and disturbing pattern of incorrect procedures, mishandling, mislabeling, misrecording, and inadequate security in storing this evidence.

A weak and vulnerable witness for the state's case, Fung was mercilessly attacked by the defense lawyer Barry Scheck. Scheck, the aggressive law professor and DNA expert, highlighted every example of sloppy collection of evidence, underscored every potential instance of cross-contamination of blood samples from O. J. and the two victims, and hammered away at the alleged "missing" 1.5 cubic centimeters of blood from O. J.'s reference sample. It was those few drops of blood that would continue to plague the prosecution and provide fodder for the defense.

Observers were shocked but not totally surprised at the inept and incompetent performance of the Los Angeles police lab specialists. More shocking and surprising was the possibility, however remote, that all of these mistakes were actually orchestrated to strengthen the case against O. J., particularly the missing blood, which could have been sprinkled on the glove discovered at Rockingham, on the gate of Nicole's condominium, and in O. J.'s white Bronco, the car he presumably drove on the night of the murders.

The defense's conspiracy theory was beginning to sound more and more plausible, especially to blacks, who found it nearly impossible to believe that the state-of-the-art police laboratory in America's second largest city could have conducted such a third-rate investigation. It did not help to allay their suspicions when Fung, at the conclusion of his nine humiliating days on the witness stand, went over to shake hands with the prosecution lawyers and then, impulsively, warmly shake the hands of all the lawyers on the defense team and even the defendant himself. This Chinese-American criminalist had unwittingly supplied the defense with some of its strongest armor against the relentless assault of the prosecution.

Even before Scheck had completed his scathing cross-examination of Fung, Scheck's colleague Robert Shapiro was passing out fortune cookies at the courthouse, sarcastically commenting, "These are from the Hang Fung restaurant." It was one of many incidents indicative of poor taste and questionable professional judgment in the trial.

Racial Tensions and Jury Discontent

Early in the spring, rumors had surfaced that there were racial tensions within the jury and complaints from some jurors about their treatment by the Sheriff's deputies assigned to escort them and monitor the restrictions on their access to information about the case. When Judge Ito dismissed three of the deputies in late April for alleged biased treatment of a few disgruntled jurors, the majority of the jurors staged a dramatic protest by wearing black and deliberately delaying their arrival at the court. It was a jury revolt unprecedented in California courtroom history, precipitating yet another crisis in the trial and raising the specter of a mistrial. Judge Ito patiently squelched the revolt, but the incident exposed the stress that was mounting among the jurors, perhaps not a clear sign of racial disharmony but certainly a symptom of escalating tensions. It was a signal to Judge Ito to take back his courtroom, to exercise some control over the endless bickering and posturing of the lawyers, and to speed up the pace of this torturous trial.

Rumors had also surfaced that various members of the jury were being investigated, as both sides wanted to remove jurors who might have betrayed any biases toward the defense or the prosecution. Despite denials by both sides, these investigations resulted in a series of unexplained dismissals of eight jurors over a period of four months. By the time the prosecution ended its case in early July, the original jury had been substantially replaced, and only two alternates remained available for the duration of the trial.

The Defense Attack on DNA

The prosecution saved its most powerful weapons until the final phase of its case—the blood, hair, and fiber evidence. In May, the prosecutors put a series of DNA experts on the stand to instruct the jury about the nature of DNA and its significance in this case. After several numbing days of technical testimony, the prosecution convincingly demonstrated that spots of blood quite consistent with O. J. Simpson's DNA profile had been found at the crime scene, in the Bronco, on the gate at Bundy, on the glove at Rockingham, and on one of O. J.'s socks found in the master bedroom the morning after the crimes were committed.

> That so-called scientific evidence doesn't impress me. You know, whites have been pulling those tricks on blacks for decades. How do we know they didn't plant that blood just to make O. J. look guilty?
>
> B. R. Crenshaw, office administrator, Oakland

Barry Scheck and Peter Neufeld, experts on DNA for the defense, adroitly managed to undermine much of this testimony by noting that O. J. often dropped by Nicole's house and that it was impossible to date precisely the blood spots on the gate. And they minimized the discovery of drops of O. J.'s blood in the Bronco, on his socks, and at his own home—after all, it is not a crime to spill your own blood on your personal property and clothes.

These two New York lawyers, who appeared to irritate both the judge and the prosecution team with their pugnacious style and their aggressive badgering of the witnesses, took what seemed like a clearly marked trail of blood evidence and turned it into no more than a confusing path of drops and smudges. Their constant insinuations about the "validity" of the evidence, comments about the sloppy way it was handled and transferred to other laboratories for testing, and challenges to the basic techniques of DNA analysis raised significant questions for trial observers about the impact of this evidence on the jury. Although the DNA evidence convinced some doubters of Simpson's involvement in the case, many blacks were still unconvinced and unwilling to believe that O. J. was a cold-blooded murderer.

Again O. J.'s supporters felt vindicated by the testimony of Dr. Bruce Weir, a population geneticist from North Carolina State University and one of the acknowledged experts on statistical interpretations of DNA evidence. The prosecution led the confident doctor through a recital of his impressive credentials in his crisp New Zealand accent, then elicited his very authoritative testimony, which was supposed to demonstrate the statistical unlikelihood that anyone other than O. J. Simpson could have left that blood all over the crime scene. But Weir's arrogance soon turned into apology when defense attorney Peter Neufeld pointed out that he had made a major error in the calculations, an error that he admitted was to the detriment of the defendant. Even though Weir corrected his calculations, one of the prosecution's major experts had been embarrassed and his results exposed to further skepticism by the jury. Was this another example of the prosecution's eagerness to convict O. J. at any cost? For blacks, Weir's statistical error was simply another clue in the accumulating mass of clues suggesting something suspicious and even devious about the prosecution's case. Was their natural paranoia about the police and the criminal justice system going to be confirmed in the Simpson case as it had been in the King case?

The Coroner's Report

After the tortured testimony of Dennis Fung and his inexperienced assistant, Andrea Mazzola, the prosecution made a calculated decision not to call the pathologist, Dr. Irwin Golden, who had already been criticized for his incompetent handling of the autopsies. Rather than provide him as a sacrificial lamb to the defense, who would certainly capitalize on his ineptitude, the prosecution put Dr. Lakshmanan Sathyavagiswaran, the Los Angeles County coroner, on the stand. Despite his unruffled professional demeanor, "Dr. Lash," as he was dubbed by the defense, reluctantly acknowledged the numerous errors in the autopsies, so serious that it was impossible to set a precise time of death. But while the coroner spent nine days on the stand reviewing the procedures and the pathology results on two dead bodies, friends and relatives in the courtroom were remembering two attractive, youthful victims. Along with many who found this testimony particularly difficult to hear, the family and friends of Nicole and Ron must have entertained their own private doubts about the prosecution's case.

Robert Shapiro, for the defense, made mincemeat out of "Dr. Lash," peeling away layers of denial and deception until the jury could easily believe that the coroner's office was also trying to cover up its own inadequacies and incompetence. Were these errors simply unintentional, or were they links in the chain of a police conspiracy against O. J. Simpson?

The Glove

By mid June, the prosecution, frustrated at every turn by the ineptitude and credibility of their own expert witnesses, gambled on a Perry Mason–style courtroom surprise. On June 15, Christopher Darden, looking like the cat who swallowed the canary, produced a pair of brown, extra-large Aris Isotoner leather gloves, presumably identical to those Nicole had purchased at Bloomingdale's and given to O. J. in the fall of 1990. It was curious, the buyer admitted, that there was a one-digit difference in the style number of these gloves, but perhaps that had been the clerk's error. He confirmed the authenticity of the gloves in evidence.

Darden asked O. J. to come forward to try on the gloves. As the courtroom grew still and the cameras zoomed in for a close-up, O. J. dramatically tried to pull the leather gloves on his large hands. The jury was transfixed as he muttered "too tight, too tight."

Darden's gamble had backfired—the whole world could see that the gloves were too small. Or was this just one of O. J.'s better performances? While Johnnie Cochran exulted and Christopher Darden erupted, legal analysts proclaimed that the prosecution had committed a major blunder and never should have set up an experiment for which the outcome was not predictable. This was a turning point in the case, not only for the defense, but also for the many fans who were convinced of O. J.'s innocence. For the African-American community, the ill-fitting gloves provided the most tangible proof to date of the defense's hint of a police conspiracy against their hero.

Shoes and Special Fibers

The shoe demonstration by William Bodziak, another FBI expert, was more successful than the glove incident, as he showed that O. J.'s expensive Italian-made Bruno Magli shoes matched the bloody footprints left at the murder scene. The prosecution did not ask O. J. to try on the size 12 shoes.

At the end of June, the prosecutors had another setback when, because of a discovery violation in sharing the information with the defense, Judge Ito refused to allow them to introduce some very damning evidence of fibers, consistent with the custom-made carpet in O. J.'s Ford Bronco, identified on the knit cap found at Bundy and the leather glove at Rockingham. This was powerful and potentially incriminating evidence, fibers highly unlikely to come from anyone else's Bronco in Los Angeles, but the prosecution had "played chicken" with the defense just once too often, and Judge Ito seemed outraged at their continued defiance of the discovery laws. It was a slap in the face for Marcia Clark and a severe setback in the prosecution's case.

Trace Evidence and Telephone Calls

Demoralized and exhausted, the prosecution called its final witness on June 30—Douglas Deedrick, one of the FBI's foremost experts on "trace evidence." His testimony that he found twelve hairs matching Simpson's on the knit cap, the glove, and Ron Goldman's shirt was technical, unimpressive, and boring, an anticlimactic postscript to a lengthy show.

But the prosecution still had one more surprise. It did not call Juditha Brown, Nicole's mother, to be the final witness, as had been widely predicted. Showing little emotion except fatigue, Marcia Clark read Juditha Brown's statement describing her final telephone call with Nicole at 9:40 P.M. on that Sunday night and identifying Nicole's handwriting on the Bloomingdale's receipt for two pairs of men's gloves. On Thursday, July 6—after five months' time, 92 days of testimony, 58 witnesses, 488 exhibits, and 34,500 pages of transcript, the prosecution rested its case.

> Hopefully, this case survived the prosecution. They basically took a case that was overwhelming and created reasonable doubt.
>
> Harland Braun, Los Angeles criminal defense lawyer, 1995

THE CASE FOR THE DEFENSE

> There are really two trials going on simultaneously—the "scientific" trial of DNA and hair and fiber evidence and the "emotional" trial, with race and conspiracy theories as the subtext.
>
> Jeffrey Toobin, KQED-TV, July 7, 1995

The Dream Team wasted no time in mounting an aggressive counterattack to the prosecution's case. The lawyers focused on three major points: (1) O. J. did not have the "window of opportunity" to commit the crimes, (2) O. J.'s demeanor before and after the killings was not consistent with that of a murderer, and (3) the so-called evidence was not only purely circumstantial but may have been planted by the police. It was the last theme that they nurtured, manipulated, and exploited until it grew to have a life of its own, reinventing itself and magically finding its own verification as the trial wore on.

On Monday, July 10, the defense began its case by calling members of the Simpson family to describe O. J.'s reaction to Nicole's death. O. J.'s mother, his daughter Arnelle, and his older sister, Carmelita Durio, all dressed in pale yellow to symbolize hope, presented a striking picture of solidarity in the courtroom.

Johnnie Cochran, smooth and solicitous, patiently elicited testimony from Arnelle, his first witness, that flatly contradicted the testimony that her father had not shown much emotion when he first learned of his ex-wife's death. By the time she finished giving her version of the detectives' visit to the Rockingham estate in the early morning of June 13, the jury must have wondered what really transpired in that house and whose version was really accurate. Or was Arnelle protecting her father by reconstructing events to cast him in a more favorable light?

Challenging Testimony and Time Lines

Then Cochran set out to destroy Ron Shipp, who had given such incriminating testimony about his conversation with O. J. on the night after the murders. O. J.'s three women stood by their man and, one by one, insisted that Ron Shipp had been drinking all evening and that he was never alone with O. J., certainly not in his bedroom. If Shipp had sounded like Judas to O. J.'s fans, then Eunice Simpson must have sounded like the Virgin Mary to his foes. Again, the defense scored some points and placed a significant dent in Shipp's testimony about O. J.'s dream of killing Nicole.

Next the defense team turned up several witnesses who challenged the time line of the murder by raising doubts about the crucial time of the dog's barking. As Johnnie Cochran had earlier observed, this may have been the first case in legal history where the time of a murder was pinpointed by the barking of a dog.

But contradictory testimony about O. J.'s physical condition and a cut on his finger were even more intriguing and nearly backfired on the defense. When Dr. Robert Huizenga, a Harvard-educated internist, suggested that O. J.'s arthritis was so disabling that he probably could not have committed the double murders, prosecutor Brian Kelberg, in sharp and incisive cross-examination, effectively challenged his expertise as a rheumatologist and implied that he was a hired gun as the personal physician of Dream Team member Robert Shapiro.

Huizenga seemed to exaggerate O. J.'s infirmities in his testimony: "Looks can be deceiving. He looks like Tarzan, but walked like Tarzan's grandfather." Unfortunately, the prosecution, in rebuttal, played a videotape of Simpson leading a fitness class, moving and dancing more like Tommy Tune than Tarzan. And on that same tape, O. J. made two casual comments about hitting his wife—not very good news in the midst of the defense's case.

In mid July, the defense lawyers redoubled their efforts to discredit the prosecution's evidence, claiming alternately that the police collection and analysis of the evidence was incompetent and inadequate, that the criminalists had inadvertently contaminated and destroyed evidence, or that the entire police investigation was a conspiracy and a cover-up. They proceeded to parade a series of experts who disputed the blood on the sock (was it a spatter or a smudge?), the amount of blood drawn from O. J. the day after the murders (was there any missing or not?), and the condition of the blood on the back gate (was it planted or not?).

The Sock, the Glove, and the Gate

> O. J. Simpson is a man who personifies the American dream. He believes in the system and he keeps the faith. He believes in the end he will be found innocent.
>
> Johnnie Cochran, defense attorney, July 7, 1995

After months of hints, promises, and leaks to the press, the defense finally had to put up or shut up. They had to discredit the prosecution's powerful forensic evidence that tied O. J. to the crime—the blood on the sock, the glove, and the gate. And to discredit the blood evidence, they had to convince the jury that there was, in fact, a police conspiracy to frame O. J. Simpson for these two brutal murders.

On the morning of July 24, Robert Blasier, the defense's expert on forensic evidence, was ready to challenge the prosecution's case further with Dr. Frederic Rieders, a toxicologist, on the stand. Rieders, with his impressive credentials and Austrian accent, electrified the courtroom when he testified that EDTA, a chemical preservative used by police criminalists to store blood evidence, was present in the bloodstain samples from O. J.'s sock and from the back gate at Rockingham. He further stated that EDTA was also present in a sample of Nicole's blood found on the sock. If Rieders's conclusion was correct, it strongly suggested that the blood was planted by the police *after* it was collected from O. J. and from Nicole's autopsy. Was this not, in fact, proof that there was a police conspiracy to implicate O. J., or could there be any other reasonable explanation of the presence of this preservative in the bloodstain sample?

On cross-examination, Marcia Clark attacked Rieders with such ferocity that Judge Ito had to warn her against bullying the witness. In a few heated exchanges, Clark succeeded in questioning Rieders's qualifications, pointing out an error in his calculations about the normal levels of EDTA in the bloodstream of an American adult, and forcing him to admit that his entire analysis was based on the report of an FBI agent who had arrived at an opposite conclusion.

The EDTA Controversy

The FBI agent, Roger Martz, initially a reluctant defense witness, was quickly transformed into a hostile witness when he appeared to contradict not only Rieders's analysis of the blood evidence but also his own statement that the highly sophisticated spectrographic analysis yielded patterns that were "consistent with the presence of EDTA" in the blood samples. By the end of his testimony, Martz was visibly annoyed with Defense Attorney Blasier, who repeatedly insinuated that he was biased for the prosecution and had tailored his testimony accordingly. Martz's courtroom demeanor and behavior had certainly given aid and comfort to the prosecution, but he insisted that he did not find sufficient EDTA in the blood sample to confirm the presence of the chemical preservative—no more, in fact, than he had found in an analysis of his own blood in a concurrent experiment. The irony of this very unscientific, uncontrolled experiment by a federal law enforcement officer, testing his own blood for EDTA, in the most celebrated criminal trial of the decade, did not seem immediately obvious to the lawyers on both sides, the judge, or the press.

The EDTA testimony was very complex, very controversial, and very difficult for a layperson to evaluate. At the end of the day, would the jurors be convinced by the defense that the blood was planted on O. J.'s sock and on his back gate, or would they be persuaded by the prosecution that the blood was inadvertently dripped by O. J., the perpetrator of the crime?

> The evidence is pretty strong, even though it's circumstantial. If it was anyone else but O. J., he would be convicted. But I don't

> believe any jury is going to convict O. J. People love him and can't believe he could commit such a horrible crime. So I think he may be guilty, but I don't think he'll ever be convicted.
>
> Black male radio caller, San Francisco, July 6, 1995

But the defense team was not finished with O. J.'s socks or with the other blood evidence. In late July, they called Herbert McDonell, a forensic expert, who testified that the pattern of the bloodstain on O. J.'s sock was not consistent with a "spatter pattern," as previously established by the prosecution's expert witness, but was most likely caused by being pressed against the sock while it was not being worn. Again, this testimony seemed to lend support to the defense's conspiracy theory by implying that the blood had deliberately been applied to the sock by someone trying to frame O. J. Simpson.

And again Marcia Clark, the prosecutor, mounted an aggressive attack on McDonell's credentials, his credibility, and his conclusions.

Trial Fatigue and Ferment

From July 10 to July 28, the weather in Los Angeles was abominable. The city suffocated under the double burden of a record heat wave and a blanket of smog—there were dozens of reported heat-related hospital admissions. Judge Ito's courtroom was a microcosm of the city—lawyers, jurors, and witnesses were uncomfortable, moods were volatile, and tempers were short.

Judge Ito had grown increasingly autocratic as he tried to move the trial along, but now he was becoming increasingly impatient and irritable. He snapped at lawyers and at witnesses alike, made sarcastic comments from the bench, and generally seemed exhausted and dispirited from the arduous pace of the trial. His tolerance for Marcia Clark's assertiveness and acerbic tongue was rapidly declining to zero, finally erupting in frustration and a fine of $250. The defense lawyers seemed mildly amused, but they, too, felt the sting of Ito's wrath with a series of unfavorable rulings and sharp warnings about their legal strategies.

On July 27, the only black male juror was rushed to the hospital with minor heart attack symptoms, bringing the trial to a halt for two days. By the end of July, commentators wondered if this case could be completed and turned over to the jury while there were still twelve healthy jurors, before they all collapsed from exhaustion or heat prostration. At this point, it seemed that even nature was conspiring against the defendant.

Mystery Tapes and TV Leaks

During the last week of July, the defense lawyers made a startling announcement—they had learned about some tapes made by Detective Mark Fuhrman in conversations with Laura Hart McKinny, an aspiring scriptwriter from North Carolina. McKinny had taped those conversations between 1985 and 1994, and Fuhrman had allegedly used the "N-word" many times. Johnnie Cochran flew to North Carolina for a hearing to subpoena the tapes, but Judge William Wood of the Forsyth County Superior Court denied the subpoena on the grounds that the tapes were fictional, simply suggestions for a script about urban police life. Cochran, temporarily stymied, returned to Los Angeles and launched an intensive media campaign and legal battle to obtain those tapes, claiming that they would prove that Fuhrman was both a liar and a conspirator against O. J. Simpson.

On Monday, July 31, another permutation in the case occurred that was to raise even more suspicion about the police handling of the case. The defense had asked Judge Ito to issue a subpoena to obtain testimony from Tracie Savage, a news reporter for KNBC, a Los Angeles TV station. Savage had achieved her own fifteen minutes of fame when she reported on September 21, 1994, that DNA blood evidence had been found on O. J.'s socks, linking him directly to the murders. Since the socks had not been sent out for testing until three weeks later, the defense seized on this broadcast as yet another piece of evidence of a police conspiracy against O. J.

The attorney for Savage strongly protested the subpoena as an infringement on the freedom of the press, claiming that Savage could invoke that right and refuse to reveal her "confidential sources." Although Judge Ito seemed skeptical of the probative value of her testimony in view of its inaccuracy, he allowed some limited testimony to establish that she was claiming that she received the information from "confidential sources" who were "closely connected to the case," leaving observers to consider several tantalizing possibilities before he issued a ruling on whether or not this witness was covered by the "shield law" and thus would not have to divulge the source of her information.

The prosecution had earlier suggested that Savage may have fabricated the story in an effort to outstrip the competition. Or was it possible that she had a bona fide source in the police department or the criminalist's lab who had anticipated the results of the tests? Was it even remotely possible that she had extrasensory perception and had accurately predicted the outcome? In any case, this development created yet another tangential issue and caused yet another delay in this interminable trial.

Judge Ito ultimately rejected the defense motion on the grounds that the information was false and therefore had no probative value to the case. Although the jury was not present during the hearing, the media had a field day about its own involvement, and the public had yet another doubt to raise on the talk shows.

> What's happening to O. J. Simpson in that courtroom is not kosher, man. In this country, aren't you supposed to be presumed innocent?
>
> Mike Tyson, heavyweight champion, August 17, 1995

LAPD Lab Contamination

By early August, the defense's case was beginning to build momentum. Dr. John Gerdes, a molecular biologist from Denver, testified on August 2 that the Los Angeles Police Department forensic laboratory had serious problems of "chronic" and "substantial" contamination, thereby calling into question the validity and reliability of any of its DNA evidence. Gerdes scathingly criticized the competence, the procedures, and even the analytical methods of the criminalists but particularly emphasized the problem of interpreting the ratios derived from the DNA analysis. He was an effective witness with a calm, deliberative style, in contrast to the brusque style of Dr. Rieders.

However, under an equally calm and thorough cross-examination by the polished prosecution lawyer George Clarke, Gerdes did not seem quite so authoritative. Clarke, who looks like a Hollywood version of a successful lawyer, successfully attacked Gerdes's credentials, his credibility, and his motivation to appear as a defense witness, thus undercutting his four days of convincing testimony. Clarke caught Gerdes in several inconsistencies and forced him to admit, quite reluctantly, that there were some blood samples of both the defendant and the victims that had been sent promptly to two other laboratories and thus could not have been contaminated at the Los Angeles police laboratory. But court observers noted that the jury assiduously took more notes when the defense experts testified than when the prosecution experts were on the stand. Was this an indication of the jurors' sympathy for the defendant, or were they just more attentive to the more spirited exchanges?

THE FUHRMAN TAPES

> I am the key witness in the biggest case of the century. And if I go down, they lose the case. The glove is everything. Without the glove—bye bye.
>
> Detective Mark Fuhrman on tape, 1995

The Fuhrman tapes would not go away. Cochran finally persuaded Judge Ito to consider the admissibility of the tapes, claiming dramatically in court, "This is a bombshell—the tapes are the most important event in this trial or any trial in this decade."

Through a series of carefully orchestrated leaks, excerpts of the tapes appeared in the *Los Angeles Times*, the *New York Times*, and several major weekly magazines. They did, in fact, provide a "bombshell" for the prosecution, for they clearly revealed Fuhrman making offensive comments about blacks, Hispanics, other minorities, women, and homosexuals. Did these tapes prove the detective was a racist, misogynist, and homophobe as well as a liar, or were the comments simply examples of artistic license to assist a playwright?

The drama of the Fuhrman tapes took an unexpected turn during the week of August 14 when the prosecution informed Judge Ito that they contained some derogatory comments about his wife, Captain Margaret York, the head of the Internal Affairs Department and the highest-ranking woman in the LAPD. Marcia Clark threw the court into an uproar when she proposed that Judge Ito might have to excuse himself because of that potential conflict of interest. An emotional Judge Ito, admitting the appearance of bias if he were to rule on the admissibility of tapes containing offensive references to his wife ("I love my wife dearly . . . and would be wounded by any criticism of her"), recessed the court to consider this critical decision in the case.

After a night of frantic consultations between District Attorney Gil Garcetti and the prosecutors and discussions between the defense lawyers and their client, all parties returned to court on Friday, August 18, prepared to compromise to avoid the real possibility of a mistrial. On one of those rare occasions in the trial, the prosecution and the defense agreed that Judge Ito should remain in charge of the case, but he should excuse himself from the decision as to whether his wife would be called as a material witness to testify about her past contacts with Mark Fuhrman.

Judge John Reid, a colleague of Ito's on the Superior Court, ruled expeditiously that Captain York was not relevant to this case, allowing all parties to breathe a collective sigh of relief. That relief, however, was short-lived. Judge Ito had requested the defense to prepare an "offer of proof" detailing the relevant portions of the tapes to be examined for their admissibility. This was clearly one of the most important motions in the case, with the verdict literally hanging on its outcome. The "talking heads" had overwhelmingly predicted that admission of the tapes would so inflame the jury that it would probably result in an acquittal, or at the very least a hung jury. Given this level of intense speculation about the impact of the tapes on the outcome of the case, Judge Ito's decision on Monday, August 21, to reject the defense's offer of proof about the relevance of the tapes, citing poor documentation, was a shocking setback to the defense.

On August 22, the day after Judge Ito embarrassed the Dream Team by publicly criticizing its legal documentation, Johnnie Cochran was never more humble and subdued, Marcia Clark was never more feisty, and His Honor was never more cranky. The trial had taken a heavy toll on all the players, and tempers flared when Clark objected to Blasier's request to recall a defense witness who had harshly criticized the police department's investigation of the case. Sustaining Clark's objection to the recall, Judge Ito used the opportunity to upbraid Clark for her intemperate remarks, criticize the defense for trying to extend the trial unnecessarily, and suggest that he might terminate the television coverage to reduce the histrionic grandstanding and pandering of both teams of lawyers. When court resumed after a brief break, Clark apologized to Judge Ito for her outburst, and he responded, "We're all tired." The trial of the century had become an albatross around the court's neck.

9

Ambushing the Prosecution

Playing the Race Card

Rodney King is the thirteenth juror in this trial.

Jeffrey Toobin, July 7, 1995

During the weekend of August 18–20, the Dream Team saturated the talk shows, from Larry King on CNN to Ted Koppel on ABC's *Nightline*. They were eager to reveal the contents of the Fuhrman tapes and just as eager to indict the entire Los Angeles Police Department. Willie Williams, the black chief who was himself in trouble with his police commission, took to the airwaves to defend his troops. Unfortunately, his comments rang rather hollow in view of some very upsetting facts in circulation.

Chief Williams had a difficult time, for example, explaining why thirty-three of the forty-four police officers identified in 1991 by the Christopher Commission as most involved in incidents of brutality were still active members of the LAPD. He did not seem enthusiastic about discussing the number of successful suits against the department for excessive force, the most recent being an out-of-court settlement of $100,000 awarded to a black male arrested for a robbery who, while lying prone, was repeatedly shot by Mark Fuhrman.

Chief Williams, with all his candor and diplomacy, was caught in a double bind, and the media were enjoying watching him try to extricate himself. Some legal analysts were also questioning the motives of the defense lawyers. Peter Keane, legal commentator for

KPIX radio in San Francisco, opined that they were conducting a public relations blitz in order to repair Simpson's image in the world marketplace as well as in the courtroom. Perhaps the defense lawyers had another, more subtle agenda in mind as they made the rounds of the talk shows. Perhaps they were sending a message to the public, particularly the black community in Los Angeles, to invoke the memory of Rodney King, the most recent and most visible victim of police misconduct.

> The specter of Rodney King has haunted this trial. The defense has cleverly manipulated their case so that Rodney King is now center-stage in this trial.
>
> Jeanine Ferris-Pirro, district attorney,
> Westchester County, New York

On August 22, the defense called its star witness, Dr. Henry Lee, the legendary medical examiner from Connecticut. With his impeccable reputation, his ability to translate technical jargon, and his elfin sense of humor, Lee proved to be a formidable witness for the defense. He criticized the work of the LAPD criminalists, discovered new pieces of evidence from the victims' clothing, and raised unsettling questions about the prosecution's version of the crime, including the possibility that there was more than one assailant.

An acknowledged master of crime scene reconstruction, Lee on the stand was precise, cautious, and virtually unassailable. Even Judge Ito advised the prosecution to make the cross-examination brief "given the reputation of this witness." To most of the legal analysts, where previous defense experts had only made dents, Lee had succeeded in punching a considerable hole in the prosecution's case. He had also provided the jury with a number of scenarios to create reasonable doubts about O. J. Simpson's guilt, with or without a police conspiracy.

RETURN OF THE FUHRMAN TAPES

> These tapes are ugly. Fuhrman is ugly. I would hope that if any good comes out of the painful process of this trial, it is that we confront that ugliness—that we look it in the face and we deal with it. And we think the jury is capable of doing that.
>
> Gerald Uelmen, attorney for the defense,
> August 29, 1995

> The content of these tapes is so repugnant and so offensive that this may be the most difficult thing I've ever had to do as a prosecutor. These tapes will only serve to mislead and confuse the jury.
>
> Marcia Clark, deputy district attorney,
> August 29, 1995

Johnnie Cochran was right—the "bombshell" of the Fuhrman tapes exploded in the courtroom on August 29, 1995. Pressed by the defense, Judge Ito reluctantly allowed Laura Hart McKinny to validate the authenticity of the tapes without the jury present. The courtroom overflowed, reporters scribbled furiously, and the crowd was absolutely attentive and amazed as the defense played sixty-one excerpts from the Fuhrman tapes. Fuhrman's tone was casual and confident as he described, in graphic and callous language, the many incidents in which he and his uniformed colleagues had beat up suspects, planted evidence, and harassed blacks and Latinos just for kicks.

The "N-Word"

Fuhrman, who had sworn under oath that he hadn't used the word *nigger* in ten years, could be heard saying it at least forty-one times in those excerpts. He revealed himself, as defense lawyer Gerald Uelmen noted, as "a liar, a bigot, and a lawbreaker." At the prosecution table, Marcia Clark and her colleagues were visibly shocked and obviously angered by the total discrediting of one of the state's key witnesses. Yet she argued forcefully against admitting any of the offensive tapes, pointing out to Judge Ito that "the admission of this evidence is telling the jury, 'Disregard the case. Look somewhere else.' . . . This is a murder trial where none of this is relevant. It is manipulative. It is cunning, but it is not relevant."

District Attorney Gil Garcetti, facing another major setback to his political ambitions, was penitent: "I'm embarrassed for the city and for the Los Angeles Police Department. . . . The vast majority of what they [the defense] seek to introduce is totally irrelevant and certainly highly inflammatory."

At a news conference after the trial, Fred Goldman, the father of victim Ron Goldman, could hardly contain his rage and grief. "The judge helped create more hate, and I think it's disgusting. This is now the Fuhrman trial. It's not the trial of O. J. Simpson."

At the end of a lengthy day of testimony, Judge Ito faced perhaps the most difficult decision of his professional life. Whatever ruling he handed down on these tapes might very well influence the jury's verdict. He did not have to listen to the talk shows or read the next morning's papers to know that the world was watching and waiting for his decision. He must have felt like Solomon, searching for a fair and just decision but knowing that he could never fully satisfy either side of this controversial case. To wrestle with the case law and his conscience, Judge Ito recessed the court for two days to decide the admissibility of Detective Mark Fuhrman's tapes.

Judge Ito's Decision

On August 31, Judge Ito ruled that he would allow only two brief excerpts from the Fuhrman tapes to be played in the jury's presence, both innocuous reference to places where "niggers" live. Ito based the ruling on his conclusion that the racially biased statements were not relevant to the defense's theory that Fuhrman planted evidence in this case and that "the probative value of the remaining examples is substantially and overwhelmingly outweighed by the danger of undue prejudice." Reflecting agreement with Christopher Darden's earlier objection to the use of the term, Ito noted that many of Fuhrman's comments might anger the jury because the term *nigger* is "perhaps the single most insulting, inflammatory, and provocative term in use in modern-day America."

The defense team immediately called a press conference, and Johnnie Cochran blasted Judge Ito's ruling, calling it "one of the cruelest, [most] unfair decisions ever rendered in a criminal court in this country." The ruling was a severe setback for the defense, but Cochran and his colleagues were determined to make the most of the two snippets and continue to build their case against the LAPD.

Meanwhile, the Fuhrman tapes had attracted the attention of a number of other interested parties who had raised their voices in protest, including the heads of the NAACP and the Los Angeles Urban League. The American Civil Liberties Union had filed a brief asking Judge Ito to release a complete transcript of the taped interviews to "ensure public confidence in the integrity and soundness of this Court's decision-making process." But perhaps the most surprising voice of all was that of California's governor, Pete Wilson, who denounced Fuhrman's statements, saying: "There is no condoning that, and no excuse for it. I think that the shock the public has experienced is a natural reaction." These words seemed slightly hypocritical coming from Wilson, a declared presidential candidate who at that very moment was running on a campaign platform to revoke affirmative action programs and to deny basic services to illegal immigrants in California.

Building the Case Against Fuhrman

After the Labor Day holiday, the defense team ratcheted up its attack on the credibility of Detective Fuhrman by calling two white women who testified about his racist views. Kathleen Bell, who had known the police officer casually ten years previously, reported that Fuhrman had boasted that he would find any excuse to stop a car with a black man and a white woman, and when she challenged the statement, he angrily replied: "If I had my way, they would take all the niggers, put them together in a big group, and burn them." Then Natalie Singer, a former personal assistant to actor Christopher Reeve, quoted Fuhrman as saying, "The only good nigger is a dead nigger." The defense painted Fuhrman into a very tight corner with the testimony of a third witness, Roderick Hodge, a handsome black man who had once complained that Fuhrman falsely arrested him and gloated: "I told you we'd get you, nigger." By the time these three witnesses had recited the litany of Fuhrman's racist language and behavior, the defense knew it had scored a major point with the jurors, who were avidly taking notes.

Refocusing on the Crime

> We have heard that Mark Fuhrman espouses genocide of African-Americans. We have heard about his racial hatreds, his sexism, his hatred for interracial couples; he wants to burn all African-Americans, or bomb all African-Americans. Everything that they wanted to accomplish today I think is done. Let's get back to the matter of trying O. J. Simpson for killing these two people.
>
> Christopher Darden, prosecutor, September 6, 1995

After all the *Sturm und Drang* over the Fuhrman tapes, it was not an easy task for the prosecution to refocus on the real defendant in this case. In fact, Marcia Clark and Christopher Darden, who had eagerly embraced Detective Fuhrman as one of their principal witnesses to describe the crime scene and to identify crucial evidence, now realized that he had been utterly discredited and had become a major liability to their case.

They were discouraged, but not defeated, so they quickly regrouped and decided not to mount aggressive challenges to any of the witnesses who had simply corroborated Fuhrman's racial views. But Darden's decision to attack Laura Hart McKinny as the messenger of the bad news backfired. The soft-spoken playwright, looking feminine and fragile with her long dark hair and her bohemian-style outfit, resisted his efforts to impugn her motives or question her integrity in using Mark Fuhrman as an informant in her work. The more Darden pressed her about the tapes, the more McKinny opened up other revealing topics about the LAPD. In one of his several strategic errors, Darden inadvertently got McKinny to bring up the issue of "police cover-ups" in the LAPD. It was a costly mistake and one that Johnnie Cochran lost no time in exploiting.

Although Judge Ito would not allow the defense to explore the general subject of cover-ups in the LAPD, Cochran was able to find a way to draw more comments from McKinny on the sexism and "certain cover-ups" in the department, leaving an indelible impression in that courtroom that the Fuhrman tapes could reveal much more than some racial epithets and leaving the jurors to wonder what those "certain cover-ups" might entail.

On September 6, the courtroom seemed charged with electricity when Mark Fuhrman, appearing confident and impervious to the hostile stares, strode into court with his lawyer. With the jury out of the room, defense attorney Gerald Uelmen asked Fuhrman: "Did you plant or manufacture evidence in this case?" Fuhrman, looking somber, replied: "I wish to assert my Fifth Amendment privilege." For the record, Uelmen would ask Fuhrman two more questions: if he had given truthful testimony at the preliminary hearing in the case and if he had ever knowingly falsified any police reports. For the record, Fuhrman twice again invoked his Fifth Amendment privilege against self-incrimination and notified the court that he intended to refuse to answer any further questions.

The high drama that held the courtroom enthralled was over in less than five minutes, and Judge Ito excused the retired LAPD detective. Observers noted that O. J. Simpson reacted very emotionally to Fuhrman's brief appearance, actually wiping tears away, but were they tears of anger, relief, or guilt?

Judge Ito assured the prosecution that Fuhrman would not be recalled to the witness stand and that, in keeping with California law, he would not inform the jury that Fuhrman had taken the Fifth but that he was simply "not available for further testimony as a witness in this case." However, the judge planned to add another key sentence: "His unavailability on cross-examination is a factor that you may consider in evaluating his credibility as a witness." This time, the prosecution reacted as if it had been run over with a steamroller. Marcia Clark, in high dudgeon, announced that she would file an emergency appeal to a higher court to overturn that instruction, which she thought unfairly undermined all of Mark Fuhrman's testimony in the case.

This time, the defense smelled an important victory, and Johnnie Cochran merely reminded Judge Ito, "We have a jury that is going to be mutinying shortly." The judge did not need to be reminded, for that very morning the jurors had again complained to him about the length of the trial. They had been sequestered for 239 days, and they were frustrated, bored, and very annoyed with the delays and the debates. The "trial of the century" was beginning to unravel, thanks to a frazzled judge, a frustrated jury, and two fractious teams of lawyers.

The Regrouping of the Prosecution

On September 8, to the amazement of most expert commentators, who had dismissed Marcia Clark's challenge to Judge Ito's ruling, the state court of appeals reversed Judge Ito's ruling on the grounds that it would penalize Mark Fuhrman for invoking his constitutional right against self-incrimination. Judge Ito, publicly rebuked, promptly vacated his order, yielding a victory for the prosecution but a setback for the defense. Marcia Clark and colleagues had won that round, and now they faced their final battle of wills and skills with the Dream Team. But the defense refused to rest its case, still looking for a dramatic denouement.

On Monday, September 11, the prosecution began its rebuttal to the defense's convoluted case. Marcia Clark, sensing that momentum was on the prosecution's side, revisited the issue of the infamous leather gloves. She showed videotapes of Simpson wearing very similar gloves as a sports commentator at various football games and called several witnesses to identify the model of the unusual gloves, but the defense objected strenuously to this line of evidence, trying to exclude it on the grounds that none of Fuhrman's testimony about finding the gloves was credible.

Was this new evidence so compelling that the jurors would be swayed after seeing the glove-that-didn't-fit demonstration? Unfortunately, Richard Rubin, the glove expert, weakened his own credibility when defense lawyer Robert Blasier read from a letter Rubin had sent to the prosecutors in July, after his earlier appearance as a witness, commenting: "Maybe I can make it to the victory party." It seemed at that point that the only victory belonged to the defense.

On September 13, the volatile situation in the courtroom erupted into a battle of wills among Judge Ito, Marcia Clark, and Johnnie Cochran. The defense had appealed the judge's decision that Mark Fuhrman could not be recalled as a witness, but the appellate court ruled that the request was premature and would be relevant only if O. J. Simpson were to be convicted. In a frenzy of activity, the prosecution withdrew two of its motions: one to introduce evidence about the infamous Bronco chase that ended in O. J. Simpson's arrest and the other to speed up the trial by holding longer sessions.

But on that Wednesday, Judge Ito was not a happy camper. The prosecution had failed to appear for an early morning hearing on the second motion, so he angrily levied a fine of $250 on the district attorney's office. When Marcia Clark objected, he increased the fine to $1,000, which provoked District Attorney Gil Garcetti to criticize the judge and the fine as "petty" and "outrageous" at a hastily called press conference. Increasingly under fire from a critical press for his conduct of the case and concerned about his tarnished judicial image, Judge Ito relented later that afternoon and reinstated the lower fine.

Meanwhile, the prosecutors felt mounting pressure to bring their rebuttal to a close before the jury actually mutinied, so they drastically reduced their witness list and announced that they would complete their case within two days. However, before this day was over, they would present two more rebuttal witnesses, whose testimony would cancel each other out. The first witness, Gary Sims of the California Department of Justice, testified that he had used the very sophisticated and highly reliable RFLP method to confirm the less reliable PCR results that identified genetic markers consistent with the blood of O. J. Simpson and Ronald Goldman found on the center console of Simpson's Bronco.

Though this testimony was very incriminating, the second witness, Thano Paratis, the nurse who initially drew the sample of Simpson's blood for police laboratory tests, testified that he had incorrectly estimated the blood as 8.0 cubic centimeters in his initial testimony but now recalled that the amount was approximately 6.5 cc. This convenient recall helped the prosecution account for the "missing" 1.5 cc of blood that the defense had used as a bludgeon to pound away at the theory of a police conspiracy to frame O. J. Simpson. Not only did this late discovery appear highly suspicious, but it was a taped interview, and the defense was unable to cross-examine the nurse, who claimed that serious health problems prevented his appearance in court. By the end of the day, the prosecution seemed to be in disarray and desperate to try any trick that would revive their case.

By September 14, the prosecutors were running out of energy and out of witnesses but still managed to create yet another side issue. They called two FBI witnesses to rebut the testimony of Dr. Henry Lee, the icon of forensic scientists, who had earlier suggested that there might have been a second set of footprints at the scene of the crime. After Barry Scheck had attempted to discredit the expertise of FBI agents Douglas Deedrick and William Bodziak, who tenaciously held their ground, Lee was asked to comment on Deedrick's contradictory testimony that there was no second set of shoe prints at the Bundy crime scene.

Like British royalty, Lee was not amused and responded to reporters that he would not return as a witness for the defense "surrebuttal" case, sarcastically saying in his accented English, "One-time experience is more than enough. Life has to go on besides the O. J. Simpson case. Once a trial becomes a game, I am not going to participate. . . . The emotional and physical trauma to an individual, to their family . . . not worth it."

On Monday, September 18, the prosecution completed its rebuttal arguments with a stipulation agreed to by both sides that "the moon on June 12, 1994, was a waxing crescent with 12 percent of its surface illuminated." Marcia Clark made the proviso that the prosecution reserved the right to resume rebuttal after the defense completed its case-in-chief, a very unusual arrangement permitted by Judge Ito to facilitate the progress of the case. But the prosecutors were not prepared for the ambush that would derail their case within the next forty-eight hours.

The Defense Ambush

> We expect to end this case with some fireworks.
>
> Johnnie Cochran, defense attorney,
> September 17, 1995

The Dream Team had promised to produce some last-minute surprise witnesses, and true to their word, they ended their case-in-chief in a brilliant display of legal fireworks on September 19. In one of the most bizarre incidents in the trial, the defense called Craig Anthony ("The Animal") Fiato and Larry Fiato, two reputed Mafia mobsters, to impeach the testimony of Detective Phillip Vannatter, the lead investigating officer in the case. Tony Fiato, a former boyfriend of Denise Brown, was an FBI informant and had been implicated in mob killings, yet he and his brother had chatted over drinks with Vannatter the previous January when they were staying at a hotel in Los Angeles, preparing to testify at a federal trial.

According to Larry Fiato, who swaggered up to the witness stand with supreme brio, Detective Vannatter had casually commented that the police entered O. J. Simpson's Brentwood estate because they initially considered him a suspect in the murders. Fiato's account was not only corroborated by his brother Tony, who repeated Vannatter's comment that "the husband is always the suspect," but also by FBI special agent Michael Wacks, the "handler" for the brothers, who heard a similar statement repeated by Vannatter again in March outside of the district attorney's office.

When Detective Vannatter was recalled to the stand, he vehemently denied making those statements and stood by his earlier statement that the police did not initially consider O. J. Simpson a suspect but allowed that he might have made some comment in jest that was taken out of context. Despite the detective's denial, the contradictory testimony of the three men, one an FBI agent who had earlier reported it to his superiors, lent powerful support to the defense's claim that O. J. Simpson had been set up from the first by police officers, who then conspired to build a case against him. It was ironic that it took two admitted gangsters to expose the duplicity of the LAPD and the complicity of the district attorney's office to cover up this fundamental violation of the defendant's civil rights. It was also a perfect parable to illustrate why Detective Vannatter and his partner, Detective Lange, the two major investigators in the case, were affectionately called "Dumb and Dumber" by some of their colleagues in the DA's office.

On September 20, the defense suffered a minor setback when Judge Ito denied a request to call two FBI agents to the stand to give further testimony about the forensic evidence. But Johnnie Cochran used his remaining time to hammer home the themes of police incompetence, contamination of the crime scene, and possible misconduct by Mark Fuhrman. In an even more flamboyant performance than usual, Cochran precipitated a minirebellion of the court stenographers, who complained to the judge that they could not keep up with his "rapid speech and his habit of talking over witnesses." Cochran was feeling very confident; he was on a roll, and he planned to end this case while still gaining momentum.

On September 21, as another week ended, Judge Ito ruled that the jurors could consider two charges against O. J. Simpson in their deliberations: a charge of first-degree murder, if they found that the crimes were premeditated, or a charge of second-degree murder, if they found that the crimes were committed during "an uncontrollable rage or a fit of passion." This was a clear victory for the prosecution, allowing the jurors some degree of compromise, but a defeat for the defense.

The defense suffered another defeat when the California Supreme Court rejected its request to rule that Judge Ito should reinstate his proposed instruction to the jurors about Mark Fuhrman's unavailability to return as a witness. The judge announced that the court would recess for one day to observe the Jewish holiday of Rosh Hashanah at the request of the Goldman family and several of the lawyers. Despite the defense team's frustration at the two unfavorable rulings, the case was obviously sputtering out. Johnnie Cochran and Robert Shapiro were not even present in court that day. It seemed like the March wind—the case had come in like a lion and was now going out like a lamb.

The Denouement: Both Sides Rest

> I am mindful of the mood and stamina of this jury. I have confidence, a lot more than it seems Ms. Clark has, of their integrity, that they will find as the record stands now that I did not, could not, and would not have committed this crime.
>
> O. J. Simpson, defendant, September 22, 1995

The defense had one last surprise for the court before officially resting their case. On Friday, September 22, when Judge Ito asked O. J. Simpson if he knowingly waived his right to testify in his own defense, the defendant seized the opportunity to turn a brief answer into a plea of innocence. For the first time since the trial had begun nearly a year earlier, the celebrity pitchman proclaimed his innocence and complained about the "misrepresentations about myself and my . . . Nicole." Over Marcia Clark's furious objections and Judge Ito's stern interruptions, Simpson finished his self-serving statement and sat down, comforted by mentor Johnnie Cochran.

It was a bravura performance, perfectly scripted and sprinkled with just the right touch of emotion and drama. Although the jury was not present to hear his plea, the district attorney and the prosecution team were incensed because Simpson had managed to outwit them without ever taking the stand to subject himself to cross-examination. Fred Goldman, whose press conferences had become as predictable as the L.A. smog, was livid with anger when he spoke: "It's disgusting what he did . . . and it's disgusting to me also that the judge tolerated it. That was part of the normal orchestrated defense, throwing garbage out there on a regular basis to influence this jury above and beyond [the] testimony."

With that one last twist in a case of many unpredictable turns, Judge Ito called in the jury, and with gracious smiles and grateful words, Marcia Clark, for the prosecution, and Johnnie Cochran, for the defense, officially rested their cases. At that point, the judge appeared to breathe a sigh of relief (or perhaps thanksgiving) and proceeded to read his instructions to the fourteen remaining members of the jury panel, two of whom would continue to serve as alternates until the final decision was rendered.

It took Judge Ito a full thirty-six minutes to read the complex set of instructions, carefully defining terms and expressions like "beyond a reasonable doubt" and cautioning that "anyone caught lying on one issue could be disbelieved on other issues." Some observers wondered if the instruction was meant to apply to Mark Fuhrman or Philip Vannatter—or both. Some jurors may have fleetingly been reminded of Rodney King and the web of lies that the LAPD had constructed to cover up his brutal beating. They might have wondered how many of the police in this case had lied or covered up evidence in order to incriminate O. J. Simpson.

As he read the lengthy instructions, Judge Ito seemed unusually nervous, stumbling so badly over two instructions that he was asked to restate them. As he methodically explained the fine points of the law to the jury, O. J. Simpson seemed almost immobile, listening intently with a frown on his face, his jaw thrust forward, and his shoulders hunched with tension. In the last two weeks of the trial, he had seemed increasingly depressed, particularly since the prosecution had shown the video clips of his sportscasting days. Watching those clips, perhaps he realized for the first time during the trial how far he had plummeted. In just one year, O. J., legendary athlete and media personality, had become Orenthal James Simpson, murder defendant and media freak.

Judge Ito recessed the trial for the weekend, weary but relieved that the closing arguments would be delivered on the day after Rosh Hashanah, so the end of this interminable trial was in sight.

THE CLOSING ARGUMENTS

On Tuesday, September 26, exactly one year after the potential jurors reported to the court for the jury selection process, the prosecution began its closing arguments. During the preceding weekend, the print and broadcast media had had a virtual orgasm of opinions, predictions, debates, and diatribes over the case. All the pundits were vying with one another to make the most profound, the most controversial, or the wittiest comments about the case, ranging from an analysis of Marcia Clark's "hysterical" personality to a critique of Johnnie Cochran's flashy wardrobe.

The Views of Blacks Versus Whites

Poll takers had a field day, with strikingly different results in the opinions of blacks and whites as to O. J. Simpson's guilt or innocence, the credibility of the evidence against him, and the conduct of the case. In a poll of five hundred San Franciscans, who had always considered O. J. their native son, 58.2 percent believed he was "probably guilty of the crimes," 10.6 percent said "probably not guilty," and 31.2 percent said they "didn't know." But whites were about four times more likely than blacks to call him "guilty" (65.2 percent to 17.8 percent), and blacks were four times more likely than whites to call him "not guilty" (31.1 percent versus 8.4 percent). Similar results were reported in Los Angeles and New York and in national polls taken by CNN, CBS, ABC, and the Gallup Organization. The racial divisions that had surfaced from the moment of O. J.'s arrest had grown, and opinions had become more polarized as the trial reached its climax.

The Prosecution Summary

> When you look at these pictures, you see rage, you see fury, you see overkill. . . . These are murders that are really slaughters, that are personal. . . . No stranger, no Columbian drug dealer, but a man who was involved with his intended victims . . . and that man is this defendant.
>
> Marcia Clark, prosecutor, September 26, 1995

Marcia Clark, dressed in a two-piece tailored white suit, looking pale and drawn, started haltingly, but her voice and her confidence grew stronger as she summarized the "mountains of evidence" in the case of *The People of California* v. *Orenthal James Simpson*. To distill that mountain of 723 pieces of evidence from fifty-eight witnesses for the prosecution, Clark set up an impressive time-line chart (in red, white, and blue, with the time of day highlighted in yellow) to demonstrate that O. J. Simpson had seventy-eight minutes unaccounted for on the night of June 12, 1994, from 9:36, when he returned home with Kato Kaelin, until 10:54, when he was (allegedly) seen by the limousine driver entering the front door of his home. She appealed to the jurors to "ignore the sideshow" and to look at the actual evidence against Simpson. She disowned Mark Fuhrman and criticized the LAPD for its sloppy police work, its criminalists, and its coroner's office. She described in detail the prosecution theory of the crime, highlighted the blood and forensic evidence connecting Simpson to the crime, and debunked the conflicting defense versions of a drug-related killing or a police conspiracy against O. J. Simpson.

Building up to her climax, the petite deputy district attorney painted a powerful picture of the brutality of the two killings and the rage of the killer. She followed the trail of blood from the sidewalk on Bundy Drive to the console of Simpson's Bronco. She began with a time-line chart and ended with a life-size puzzle, filling in the pieces of the incriminating evidence against the defendant, slowly filling out the face of O. J. Simpson. It was a stunning device with a significant impact on the courtroom.

Marcia Clark had pulled her case together and presented a convincing argument, albeit much of it circumstantial, to prove that O. J. Simpson was indeed the person who butchered Nicole Brown Simpson and Ronald Goldman. When she finished her summation and turned the podium over to her colleague Christopher Darden, millions in the television audience were absolutely convinced that she had preempted the defense and had proved her case.

The Time Bomb Waiting to Explode

Christopher Darden, who had taken the hardest hits during the trial, was anxious to redeem himself and to build an airtight case against O. J. Simpson, whose defense team had come to symbolize for him all that was wrong with the adversarial nature of the criminal justice system. He depicted Simpson as a violent wife beater, a jealous spouse, a "time bomb" waiting to explode. Clark had laid out the blueprint; now Darden filled in the specifications. He built up the image of O. J. Simpson as a controlling, abusive, and vengeful man. He documented the many incidents of physical and psychological abuse inflicted on Nicole by O. J., the constant humiliation and hostile behaviors, his need to dominate, and his fear of losing control over his former wife.

The next day, Darden hit his stride and held the courtroom rapt as he pointed to Simpson and named him as the killer. It was the only time in the trial that anyone had confronted Simpson so directly, and he did not seem to enjoy the brief confrontation. By the time Darden had concluded the prosecution's closing statement, he had proved to the courtroom and to the world that he was a first-rate prosecutor and, even more, a decent human being deeply committed to justice. He believed in the righteousness of his case, and with unflinching honesty and integrity, he had shown his admirers and detractors that there must be one standard of justice for blacks and whites, a system of justice that is truly color-blind for the victims, the defendants, and their counsel.

The Defense Summary

On Friday, September 28, Johnnie Cochran, colorful and cocky in a periwinkle blue suit, rose to give the closing arguments for the defense. With his mellifluous baritone voice filling the courtroom, Cochran stalked and strutted like a Baptist preacher in the pulpit while he mounted his final defense of O. J. Simpson. He called Detectives Fuhrman and Vannatter "twins of deception" and pointed to the many inconsistencies, incompetencies, and inaccuracies in the prosecution's case. He subtly manipulated the black members of the jury by quoting familiar scriptures from the Bible, invoking the name of Martin Luther King, Jr., and a pantheon of African-American heroes, and returning again and again to the three themes of police misconduct, police incompetence, and police conspiracy to take down another black hero.

Perhaps he got carried away with his own rhetoric, but Cochran stepped very close to the ethical line when he compared Mark Fuhrman to Hitler and linked his remarks to genocide against blacks, another very sensitive theme to blacks on the jury. He did not shrink from asserting that the police conspiracy was fueled by racism and urged the jury to "send a message" to the LAPD that police misconduct against a black man would no longer be tolerated.

But what would be remembered after all the smoke and mirrors, the Scriptures, and the litany of insults against the LAPD was his simple statement: "If the gloves don't fit, you must acquit."

Socks, Lies, and Videotapes

> If they manufactured evidence on the sock, how can you trust anything else? How in this country, in this democracy, can they

> come in? There's no doubt Fuhrman's a liar, and a genocidal racist, there's no doubt about that. But there's really no doubt either that they played with this sock, is there? And if that can happen, that's a reasonable doubt for the case. End of sentence. End of case.
>
> Barry Scheck, defense lawyer, September 28, 1995

After Cochran had whipped the courtroom into a state of hyperalertness with his dramatic delivery, Barry Scheck, the quintessential New York lawyer with his staccato speech and his acerbic wit, continued the impassioned arguments on behalf of the defendant's innocence. He began by characterizing the physical evidence as "contaminated, corrupted, and compromised," calling it "a cancer infecting the heart of this case." His voice dripping with sarcasm, Scheck dismissed the most significant items of prosecution evidence, from the blood-spattered sock to the blood-speckled gate, both of which were curiously not collected for testing until several weeks after the crimes were committed. Scheck waved a photograph of the bloody sock at the jury and loudly proclaimed: "Somebody played with this evidence, and there's no doubt about it." By the time Scheck had completed his summation, he had been effective in creating doubts about the validity of the evidence and about the possibility of police tampering with it—but had he succeeded in creating "reasonable doubt" in the jurors' minds?

That task would have to fall to Johnnie Cochran, lead defense attorney, who would make the concluding comments.

Concluding Comments: The Defense

> Nobody has the courage to say it's wrong. . . . Maybe you're the right people at the right time at the right place to say, "No more! We're not going to have this. This is wrong. What they've done to your client is wrong." . . . You are empowered to say, "We are not going to take that anymore."
>
> Johnnie Cochran, defense attorney,
> September 28, 1995

At the end of a very long and tiring day of closing arguments, Johnnie Cochran, speaking on behalf of the Dream Team for their client, marshaled his reserves of energy and displayed all of his considerable rhetorical skills in his concluding remarks. He complimented the jury with lavish words of praise, cited the Scriptures about the sin of bearing false witness, and even suggested that the jurors had been selected by divine intervention "to do the right thing" for this particular defendant. Beating his fist in his hand, Cochran implored the jury "to send a message to the LAPD," telling them in clear and unambiguous terms that they could not get away with police misconduct or conspiracy any longer. As he wound down, Cochran lowered his voice and said he wanted to pose a set of troublesome questions to Marcia Clark. He then read a list of fifteen questions about the prosecution's case, clearly intending to remind the jury one final time of the possibility of a police conspiracy and cover-up against O. J. Simpson—and to ask one final time, "How come the gloves just don't fit?"

At the end of the day, the defense team of Cochran and Scheck felt pleased with themselves for their impressive and impassioned closing statements; others were not so pleased. Cochran's comparison of Fuhrman's racist behavior to Adolf Hitler's anti-Semitic genocide enraged many Jews and Jewish leaders, including Fred Goldman, who called another news conference to denounce Johnnie Cochran and the defense strategy. Goldman, visibly agitated, responded:

> This man ought to be ashamed of himself to walk among decent human beings. He is one of the most disgusting human beings I have ever had to listen to in my life. Because of racism, we should put aside all other thoughts, all other reason, and set his murdering client free?

Goldman's anger had also been inflamed earlier that week when Johnnie Cochran began appearing at the courthouse, flanked by a phalanx of bodyguards from the Nation of Islam, a group whose leaders were reputed to be virulently anti-Semitic. But Goldman's attacks this time were countered by O. J. Simpson's family, who called their own news conference to reject criticism of the defense team's strategy and to affirm their support of their brother, Johnnie Cochran, and the Nation of Islam, who had, in the words of Shirley Baker, O. J.'s older sister, "offered to embrace us and help us."

The Race Card

The Dream Team had completed its mission to provide O. J. Simpson with the best possible defense that money could buy. The members of the team had recovered from their disagreements and disarray at the beginning of the case and had worked effectively together to expose the weaknesses in the prosecution's case and to support their own theory of a possible police conspiracy against their client. Critics accused Johnnie Cochran of "playing the race card" in his closing argument, but their harsh criticism was only partly justified; in fact, it was a far more sophisticated argument and complex card that he played.

Race had been an integral and inevitable factor in this case from the very beginning. Cochran had simply made a deliberate decision to use it to his client's advantage, as any good defense lawyer would have done. Subtly and subliminally, Cochran had manipulated the negative attitudes of the black jurors toward the LAPD. He had played on their fears and anxieties about a genocidal conspiracy against African-Americans. More than any single factor, Cochran had evoked the memory of Rodney King, the innocent victim of a vicious LAPD beating, police conspiracy, and subsequent cover-up only four years previously.

Like Rodney King, O. J. Simpson was a black man; like Rodney King, O. J. Simpson had tried to escape from a posse of patrol cars pursuing him on the freeway; like Rodney King, O. J. Simpson had been treated with disrespect and demonized by the police before he was arrested and even before he was an official suspect. Despite their differences in accomplishments, access, and aspirations, Rodney King and O. J. Simpson were still two sides of the same coin, two black males in a racially divided society, vulnerable to the vagaries and the violence of the notoriously racist Los Angeles Police Department. For the defense during the yearlong trial, Rodney King was indeed the thirteenth juror, unobserved in the jury box but clearly visible in the imaginations of the black jurors.

Concluding Comments: The Prosecution

> They have to attack our science because all the science points to O. J. Simpson, to the defendant, it all points to him as a killer.
>
> Christopher Darden, prosecutor, September 29, 1995

In the American criminal justice system, the prosecution carries the burden of proof to convict criminal defendants, so prosecutors have the privilege of opening and closing a case. Thus on Friday, September 29, as summer gradually turned into autumn in Los Angeles, Deputy District Attorneys Marcia Clark and Christopher Darden made their final appeal to the jury in the O. J. Simpson double-murder case.

Darden, in his low-key laconic style, borrowed some tactics from his estranged mentor, Johnnie Cochran, with whom he had jousted frequently during the trial. He quoted from Martin Luther King, Jr., Malcolm X, the Bible, and the United States Constitution, hoping to sway the jurors that his case was convincing and that his cause was righteous. He advised the jurors to "look at all the evidence," to ignore the "red herrings" and "wild goose chases" offered by the defense, and to avoid "quantum leaps of logic" based on racism. Darden did not talk very long, but he advised the jurors not to "choke on smoke" and reminded them that Nicole Brown Simpson and Ronald Goldman had been deprived of their "right to liberty . . . and the right to life." He reminded them that O. J. Simpson was not "above the law" and cautioned them against "sending a message" to Fuhrman or to the LAPD.

Ultimately, Darden challenged the jury to deliver a guilty verdict because "everybody knows he killed—everybody knows. The evidence is there." With his soft voice and his intense manner,

Darden himself left a powerful message with the jury, but his message was about courage, about duty, and, above all, about justice for the silent victims in this case.

The Voice for the Victims

> Usually I feel I'm the only one left to speak for the victims. But in this case, Ron and Nicole, they're speaking to you. And they're telling you who murdered them. . . . He did it. Mr. Orenthal Simpson. He did it.
>
> Marcia Clark, prosecutor, September 29, 1995

It was left for Marcia Clark, the lead prosecutor, to speak for the two silent victims in her final comments to the court. Exhausted and plainly dispirited, Clark summoned up all her strength to reach the impassive jurors for the last time. She set up another impressive display of an oversized pyramid, spelling out all the "unrefuted facts" of the prosecution case and building a persuasive argument of O. J. Simpson's guilt by inference. Clark ignored the fifteen questions posed by Johnnie Cochran the day before but proceeded to raise numerous questions of her own. She challenged the motives and the methods of many of the defense experts, ridiculed the "crazy conspiracy theories," and pointed to the physical evidence of blood, hair, and clothes as telltale clues to the killer.

Clark saved her most dramatic piece of evidence until the very end, when she played the tape of the 911 emergency call from Nicole Brown Simpson, her voice full of fear, screaming, "He's back. He's O. J. Simpson. I think you know his record." As Nicole's voice echoed in the eerily quiet courtroom, the muffled sobs of her three sisters and Ron Goldman's family could be heard, anguished in their grief and desolate in their loss.

When Clark completed her summation, she uttered a little sigh, thanked the jury, and sat down next to her colleague Christopher Darden. The two of them smiled at each other, pleased that they had ended on an emotionally compelling note and happy that the case was finally over. At a press conference after the court adjourned, they seemed upbeat and confident that they had proved their case "beyond a reasonable doubt." Strangely, the defense team members were a little more subdued but professed confidence that their client would be acquitted, but it was unclear whether this was yet another example of their tendency to put a favorable spin on events just to keep the press and public guessing.

To the Jury at Last

Meanwhile, Judge Ito referred the case to the jury, informed the jurors that they would no longer be able to enjoy conjugal visits or unmonitored phone calls until they had reached a verdict, and instructed them to elect a foreperson before court adjourned for the day. In just a few minutes, the jurors announced that they had selected a forewoman, the first clue that they might be more cohesive and more collegial than observers had predicted. Judge Ito quickly adjourned court until the following Monday, when the jury would begin its long-awaited deliberations.

By the end of the day, the sheriff of Los Angeles County had announced that his seven thousand–member department would be placed on tactical alert throughout the period of jury deliberations. Along with the LAPD, this force would be nearly twice as large as the force available when the verdict was announced in the trial of the four white LAPD officers for violating the rights of Rodney King. The pundits predicted that the jury would be out for days, even weeks, to sift through all the complicated evidence and the competing claims. Even the most astute analysts and omniscient observers could not have anticipated the surprising speed of the verdict and the tremendous chaos it would provoke.

10

The Color of Justice, II

The Verdict, the Response, the Aftermath

Race plays a role in everything in America and people need to stop ducking and dodging away from it. . . . We played the credibility card, not the race card.

Johnnie Cochran, defense attorney, October 3, 1995

We not only played the race card, we dealt it from the bottom of the deck.

Robert Shapiro, defense attorney, October 3, 1995

On September 29, the last Friday of the month, the jurors in the Simpson case hoped that this would be their final weekend sequestered in a hotel; the prosecution and defense lawyers looked forward to two days of unwinding from their intense contest of wills; the mass media went into overdrive predicting the jury's verdict; and the public began to cope with withdrawal symptoms from the daily diet of Simpson mania. The whole nation was poised for the final act of this national tragedy.

THE CONCLUSION OF THE CASE

On Monday, October 2, a subdued and exhausted Judge Lance Ito referred the case to the jury, sternly admonishing the jurors of their solemn duty to follow his instructions in their deliberations and to take their responsibilities seriously. After the jury retired to discuss the case, people in the courtroom seemed suspended, at loose ends and unsure of what to do with themselves while the jury was out. Feelings on both sides were intense, particularly since the Goldman family had objected so strenuously to parts of Johnnie Cochran's closing arguments comparing Mark Fuhrman to Adolf Hitler. Both sides had spent the weekend spinning their cases with the media and positioning themselves to win or lose gracefully.

The polls reflected growing polarization between blacks and whites, not only on the question of O. J.'s guilt or innocence but also on the tactics used by both sides to bolster their case. The racial split was further exacerbated by the ethnic tensions between blacks and Jews, fanned by Cochran's provocative use of security guards from the Nation of Islam and his gratuitous comments about racial genocide.

After one year of intense discussion and debate, it was clear that there was a deep fault line in the society over this case and that there would be an inevitable upheaval in the community no matter what verdict was rendered.

> O. J. will probably be acquitted because of the Fuhrman tapes. They certainly raise reasonable doubt, and that jury has many blacks who have probably experienced the racism of the LAPD. It will serve [the police] right because they never should have tampered with the evidence and lied about the search warrant.
>
> Arthur B. Walker, professor of physics,
> Stanford University

Reporters were beginning to close down their portable computers and lawyers were making their lunch plans as Judge Ito abruptly reconvened court to respond to the jury's request to read the testimony of Alan Park, the limousine driver who picked up O. J. Simpson on the night of June 12. This request caused considerable anxiety in and around the courthouse as both teams of lawyers and all the reporters tried to second-guess the jury's intent. The consensus seemed to be that this was favorable for the prosecution, particularly since the defense looked visibly distressed.

Shortly after 3:00 P.M. (Pacific Daylight Time) and before the reporters could complete their stories on this development, Judge Ito made an even more surprising announcement. The jury had notified the judge that they had reached a verdict—after less than four hours of deliberation! Pandemonium broke out in the courthouse as Judge Ito, noting that several of the principal lawyers were out of town, decided to postpone the reading of the verdict until the next day. He also wanted to give the Los Angeles Police Department ample time to place officers on a contingency plan to avert any potential replay of the 1992 civil disturbances after three of the four officers were acquitted in the Rodney King case.

Again the media rose to the challenge and filled the evening news, talk shows, and morning newspapers with predictions of O. J.'s verdict. Expert defense lawyers and prosecutors pronounced diametrically opposing opinions: that it would be a "guilty" verdict because the jury reached a decision so quickly (prosecutors) or that it would be a "not guilty" verdict for the same reason (defense lawyers). Previous experience with brief deliberations actually seemed to favor the defense viewpoint, but logic was overcome by emotion for those who strongly felt that O. J. deserved to be convicted of these two heinous murders. More polls were taken in anticipation of the verdict, and blacks and whites were again on opposite sides of the issue. Predictably, the verdict was like a Rorschach test—prosecutors, conservatives, and most whites believed that the jury would find O. J. guilty; defense lawyers, liberals, and most blacks believed that he would be acquitted.

One indisputable fact emerged in all of the polls—the American public had faithfully followed this trial, had heard even more evidence than the jury, and had reached a decision about O. J. Simpson's guilt or innocence. Though dramatically divided, the public had judged O. J. Simpson and was simply waiting to hear that judgment confirmed by the jury.

> In a CBS poll conducted the week-end before the verdict was announced, 64 percent of whites said they thought that O. J. Simpson was probably guilty of the crimes but only 12 percent of blacks believed he was guilty.
>
> *New York Times*, October 2, 1995

THE VERDICT

At 10:00 A.M. PDT on Tuesday, October 3, the country came to a virtual standstill as 150 million people watched television sets at homes and department stores or tuned in to portable radios in offices and on construction sites, all anxiously awaiting the verdict. In San Francisco, friends and former neighbors of the Simpson family gathered at the Potrero Hill Neighborhood Community Center to hear the verdict. In Los Angeles, Rev. Cecil Murray of the First African Methodist Episcopal Church (FAME) had again invited his parishioners and community leaders to gather at his church to await the verdict, as they had done after the trial of the police officers in the King beating. Members and friends of the Brown and Goldman families had gathered in the prosecutor's office on the eighteenth floor of the Criminal Courts Building, where they did not have to face the inquisitive and invasive probes of the press.

AT&T reported that the volume of phone calls between 10:00 and 10:10 A.M. plummeted by 58 percent as the business and social calls of the nation were put on hold. On Wall Street, the brokers had placed personal bets on the outcome with a payoff of $18 for a verdict of guilty in the first degree and $10 for a verdict of guilty in the second degree; Wall Street was betting on a conviction, and the price was still rising at noon on the East Coast (9:00 A.M. PDT), an hour before the verdict would be announced in Los Angeles. Airplane flights at the Hartsfield International Airport in Atlanta were delayed as passengers boarded late so they could watch the verdict. Even President Clinton left the oval office to join his aides, who were gathered around a television set in a nearby office. The climax of the long-running Simpson serial drama was imminent; the suspense was palpable as people waited for the final curtain to come down on this infamous case.

As the jurors filed into the jury box, their faces impassive, they studiously avoided eye contact with the defendant. A nervous Judge Ito asked O. J. Simpson and his lawyers to stand while the court clerk read the verdict, and he cautioned the courtroom to remain calm and to refrain from any disruptions during the reading. Observers and participants alike seemed to hold their collective breath as the suspense became nearly unbearable. Deirdre Robertson, the court clerk, also nervous, stumbled over Simpson's full name, then solemnly read the verdict: "We, the jury, in the above entitled action, find the defendant, Orenthal James Simpson, not guilty of the crime of murder . . . upon Nicole Brown Simpson." Before she could read the second count, the courtroom erupted in a dramatic display of pent-up emotions. O. J. Simpson, the celebrity defendant, at first looked stunned, then let out a deep sigh of relief and smiled broadly when he grasped the full impact of the verdict. Johnny Cochran, his celebrity lawyer, hugged him and punched a victorious fist in the air. Behind the defense table, O. J.'s mother, sisters, and two older children alternately cried, smiled, and lifted their hands in thankful prayer.

But on the prosecutor's side of the courtroom, the camera showed the stunned expressions of Marcia Clark and Chris Darden, looking dazed and disbelieving that the jury had failed to convict this defendant in spite of all the incriminating evidence against him. Sitting behind the prosecution table, the members of the Goldman family were also shocked by these "not guilty" verdicts. Ron Goldman's father tried to comfort his sister Kim, sobbing uncontrollably, and was heard to mutter "murderer, murderer" as O. J. Simpson looked over in their direction. Nicole's parents sat there in stoic silence, seemingly resigned to this outcome, but Nicole's sisters looked angry as they turned to comfort each other.

The Public Response: Blacks Versus Whites

> This jury sent a message that the time has come here in Los Angeles and in America that there must be a level playing field for everybody.
>
> John W. Mack, president, Los Angeles Urban League, October 3, 1995

> After the Rodney King incident and after the riots, black people have been on a downward spiral, with a new mood in the nation which is basically antiblack. We were desperate for any kind of victory, no matter what it was.
>
> Myles Goodson, retired pharmaceutical salesman, October 3, 1995

Outside the courtroom, pandemonium reigned. Blacks, dressed in African liberation colors and brandishing banners professing Simpson's innocence, were shouting for joy, raising their fists in victory, and dancing in the streets. Whites, standing symbolically on the other side of the barricades, seemed shocked and bewildered at first, then frustrated and angry, women crying and hugging each other to seek solace from their pain at this miscarriage of justice. With the instant access of cameras and satellite feeds, television screens showed the reaction of people in Los Angeles, San Francisco, New York, Washington, Atlanta, and Buffalo.

This time, the congregants at Rev. Murray's church were celebrating the verdict, clapping their hands and singing "Hallelujah!" On Potrero Hill, O. J.'s old friends and neighbors were jumping up and down, yelling that their homeboy had been vindicated. Black law students at Howard University in Washington, D.C., were overjoyed, loudly proclaiming that the system had finally worked for a black man.

> For once in a lifetime, a black man was able to afford adequate representation. We can now do what white people have been doing all the time.
>
> Student, Howard University, School of Law, October 4, 1995

This sentiment was repeated over and over by blacks shown greeting the verdict with jubilation or resignation in bars, beauty shops, department stores, and subway stations. They were celebrating the verdict of a jury that could not find Simpson guilty "beyond a reasonable doubt." Despite their obvious excitement and enthusiasm, many blacks quite seriously and emphatically made it clear to reporters that they were not celebrating the brutal murders of two innocent people but rather the release of a black celebrity whose guilt had not been proved in a court of law.

> When O. J. gets off, the whites will riot the way we whites do: leave the cities, go to Idaho or Oregon or Arizona, vote for Gingrich, . . . and punish the blacks by closing their day-care programs and cutting off their Medicaid.
>
> Ben Stein, lawyer, Los Angeles, October 3, 1995

> Understandably and rightly, the black community in Los Angeles abhors the years of racism directed against them from the LAPD, but that doesn't justify this verdict.
>
> Steven Yagman, Los Angeles defense attorney, October 4, 1995

Whites all over the nation initially responded to the verdicts with shock, anger, and outrage. Scenes of whites in corporate offices, suburban shopping malls, and upscale restaurants showed expressions of dismay, disgust, and even despair. White women, like their counterparts in front of the Los Angeles Criminal Courts building, seemed particularly upset about the verdict, protesting that O. J. had gotten away with spouse abuse and murder, sending a chilling message to battered women everywhere.

At the coffee bars and boutiques in Brentwood, casual acquaintances of Nicole and Ron were visibly distressed, denouncing the verdict, the defendant, and Simpson's defense team for this "travesty of justice." In New York's Times Square, where people watched the verdict as it flashed on the huge Sony television screen looming among the skyscrapers, the large, frenetic crowd of shoppers, tourists, and bike messengers suddenly turned into two opposing camps, people of color and whites—one group enjoying the ecstacy of victory, the other feeling the agony of defeat. It appeared that blacks and Latinos were hugging each other and exuberantly exchanging high fives, while whites were momentarily stunned and immobilized by the news. In corporate law offices in Chicago and Atlanta, young white lawyers seemed surprised at the verdicts, injudiciously criticizing the jurors for their hasty deliberations and the judge for his conduct of the case.

Meeting the Press: Victors and Vanquished

> We said if we could shatter the prosecution's time line so that O. J. Simpson couldn't have committed this crime, that there would be a reasonable doubt.
>
> Johnnie Cochran, defense attorney, October 3, 1995

> I was always in prayer. I knew that my son was innocent and I had the support of so many people all over the world. I know that the prayer of the righteous prevaileth much and I believed in that.
>
> Eunice Simpson, October 3, 1995

While the television crews and newspaper reporters were seeking sensational sound bites around the nation, the focus of the major networks returned to the courthouse for postverdict press conferences with the defense and prosecution teams. The victorious defense team, with Robert Shapiro notably absent, lined up at a table flanked by O. J. Simpson's family—his mother, two sisters, and two older children. His son Jason, who had been conspicuously missing during most of the trial and had cried copiously at the announcement of the verdicts, read a statement from his father:

> When things have settled again I want to pursue as my primary goal in life the killer or killers who slaughtered Nicole and Mr. Goldman . . . whatever it takes to identify them and bring them in I'll provide somehow. I can only hope that some day, despite every prejudicial thing that has been said about me, people will understand that I would not, could not, and did not kill anyone.

O. J.'s mother and sisters reaffirmed their faith in his innocence and their faith in God for this happy outcome. Johnnie Cochran, looking as if he had swallowed both the cat and the canary, graciously and charmingly responded to reporters' questions, continuing to put a favorable spin on his client's innocence even though it was no longer necessary.

Several of the other defense lawyers fielded questions, reacting with equanimity but skillfully trying to defuse some of the hostile and derisive questions about their defense tactics, their defendant's future civil trials, and their concerns about the victims' families. It was a tour de force, another staged event in the ongoing saga of the O. J. Simpson story, yet beneath the facade of smiling faces and sanctimonious statements was the subtle suggestion of a shared "family secret," suppressed from conscious awareness but hovering in the recesses of their minds and festering in the depth of their souls. The Dream Team had unraveled in its moment of triumph, with Robert Shapiro publicly distancing himself from Johnnie Cochran. Not only had Shapiro exposed their bitter personality conflicts and their disagreements over strategy, but he had also revealed the undercurrent of doubts and ambivalence of some of the team's members about their client's innocence and integrity from the outset of the case.

The Prosecution's Response

> June 13, 1994, was the worst nightmare of my life. This is the second. This prosecution team didn't lose today. I deeply believe that this country lost today. Justice was not served.
>
> Fred Goldman, October 3, 1995

> We came here in search of justice, and you will have to be the judge, as I expect, as to whether any of us found it today.
>
> Christopher Darden, prosecutor, October 3, 1995

Meanwhile, the Brown and Goldman families had gathered upstairs in the prosecutor's office to hold their press conference. This was also an emotion-filled session, with District Attorney Gil Garcetti praising the prosecution team, the support staff, and the witnesses for their hard work and their commitment to the pursuit of justice yet strangely downplaying the central roles of Marcia Clark and Chris Darden, the principal prosecutors.

This case was another major public loss for Garcetti's office, and it was bound to weaken his chances for reelection, so perhaps he could not afford to be too fulsome in his praise of the losing attorneys. Marcia Clark, subdued and dispirited, spoke briefly about the prosecution's efforts, but it was Christopher Darden, the only black prosecutor, who was so disappointed and depressed that he broke down in tears as he tried to speak. Overcome by the loss of his biggest case, Darden seemed embittered by the verdict and disenchanted with the legal system.

Knowledgeable observers could empathize with Darden's pain; he had suffered a double loss: first the rejection by many in the black community for aggressively prosecuting a bona fide black hero and now the loss of face for ultimately losing the case. The sight of Darden being comforted by Marcia Clark and the Goldman family was both sad and ironic. Fred Goldman spoke vehemently against the verdict, against O. J., and against the system. His rage was implacable, his grief forever unresolved, his demeanor that of a truly tragic figure. By contrast, the Browns spoke in somber but measured tones about their disappointment at the verdict, but Juditha Brown, always the pragmatic realist, recognized the need to heal the family's pain, to move forward, and to have some kind of reconciliation with O. J., the father of Nicole's children.

The Spectrum of Reactions

> I never thought he did that horrible crime. I think he may know who did it—perhaps it was drug-related. He may have beat her and he may be a terrible person, even a Dr. Jekyll and Mr. Hyde, but I never thought he was capable of killing his ex-wife in cold blood and mutilating her so badly. Secondly, the prosecutor did not prove beyond a shadow of doubt that he was guilty. The time frame was extremely ambiguous in view of planted evidence by Mark Fuhrman.
>
> Sara McNeil Boyd, former school administrator, Palo Alto

The African-American community in cities and suburbs, in schools and offices, in barber shops and pool halls had felt a great sense of relief and satisfaction—for the first time in memory, black Americans had witnessed something unusual, something that had restored their faith in American justice. No matter what their personal beliefs or doubts about O. J.'s culpability for these crimes, he had been tried and found not guilty by a jury of his peers and the system had set him free.

In Brentwood, O. J.'s neighbors kept a low profile but made it clear that they were not pleased with the outcome and that he was no longer welcome in their neighborhood. Likewise, members of his exclusive country club, where he had been a frequent golfer with some of the Southern California gentry, sent word that he would be asked to resign his membership. His neighbors and golfing buddies were unimpressed with the jury's verdict; they were convinced of his guilt and wanted to exclude him as quickly as possible from their privileged enclaves.

While reporters on the ground were searching for significant sound bites, reporters following Simpson from the courthouse to the jail produced the most riveting photos of the day. After his release from custody, a news helicopter showed the white Ford police van driving up Freeway 10, then turning onto Freeway 405 to return O. J. to his Rockingham Avenue estate. It was an eerie scene, so reminiscent of the white Bronco chase that had captured the nation's imagination as Al Cowlings led a procession of police cars waiting to arrest his friend just over fifteen months earlier.

This time, the Los Angeles Police Department was escorting O. J. home as a free man after 473 days of incarceration at the Los Angeles County Central Men's Jail. It was only fitting that Al Cowlings, his lifelong friend and protector, would be there to meet him when the van arrived in the driveway. Al embraced O. J. with a bear hug and, with tears in his eyes, led him into his Brentwood home. The nightmare was over. The Dream Team had restored O. J.'s dream.

THE AFTERMATH

> A lot of white folks will think the racial composition of the jury is the cause of an acquittal in this trial.
>
> Mary Tillotson, CNN talk show host, October 3, 1995

> I'm sick and tired of the arrogance of these white commentators who have lived a life of privilege, power, and insulation from

> poverty and racism. How dare they presume to second-guess this jury's verdict!
>
> Z. G., social worker, Los Angeles, October 4, 1995

In many circles, the superficial congeniality between blacks and whites, gained at considerable expense since the Rodney King beating, was shattered by this verdict in the Simpson murder trial. The races divided almost seamlessly into two camps: whites who believed that the verdict was a travesty of justice and blacks who believed that the verdict was a triumph for the criminal justice system. Voices of reason and moderation in both groups could not be heard above the shouting, the name-calling, and the vituperation. Blacks who believed that Simpson was guilty and whites who agreed that there was reasonable doubt were drowned out by the angry debate between the true believers on each side of the racial divide.

The Public and the Polls

> In a poll taken immediately after the verdict, 85 percent of blacks agreed with the "not guilty" verdict and 80 percent thought the jury was fair; only 32 percent of whites agreed with the verdict, but 50 percent thought the jury was "fair and impartial."
>
> *Newsweek*, October 16, 1995

Polls taken immediately after the verdict confirmed that the racial divisions were not simply manufactured by the media. The poll results reflected quite disparate views of the prosecution's case, of the defense team's strategy, and of the outcome. White women emphatically declared their outrage that Simpson, an admitted wife beater caught in a web of convincing circumstantial evidence, was exonerated. Black women indignantly responded, echoing the words of juror Brenda Moran, that Simpson was not on trial for spousal abuse; he was on trial for murder.

As days grew into weeks without any surcease from the charges and countercharges, the smoldering tensions between blacks and whites bubbled closer and closer to the surface. As magazine and newspaper feature articles solemnly reported, neighbors stopped speaking to each other, colleagues stopped having lunch together, store clerks and customers stopped exchanging pleasantries, and even college students on well-integrated campuses exchanged hostile glances. The verdict in the O. J. Simpson murder case, much like the verdict in the Rodney King assault case, had again exposed the fault line in American society—the deep and dangerous division between blacks and whites. And again this society had to confront the reality that we inhabited one country geographically but were divided into two nations racially, culturally, economically, and politically. There was no consensus and no common ground.

> White people are feeling now the same anger and frustration over the justice system that black people have felt for a long time. I fear the reaction will be . . . "Let's get back."
>
> N. Don Wycliff, *Newsweek*, October 16, 1995

The Jury: Saints or Sinners?

What was most striking about the prolonged and acrimonious debate about the Simpson verdict was not just the level of racial rhetoric but the fact that most of it was directed against the jury. People described the jurors as "that all-black jury" and "that bunch of dummies," excoriating them for reaching their decision in less than four hours. How could a jury sit through nearly a year of testimony from over a hundred witnesses, some of it highly technical and complex, and review it in less than half a day? One critic opined that this jury "didn't know the difference between PTA and DNA."

The jurors were verbally attacked from Boston to Birmingham for the speed of their deliberations, for their inability to comprehend the scientific testimony, and for their rejection of the strong circumstantial evidence. They were even criticized for coming to the courthouse dressed in leisure clothes on the first day of deliberations, as if they had decided the case in advance. But far and away the most damning charge against the jury was that race had been the key factor in their decision to acquit O. J. Simpson.

This charge of jury bias seemed to resonate with the public, the press, and even the politicians, who made their usual mealy-mouthed nonstatements after the verdict was announced. Veteran television news anchors like Tom Brokaw of NBC, Dan Rather of CBS, and Ted Koppel of ABC, usually cool and composed, seemed caught unaware by this verdict, rattled that their own expert opinions and confident expectations of a guilty verdict had been shattered. To these arbiters of public opinion and their colleagues in the print media, the verdict was incomprehensible except through the lens of racial politics. It was simply inconceivable to them that any reasonably competent, mature, and "objective" jury could have reached anything other than a guilty verdict in this case.

> The verdict stunningly affirmed the recognition that, along with the nonblacks, the black people on the jury practiced the law-abiding behavior they had been socialized by and conditioned to: they believed they were obligated to follow both the judge's instructions and the letter of the law. For them, the "mountain of evidence" was, at best, a sand castle of possibilities.
>
> Shirlee T. Haizlip, author, October 5, 1995

But this intense scrutiny of the jury began to seem, as Alice in Wonderland would say, "curiouser and curiouser." If one were truly objective in appraising the jury and its decision, the very first point would be to describe the jury accurately. This was not an "all-black jury" by any means, but a jury of nine blacks, two white women, and one Hispanic male. Nor was it a jury that would be insensitive to the issue of domestic violence, since ten of its members were women. However, in their initial screening questionnaires, 33 percent of these jurors reported having a friend or relative who had been a victim of domestic violence, and 42 percent believed that it was acceptable to use physical force on a family member, thus contributing to their skepticism about spousal abuse as a motive for murder. Moreover, this was a jury whose educational level was typical of American juries; the jurors were not Nobel laureates or computer scientists, but they were competent enough to understand and evaluate the significance of the expert scientific testimony that had been presented by the prosecution and vigorously challenged by the defense.

Perhaps this jury was not a cross section of America, but it was a cross section of the jury pool in that jurisdiction in Los Angeles, the standard of fairness in the American criminal justice system for all defendants. And what was most apparent to the truly objective observer is the sheer irony of the unparalleled attacks on this particular jury for rendering its verdict quickly when it was perfectly obvious that most Americans who had followed the trial for just a few weeks had reached their own verdicts! What could account for this mass hypocrisy, this demeaning display of disrespect for the jury, this shrill call for immediate reform of the jury system?

The Press: Scapegoating the Jury

> Yesterday's verdict was a horror, too. While there was no videotape of the murder, the proof against O. J. Simpson was overwhelming. Perhaps the verdict can be attributed in part to the jurors' belief that the prosecution just didn't make its case—and jurors had some grounds, if feeble ones, to so find—but race was the trump card.
>
> Debra J. Saunders, *San Francisco Chronicle*, October 4, 1995

> Incited by Johnnie Cochran to turn the trial into a political caucus, the jurors did that instead of doing their duty of rendering a

> just verdict concerning two extremely violent deaths. The jurors abused their position in order to send a message about racism or police corruption.
>
> George Will, *Washington Post*, October 4, 1995

Just as the media had rushed to judgment about O. J.'s involvement in the murders, they now rushed to judgment about the jury's racial bias. One might expect unsophisticated and unenlightened remarks about the verdict from Rush Limbaugh and Gordon Liddy, whose ratings depended on crude comments and shocking sound bites, but one would expect more in-depth analysis and thoughtful commentary from the columnists and op-ed writers of the leading newspapers. At the end of the day, the editorials and slanted news articles shed much more light on the writers' ambivalence about blacks, and particularly about black males married to white females, than on the motives and meaning of the jury's verdict.

One question frequently asked by blacks was, if O.J. had been accused of murdering a black wife and her black friend, how long would this story have been on page one? And if an aging white former football hero had killed his white wife and her friend, would CNN and Court TV have televised the trial for a year? Race was a major part of this story from the minute those two bodies were discovered, so why were the press and the public just discovering the racial factor in the verdict? Or was this just America's dirty little secret—the obsession with race and sex that had haunted the nation since the days of slavery and was always just below the surface of civilized discourse between blacks and whites? Johnnie Cochran had exposed the secret, but he was only a messenger delivering a very powerful message.

Divergent Agendas, Divergent Voices

> It is a dilemma for those of us who can relate to both sides' theories of the case; the parallel between the racism the [black] community is decrying and the violence against women it is largely ignoring does not escape us. Whatever you think of Simpson's

> guilt or innocence, there was uncontroverted evidence about his abusive behavior. Lest the message be to disregard domestic violence, we ought to pause and recognize our interest in ending this form of abuse.
>
> Anita Hill, legal scholar

> This is a story about race and gender and how they intersect. It's about a black man married to a white woman, being judged by black women.
>
> Susan Reverby, professor of women's studies, Wellesley College

---

Race was the primary theme, but sex was the secondary theme that dominated the debate over the verdict. Leaders of women's organizations, celebrity feminists, and staff members of battered women's shelters held news conferences and appeared on talk shows to decry the verdict as a vindication of wife beating and a misbegotten message to send out to male batterers. They predicted that men would now feel that since O. J. could get away with beating and killing his ex-wife, this verdict would give them license to assault their spouses and partners. Even as they added their voices to the cacophony of criticism, it became apparent that there were at least two subtexts underlying their strong rhetoric. For one thing, apparently none of these leaders had ever before come forward in defense of a black female victim of domestic violence whose partner had been tried and exonerated for murder, so they seemed to be directing their message toward white women with a metamessage that targeted yet another black male as the stereotypical brute.

> I was thinking about all the battered women whose abusers are saying to them: "I'm going to kill you and get away with it!"
>
> Deb Spangler, outreach coordinator, Domestic Violence Clinic, Madison, Wisconsin

---

Another subtext underlay these protestations from the spokespersons against domestic violence. While heaping sarcasm and shame upon the predominantly female jury, they themselves shamelessly used Nicole Brown Simpson's murder as a rallying call to promote their own agenda, that is, to advocate for better laws and greater financial support for programs to reduce domestic violence and provide resources for battered women. Though their cause is important and worthy of significant support, their timing and taste raised many questions about their own motivations and judgment in criticizing the jury's verdict in this case.

Responses from the Jurors

> [Vannatter] was my biggest doubt. Him carrying that vial of [Simpson's] blood around for hours. There was an opportunity to sprinkle it here or there. . . . It was all about blood and believability.
>
> Brenda Moran, Juror 7

> Things just didn't add up. . . . On our last vote we all agreed.
>
> David A. Aldana, Juror 4

Fed up with the attacks on their character and their competence, the jurors began to speak for themselves. Juror 7, Brenda Moran, a forty-five-year-old black computer technician who had been one of the dominant members of the jury, was the first to hold a brief news conference. Standing on the roof of a parking garage with her lawyer, Moran fiercely defended the intelligence and integrity of her fellow jurors. In a no-nonsense, in-your-face style, Moran deftly fielded reporters' questions and seemed to surprise them with her succinct and straightforward responses. She emphatically denied that O. J.'s race or celebrity status had in any way influenced the jury's decision. She also deflated the analysts' puffed-up pronouncements that the jury had been swayed by Mark Fuhrman's testimony and had "nullified" the evidence to send a message to the Los Angeles Police Department about police misconduct. She insisted that the jury did not hear about Fuhrman's extensive racial comments through "pillow talk" during conjugal visits and that his brief testimony had very little impact on their decision.

As Moran made perfectly clear, the jurors simply did not think the prosecution had proved its case beyond a reasonable doubt. They found some of the prosecution's witnesses to be less than credible, they did not think the police investigation was competent, and they believed that the police might have planted the bloody glove and the blood on the back gate of Nicole's condominium. In the final analysis, the prosecution lost its case because its evidence failed on three counts: credibility, competence, and possible police conspiracy. The jury thought the prosecution had missed the mark on presenting spousal abuse as a motive for murder. In Brenda Moran's view, this was not a case of domestic violence; it was a case about murder, and the prosecution did not prove its circumstantial case. Finally, she shrugged her shoulders in a gesture of disdain and dismissal and then simply said, "In plain English, the glove didn't fit."

Within the next two weeks, several other jurors spoke out to defend themselves and their verdict against the continued criticism of the Monday morning quarterbacks. Anise Aschenbach, a retired sixty-one-year-old, one of the two white female jurors, obviously in turmoil over her vote, confided to her daughter that she believed that O. J. had probably committed the crimes, but the Fuhrman tapes had been sufficiently disturbing that she was not convinced of O. J.'s guilt "beyond a reasonable doubt." That phrase was repeated again and again by jurors who were willing to submit themselves to the merciless scrutiny of the press and public.

Juror 4—the lone Latino male, David Aldana, a thirty-three-year-old Pepsi-Cola truck driver—was adamant that race was never mentioned in the jury deliberations; he and his fellow jurors did not think the prosecution's evidence was compelling "beyond a reasonable doubt."

The demeanor and the discussion of these jurors belied the derogatory descriptions of them by their critics—these people were at least of average intelligence, they were fairly articulate, and they managed to make a perfectly reasonable argument for their decision.

To these twelve citizens who had reluctantly devoted over one year of their lives and patiently endured months of repetitive and often repugnant testimony, the prosecution's case was unfocused, had too many inexplicable holes, and was based primarily on circumstantial evidence. Without the murder weapon, bloody clothes, or any witnesses, and with a time line that was difficult to believe and impossible to corroborate, these jurors had, in good faith and in compliance with the judge's instructions, reached consensus on the two not-guilty verdicts. When a skeptical reporter asked one juror, Brenda Moran, if she would be able to "live with her conscience" over the verdicts, she looked directly at him with a sober expression on her face and responded: "Yes, I believe we did the right thing."

THE COLOR OF JUSTICE: BLACK VERSUS WHITE

> These white feminists who've spent their careers running away from the problems of poor and minority women are now racing and falling all over each other to exploit the death of a wealthy white woman who just happened to be married to a black man.
>
> H. G., junior college instructor,
> Los Angeles, October 5, 1995

To understand the wide gulf between the predominantly black jurors who believed that they had "done the right thing" and the primarily white critics who believed that they had nullified the evidence to set a guilty black man free is to gain some insight into the wide chasm that separates blacks and whites in their reactions to the Simpson verdicts. Further, in reaching such an understanding, it is instructive to bear in mind that, like members of the Simi Valley jury, ten of the twelve jurors in the Simpson trial had lived most of their lives as minorities in a separate world circumscribed by invisible but intractable boundaries of race and class.

Within their predominantly black and Latino communities, many of these jurors had probably been spatially separated from middle-class Anglo-American society in their neighborhoods, educationally separated in their schools, economically separated in their jobs and opportunities, culturally separated in their leisure time and recreational pursuits, and socially separated in their most intimate family and friendship activities. For most blacks and Latinos, Sunday morning is the most segregated day of the week. They attend churches in their neighborhoods and hear sermons dealing with the "social gospel"—economic and political concerns—that may offer very different perspectives from the sermons heard by middle-class and affluent whites in their churches.

Living in the encapsulated but often exposed world of the inner cities, blacks and Latinos experience a daily reality very different from that of more advantaged whites who live in gated urban neighborhoods and suburbs. And one of these more pervasive and painful realities is the persistent presence of police harassment and brutality. Those police practices in Los Angeles and other cities have been well documented in the McCone Commission report after the Watts riots in 1965, the Kerner Commission report in 1968, and the Christopher Commission report after the Los Angeles riots in 1992 following the acquittals in the Rodney King beating. For the rest of Los Angeles and the rest of the nation, these reports were unwelcome reminders of police misconduct, but for the African-American and Latino communities, they were regarded merely as official efforts to appease their communities, raising little expectation of real change or improvement.

Whereas the Simi Valley jurors perceived the police as their familiar neighbors and friends, the majority of the Simpson jury might well have perceived the police as an occupying force of strangers and enemies. Whereas the Simi Valley jurors believed that the primary mission of the police was to protect and to serve their community, the majority of the Simpson jury probably believed that the police force's major goal was to repress and control their community. Whereas the Simi Valley jurors were usually treated with courtesy and respect by the police, the majority of the Simpson jurors were more likely to have encountered discourtesy and disrespect from police officers. Whereas the Simi Valley jurors probably had few relatives or acquaintances who had experienced physical or verbal abuse from the police, 42 percent of the Simpson jurors reported that they themselves or a family member had had a negative experience with law enforcement.

Not only had these two sets of jurors had very different experiences with police officers, but they had had very different experiences with the courts and the criminal justice system. Whereas most Simi Valley jurors would expect a fair trial in the event of an arrest and a just sentence if convicted of a crime, most blacks on the Simpson jury might know from personal experience that minority defendants could never take these assumptions for granted. Moreover, minority members of the Simpson jury could probably all remember the stories of Eulia Love, Ron Settles, and Leonard Deadwyler, all killed by police officers who were later acquitted on the grounds of "justifiable homicide." But most damning of all, everyone on that jury, black, white, and Latino, could certainly remember the videotaped beating of Rodney King by four officers of the Los Angeles Police Department, witnessed by twenty-three other uniformed peace officers who stood by, watched, and did not intervene to stop it.

Blacks and the Criminal Justice System

> Blacks and whites have very different realities and different experiences in America, so they had different perceptions of the evidence in this case. Whites just can't comprehend that a jury could believe that the police could cover up or plant evidence

> against anyone. But police have been doing this to blacks ever since the days of slavery. There is a total difference in the way the two communities view the verdict because of the differences in our experiences.
>
> Barbara Solomon, vice provost,
> University of Southern California

From these different experiences with the police in their respective communities, it is logical and reasonable to predict that blacks and whites would develop different attitudes, expectations, and feelings toward police officers and the entire criminal justice system. When people serve on juries, they bring a lifetime of experience with them, and they will perceive the evidence and process the testimony according to their own personal framework of prior experiences, knowledge, and beliefs about the world. They will try very hard to process all of the evidence so that it is internally consistent with their prior experiences, knowledge, and beliefs.

In fact, there is a famous principle in psychology that governs the way all human beings process new information—the principle of cognitive dissonance. This principle states that people more easily assimilate information that fits in with or is consistent with their prior knowledge, beliefs, and experiences and will tend to reject information that is not consistent with their prior understanding of the world. Thus the jurors in Simi Valley were *inclined to believe* the police officers' defense because it was consistent with their prior experiences and beliefs about the police. In contrast, the jurors in the Simpson case were *inclined to disbelieve* the testimony of the police because of their prior experiences and beliefs about police misconduct. In both cases, these jurors viewed the evidence, processed it, and evaluated it in terms of their own worldview and personal experiences.

The jury's verdict in the Simpson case was not an example of nullification of the evidence, nor was it an example of racial bias in favor of a black defendant. The jury's verdict, in fact, was a classic example of the principle of cognitive dissonance. It was not the color of their skin that influenced their skeptical appraisal of the prosecution's witnesses; it was their life experience that caused them to doubt the credibility of the witnesses, to question the integrity of the evidence, and to entertain the possibility of a police conspiracy against O. J. Simpson.

In the final analysis, this jury found the defense claims of police misconduct and conspiracy against a black male not only within the realm of possibility, but—from their perspective of years of police hostility and abuse against minorities in Los Angeles—resonating with plausibility. With these serious doubts about the building blocks of the prosecution's case, this jury brought back the only verdicts that were defensible to them—not guilty beyond a reasonable doubt.

Implications of the Verdict

> In the sweep of history, maybe the most important contribution this case can make is to really open the eyes of white people to the double standard of justice in this country. Blacks know about police misconduct and police bias against them, but whites don't believe it. The Fuhrman tapes prove that police frame blacks all the time. If you weigh one man getting away with murder against all the years that the police have "gotten away with murder" as far as black people are concerned, then it all balances out in the long run.
>
> James Lowell Gibbs, Jr., professor of anthropology, Stanford University

---

Just as the press and many whites misinterpreted the jury's verdict, they also misunderstood the enthusiastic endorsement of the verdict by so many blacks. Having seen so many black defendants convicted because of tainted testimony or lack of resources to hire competent counsel, blacks were relieved that O. J.'s defense team had mounted an aggressive defense to expose the serious deficiencies in the prosecution's case. Having known so many black males who had been victims of false arrest, planted evidence, and police abuse, blacks were pleased that O. J.'s defense team had highlighted those issues and raised doubts about those practices in this case. Having shared the frustrations of seeing countless wealthy white defendants acquitted of major felonies and capital crimes, blacks were consoled that a rich black defendant could receive equal treatment under the law. While many whites may have assumed that blacks were celebrating the acquittal of a guilty man, many blacks understood that they were celebrating the affirmation of a fair trial for a black defendant.

Learning the Game, Changing the Rules

> O. J. became a symbol of attacking the system. When I go into work, white officers will hit the soda machine and get a free soda. When I hit the machine and get a free soda, they say, "We need to fix that machine." When I heard the O. J. verdict, it was as if all black America hit the soda machine. And now that we got our free soda, everybody wants to fix the machine.
>
> Eric Adams, chairman of the Grand Council of Guardians, New York City

---

> There's an old saying in the black community: whites make the rules so they can win all the games. When blacks learn how to play the game, the whites change all the rules. Now that a black man beat them at their own game, they're such sore losers that they want to change the whole jury system.
>
> T. N., female paralegal, Los Angeles

Many blacks could not comprehend why so many whites were not only bitterly opposed to the verdict but also immediately proposed that the criminal justice system should be radically restructured, most particularly by changing the criteria for unanimous jury sentences in major felony crimes. While whites were fixated on the "unjust verdicts" in this one case, blacks were puzzled over their lack of outrage at previous acquittals of celebrity defendants in other highly publicized cases of murder or attempted murder like those of socialite Claus von Bülow in Rhode Island and millionaire Clive Davis in Texas. Why was there such a double standard for this defendant and this jury? Why was there no groundswell for jury reform in those other cases? What was it about this Simpson case that generated so much heat and hostility and seemed to cloud the judgment of so many usually logical and dispassionate commentators?

Not surprisingly, opinion in neither the black nor the white community was monolithic. There were many blacks who rejected the verdict, and there were many whites who supported it. In both communities, however, there were pressures to present a united front. For blacks, it was viewed as a litmus test of one's loyalty to the race; for whites, it was viewed as a measure of one's commitment to justice. It took courage for blacks and whites to voice opinions counter to the prevailing sentiments of their friends, neighbors, and coworkers. As time elapsed and the analysis of the verdict became more sophisticated and the media commentary more balanced, these voices began to emerge from the pack and began to assert themselves—voices of the black feminists in concert with white feminists, abhorring the verdict; voices of white and black civil libertarians upholding the jury system; voices of all races pleading for reconciliation and reasoned discourse over the racialized debate.

The Lawyers' Reactions

> Our urban policy for blacks is the criminal justice system and for many blacks, it is not a fair system. . . . The rejoicing is not that somebody got away with murder, but that somebody beat the system.
>
> Lani Guinier, professor of law,
> University of Pennsylvania

> If you know that the most important witness had a history of racism and hostility against black people, that should have been a relevant factor of inquiry even if the jury had been all white.
>
> Leon A. Higginbotham, retired federal judge

Almost smothered by this avalanche of outrage were the occasional supportive comments from legal experts defending the jury's verdict and confirming their critical view of the prosecution's case. Despite attempts of the media to drown out this chorus of voices, it grew louder after several weeks and began to restore a semblance of sanity to the debate.

Trained to be logical and dispassionate, lawyers on both sides of the aisle criticized the prosecution's case, particularly on four points: the overreliance on complex DNA testimony, the failure to introduce evidence about the infamous freeway chase and the disguise items and cash found in the Bronco, the eager embrace of Detective Mark Fuhrman, and the unrehearsed and disastrous glove experiment.

Defense lawyers lauded the Dream Team's overall strategy, with special praise for Johnnie Cochran's decision to put the Los Angeles Police Department on trial by attacking the credibility of its witnesses (Fuhrman, Lange, and Vannatter) and the competence of its forensic investigators (Fung and Mazzola). Although some prosecutors agreed with Robert Shapiro that Cochran had "played the race card . . . from the bottom of the deck," the defense lawyers were emphatic that Cochran was ethically obligated to challenge Fuhrman's racial attitudes in view of his perjured testimony and crucial role in collecting incriminating evidence against Simpson.

Not surprisingly, a great many experienced trial lawyers and prosecutors were quick to proclaim that the jury had reached the only verdict that was defensible in view of the doubts raised about the quality of the evidence and the integrity of the witnesses. As one legal expert pointed out, Judge Ito had instructed the jurors to weigh the evidence carefully and, if they should find reason to give equal weight to the evidence pointing to the defendant's guilt and the evidence pointing to the defendant's innocence, they would be obligated to find for the defendant. In the case of *The People of California* v. *Orenthal James Simpson*, the jury had taken this charge very seriously, had discharged its duties diligently, and had found for the defendant.

The verdict, so unexpected and so controversial, would be intensely debated in public forums and private gatherings for months to come. And one of the issues that would continue to divide blacks and whites was the impact of the defense's "conspiracy theory" on the predominantly black jury. Had jurors been unduly influenced by the cornerstone of Johnnie Cochran's "three C's" attack on the police testimony—conspiracy, contamination, cover-up—or had they simply been unconvinced of the prosecution's compromised case?

Part III

Race and Justice

11

"Bad Blood"

Conspiracy Theories and the Black Community

> At times, the conclusion seems all but self-evident that white America has no desire for your presence or any need for your people. Can this nation have an unstated strategy for annihilating your people? How else, you ask yourself, can one explain the incidence of death and debilitation from drugs and disease; the incarceration of a whole generation of your men; the consignment of millions of women and children to half-lives of poverty and dependency? . . . You cannot rid yourself of some lingering mistrust.
>
> Andrew Hacker, *Two Nations*, 1992

Conspiracy theories have a long and well-documented history in the African-American community, from the earliest days of slavery through the generations of lynching to the decades of civil rights protests. The history of blacks in America is an indictment of the criminal justice system, a coordinated effort, sanctioned by the state and local governments and enforced by their police surrogates, to deprive a whole segment of Americans of their rights to life, liberty, and the pursuit of happiness. The uncontested record and unrefuted facts document a history of deliberate destruction of slave families, hundreds of unsolved public lynchings, scores of unpunished murders and assaults of civil rights workers, blatant violations of the rights of peaceful protest groups, and wanton police brutality against unarmed and unresisting black males. Thus it is not without ample experience and past provocation that blacks on the Simpson jury might well have been swayed by defense theories of conspiracy and cover-up against O. J. by a cabal of racist cops, incompetent criminalists, and complicit prosecutors.

In her provocative and thoughtful book *I Heard It Through the Grapevine*, Patricia Turner uses a folklorist's keen ear and a social scientist's discerning eye to document and deconstruct the persistence and power of conspiracy theories in the African-American community. As she convincingly demonstrates, American blacks have historically constructed explanations of racial discrimination and traumatic social and political events in terms of their worldview as an oppressed and powerless people. This perspective inevitably perceives those in power as manipulative and completely Machiavellian in their motivations to maintain the status quo of the white majority at all costs.

Since the Emancipation Proclamation released blacks from the bondage of slavery in 1863, the oral tradition, developed on the plantations to facilitate communication, has remained a strong force in keeping the African-American community connected through the common bonds of shared stories, music, and cultural traditions. It has also been the vehicle for forging bonds of unity, solidarity, and resistance among blacks in the face of harsh discrimination, abject poverty, and exclusion from the opportunities and privileges of mainstream American society.

Conspiracy theories have proved to be one of the most enduring legacies of the oral tradition, as they have enabled blacks both to explain and to endure the prejudice, the poverty, and the injustice that have always seemed so inexplicable, so unpredictable, and so unjustified—from the barbaric cruelty of the plantation overseers to the lynch mobs in the South to the police brutality of urban ghettos.

CONSPIRACY THEORIES: MOTIFS AND MYTHS

The motifs of conspiracy theories, widely disseminated in the black community through the black media, music, political leaders, churches, and civic and social organizations, cluster around certain major themes. Those themes defy simple classification, but for our purposes they can be sorted into four major categories of conspiracies:

- *Contamination and disease*—theories that portray blacks as victims or guinea pigs of the government (or of scientists, multinational corporations, the military, and so on) to test out a new virus or spread a disease in a vulnerable population

- *Criminalization and drugs*—theories that suggest that the government (or the police, FBI, CIA, and so on) has deliberately flooded the black community with drugs in order to increase criminal activity, arrest drug users and pushers, and thus destroy the community; this theory is frequently paired with the related hypothesis that blacks are targeted by the police and the criminal justice system for the specific purpose of criminalizing young black males, further weakening the black family by eviscerating the male population and destroying potential resistance

- *Destruction of black leaders and civil rights organizations*—the theory that the government (or the police, FBI, powerful politicians, and so on) deliberately targets effective black leaders and their organizations, exposes their frailties, and sets them up for failure, illegal activities, or even assassination; this theory also embraces black entertainers, athletes, successful professionals, and even local officials

- *Racial and cultural genocide*—the theory that the government (the power structure, the police, the medical establishment, and so on) has supported Ku Klux Klan lynchings, police killings of blacks, forced sterilization, and involuntary birth control as a means of eradicating

> or decimating the black population and destroying black culture; these attacks are often viewed as assaults on black male sexuality and female reproduction as symbolic of the broader agenda to eliminate the black race in America

For the majority of black Americans, particularly those who have experienced the rigid segregation of the South or the ghettoization of the urban North, these theories are not just plausible but supported by evidence that they selectively screen through the prism of their racial experiences. For example, in the 1990s, it was plausible for blacks to believe that AIDS was a virus designed by white scientists, tested on unsuspecting Africans, and intended to decimate "undesirables," such as people of color, homosexuals, and drug addicts, in America. After all, hadn't the government earlier in this century planned and executed the Tuskegee Study in rural Alabama, leaving poor, uneducated black males with syphilis untreated for over forty years?

It was also plausible in the 1990s for blacks to believe that there was a conspiracy to saturate the urban ghettos with drugs and to target young black males for arrest and imprisonment. After all, hadn't the government been accused of cozying up to Manuel Noriega of Panama and other right-wing dictators of Central American countries where cocaine was the major export crop while shipments of the drug managed to elude customs inspectors at the U.S. border? Hadn't the federal government and some states spent more on building prisons than on educational programs in the early 1990s? Weren't the prisons replacing the projects as the major form of public housing for young black males in the 1990s?

And it was plausible in the 1990s for blacks to believe that the government had targeted black political leaders to destroy any effective organized protest and economic empowerment of African-Americans. Hadn't they heard persistent rumors that the FBI had helped engineer the assassinations of Medgar Evers, Martin Luther

King, Jr., and Malcolm X in the 1960s? Hadn't they read about the FBI's Cointelpro program in the 1960s and 1970s to infiltrate and destroy the Black Panthers, to discredit the NAACP, and to cripple the civil rights movement? And in more recent years, they had seen an elaborate sting set up to entrap the mayor of Washington, D.C., the impeachment of a prominent Florida federal judge, the prosecution of several black congressmen, and the indictment of several black mayors.

Finally, it was entirely plausible that there were powerful forces intent on racial and cultural genocide to eradicate blacks as a race and to destroy their culture, both increasingly viewed as a threat to the purity and piety of the nation's European heritage. Hadn't blacks been the victims of hundreds of unsolved lynchings since Reconstruction, widespread forced sterilization among welfare recipients and institutionalized women, and involuntary birth control for urban teenage mothers? Hadn't white policemen in every major city been legally exonerated over and over again for killing unarmed and noncombative black men and women, often under mysterious circumstances after they were taken into custody?

Urban Myths and Collective Memories

These conspiracy stories circulated in the African-American community from the urban inner cities to the rural southern hamlets, from the ghetto projects to the sprawling suburbs. They spread in the beauty shops and barber shops, the pool halls and the after-hours clubs. For residents of Los Angeles, a community with southern roots and western ways, these conspiracies assumed the status of urban myths, replicating themselves rapidly and finding reinforcement in every household as they mirrored the lived experiences of these people and the memories of their collective history.

And it was this collective history, this collective memory, that was shared by all the black jurors as they listened to the prosecution and defense versions of the murders in the O. J. Simpson trial. As these jurors listened to the witnesses and evaluated the mountains of evidence in the trial, they might all have been reminded of any one or all of these theories.

First, they might have thought about the *blood evidence* that had mysteriously appeared on the socks, on the back gate, and on the white Bronco. Had this blood been contaminated or compromised by Detective Vannatter, who carried it around in his pocket for hours before booking it properly in the police crime laboratory? Was it not possible for someone to tamper with the blood to frame O. J. Simpson? Wouldn't that explain the few drops that seemed to be missing from the test tube sample?

Second, they might have been disturbed by the initial *behavior of the police*, entering O. J.'s home without a warrant, searching for evidence, and then handcuffing O. J. even before he was an official suspect in the crime. The comments of Detective Mark Fuhrman, moreover, were sure to raise their anxiety and provoke their anger at the real possibility of police misconduct against O. J. simply because he was a black man. It was an all too familiar scenario to them.

Third, they might have wondered if O. J. had been *targeted as a suspect* so early in the investigation because he was Nicole's former husband or because he was a black celebrity, a role model for his people, and a symbol of success in the white man's world. They had read about the black Hollywood celebrities who had been harassed by the LAPD—entertainers like Blair Underwood and athletes like Jamal Wilks—just for being in an exclusive neighborhood or driving an expensive sports car. Could O. J. be another target of their racist attitudes?

Most important, the police testimony might have reminded them about the brutal beating of Rodney King, the conspiracy to cover up the beating, the police lies contradicted by the videotape and the eyewitness accounts, and the surprising acquittal of the four police officers by an insensitive, predominantly white suburban jury. For the blacks on the O. J. Simpson jury, the memory of Rodney King's beating would trigger their deepest anxieties about their physical vulnerability to the whims of the guardians of the status quo and their strongest fears about the threat of racial genocide. In 1991, the LAPD had almost lynched King, a poor black man, and nearly walked away without punishment or remorse. Had the LAPD selected O. J. Simpson, a wealthy black celebrity, to cut down to size in 1994, not by assaulting him physically, but by destroying his reputation, his family, and his career?

This jury was unusually attentive and particularly susceptible to the twin mantras of "conspiracy" and "cover-up," repeated throughout the trial by defense attorney Johnnie Cochran and his Dream Team. Unlike the Simi Valley jury, most of the members of the Simpson jury had absorbed conspiracy theories from early childhood in the very air they breathed. For the black jurors, there was probably no conspiracy involving African-Americans that was too far-fetched, too fantastic, or too convoluted. All they had to do was to close their eyes and recall the litany of past conspiracies that traumatized the black community and destroyed its leaders.

BAD BLOOD: THE TUSKEGEE SYPHILIS STUDY

> The Tuskegee Study was, in the words of a North Carolina newspaper editor: ". . . a reminder that the basic rights of Americans, particularly the poor, the illiterate, and the friendless, are still subject to violation in the name of scientific research."
>
> James H. Jones, *Bad Blood,* 1982

No single incident could have confirmed these apparently paranoid beliefs of African-Americans more than the astounding revelations of the Tuskegee Syphilis Study. When the news media first reported the story in July 1972, most of the nation was shocked to learn the U.S. Public Health Service had conducted an experimental study for forty years of a group of six hundred rural, largely uneducated black men in Macon County, Alabama, to investigate the effects of untreated syphilis on their health and overall functioning.

When the study began in 1932, some 399 of the men were in the tertiary (late) stage of syphilis, while a control group of 201 men were free of the disease. The men recruited into the study were told that they had "bad blood," a black folk term for syphilis. These men were promised free medical treatment and burial expenses for participating in the study. A black nurse, Eunice Rivers, helped recruit these men and served as the liaison with the white doctors and bureaucrats from the Public Health Service in Tuskegee and in Washington, D.C. The participants in the study became known as "Miss Rivers's boys," as she was the human face of the study who faithfully made the rounds to see her boys, monitored their vital signs, and made them feel like members of a very special club.

But Nurse Rivers did not tell her boys the truth about the study. She did not tell them that the real purpose of their medical checkups was to monitor the progress of syphilis, not to give them any treatment or to intervene in any way to alter the inevitable course of the disease. She did not tell them that many of them would become crippled, blind, or mentally disturbed due to the disease. Nor did she tell them that many would die a painful premature death after years of debilitating symptoms and emotional stress for their families and friends.

Even when penicillin was introduced in the early 1940s as a miracle cure for the disease, Nurse Rivers did not challenge the decisions of the investigators to withhold treatment from her boys. Nurse Rivers proved herself to be a loyal assistant in the service of scientific research, continuing for forty years to minister to her ever dwindling group of disease-ridden patients.

Nurse Rivers was highly visible, but she became an unwitting scapegoat for the Public Health Service, for the Centers for Disease Control in Atlanta, and for the Tuskegee Institute and the U.S. Veterans Administration Hospital, two all-black institutions that had cooperated with the study and never challenged its basic premises or its procedures during those four decades when lifesaving medication was deliberately withheld from these ailing African-American men.

By 1960, the effects of untreated syphilis could be fairly well documented, but the study was not terminated by the Centers for Disease Control until 1972. By that time, the researchers had found that mortality rates were significantly higher among the syphilitic subjects than among the controls. By that time, they knew that at least one hundred men had died as a direct result of complications from the disease, and many others had died from heart conditions related to the infection. But the researchers were quite reluctant to estimate the total mortality rate from direct or indirect consequences of syphilis. The one indisputable fact that emerged in U.S. Senate hearings held in 1973 was that only 56 men of the original 399 experimental subjects were still known to be alive, most in very poor health and with obvious signs of the ravages of the unchecked disease process.

On August 24, 1972, the Department of Health, Education and Welfare set up an ad hoc panel to investigate the Tuskegee Syphilis Study. The nine-member committee was chaired by a black college president and included four other distinguished blacks. The panel's findings that the study had failed to obtain informed consent from the subjects and was "highly unjustified" were published just two months after Senator Edward M. Kennedy convened hearings on the study in the U.S. Senate in February 1973. The combined impact of the hearings and the panel's report created a firestorm of controversy about the use of these vulnerable, poor black men as human guinea pigs in an experiment in which their medical needs were sacrificed on the altar of scientific inquiry.

Impact of the Tuskegee Study

The Tuskegee Study will always be more than a footnote in the annals of the history of scientific research because it had two very significant and ultimately lasting impacts on the nation's scientific community. First, the scandal of using these men as human guinea pigs without their informed consent provided a major impetus in revising and strengthening the ethical guidelines for human experimentation in government and university sponsored research. Second, and more relevant to the cases of Rodney King and O. J. Simpson, it provided a classic case study of the willingness of the government and major health and educational institutions to manipulate black people for their own ends, even if it entailed a conspiracy to deny them needed health care and to deprive them of their legal rights. The "bad blood" of Nurse Rivers's boys in the Tuskegee Study has left a terrible legacy of fear, distrust, and suspicion of the government and its representatives, whether they are researchers, health professionals, bureaucrats, or law enforcement officials.

If all of these well-educated scientists, doctors, and civil servants could engage in such deception and betrayal for forty years, how could the black community place its trust in these institutions and their agents ever again? These questions must have been in the minds of millions of blacks who listened to the testimony of police defense experts who minimized Rodney King's bloody wounds. And they must have been lurking in the subconscious minds of the black jurors who listened to the testimony of the prosecution experts who maximized the blood evidence against O. J. Simpson. Blood evidence was a thread running through both of these cases, raising the specter of the Tuskegee experiment over and over again.

DESTRUCTION OF BLACK LEADERS: CONSPIRACY OR COVER-UP?

> For the conscious observer, it should be quite obvious that this society is bent on destroying Black people, especially Black men, as quietly and efficiently as possible."
>
> Haki R. Madhubuti, *Black Men*, 1990

Medgar Evers, Malcolm X, Martin Luther King, Jr.—the names are familiar. They are recited in every litany of African-American heroes, martyrs in the civil rights crusade. The dates and places of their assassinations are engraved in the memory bank of the black community: Medgar Evers, 1963, Jackson, Mississippi; Malcolm X, 1965, New York City's Harlem; Martin Luther King, Jr., 1968, Memphis, Tennessee. And in every one of their murders was the specter of a conspiracy or a cover-up to protect the real perpetrators of these heinous crimes.

The Assassination of Medgar Evers

In the early 1960s, at the beginning of the civil rights movement, Medgar Evers, the courageous leader of the NAACP in Mississippi, was a prophet of racial equality in a deep southern state resistant to change and resentful of "agitators." On the hot night of June 12, 1963, in Jackson, Mississippi, when Evers was returning from a NAACP meeting, his wife, Myrlie, and his three small children heard his car in the driveway, then a shot; they ran outside to find his body slumped and bleeding on the ground in front of their modest home. Although there was strong evidence implicating Byron de la Beckwith, a rabid racist and member of the White Citizens Council, he was acquitted in 1964 in two trials by all-white juries, which deadlocked on the charges.

After three decades of patient and persistent investigation, Byron de la Beckwith, at age seventy-three, was finally convicted of the murder of Medgar Evers by a racially mixed jury in March 1994 and sentenced to life in prison. The cover-up was uncovered and the system corrected itself, but it took thirty years and a lifetime of pain for the Evers family to obtain equal justice in the courts.

But for black Americans who shared this burden of pain there remained many unanswered questions and unresolved anger at the charges that the FBI had targeted Medgar Evers as a troublemaker and that local agents had aided and abetted his murder by openly sympathizing with segregationist leaders and their policies.

The Assassination of Malcolm X

When Malcolm X was cut down in a crossfire of bullets from three assassins while he was speaking from the podium of the Avalon Ballroom in Harlem on February 21, 1965, the New York City police quickly pointed to members of a rival faction of the Black Muslims as the triggermen. These alleged killers were arrested, brought to trial, and convicted with dispatch. But Malcolm's widow, Betty Shabazz, had lingering doubts that the real killers had been apprehended or that the conspiracy against her husband had been unmasked.

It was not long before Betty learned that Malcolm, too, had been on the FBI list of "suspicious people" who were a threat to the security of the United States. It was not long before black politicians and civil rights organizations began to question the role of the FBI in Malcolm's murder, since his increasing moderation had made him more visible and viable as a national black leader. FBI chief J. Edgar Hoover, clearly not in sympathy with the goals of the civil rights movement, might have viewed Malcolm X as a major threat to the status quo as he talked more and more about joining forces with other black organizations to combat segregation and discrimination in American society. A government-led conspiracy against Malcolm X has never been documented, but many blacks remain convinced that the FBI, the New York City police department, or both were somehow implicated in his premature death.

Ironically, these lingering doubts were revived just a few months after the Simpson trial began when Malcolm X's middle daughter, Qubilah Shabazz, was arrested in Minneapolis, Minnesota, and indicted for conspiring to kill Minister Louis Farrakhan, the current leader of the Black Muslims in America. Before a trial was scheduled, her lawyers claimed that she was actually a victim of a government conspiracy to discredit and divide the Black Muslim movement in the United States. Sufficient evidence existed to show that Qubilah had been set up by a young white informer with a long and unsavory reputation as a radical provocateur and a petty criminal who acted as a police snitch when it served his purposes. So nearly thirty years after Malcolm X's assassination, his daughter was entrapped in a scheme to kill his successor by the same government agency that had denied involvement in her father's 1965 murder.

Black Americans were amazed at the government's duplicity and appalled at its arrogance, but they were not surprised that their own government had once more conspired against the family of a prominent African-American whose legacy, even after three decades, appeared to threaten the status quo of an increasingly polarized nation.

The Assassination of Martin Luther King, Jr.

On April 3, 1968, Martin Luther King, Jr., had traveled to Memphis to support striking garbage and sanitation workers. Though exhausted and depressed over the deepening schisms in the civil rights movement and the competing demands of the Vietnam War protesters, King had agreed to speak to a major rally on April 4, the following evening. But after dinner, he stepped out onto the balcony of the Lorraine Motel, located in a poor black section of the city, and was shot by a sniper's bullet.

In the rage and riots that followed his assassination, the police soon apprehended the alleged gunman, a white drifter named James Earl Ray. Ray consistently denied his guilt, but the evidence was overwhelming, and he was convicted of the crime. But once again, doubts began to surface almost immediately after his arrest. How could this man have planned this shooting alone without some inside knowledge of King's schedule and social habits? Where did he obtain the funds to buy an expensive rifle, to finance his trip to Memphis and his escape from the scene of the crime?

Soon after King's assassination, black Americans were shocked to learn that he had been a prime target of FBI surveillance for years. The agency had collected extensive files on him, his family, his friends, and his intimate affairs. Dr. Martin Luther King, Jr., scholar, clergyman, civil rights leader, and Nobel Prize recipient, was just another black radical to the FBI and to numerous southern local law enforcement agencies. They had no qualms whatsoever about surreptitiously following him, clandestinely photographing him, secretly taping his phone conversations, and bugging his hotel rooms. For many black Americans, this revelation was too outrageous to believe and too sinister to accept. Yet it did not take a rocket scientist to speculate that there might be some connection between the FBI surveillance and the assassination of this most revered black leader.

Although the possibility of a government-sanctioned conspiracy to assassinate Martin Luther King, Jr., has never been substantiated, there are persistent and recurrent rumors in the black community that the FBI was an accessory to his murder, perhaps through rogue agents or intermediary double agents. Whether or not the full circumstances of his assassination will ever be revealed, most blacks are quite willing to believe that King was the victim of a conspiracy by powerful persons who perceived him as the most effective and most popular leader of a burgeoning civil rights and antiwar movement, a combined mass movement with the potential of causing fundamental change and redistributing power and privilege in American society.

Targeting Black Leaders: The Bigger the Better

Medgar, Malcolm, and Martin are the three best-known martyrs of the civil rights movement of the 1960s. Targeted by the FBI and harassed by police officers and deputy sheriffs in the North as well as the South, they were all victims of racial injustice and all possible victims of conspiracies by groups or persons unknown. Their lives will be remembered for their unyielding commitment to the cause of racial equality and empowerment; their deaths will be remembered for exposing the hypocrisy, venality, and absolute corruptibility of the American criminal justice system. And that is the legacy that has surfaced to haunt the trials of Rodney King's police assailants and O. J. Simpson, murder defendant.

> If I learned one thing in black history, it is the systematic effort of the U.S. government to discredit and destroy black leadership in this country, from the leaders of the slave revolts to the leaders of the civil rights movement.
>
> E. J., junior college student

There is a persistent belief among African-Americans in a widespread conspiracy to destroy the black community. This conspiracy presumably involves a loosely organized group of powerful people and strategic institutions who feel threatened by both the growing economic and political power of middle-class blacks, at one extreme, and the rising rates of crime and welfare dependency of the black underclass, at the other end of the economic spectrum.

Proponents of this conspiracy theory claim that right-wing conservative politicians have joined forces with corporate power brokers and reactionary intellectuals to exclude blacks from the mainstream and to isolate them in urban ghettos where they can be controlled, conditioned, and ultimately subdued into a state of permanent servitude and submission to white power.

These conspiracy theorists have no trouble finding incidents and evidence to support their elaborate claims. They offer as proof the disproportionate number of black politicians and community leaders who are targeted by district attorneys and FBI agents for investigations of their tax returns, their campaign finances, their family businesses, and even their sexual habits—Congressmen Harold Ford of Tennessee and Floyd Flake of Brooklyn, Mayors Richard Arrington of Birmingham, Alabama, and David Dinkins of New York City. In most of these high-profile cases, charges have been dropped or not sustained in court, but only after serious damage has been inflicted on the leader's reputation, his family, and his financial resources.

These observers note that many white politicians are indicted for far more grievous offenses yet manage to negotiate reduced pleas and to restore their reputations and their power with far less public humiliation. They point to recent investigations of charges of unethical, illegal, or immoral conduct against Senator Edward Kennedy of Massachusetts, Senator Robert Packwood of Oregon, and Governor Edwin Edwards of Louisiana as examples to back up their claims.

> Black men are being used as the poster children for every domestic issue around: sexual harassment (Clarence Thomas), date rape (Mike Tyson), child abuse (Michael Jackson), domestic violence (O. J. Simpson).
>
> George Curry, editor in chief, *Emerge* magazine

They further offer as proof the number of black superstar athletes and celebrity entertainers who are arrested for drug use, assault, drunken driving, domestic violence, and illegal gambling. These arrests often result in suspensions from professional teams, criminal convictions, and the loss of valuable product endorsements. Yet while these critics do not seem to condone or apologize for such antisocial behavior, they raise an interesting question about the differential treatment of white athletes and celebrities who are rumored to be addicted to drugs, arrested for drunken driving or spousal abuse, or involved in illegal gambling or questionable business deals. How many of them are convicted, given harsh punishments, and pilloried by the mass media?

> Chuck Berry went to prison for fooling around with young girls, and Daryl Strawberry was suspended from baseball for using drugs. But when Jerry Garcia, a known heroin addict, and Mickey Mantle, an admitted alcoholic, died, they were treated like heroes.
>
> B. R., black male lawyer, San Francisco

TARGETING CIVIL RIGHTS ORGANIZATIONS AND PROTEST GROUPS

Conspiracy theorists also offer as proof the dismal record of the FBI in failing to protect civil rights workers in the South during the 1960s and 1970s. In fact, there is ample documentation that FBI agents not only infiltrated the movement but also gave crucial information to members of the Ku Klux Klan and White Citizens' Councils that resulted in many unsolved beatings, killings, and bombings. Local FBI agents were reluctant to investigate the most egregious hate crimes, such as the murders of Ben Chaney, Andrew Goodman, and Michael Schwerner in Mississippi and the bombing of the Sixteenth Street Baptist Church in Birmingham, Alabama, in 1963. Rather than support the movement for racial equality in this country, critics complain that J. Edgar Hoover and his associates did everything in their power to sabotage it. How could blacks ever be expected to trust the very law enforcement agency of the federal government that was officially entrusted with and responsible for enforcing and protecting their civil rights?

Black militants of the 1960s and 1970s assailed the conspiracy of the FBI and law enforcement groups against the Black Panthers, the Oakland, California–based group that confronted the police with angry rhetoric and menacing guns. The police were neither amused nor intimidated. In less than a decade, they broke the back of the Black Panthers through a series of informants, harassment, and surprise attacks on the group's headquarters and "safe houses."

Years after most of the Panther leaders were either in prison, in exile, or dead, the public learned that some of those surprise attacks were unprovoked assassinations of unarmed members of the movement. Johnnie Cochran, in one of his early cases as a defense lawyer, also learned that the FBI played a major role in the 1972 murder conviction of Geronimo Pratt, a twenty-four-year-old Panther whose case raises troubling questions of a police frame-up, seeing that there were reliable witnesses who confirmed that he was in

Oakland, California, when the murders were committed in Los Angeles.

Younger blacks who did not live through the tumultuous years of the civil rights movement can point to contemporary incidents of police conspiracies and cover-ups against blacks and other minorities in the inner cities. They can document reports of widespread corruption, police brutality, and blatant misconduct in the metropolitan police forces of New York, Chicago, Detroit, Philadelphia, and New Orleans. They can discuss the criminal behavior of many officers in the New Orleans police department, characterized as one of the most corrupt and most brutal in the United States, where police have been indicted for killing witnesses willing to testify against them. They can show the videotape of white racists in Greensboro, North Carolina, methodically attacking and killing several blacks who were marching in 1979 in a protest demonstration against the Ku Klux Klan. Television cameras were there to record the attacks, but police did not show up until five people had been killed and eleven seriously injured. Their easily identifiable assailants were twice acquitted by all-white juries.

It is not difficult to make the case for a police conspiracy against African-Americans in the face of so much overwhelming evidence. What is more difficult is to suspend disbelief, cynicism, and healthy paranoia for an objective and dispassionate analysis of each situation and its racial and social context. But it is also important to remember that even paranoid people do have enemies!

KILLING BLACK MALES: LEGAL LYNCHING OR MURDER?

> The National Black Police Association sent a letter to U.S. Attorney General Janet Reno in September 1994 with complaints about ". . . the continuing trend that appears to have gained momentum over the past five years—an aggressive criminal assault on the African-American community. We believe this trend is directly

related to the notion that African-American males are criminals, due in part to "police profiles," and extremely unfortunate for African-American police officers working undercover.

Nick Charles and Chrisana Coleman,
Emerge, September 1995

Black Americans know about the many shootings and beatings of undercover black police officers by their white colleagues in New York, Nashville, Chicago, Detroit, and Oakland. In case after case, the police officer claims he did not "recognize" his undercover black counterpart or that the black undercover officer was engaged in "suspicious behavior" or that his gun was fired accidentally and not with the intention of harming anyone.

The excuses were all too familiar—"mea culpa" does not exist in the vocabularies of these policemen who wound or kill their black fellow officers. And in nearly all of these cases of "accidental" shootings, the white officers are not charged with any crime. They are vindicated; their victims are twice victimized. To blacks, this seems like a conspiracy of the police establishment to protect their white colleagues against legitimate claims of severe injuries or fatal wounds inflicted on their black colleagues.

Black Americans know about police killings of unarmed black males in nearly every major city in America and, increasingly, in smaller cities, towns, and suburbs. They have read about William Lozano, the thirty-year-old Miami, Florida, Latino policeman who in January 1989 shot a young black engineer riding on a motorcycle with his friend, both of whom were killed when the motorcycle went out of control. Despite consistent testimony from several witnesses that the police officer did not give them any warning and pointed his gun directly at the driver's back, the jury believed the officer's story that it was all a regrettable accident. After two trials and a change of venue to a more conservative city in Florida, Officer Lozano was acquitted in May 1993.

Blacks have also read about the four Detroit police officers who stopped Malice Green, a thirty-five-year-old black man with a record of drug offenses, dragged him out of his car, and beat him to death with their flashlights in November 1992. Witnesses contradicted the officers' claims that Green was resisting arrest and threatened the police with a weapon. No weapon was found, but three officers were ultimately indicted; two were convicted of second-degree murder, and one was acquitted of felony assault charges. Walter Budzyn and Larry Nevers, the two convicted officers, had a long history of brutality complaints lodged against them, but they had never been disciplined by the Detroit police department.

Justifiable Homicides: Police and Klan Killings

The images imprinted on the brains of black folks reveal past conspiracies of police killings of unarmed black youth in New York, Detroit, Atlanta, and New Orleans, only to be exonerated time after time, their fatal shootings excused as "justifiable homicide." And how many black males have been convicted of felony crimes on the basis of circumstantial evidence and no eyewitnesses, even in the face of strong alibis? How often have judges passed death penalty sentences on black defendants whose major crime was the color of their skin and not the severity of their actions? Why do black male defendants frequently receive harsher sentences and spend longer prison terms for the same or similar offenses committed by whites? And blacks vividly recall the indelible image of the Scottsboro boys, languishing in jail for years for the alleged rape of two white girls, who later recanted their testimony far too late to restore the youth and health of their black male victims.

The memories recalled in the minds of black folks encompass the cold-blooded murder of Chaney, Schwerner, and Goodman, three young civil rights workers ambushed on a rural Mississippi road and buried like garbage in a construction pit. Memories of Freedom Riders attacked, their buses burned, their lives threatened both by the Ku Klux Klan and the local police officials in the summer of 1961. One especially vivid memory of the bombing of the Sixteenth Street Baptist Church in Birmingham, where on September 15, 1963, four little black girls dressed in their Sunday best were incinerated in the ashes of white supremacy. Memories of police dogs and fire hoses turned against the marchers at Selma, Alabama, in 1965, viciously attacking them and injuring their bodies just for asserting their right of peaceful assembly.

"BAD BLOOD" AND CONSPIRACY IN THE BLACK COMMUNITY

> Rodney King's bruised body had come to symbolize the collective body of African-Americans in the 1990's. . . . The chaos and uncertainty that followed the verdict fueled the perpetuation of rumors that reveal the extent of suspicion and mistrust that persist between the races.
>
> Patricia A. Turner, *I Heard It Through the Grapevine*

Blood and bruised bodies have always been at the heart of conspiracy theories in the black community. If there is a Jungian collective unconscious operating among African-Americans, then they are all aware at some subliminal level of the countless conspiracies involving blood, police brutality, and the criminal justice system. This collective unconscious is the repository of the shared images of police brutality, of hanging judges, of unfair convictions. This collective unconscious is the reservoir of memories of Klan lynchings, of police dogs attacking, of buses burning, of bombed-out churches. This collective unconscious is the receptacle of broken promises, frustrated ambitions, unfulfilled dreams.

Blacks remembered the shocking photographs of fourteen-year-old Emmett Till's bloody, mutilated body, dragged from the Tallahatchie River, where he had been dumped after he was brutally murdered in August 1955. "Bo" Till, a Chicago teenager on a summer visit to his relatives in Money, Mississippi, had made the fatal mistake of seeming too familiar with Carolyn Bryant, a pretty white grocer's wife, whose husband, Roy, and his friend, J. W. Milam, kidnapped him in broad daylight, tortured him, and then killed him. Despite the eyewitness testimony of Emmett's relatives and Bryant's admission that they had kidnapped the boy, the all-white, all-male jury acquitted the two defendants after deliberating for sixty-seven minutes. Emmett Till's murder became a cause célèbre, not only because it exposed the dual system of southern justice, but also because it galvanized a national movement for antilynching legislation and ushered in the modern civil rights protests.

AIDS and the Black Community

> AIDS origin stories . . . reveal several facets of the contemporary African-American worldview. Those individuals who find these stories credible consider the "powers" that run America . . . to be consistently ambivalent and even hostile to African-American well-being.
>
> Patricia A. Turner, *I Heard It Through the Grapevine*

So powerful was the impact of the Tuskegee Study scandal on the consciousness of African-Americans that it became permanently embedded in their collective unconscious, even among uneducated and unsophisticated blacks who are beyond the reach of the media and beyond the boundaries of the scientific community. Its impact was so pervasive that a decade later, when the AIDS epidemic emerged as a major threat to the black community, the specter of conspiracy reared its head again.

African-Americans, many of whom had dismissed AIDS as a disease of gay white males, could not comprehend its rapid spread among black male drug users and their female partners. By 1983, rumors had begun to circulate that AIDS was an artificially created virus introduced by diabolical politicians to kill homosexuals and people of color, thus ridding the country of its most unwanted groups. When a group of scientists speculated that the virus may have been transmitted to humans from an African monkey, blacks' worst fears were confirmed. Now not only were scientists in league with politicians to exterminate American blacks, but they also planned to blame the origin of the virus on African monkeys, spread throughout the world through contact with Africans in remote jungle villages.

In a 1990 survey of 1,054 members of black churches in five cities (Atlanta; Charlotte, North Carolina; Detroit; Kansas City, Missouri; and Tuscaloosa, Alabama), Dr. Sandra Crouse Quinn found that over one-third (33.9 percent) agreed or strongly agreed with a statement that "the AIDS virus was produced in a germ warfare laboratory," and another 44 percent were unsure. Moreover, 35 percent of the sample believed that "AIDS is a form of genocide against black people," and 30 percent more were unsure. Thus in this group of religious blacks, no more than one-third were willing to dispute either one of these statements.

As preposterous and paranoid as these beliefs about AIDS may seem, a surprising number of well-educated, professional blacks subscribe to a full-fledged or modified version. Black journalists have raised the issue in their columns and on talk shows, black politicians have tried to allay the anxiety of their constituents, black health professionals have offered reassurance to their patients, and black ministers have preached abstinence and fidelity to their congregations. If this dreaded disease was contaminating the nation's blood supply and ravaging the homosexual community, why was it also decimating young blacks and Latinos in the inner cities just as they were beginning to escape the confines of the ghettos and move into the mainstream? What was the sinister connection, if any, between the "bad blood" in the Tuskegee patients and the "bad blood" in the AIDS patients?

CONSPIRACY THEORIES AND THE LAPD

Against this historical pattern of government deprivation, deception, and discrimination, the idea of a police conspiracy in the

O. J. Simpson case seems not just plausible but probable to African-Americans. From the perspective of members of the black community, the police in Los Angeles are "just another gang that wears blue colors." They know from their experiences that the Los Angeles Police Department does not come into their neighborhoods "to protect and serve" but rather to harass and intimidate. They know from their collective memories that the police do not need any reasonable cause to stop and search them, to invade their homes without a search warrant, or to arrest them and rough them up in their patrol cars. For blacks in Los Angeles, the police are to be feared, avoided, and, if encountered, treated with the utmost caution.

> The idea of a potential conspiracy seems like a bizarre plot to much of the white community because their experience has been much different with the Los Angeles Police Department. But with the black community, as a product of their experience, they don't think that a conspiracy is such a bizarre phenomenon.
>
> John W. Mack, president of the
> Los Angeles Urban League

African-Americans in Los Angeles can point to the evidence of a police conspiracy in dozens of cases, some well documented and others not, most involving unarmed young black men. They can tell you about Leonard Deadwyler, running red lights to get his pregnant wife to the hospital, stopped by the police, and fatally shot because they thought he was threatening them with a gun. No gun was ever found, but the two policemen were found innocent by virtue of "justifiable homicide." This was one of Johnnie Cochran's first cases in 1996, and it taught him an unforgettable lesson about the LAPD.

They can tell you about Ron Settles, the twenty-one-year-old black football player from California State University, Long Beach, who was arrested one morning in June 1981 for speeding in Signal

Hill, a conservative white suburb of Los Angeles. Three hours later that same day, Settles, a perfectly healthy young man with no history of psychological problems, was found hanging from a mattress cover in his cell, an apparent suicide. Settles's family hired their own independent pathologist to challenge the official autopsy report, and he found that this popular athlete had been killed "by other than his own hand." The family sued and in 1983 won a settlement of $760,000 for wrongful death against the Signal Hill police department. The lawyer who successfully won this award for the Settles family was also Johnnie Cochran, who was rapidly developing a practice specializing in defending victims of police brutality and misconduct.

Blacks in Los Angeles can recall the graphic TV images of Donald Jackson, a black Long Beach police officer, who was thrown through a plate glass window in 1989 by several white policemen after he complained that the Long Beach police department had a pervasive pattern of harassment and brutality against the black community in that city that stretched somnolently along the Pacific Coast shoreline just north of Los Angeles. Despite clear visual evidence of the assault, the police defendants accused Jackson of throwing himself through the window to garner publicity. They were acquitted by a predominantly white jury.

Blacks in South Central still had a vivid recollection of the LAPD raid on a block of four apartments at Thirty-Ninth Street and Dalton Avenue on August 1, 1988, by eighty-five police officers from the Southwest Division. Searching for drugs, this army of officers assaulted the tenants, used shotguns and sledgehammers to destroy their apartments beyond repair, and arrested thirty-two residents, who were made to run through a gauntlet of police baton blows and racial epithets. Although the police commission declined to investigate this highly publicized raid, the department brought charges against thirty-eight of the officers, including two of the supervising officers who had instructed their subordinates to "level" the apartments and make them "uninhabitable." In this Rambo-style raid, the LAPD seized less than one ounce of crack cocaine and less than six ounces of marijuana in the four apartment units. In May 1991, when three of the senior officers were finally brought to trial on charges of conspiracy to commit vandalism and misdemeanor charges of vandalism, Deputy District Attorney Christopher Darden commented: "They didn't do a search-and-destroy mission. They did a destroy mission." After three weeks of deliberation, in June 1991, the jury acquitted the officers on five of six charges and deadlocked on the sixth charge, which was subsequently dismissed. Although the tenants at Thirty-Ninth and Dalton never found justice in the criminal courts, they successfully sued the LAPD in civil trials and were collectively paid $3.4 million in damages by the City of Los Angeles.

Young Black Males and the LAPD

> A major strategy in the war against the Black collective is the killing of Black males. Black males are being killed daily, in ever-increasing numbers across the country. . . . These black and other non-white males are being killed by white males in uniforms who have been authorized to carry guns. This particular form of murder and slaughter is called "justifiable homicide."
>
> Dr. Frances Cress Welsing, 1993

Between 1965 and 1992, long before the Rodney King incident, nearly every black family in Los Angeles knew some young black man who had been beaten or fatally injured in police custody. During the 1980s, at least sixteen blacks had died from police choke holds, many on the streets and in police patrol cars, arrested for "suspicious behavior," "loitering," or, ironically, "resisting arrest." The coroner managed to rule that most of these cases were unfortunate "accidents," not really cases of excessive police force or misconduct.

Nearly every black family in South Central Los Angeles had also witnessed "Operation Hammer," launched in February 1988, when Chief Daryl Gates deployed his officers in military-style units to surround the projects on weekend evenings and round up all the young black males in sight. They were searched without warrants, harassed without justification, and hunted like animals. No single act of brutality or injustice enraged the black community more than these frequent weekend invasions, sanctioned by police officials and condoned by politicians. According to one study, in 1990 alone, the LAPD arrested over twenty-five thousand minority youth, "yet fewer than 1,500 of them were ever actually charged with a criminal offense." Under the pretext of crime prevention, thousands of innocent young black men, just hanging out in front of their own homes or cruising down their own familiar streets, were stopped, searched, and humiliated by L.A.'s finest for no reason other than the color of their skin.

If the Los Angeles Police Department was hated and feared by blacks, the Los Angeles County Sheriff's Department was even more distrusted and despised. In 1991 alone, the same year Rodney King was brutally beaten by four policemen, fifty-seven unarmed citizens, most of them people of color, were killed by the Los Angeles County Sheriff's Department. Black and Latino males were the most frequent victims, shot to death in the most mundane of circumstances when they were driving along less traveled roads at night, strangely always found to be resisting arrest or threatening to assault a police officer. Rarely were there any reliable witnesses to these inexplicable shootings, and even more rarely were any officers disciplined for killing unarmed civilians.

Of the four families who sued the sheriff's department in 1991 for wrongful death, not one case resulted in a successful prosecution or even a settlement for damages. Blacks in Los Angeles County understood perfectly well that a young black male driving alone on a county road at night, especially in a late-model car, was placing himself in a high-risk situation with no guarantee of safe passage or due process if stopped by a sheriff's deputy.

Even L.A.'s infamous gangs, the Crips and the Bloods, were not immune from the wide web of conspirators in the Los Angeles

Police Department, as they soon learned after the 1992 uprising. True to their pledge, the members of these two major gangs made a number of good-faith efforts to maintain their truce—"to stop the killings and keep the peace." Yet whenever they planned a joint meeting or social affair, curiously, the police always showed up in full force, in patrol cars with lights flashing and batons in readiness.

Was it sheer coincidence that the police always knew the exact time and place of the meeting and always arrived in time to create a show of force and to intimidate the crowd? Was it simply accidental that the police were equipped with riot gear and frequently waded into a peaceful crowd of gang members, hoping to provoke some counteraggression? Was it even remotely possible that the police were actually opposed to the gang truce and had decided to sabotage it because the gangs provided the police with a justification for official violence and repression against the black community? In fact, the gangs provided the police with a mirror image of themselves—a bunch of frustrated, macho males who needed to vent their anger and aggression on vulnerable, powerless targets. If the gangs cleaned up their act and stopped victimizing the community, what excuse would the police have to continue victimizing the victims?

And it wasn't just the wanton war against the gangs that fueled African-Americans' suspicion and distrust of the Los Angeles Police Department. Nearly every black woman in Watts and South Central had a son, brother, or nephew who had been followed, stopped, or arrested by a policeman for no apparent reason. They knew that Mark Fuhrman was telling the truth on those notorious tapes when he said that "cops found any excuse to stop a nigger in a Porsche and not wearing a hundred-dollar suit." How many celebrities had complained about being arrested while driving or jogging in their own West Los Angeles neighborhoods? They understood completely when Fuhrman admitted that the Los Angeles Police Department often planted evidence on suspects because so many of their family members had been falsely accused and unjustly convicted. And most of all, they could relate to the helplessness and hopelessness that these young black males must have felt when their lives were disrupted by a policeman's prejudice, when their reputations were destroyed by a prosecutor's passion, when their future was stolen by a judge's vindictiveness.

> Black people in L.A. don't trust the cops or the courts. We know that cops arrest innocent people. We know that cops brutalize young black males. We know they would like nothing more than to bring down O. J. Simpson, even if they have to frame him for these murders.
>
> O. L., black female psychologist, Los Angeles

The Cycle of Violence: Criminalization of Young Black Males

Blacks in Los Angeles recognized that the criminal justice system has its own inexorable cycle of violence: false arrests, unfair convictions, and illegal incarcerations. But for young black males in Los Angeles, as in the rest of the nation, the cycle begins with higher arrest rates than whites for comparable crimes, higher conviction rates, and longer periods of incarceration. In Los Angeles, as in the rest of the country, disparities in sentencing for drug offenses discriminate against black youth, who are more likely to possess crack cocaine, than white youth, who are more likely to possess powdered cocaine.

It was no surprise to African-Americans that black defendants in Los Angeles courts received longer prison sentences than whites or Latinos for all major felony crimes committed in the 1980s. By 1995, it was a shocking indictment that the United States had imprisoned more people than any other nation, including South Africa, and that more young black males were in jail or prison than were enrolled in colleges and universities. Was this, in fact, a reasonable response to crime in the black community, or was this an even more pathological sign of a widespread conspiracy against black males in America?

Against this backdrop, one can begin to comprehend the power and potency for African-Americans of the idea of a police conspiracy in the O. J. Simpson case. It is embedded in the fertile soil of the black American experience, from the betrayal of the first coffles of

West African villagers, sold into slavery by their venal chieftains and bartered for sugar and coffee in the Middle Passage.

> The LAPD is still boiling about the Rodney King case. They got caught in the act, and they finally got punished. They've been waiting to get their revenge on the black community. So even if O. J. committed the crimes, those racist cops cooked the evidence to be sure he was convicted. The King beating backfired, but they retaliated and brought down a black hero.
>
> A. B., educator, Los Angeles, September 15, 1995

Justice is not color-blind in Los Angeles; it is color-coded. African-Americans were neither surprised nor shocked to hear excerpts from Detective Mark Fuhrman's tapes. As far as most blacks are concerned, the racial epithets, admissions of police misconduct, and biased treatment of people of color were just business as usual in the United States of America. To white Americans, these statements were shocking, beyond belief, utterly difficult to fathom. Perhaps the Fuhrman tapes offered whites a glimpse into the world of black America and what it means to be a black man in a white man's world. Perhaps those tapes offered whites an insight into the paranoia and prejudice of the police force that they view as society's protectors. Perhaps those tapes gave them pause to think about what little distance really separates the criminals and antisocial elements in society from the "thin blue line" of law and order.

Perhaps, at the end of the day, white Americans can really begin to understand the obsession with race in this society—how it has divided blacks and whites, how it has led to unequal treatment and unequal chances for blacks, and how it has perverted every institution in this society in order to maintain white privilege and white power. Perhaps then, and only then, will whites be truly able to comprehend why the polls reflect such racial differences in opinions of the innocence or guilt of O. J. Simpson.

12

A House Divided

Healing the Wound, Restoring the Dream

A house divided against itself cannot stand.

Abraham Lincoln, June 16, 1858

We are at a crucial crossroad in the history of this nation—and we either hang together by combating these forces that divide and degrade us or we hang separately.

Cornel West, *Race Matters*

From all external signs and signals, Los Angeles had returned to normal by January 1996, the beginning of the new year. The weather, usually mild and overcast during the winter months, had been unusually warm and sunny. During the holiday season, the shopping malls in the suburbs and the strip malls in South Central had been full of harried shoppers and hyperactive teenagers. Hollywood had released the annual quota of Christmas movies, with *Waiting to Exhale* a surprise hit at the box office. It was a story about four middle-class black women and their unsatisfactory relationships with black men, a "crossover" movie that appealed to white and black audiences with its universal themes of male-female communication problems, unrequited love, rejection, and revenge. The movie premiered at the impressive new multiplex theater owned by Magic Johnson, another black superhero who had joined a group of investors to build the first major entertainment center in the South Central–Crenshaw area since the Watts riots of 1965.

Most critics failed to notice that here was a movie that transcended race, class, and cultural differences. It spoke to the human condition, the age-old conflicts between men and women, the unending battle between the sexes, the strangely familiar but unrecognized agendas and unfulfilled needs in the uncharted territory of sexual relationships in the 1990s. And yet, while millions of women and their reluctant dates were finding common ground in this contemporary urban drama, the citizens of Los Angeles were still obsessing over the ugly racial divisions that had been exposed by the verdict in the O. J. Simpson trial. Columnists were still analyzing, commentators were still discussing, and politicians were still bemoaning the bitter discourse and the hostile confrontations between blacks and whites over Simpson's acquittal.

> Race is the most explosive issue in American life precisely because it forces us to confront the tragic facts of poverty and paranoia, despair and distrust. . . . A candid examination of race matters takes us to the core of the crisis of American democracy.
>
> Cornel West, *Race Matters*

The Simpson trial had been a *mirror* in which Americans could see their larger social problems reflected—it had portrayed the unflattering and harsh realities of spousal abuse, marital infidelity, drug use, sports hero worship, interracial conflicts, black-Jewish tensions, and lethal violence. It had also shown how a rags-to-riches fairy tale could turn into a tawdry tale of "rich man's justice." The O. J. Simpson odyssey was also a saga of the inextricable intersection of race, class, and sex in the American social discourse.

If the Simpson trial held up a mirror to reveal the contradictions and conflicts in American society, the cases of Rodney King and O. J. Simpson, in tandem, could be viewed as a *metaphor* for black males involved in the criminal justice system. Despite their obvious differences in talent, status, and lifestyle, King and Simpson shared a surprising number of background characteristics and personal attributes. Both were sons of southern migrants to Northern California; both were reared in working-class families with strongly religious mothers; both were mediocre students; both participated in high school sports; both were involved in delinquent activities and had contacts with the police. But fate dealt them very different hands: O. J.'s superior athletic ability and charismatic personality won him a college scholarship and a ticket out of the ghetto, whereas Rodney never was able to finish high school or to realize his dream of becoming a professional baseball player.

Though the lives of the two men followed very different trajectories, with Rodney remaining mired along the margins of society and O. J. moving effortlessly into the mainstream, the vagaries of chance brought them both back into contact with the police in two of the most celebrated cases of the decade. As black male adults involved in the criminal justice system in Los Angeles, their superficial differences disappeared, and both were transformed into the "other," mishandled by their arresting officers, misrepresented by the media, and mistreated by the Los Angeles Police Department in both subtle and flagrant ways. In both of these cases, the media reduced King and Simpson to stereotypes of aggressive and sexualized black male symbols, stripped of their essential individuality, their inherent dignity, and their basic humanity.

South Central Los Angeles became a *microcosm* of the African-American community in its response to the acquittal of the white officers for beating Rodney King and the subsequent acquittal of O. J. Simpson for the murder of his wife and her friend. South Central was the repository of the recovered memories of racism, discrimination, and police brutality against all blacks—young black males, adult black leaders, and black celebrities. For people in the black community, their identity and empathy with the plight of Rodney King and O. J. Simpson, as two black males ensnared in the criminal justice system, transcended issues of facts and evidence, uniting blacks in a way that no other event had done since the assassination of Martin Luther King, Jr., in 1968.

South Central had become a synonym for black America, a collective consciousness, a shared identity, and a sense of solidarity in the face of persistent distrust of the criminal justice system. The members of the African-American community rallied behind Rodney King and O. J. Simpson because they saw the images of their fathers, uncles, brothers, and sons, and they viewed these black men, rightly or wrongly, as two more victims of white America's brand of justice. And in the aftermath of their ordeals with the criminal justice system and the LAPD, while whites were ridiculing Rodney King and reviling O. J. Simpson, blacks found all the more justification for embracing these two prodigal sons and praying for their redemption and rehabilitation.

A HOUSE DIVIDED

> African-Americans have been abused by police as if it was common practice. . . . We've got to stop allowing things like "three strikes, you're out" laws. We've got to stop allowing bad bills to get out of committee in the state legislature. We can't get complacent. . . . We need to stay here and clean our neighborhoods up. We need a decent civil rights bill. And we need to see that the same policy that applies to white folks applies to black folks—in Beverly Hills or South Central. We have to hold white folks accountable for how awful they have let the system go.
>
> Duane B. Bremond, public relations director,
> AIDS Project, Los Angeles

The bitter controversies surrounding the jury decisions in the acquittals of the white police officers and the black sports celebrity send a clear and sober message. The criminal justice system in Los Angeles is not well served as long as it is permeated at all levels with bias, brutality, and discrimination against minorities. Moreover, the members of the African-American community have served notice to the LAPD and to community leaders that they will no longer tolerate two standards of justice—one for whites and one for people of color. To heal the wound between blacks and whites in this society, the system of justice must become truly color-blind, not just in Los Angeles but throughout America.

Black Americans understand—much better than most other Americans—that the criminal justice system represents the values of the dominant society. Its major function is not only to enforce the laws but also to preserve the status quo. The function of the police is indeed "to protect and serve"—to protect the institutions that control the society and to serve the leaders who control the institutions. Thus police officers are the front line, the guardians of the prevailing and predominant norms, attitudes, values, and beliefs of the society, whether those beliefs are expressed in the Bill of Rights or in the voting booth.

Police clearly understand that their function is one of social control—to carry out the unspoken message and the hidden agenda to deal with groups deemed undesirable, unworthy, or unequal by the dominant society. They clearly understand that their mission is to keep these people in their place, to minimize their intrusion into the mainstream, and to make their presence as invisible and as innocuous as possible. The police clearly understand that they must insulate the dominant society from the undesirables—the people of color, the immigrants, the poor, the homeless, the homosexuals (not to mention the criminals, the prostitutes, and the drug addicts)—all those who would threaten their identity, their security, their privilege. The police, as poorly paid agents of the establishment, understand that it is their "thin blue line" that ultimately isolates and separates the throwaways and the undesirables from those who claim to be the rightful heirs to American culture and civilization.

But the police in Los Angeles are just the lowest rung in the ladder of the criminal justice system, which also represents "the people," albeit the majority of the people. With each rung of the ladder, the message is transmitted, sometimes subtly and sometimes overtly, that the full protection of the law is reserved for those who are white, well-to-do, and well connected. The message is transmitted, from the police to the lawyers to the judges to the probation officers, that there are two systems of justice, one for the majority and another for the minority.

It is this silent conspiracy that allows the police to violate the rights of people of color, to arrest black youth without sufficient cause, and to beat suspects into submission. It is this unspoken contract among the police, the criminal justice system, and the dominant majority that allows rampant police brutality to proceed unchecked in the inner cities of America.

HEALING THE WOUND

> Community policing means more than a police presence. It means a different style of policing, where you sit down and you talk with people who live and work in your community, and you find out what's important to them, what it is they want, and you try to tailor some of your services to meet those demands.
>
> Willie Williams, chief of the
> Los Angeles Police Department

Attention must be paid first to the criminal justice system in Los Angeles and to the segments of the community that have supported it and allowed it to trample the rights of minorities, the poor, and the other "undesirables" in the society, just as the twenty-three officers stood silently by while Rodney King was brutally beaten by four of their colleagues. If the racial divisions in Los Angeles are to be healed, the community leaders must insist that the criminal justice system operate as a color-blind system, that minorities should have the right and the expectation to be treated with dignity, fairness, and due process in that system. Equal justice under the law should be more than empty rhetoric; it should be an absolute right and a welcome reality for people of all colors.

Since the police in Los Angeles seem unable to police themselves, the recommendations of the Christopher Commission must be implemented. Three of those recommendations are crucial to help heal the wound in the African-American community: community policing, upgraded recruitment and training programs, and accountability of police to a civilian review board. Willie Williams, the chief of the LAPD, has met serious resistance within the police force to any substantial reforms or changes in their culture and code of silence. Despite the heralded claims of change and promises of reform in bringing the police closer to the community through local substations, increased foot patrols, and more police involvement in community activities and youth programs, change in the LAPD has been slow and painful. As has been noted, of the forty-four officers who were identified in the Christopher Commission report as repetitive violators of police regulations against the use of excessive force, thirty-three were still active members of the force at the end of the O. J. Simpson trial, more than four years after Rodney King was beaten and the report was issued.

If the LAPD does not clean up its act and reform its image in the black community, there will be serious consequences for the criminal justice system. As the nonwhite population of Los Angeles County grows, juries will become dominated more and more frequently by people of color who will bring with them the same kinds of beliefs and attitudes about the police that probably influenced the verdicts in the O. J. Simpson case and the Denny assault case. Jury experts have already predicted that it will become more and more difficult for prosecutors to obtain convictions of minority defendants in urban jurisdictions with a history of police misconduct and brutality. In effect, minority jurors will be disinclined to believe police testimony and will be inclined to view the defendants as victims of an oppressive criminal justice system rather than as offenders who deserve punishment.

Institutionalized Injustice

> When you don't own things where you live, you don't have any respect for it. If you don't work there, and when you go in and spend your money, you're not respected, then you can't respect yourself. When you're brought up in a society that says you're still a visitor and none of this belongs to you, then you don't respect it. . . . That's the kind of thing we're trying to instill in our kids—to take pride in where you live and then you can have some ownership in it. That hasn't happened yet, but we're working on it.
>
> Lillian Mobley, executive director, South Central Multipurpose Senior Citizens Center, Los Angeles

---

The criminal justice system is the most visible and most victimizing social institution for minority males, but there are many forms of injustice in American society, and they all have their most direct and most severe impact on blacks and other people of color. What makes blacks so willing to embrace conspiracy theories is that in their daily lives they experience so much deprivation, discrimination, and despair at the mercy of the mainstream society. In just the past decade, African-Americans have become painfully aware of a growing gap between the income of whites and blacks, an increasing rate of young black males involved in the criminal justice system, a growing hostility in the society toward all social welfare programs, an increasing retreat from affirmative action by politicians and employers, an increasing neglect of urban policy and inner-city problems, and an escalating mean-spiritedness of politicians toward programs for assisting the poor, the homeless, and minority families.

African-Americans are exposed to inequities and injustice in every major institutional system in American society: the social welfare system, the educational system, the employment system, the health care system, and the political system. Major industries in this country openly and flagrantly discriminate against blacks, including businesses connected with banking and finance, real estate and construction, manufacturing, transportation, retail trade, and even the service industries.

Blacks experience daily injustice in inadequate transportation systems, exposure to environmental pollution, substandard housing, inadequate recreational facilities, and unequal access to consumer goods and services.

Attention must be paid to the systemic racism and endemic inequities that permeate every institution of American society, reproducing inequality from generation to generation and replicating social problems from rural areas to inner cities. Political leaders must demonstrate the courage, business and financial leaders must provide the resources, professional and community leaders must dedicate the commitment to rooting out the systemic supports for inequality and restructuring these basic social institutions to promote equal access and equal opportunity in education, employment, housing, health care, transportation, recreation, and consumer services. Without opportunities for social and economic mobility in the mainstream society, black Americans will continue to be disproportionately involved in the criminal justice system as legitimate avenues of achievement and economic security are blocked.

The Mass Media

> Recently, a group of local leaders met with the media, and we urged them to be more responsible. . . . We talked about adopting a set of voluntary guidelines of restraint. They don't really want to hear that, but we have entered into a dialogue, and we're beginning to see, in some small ways, some improvement here and there. They have been criticized all over the place and have caught so much flak that we're beginning to see some changes.
>
> John W. Mack, president, Los Angeles Urban League

The entertainment industry and the mass media occupy a special place in the dehumanization and demonization of blacks and other people of color, as they are the main purveyors of stereotypes, negative images, and subliminal messages that reinforce the notions of black inferiority, hypersexuality, criminality, and deviance.

Definitive accounts of both the Watts riots in 1965 and the South Central riots in 1992 have severely criticized the print and broadcast media for their roles in publicizing the looting and arson as they happened, inciting others to join in, spreading rumors that inflamed the community, and presenting very biased views of the causes and consequences of the riots. More recently, the mass media have continued their inglorious record of biased and sensationalized coverage of the trials of Rodney King's police assailants and O. J. Simpson, often intruding on the stories so unprofessionally that the media themselves became the story, particularly when they printed unconfirmed rumors as fact, quoted unreliable sources for a scoop, and slanted stories to place the defendants or the victims in a more favorable light. In many instances, the media shed more heat than light on the two trials and performed a grave disservice to the public, which expects balanced and accurate information.

Attention must be paid to the mass media, which do not always adhere to their own code of ethics on accuracy, objectivity, and accountability, particularly in reporting on the sensitive area of race relations and racial conflicts. If the racial rift in our country is ever going to be healed, the media need to recognize and remedy their role in promulgating negative stereotypes about blacks and other people of color, most particularly about young black males. The media need to examine their own contribution to the public paranoia about crime and violence in the community, which is highlighted and exaggerated in the morning headlines and the nightly news broadcasts, provoking irrational fears of blacks among whites and reinforcing punitive policies in the criminal justice system, such as "three strikes" laws and wide disparities in penalties for possession of powdered and crack cocaine, which fall most heavily on black males.

Only when the media begin to portray African-Americans in all their diversity and their complexity will blacks feel fairly represented and fairly treated, and only then will whites feel motivated to look beyond the stereotypes to discover the common humanity shared with their darker neighbors. The media, often referred to as the fourth branch of government, has a moral and ethical obligation to use its formidable power and influence to elevate the public discourse about racial issues, to stimulate informed and responsible debate about these issues, and to play a proactive role in bridging the gulf between blacks and whites in the community.

MOVING TOWARD JUSTICE

> Blacks just need a hand, not a handout. Enable the black community. The white corporate world can assist the black community. We cooperate with "Operation Hope," taking bankers on a bus tour of South Central to consider investing in the community. Economics is the locomotive of history. If people can eat and live, they will have solid families and will rear their children well. And if children can work, they will have [alternatives] to the streets. You have to give young people alternatives and options.
>
> Rev. Cecil L. Murray, senior pastor, First African Methodist Episcopal Church, Los Angeles

---

To move toward a color-blind society will require more than institutional change in the white community, but active efforts in the African-American community are also required. In South Central Los Angeles, there are many organizations and individuals that have dedicated years of effort to improving their community and to narrowing the gulf between blacks and whites. These organizations include churches, civil rights groups, social agencies, youth development programs, and gang prevention services. The racial animosities that surfaced after the trials in the Rodney King beating case and the O. J. Simpson murder case were especially troubling and discouraging to these groups and their leaders, unheeded and unsung in their lifelong struggle to achieve racial justice.

These organizations and their leaders represent constructive forces for change in South Central, but they also represent the vanguard of a community still in shock over the beating of Rodney King. They represent a community still reeling from the aftermath of the riots of 1992, only to be freshly assaulted by the verbal invective from the white community after the acquittal of O. J. Simpson. They represent a community that heeded the call for hundreds of thousands of African-American men to attend the Million Man March on October 16, 1995, just a few days after Simpson was set free, seeking to strengthen the bonds of racial solidarity and community in the face of the nation's relentless retreat from equal opportunity and social justice.

TO RESTORE THE DREAM: A VISION FOR THE TWENTY-FIRST CENTURY

> In a real sense, America is essentially a dream, a dream as yet unfulfilled. It is a dream of a land where men of all races, of all nationalities, and of all creeds can live together as brothers.
>
> Martin Luther King, Jr., June 1961

At the dawn of the new century, it will be 220 years since the *pobladores* first glimpsed the fertile fields of the city they named after the Queen of the Angels. It will be just over two centuries since the racially diverse group of thirty-two founders signed their *X*'s to the city's charter. Somewhere along the way in these last two hundred years, the citizens of Los Angeles have lost the vision of a truly harmonious multiracial and multicultural society; they have betrayed the dream of equal opportunity and equal justice for all Angelenos.

The community's dramatic and polarized responses to the jury decisions in the cases of Rodney King and O. J. Simpson have exposed the deep racial divisions between blacks and whites in the United States. Los Angeles, a microcosm of the nation, is the second-largest city in the country, but it will be the first city of great size to achieve a nonwhite majority by the end of the twentieth century. It is time for the community's leaders to bring together people of all colors and classes to talk frankly about race and culture; to confront the stereotypes and symbols that divide groups; to develop a new vocabulary of tolerance, trust, and inclusion; and to promote a new spirit of conciliation, cooperation, and collaboration among all groups. It is time for Los Angeles to recognize the strength of its multicultural mosaic, to use that strength to build a model city for its citizens, to celebrate its diversity, and to demonstrate that "we all can get along."

Los Angeles has been called "the city of the future" by its cheerleaders and by its critics for its trend-setting role in the areas of the arts, fashion, entertainment, and contemporary culture. Just as it takes pride in its role as a cultural innovator, the city could effectively embrace the role of social innovator in creating a dynamic and diverse community where people of all colors and ethnic groups are welcomed, nurtured, and afforded opportunities for life, liberty, and the pursuit of personal fulfillment. If Los Angeles can solve the problems of racial divisions, if it can provide the political and economic context for multiracial and multicultural harmony, then the rest of the nation will have a model to follow as people of color will constitute nearly half of all Americans by the middle of the next century. With growing economic leverage and increasing political power, these people of color will demand equal treatment, equal opportunity, and equal justice in every aspect of this society.

The challenge for the citizens of Los Angeles is to restore the founders' vision of the city as a mecca for people of all colors, to restore the promise of the city for those seeking a new beginning, and to restore the dream of the city as a place where justice would not be determined by the color of one's skin or the wealth of one's estate. As the new century dawns, Los Angeles will remain a beacon for those seeking a new vision, a renewal of hope, and a dream of opportunity. May it keep the faith with its founding families and restore the dream for all those who enter the City of the Angels.

Epilogue

February in Los Angeles is always a harbinger of spring, with the usual signs of weekend gardening, leisurely patio lunches, and bets on the basketball playoffs. The media hype generated by Magic Johnson's return to the Los Angeles Lakers basketball team dominated the news for several weeks, relegating most other stories to second billing. Johnson, living with AIDS, had transformed his personal tragedy into a message of hope for all his fans, black and white, as he demonstrated his determination to challenge the odds and live out his dream.

But there were two stories in Los Angeles in February 1996 that would not disappear, and these stories continued to frustrate, fascinate, and fracture the community. And in some inexplicable fashion, these two stories continued to be inextricably linked as they unfolded in unpredictable moments of high drama and low comedy. During the third week of February, Angelenos were once again reminded of the continuing saga of Rodney King and O. J. Simpson, the two black males whose cases had polarized the community and whose issues were still unresolved in the courts.

On February 20, 1996, the U.S. Supreme Court heard the final appeal of the two white police officers who had been convicted of assaulting Rodney King and had served their sentences in prison. Lawyers for Laurence Powell and Stacey Koon had appealed the decision of the Ninth Circuit U.S. Appeals Court that Judge John G.

Davies had not presented valid reasons for imposing sentences below the federal minimum guidelines on the two convicted officers, thereby returning the case to the lower court for resentencing. The Supreme Court, in accepting the appeal, had placed itself squarely between a rock and a hard place. If the Court were to uphold Judge Davies's discretion to ignore the minimum guidelines, it would be undermining the federal judicial commission that had worked so deliberately and diligently to develop a more uniform and more equitable system for sentencing people convicted of federal crimes, thus opening the floodgates to judicial bias and abuse against minority and low-income defendants. If the Court were to uphold the decision of the appeals court, it could create a backlash of sympathy for Powell and Koon and contribute to renewed hostilities between the LAPD and the African-American community. In light of the conservative Court's recent pattern of decisions restricting the rights of criminals and expanding the powers of the police, it was unlikely that the decision of the Appeals Court would be upheld.

On February 16, only four days before the court hearing, the distributor of O. J. Simpson's videotape, *O. J. Simpson: The Interview*, announced that copies were finally available and had been mailed to people who ordered by phone. Despite sustained protests against the video promotion by feminist groups and others outraged by O. J.'s acquittal for the double murder, hundreds of people had apparently ordered the video out of sympathy or curiosity to hear his version of the events on the night of June 12, 1994. Several television shows rushed to air brief segments of the tape, showing O. J. recounting his alibi and retracing his steps on the night of the murders. Other stations refused to publicize the video, unwilling to lend it any aura of legitimacy or to promote its sales. The media industry that had eagerly created and cashed in on the persona of O. J. Simpson was now just as eagerly destroying and demeaning his image so that he would no longer be a salable commodity. The "golden boy" of *Sports Illustrated* and NBC-TV football fame now found himself portrayed as the dark-skinned Othello, symbol of wife abuse and homicidal jealousy. O. J. Simpson had been given his freedom by a jury of his peers, but would he be forever deprived of making a livelihood by a jury of the public?

THE AFTERMATH OF THE RODNEY KING CASE

In early March, 1996, the media, mired down in the mudslinging of the eight candidates competing in the Republican presidential primary election contests, paid very little attention to March 3, the fifth anniversary of the beating of Rodney King. While still fascinated with the continuing saga of O. J. Simpson, the media and print journalists used the Supreme Court hearing to review the developments in the King case and to note its lasting impact on the City of Los Angeles. It seemed ironic that after five years, the media paid more attention to the legal troubles of the convicted white assailants than to the traumatic consequences for the brutalized black victim. How has this case affected the lives of its principal players since that fateful encounter on the Foothill Freeway in March 1991?

Rodney King: Vulnerable Survivor

Rodney King has experienced continuous turmoil in his personal and public life since he was the victim of the violent assault. In the past five years, he has been arrested twice for drunken driving. He was also apprehended by police for soliciting a male transvestite prostitute, but charges were ultimately dropped. In 1995, his wife, Crystal, charged him with assault, obtained a court restraining order against him, and subsequently separated from him. In April 1996, a hearing was scheduled to determine the amount of child support and alimony King will have to pay his wife, who was to be represented by Gloria Allred, a well-known Los Angeles lawyer. Allred, who also represented the family of Nicole Brown Simpson during the murder trial of O. J. Simpson, is a frequent media commentator on issues of spousal abuse and women's rights.

In 1995, Rodney King moved to Upland, an integrated middle-class suburb of Los Angeles, where he feels safer and is valiantly trying to rebuild his life through tutoring to learn to read, counseling for his drinking problem, and regular daily workouts to restore his physical health. However, relatives have reported that he still suffers pain and various physical impairments from the effects of the brutal beating, including nightmares, constant headaches, dizziness, and problems of concentration and memory loss. He is unable to work and may never again be capable of holding a regular job, although he says he would like to coach a Little League team. He has become increasingly fearful, suspicious, and withdrawn, quite different from the affable and sociable "gentle giant" that he was before the beating. When those four policemen assaulted Rodney King, they not only stripped him of his dignity and humanity but also deprived him forever of his good health, his livelihood, and his peace of mind.

The Police Officers: Poetic Justice

The four white police officers who were defendants in the criminal and civil trials on charges of assaulting Rodney King with excessive force have had their own set of troubles in the past five years.

Sergeant Stacey Koon, the supervising officer at the site of the beating, served twenty-five months of his thirty-month sentence at the Sheridan Federal Correctional Institution near Portland, Oregon, and was released on December 14, 1995, after serving six weeks in a halfway house in Rubidoux, Riverside County. On Thanksgiving Day, November 23, while Koon was visiting his family to celebrate the holiday and his forty-fifth birthday, a disturbed black parolee invaded the house with a gun, captured three hostages, and killed one of them before he was killed by a police sharpshooter. He had apparently been looking for Koon but settled for an innocent bystander. In a strange twist of fate, this bizarre incident mirrored the encounter between Koon and King, with Koon playing the role of the innocent victim who gained the public's sympathy. This was the second time since the trial that Koon had garnered public sympathy; the first time, supporters had raised over $4 million dollars in a fund drive to help finance his legal and family expenses while he was in prison. Cynics noted that this successful drive generated more money for Koon than the $3.8 million awarded to Rodney King in his civil suit against the LAPD. Crime, in some cases, does pay, and justice does not always reap just rewards.

Laurence Powell, the officer who inflicted most of the baton blows on Rodney King, was also released from prison in September 1995, then spent over two months in a halfway house in Orange County until his release in mid December. A hero's welcome had been planned for him by the Legal Affairs Council, which had invited a select group to a dinner at a private club located on the grounds of the Los Angeles Police Academy. The event was canceled only after criticism from the media and pressure from city officials.

Timothy Wind, the rookie who won his case but lost his job with the LAPD was interviewed in January 1996 on CNN about his life since the infamous case. He had been hired in October 1994 as a civilian community service officer in Culver City, after much community controversy, but that job did not provide any stability or security. He admitted that he had not been able to find another regular full-time job since he was acquitted and that his family was in debt. When the reporter told him that Rodney King still wanted an apology from the officers who beat him, he responded that he didn't think he owed King an apology, but he would be happy to sit down with him over a few beers and talk about how the case had changed their lives. After nearly five years, it was clear that Wind was still unwilling or unable to take full responsibility for his participation in the beating of Rodney King, nor was he able to understand the terrible toll it had taken on all of their lives.

Theodore Briseno, the only officer who had publicly acknowledged that his colleagues were out of control in that violent encounter with Rodney King, was also fired in July 1994 after he applied for reinstatement following his acquittal in the civil trial. He was subsequently investigated for perjury for contradicting his testimony in the criminal trial, but he has kept a very low profile since he was terminated from the LAPD.

The Lawyers: Winning and Losing

As for the lawyers who were involved in the Rodney King case, on either side of the aisle, the last five years have proved to be somewhat more variable, with some gaining fame and fortune and others losing status and salaries.

Ira Reiner, the district attorney who planned the prosecution strategy in the 1992 criminal trial against the four police officers, suffered a severe political setback when his deputies lost the case. He was roundly criticized for not appealing the judge's decision to move the trial to Simi Valley, where jurors were predictably more empathic with the police defendants. In the June primary of 1992, only two months after the verdict and the South Central riots, Reiner polled fewer votes than his former deputy, Gil Garcetti, forcing them into a runoff; he subsequently withdrew before the general election and returned to private practice. During the O. J. Simpson trial, he was a regular commentator on local television with expert analysis from the prosecution's perspective. As a former district attorney, Reiner might have found himself critical of several of the strategic decisions made by the prosecutors in the Simpson case and might have experienced a feeling of déjà vu when his successor lost the case, one in a string of high-profile controversial cases mishandled by Garcetti's staff since he replaced Reiner.

Steven D. Clymer, one of the federal prosecutors in the 1993 trial of Koon and Powell on charges of violating Rodney King's civil rights, has joined the faculty of the Cornell University Law School in Ithaca, New York. As a law professor at Cornell, "far above Cayuga's waters," Clymer is far removed from the racial tensions and urban anxieties of metropolitan Los Angeles.

Steven Lerman, Rodney King's lead lawyer, presented a bill to the City of Los Angeles for $1 million plus an additional $3 million for the team of defense lawyers for King's civil suit. In January 1995, Judge John G. Davies reduced the total bill to $1.6 million, disallowing $2.8 million in expenses that included time billed for visiting King in the hospital and appearing on talk shows such as *Oprah* and *Donahue*. After a spate of articles ridiculing the bills, Lerman has disappeared from the headlines.

John Burris, the Oakland, California, defense attorney who successfully represented Rodney King in his civil trial against the City of Los Angeles, has enhanced his reputation and expanded his practice as an aggressive defender of victims of police abuse. During the O. J. Simpson trial, Burris hosted a half-hour talk show, *Legally Speaking*, on Bay Area radio station KDIA and was a frequent commentator on the TV talk show circuit.

The Police Chiefs: Passing the Baton

The tale of the two police chiefs associated with the Rodney King case is an ongoing saga in the annals of the LAPD and the African-American community.

Chief Daryl Gates, who reluctantly retired in June 1992 after the riots in South Central, a month later published his autobiography, *Chief*, promoting his own self-serving spin on the Rodney King beating and the recommendations in the Christopher Commission report. Clearly unenlightened about race relations in Los Angeles and unrepentant about his myopic leadership of the LAPD, Gates could still draw an audience as a local commentator on the O. J. Simpson case from a decidedly pro-prosecution perspective.

Chief Willie Williams, who assumed the leadership of the LAPD in the wake of the Rodney King incident, has a very uneasy relationship with his rank and file, with the police commission, and with Mayor Richard Riordan, the successor to Mayor Tom Bradley. When the police commission in 1994 accused Williams of unethical behavior in accepting free hotel accommodations in Las Vegas, his only defenders were the city council majority, which voted to overturn the police commission's censure. Although the African-American community has expressed overwhelming support for Chief Williams for his outreach efforts to bridge the racial divide between the LAPD and minority groups, they, too, are still waiting for his promised innovations and implementation of community policing. Chief Williams appears to be long on public relations and short on police reforms, but his defenders claim that the "old guard" in the LAPD and the city's political establishment have resisted structural changes and have never given him their full support for radical reforms. Pundits predicted that Willie Williams would not be appointed for a second term as chief of the Los Angeles Police Department.

The Commissions: Resisting Change

The recommendations of the two commissions that investigated the Rodney King beating and the subsequent civil disturbances following the acquittal of the police officers accused of the assault have taken their place on dusty library shelves alongside the McCone report on the Watts riots and the Kerner report on the urban civil disorder in the mid 1960s, all of which produced remarkably consistent conclusions about the need for reforms in policing of minority communities, economic investment in inner cities, and structural and policy changes in nearly all the major social institutions of American society. Most of the recommendations in the Christopher Commission report (July 1991) and the report of the Assembly Special Committee on the Los Angeles Crisis (September 1992) have yet to be adopted or implemented by the LAPD or by the City of Los Angeles, but the chairs of those committees have been able to advance their own professional and political agendas.

Warren Christopher, the chair of the independent commission on the Los Angeles Police Department, an early supporter of candidate Bill Clinton in the 1992 election, was appointed a cochair of

Clinton's presidential transition team and was then appointed secretary of state when Clinton was inaugurated in January 1993. This marked a return to the U.S. State Department, where Christopher had served as deputy secretary of state under President Jimmy Carter, thereby shifting his focus from local conflicts to global conflicts.

Curtis R. Tucker, Jr., the chair of the Assembly Special Committee on the Los Angeles Crisis, has continued his efforts to address the deeper social and economic issues plaguing South Central and its neighboring communities, but progress in attracting economic investment and generating jobs in the area has been slow. Tucker was reelected to the assembly in November 1994 with an overwhelming majority of the vote. However, Tucker, a victim of term limits, ran for a seat in the California State Senate in the March 1996 primary but was defeated by the incumbent, Teresa Hughes.

Rebuild L.A., a nonprofit organization set up after the 1992 riots to promote economic development in the South Central area, has failed to live up to its advance publicity and its great expectations. A survey of the city's riot-damaged property in October 1993 showed that 53 percent had not been rebuilt but that South Central had the lowest rate of rebuilding activity of any affected area in the city. Its first chairman, Peter Ueberroth, the enterprising organizer of the 1984 Los Angeles Olympics, found that organizing the community for social and racial betterment was a much more daunting and less rewarding task than organizing it for sports and profit. After one year, Ueberroth resigned and was replaced by his cochair, Bernard Kinsey, a black business executive, whose tenure lasted two more years.

THE AFTERMATH OF THE O. J. SIMPSON CASE

March 12, 1996, marked twenty-one months since the murders of Nicole Brown Simpson and Ronald Goldman, yet only five months had elapsed since O. J. Simpson had been acquitted of the crime. In those few short months since the trial had ended, the lives of all who had played principal roles in the drama had been irrevocably altered.

Before O. J.'s acquittal in the criminal trial, the Brown family, the Goldman family, and Ron Goldman's biological mother, Sharon Rufo, had filed civil suits against Simpson for the wrongful death of Nicole and Ron. The civil case, filed in the Santa Monica Superior Court with Judge Alan Haber presiding, began with the taking of depositions on December 14, 1995, with lawyers on both sides arguing about whether the trial would be open to the press, whether O. J. would have to reveal his complete financial holdings, and whether the plaintiffs could collect punitive damages if Simpson were to be convicted of the charges. Then the pretrial depositions began.

O. J. began his deposition on January 23, 1996, under very tight security; his testimony lasted ten days, with several interruptions due to his lawyer's schedule, and was completed on February 29. The transcripts released from the hearings suggest that he contradicted his lawyers' earlier statements on several crucial points in his alibi for the night of June 12 at the approximate time of the murders. He also denied that he had ever physically abused Nicole, even on the occasion of the infamous 911 call on early New Year's morning, January 1, 1989. Nicole's diary told a different story, but that was considered only "hearsay" evidence.

Brian "Kato" Kaelin, the prosecution's spacy and incoherent witness in the criminal trial, returned to the stand to give his deposition for the civil trial on February 14, 1996, but this time he sang a different tune. He revealed that Nicole had told him she was afraid that O. J. would kill her "with scissors" and that "he would get away with it because he was O. J. Simpson." He also testified that O. J. had in fact been very angry with Nicole after the concert on June 12, particularly incensed that she had excluded him from the family dinner party. Kaelin, whose fifteen minutes of posttrial fame had sputtered out in a series of brief and vapid celebrity cameos as a talk show host and male model, was surprisingly collected and coherent.

Robert Baker, O. J.'s new and very establishment lawyer for the civil trial, held a brief conference on February 28 to denounce Kaelin's testimony as untrue and to suggest that Kaelin might even have been present at the murder scene. Further, Baker decried the "trial by media," reasserting that his client had been acquitted of all charges against him and was entitled to be treated like any other American citizen. O. J., the aggrieved defendant, stood by silently and did not utter a word in his own defense.

On February 29, the civil trial, originally scheduled for April 2, was postponed until September 9 due to the number of depositions still to be completed. O. J.'s lawyers were hoping fervently that he would maintain a lower profile, and even his strongest supporters were pleading publicly that he should keep his mouth shut lest he choke on both feet.

The Media: Continuing Coverage

The media pursued O. J. after his acquittal, continuing to feed the insatiable thirst of the American public for O. J. news and views. They avidly reported on his reunion with his children (the *Star* was alleged to have paid a huge fee for the exclusive photos), his golf trip to Florida (his fans greeted him warmly), and his breakup with model Paula Barbieri (her father was relieved). But O. J. found an even more direct route to feed the O. J. mania of his addicted public—he finally decided to tell his side of the story on the talk shows, on video, wherever he could find a listening audience.

O. J. made a video with his version of events on June 12 (*O. J. Simpson: The Interview*), but as soon as he announced the toll-free telephone order number, militant women's groups and angry protesters blocked access to the number to prevent sales. Ever resourceful, O. J. then called in to a series of radio and television talk shows (including *Larry King Live*) to promote his video and proclaim his innocence. O. J.'s frequent calls sometimes verged on hysteria, suggesting a manic search for acceptance and absolution from the public. The $29.95 video, after several delays, was finally released on February 16, 1996, to the media and to the waiting fans; it had no earth-shaking revelations and got less than ecstatic reviews.

On January 24, 1996, O. J. had an hourlong interview with Ed Gordon on the Black Entertainment Network, his first live formal interview following his acquittal. Under Gordon's aggressive questioning, O. J. challenged Marcia Clark to a debate, reaffirmed his right to make a living, and essentially told his critics to buzz off. Despite his lawyer's urging to keep a low profile and refuse all interviews while the civil trial was pending, O. J. was determined to repair his image. Instead of improving his image, the interview only raised more questions about his alibi on the night of the murders and displayed his incredible arrogance and insensitivity to the public's anger toward him. The more O. J. talked, the more he seemed to be unraveling in a desperate attempt to restore his reputation and make himself salable again. But as the months passed, no one seemed very interested in buying what O. J.—aging athlete, second-rate movie actor, and compromised celebrity—had to sell.

The Victims' Families: Seeking Closure

The victims' family members continued to seek justice for Nicole and Ron inside and outside of the courts. They lost the criminal case, but they mounted a fierce campaign to win the civil case and to destroy O. J. Simpson's credibility and career possibilities.

Denise Brown, Nicole's older sister, had found a new and more dignified role as a crusader for improved funding of battered women's programs. She was president of a foundation to increase awareness of domestic violence, but the organization had run into some financial difficulties. Denise was still living at home with her parents, her two sisters, her son, and O. J.'s two youngest children. There were no further reports about her relationship with Tony Fiato, the Mafia mobster whose testimony had been crucial in undermining the prosecution's case against O. J. Simpson, the man accused of murdering her sister.

Fred Goldman, Ron's aggrieved father, continued his verbal assaults on O. J. Simpson at every opportunity. He confronted O. J. at the deposition, held press conferences to impugn O. J.'s integrity, and could barely suppress his rage at O. J.'s freedom. His quest for justice for his murdered son had turned into a thirst for revenge against the young man's presumed killer.

The Witnesses: Searching for Privacy

The witnesses and near-witnesses also maintained their aura of intrigue for the O. J. aficionados. Some had gained unwelcome notoriety at the expense of their privacy, while others had shunned privacy to exploit their welcome notoriety.

Mark Fuhrman, whose name had become synonymous with police misconduct, had retired from the LAPD in August 1995, this time with his supervisor's blessing. He had moved with his wife and two young children to Sandpoint, Idaho, a community nestled in the heart of militia country. Soon after arriving in Sandpoint, Fuhrman wrote a letter to the local newspaper, the *Sandpoint Bee*, reassuring the community that "I am no threat to this community. My only goals are to raise my family with as little fanfare as possible." The man who had once graduated second in his class at the police academy, then plunged to the bottom of his department, was studying to be an electrician's helper in rural Idaho.

On March 1, federal, state, and local officials who were investigating Fuhrman's claims of involvement in acts of police brutality and misconduct announced that they had found little evidence of these illegal activities after a fairly exhaustive review of police records and interviews with his colleagues. In January 1995, the Los Angeles public defender's office had concluded, after a review of thirty-five cases for which Mark Fuhrman had been the lead investigating officer since 1988, that there were almost no complaints lodged against him, not even a single charge of racial misconduct or falsifying evidence. However, this report does not quite jibe with an earlier report that at least six people had complained about being threatened or beaten by Fuhrman between 1984 and 1990 when he worked at the West Los Angeles Division of the LAPD. Could it be that Officer Fuhrman was simply a consummate liar who lived in his own private fantasyland, as suggested by some of his friends and his former wife, or could it be another cover-up orchestrated to protect the LAPD from an avalanche of lawsuits?

Faye Resnick, who gave her deposition in the civil trial but was never called in the criminal trial, had parlayed her instant notoriety into two books about her intimate friendship with Nicole Simpson, frequent stints on talk shows, and an apartment in New York City. In touting her second book, *Shattered: In the Eye of the Storm*, on *Larry King Live* in late February, Resnick accused Simpson of threatening her and expressed fears that he would harm her and get away with it "just as he did with Nicole and Ron." O. J. wasted no time in responding to her dramatic charges, labeling her a liar, a drug addict, and an exploiter of her dead friend's memory. Perhaps it was a case of the pot calling the kettle black; perhaps not.

Susan Forward, the high-profile clinical social worker who had treated Nicole for spousal abuse and had warned her to cut all ties with O. J. Simpson months before Nicole was murdered, was back in the news in late February. Although her license had been suspended in November 1995 for violating professional ethics by revealing Nicole's therapy record, her claim that Nicole was increasingly fearful of O. J.'s rage was supported by the revelation that another therapist had seen Nicole and Ron Goldman concerning the same issue just a few days before they were killed. Had they been seen together, and if so, what were the implications of such a relationship? Was this just another unconfirmed rumor floated by the victims' families, or was this another example of prosecutorial incompetence, another failure to track down essential incriminating evidence against O. J. Simpson?

The Prosecutors: Reluctant Heroes

The prosecutors, who lost the battle but won the war, had suddenly and unexpectedly become celebrities, pursued by talk show hosts and literary agents and praised by feminist groups and law-and-order politicians.

Gil Garcetti, the district attorney who orchestrated the prosecution team's losing strategy in the Simpson case, must have wondered what it would take to obtain a jury conviction in Los Angeles. Since he had replaced Ira Reiner in 1992, Garcetti's office had lost several high-profile prosecution-friendly cases, such as the first trial of the Menendez brothers for the murder of their parents. The brothers were retried and were found guilty of first-degree murder, a verdict announced in March 1996 just a week before the California primary and probably too late to affect the outcome of the district attorney's race.

In February 1996, Garcetti's prosecutors lost another case with the mistrial of rapper Calvin Broadus (also known as Snoop Doggy Dogg) and his former bodyguard on charges of manslaughter in the 1993 shooting of an Ethiopian gang member in Los Angeles. Despite these losses, Garcetti, dubbed the "million-dollar man" for his success in raising campaign funds, was considered the Teflon candidate in the March 26 California primary election, where he was opposed by five challengers, three of whom were colleagues and subordinates in his office. Unfortunately, his losses canceled out his luck, and he won less than 51 percent of the vote, so he will face a runoff with John Lynch, one of his deputies, in the November election. Garcetti might well have heeded the famous advice of baseball player Satchell Paige: "Don't look back—they might be gaining on you."

Marcia Clark, lead prosecutor and beleaguered mother, quickly became a heroine to the advocates for battered women, but she preferred the luncheon circuit to the talk show circuit. After the trial was over, she negotiated a $4.2 million contract with Viking Penguin for a book about the case, winning the early contest for the most impressive deal among the many O. J. tell-all book proposals. In early March, Clark was still on an extended leave from the district attorney's office, writing her book, ensconced in the serene surroundings of her agent's Hollywood home.

Christopher Darden, the lone black prosecutor who seemed so dejected and bitter at O. J.'s acquittal, also took an extended leave from the DA's office and announced that he had become disillusioned with the practice of law. In November 1995, he launched a lecture series at Town Hall in New York City, but his low-key cerebral style did not appeal to Manhattan audiences, and the series was canceled after one lecture. Not to be outsmarted by his friend and colleague, Darden negotiated a book contract for $1.3 million with HarperCollins and a movie contract to chronicle his life story. Shortly after he accepted a position as a full-time professor at Southwestern Law School in Los Angeles, he was honored with an award from major organizations in the African-American community at a reception attended by his role model and rival, Johnnie Cochran. Responding to the fulsome praise from prominent black leaders, some of whom had heaped scorn on him for prosecuting O. J. Simpson, Darden declared, "It is my duty to accept this award, just as it was my duty to prosecute O. J. Simpson." Darden proved once again that he was a master of understatement, just barely masking his ambivalence about this belated recognition from his own community. Darden's book, *In Contempt,* was published in February 1996, and this time he proved to be much sought after for all the major talk shows, shrewdly using the media to even old scores.

The Defense Lawyers: A Pyrrhic Victory

The defense attorneys had parlayed their dramatic victory into an even higher plane of celebrityhood. But the stresses and strains of suppressing their individual personalities for over a year of uneasy collaboration had finally surfaced at the end of the trial, ironically just at the moment of their unexpected triumph. The Dream Team had disintegrated into a nightmare of bruised egos, fractured friendships, and damaged reputations.

Johnnie L. Cochran, Jr., the charismatic team leader, had quickly leveraged his media exposure into a national reputation as a formidable advocate for difficult defendants. He was hired before the trial was over by the families of four survivors of the Oklahoma City bombing to sue the company that provided the fertilizer used to make the bomb that destroyed the federal building. Lionized by the black community and profiled in magazine cover stories as "the most celebrated criminal defense attorney" in the nation after his impressive victory, Cochran signed a lucrative $4.2 million book contract with Random House for his autobiography, *My Journey to Justice,* matching Marcia Clark's generous deal.

Robert L. Shapiro, the disgruntled team organizer, had just as quickly damaged his own credibility and impugned his professional integrity by publicly distancing himself from their successful defense of O. J. Simpson. The man who passed out fortune cookies ridiculing Dennis Fung, then donned the mantle of righteousness to criticize Johnnie Cochran for "playing the race card," closed down his solo practice to join a Century City entertainment law firm as a senior partner. Shapiro's rumored book deal for $1.5 million with Warner Books seemed to reflect his devalued status as a member of the Dream Team, but he was a popular guest on the talk show circuit after his book, *The Search for Justice,* was published at the end of March 1996.

F. Lee Bailey, the most flamboyant member of the team, found his career briefly resuscitated after his bombastic cross-examination of Detective Mark Fuhrman turned out to be one of the key weapons in the defense's arsenal against racism and misconduct in the LAPD. But by February 1996, Bailey had himself become a defendant in a complicated Florida case, sued by the U.S. government for misappropriating assets of Claude Duboc, a French-American client, who had pleaded guilty to charges of drug conspiracy and money laundering. Federal prosecutors claimed that the government had allowed Bailey to keep Duboc's forfeited stock, worth over $20 million, in order to maintain his client's homes and other property in France. Apparently, Bailey had taken nearly $3 million of the money as "fees" and contested the government's claim about the amount owed. By early March, Bailey had been charged with contempt of court for failing to return the full amount of Duboc's stock, including its quadrupled increase in value, and on March 6, he was put into handcuffs and led off to the federal detention center in Tallahassee, where he would be imprisoned for six months or until he could comply with the judge's order. On April 19, forty-four days after he was incarcerated, Bailey was released after turning over $16 million worth of stock and promising to pay an additional $700,000 to the federal government within a year. The ultimate irony is that Robert Shapiro, his former friend and colleague, was one of the principal witnesses against him. There's truth to the saying, "What goes around comes around."

Alan Dershowitz, the most voluble member of the team, who remained on his lofty academic perch at Harvard University Law School, was sighted frequently on the most highly rated talk shows, vigorously attacking all who dared to question the verdict or challenge the defense. A prolific author and tireless advocate of the American adversarial system of justice, Dershowitz was predictably the first of the defense team to complete a book on the case, *Reasonable Doubts: The O. J. Simpson Case and the Criminal Justice System*, published in February 1996.

Barry Scheck and Peter Neufeld, the DNA specialists on the team, returned to their positions as codirectors of the Innocence Project legal clinic at the Cardozo School of Law at Yeshiva University in New York City. Admired by some and annoyed by others for their pugnacious and persistent "New York style" of interrogating witnesses, Scheck and Neufeld were allegedly developing a pilot project for a television drama series based on their use of DNA genetic testing to exonerate eight inmates in serious capital cases of rape and murder convictions. Jurors revealed that Scheck had been one of their favorite lawyers, undoubtedly for his ability to keep them awake and attentive throughout the months of numbing testimony.

The Jurors: Seeking Vindication

The jurors, who had endured weeks of vilification in the mass media, finally found the courage to speak up in their own defense. Before the trial was over, several of the dismissed jurors had shared their opinions with the press, whetting the public's appetite for insider gossip about the trial and personal insights about the case. Two of the enterprising male jurors turned their rejection into rewards by publishing the first quickie books about the trial: Michael Knox, a forty-six-year-old black delivery man, wrote *The Private Diary of an O. J. Juror*, and Tracy Kennedy, a biracial Native American–white railroad employee, wrote *Mistrial of the Century*, both published in 1995 while the trial was still in progress. After a flurry of appearances to promote their books, their stars quickly faded.

In December 1995, Johnnie Cochran threw a lavish Christmas party for the jury at a downtown hotel in Los Angeles. O. J. sent his greetings via a videotape featuring himself and his four children. The two white jurors did not attend.

Amanda Cooley, the forewoman of the jury, and two of her black female fellow jurors, told their side of the story in a revealing book, *Madame Foreman: A Rush to Judgment?* published in November 1995. While they steadfastly stood by their verdict in the criminal case, in an interview on the NBC-TV *Dateline* program on January 16, 1996, two of the three authors (including Cooley) suggested that they would probably cast a "guilty" vote in the pending civil case against O. J. Simpson, given the additional information they had learned about incriminating evidence never introduced at the murder trial.

Brenda Moran, the most outspoken juror immediately following the verdict, had enjoyed her brief turn in the spotlight and was presumably working on her own book, tentatively titled *Parallel*

Universe: Inside the Simpson Jurors, which will reveal the racial turmoil and tensions in the jury.

Tracy Hampton, the youngest black juror, who had to be rushed to the hospital on a stretcher the day after she was dismissed from the jury on May 1, 1995, made a remarkable recovery from her depression by the end of the year. In late January, Hampton, a former flight attendant, was interviewed on one of the TV talk shows, where she revealed that she had posed for *Playboy* in an attempt to enhance her movie career. The photos were published in the March 1996 issue of *Playboy*. Hampton also announced that had she remained on the jury, she would have cast a "guilty" vote against O. J. Simpson. It was not clear if she thought that this announcement might also "enhance her career."

The Media: Manipulating the Message

The media, with their voracious appetite for news about the O. J. Simpson case, could never seem to be satiated. The case had launched whole new careers or enhanced old ones for several of the legal commentators who had spent endless hours analyzing the case and critiquing the lawyers.

Greta van Susteren and Roger Cossack, who had been regular commentators on CNN for the defense and prosecution viewpoints during the trial, were now cohosts of *Burden of Proof*, a daily CNN morning show on legal issues and current controversial cases. They continued their attachment to the Simpson case with frequent follow-ups, including a long call from O. J. on February 15, 1996, in which he insisted that he had never physically abused Nicole, promoting his videotaped version of his alibi, and proclaiming his innocence of the crime.

Larry King, the true ruler of the late-night talk shows, also maintained his interest in the case, featuring one session with the losing prosecutors to present their case without any challenge from the defense. King also showcased authors promoting their many books about the case, including Faye Resnick and Alan Dershowitz, balancing the claims of the prosecution and the defense versions of the case. King had also received a lengthy and unscripted call from O. J. Simpson on October 4, 1995, his first full day of freedom, expressing his anger at the many "misrepresentations" of the trial evidence. O. J. wasted no time and ruled out no ally in his frantic efforts to rehabilitate himself and resume his privileged life as a celebrity.

Tammy Bruce, the head of the Los Angeles chapter of the National Organization for Women and host of a weekend talk show on KFI-AM radio, had proved to be particularly hostile in her vitriolic attacks on O. J. Simpson's acquittal, loudly proclaiming that her focus on domestic violence was a "needed break from all that talk of racism." In early January, her defiant rhetoric resulted in her censure by the national board of directors of NOW for "racially insensitive comments."

Five months after the verdict, the inflammatory issues of race and sex were still invoked as fighting words in the press whenever the Simpson case was discussed, revealing the deep schisms that the case had exposed and that were ever present beneath the surface of American society.

THE CRIMINAL JUSTICE SYSTEM: COLOR-CODED OR COLOR-BLIND?

The impact of the Rodney King case and the O. J. Simpson case was still reverberating on the Los Angeles Police Department and the Los Angeles County criminal justice system in predictable and unpredictable ways. The embattled LAPD had made very few significant changes since the beating of Rodney King on March 3, 1991, but there had been signs of a backlash against the black community, a trend that seemed to accelerate after the acquittal of O. J. Simpson.

In September 1995, Chief Willie Williams announced the suspension of two eighteen-year veterans of the LAPD for falsifying evidence in a murder case. Detectives Andrew Teague and Charles

Markel had conspired to forge signatures on reports that identified two black suspects in a murder case, then lied about their deception in court. Prosecutors were forced to drop the murder charge against both suspects and feared that at least one hundred other felony cases investigated by these two officers were in jeopardy. Detective Teague, the actual forger, was one of the forty-four "problem officers" on the police force identified in the 1991 Christopher Commission report, thirty-three of whom were still active members of the LAPD more than four years later.

In November 1995, Sergeant Ed Kirste, a twenty-six-year veteran of the Los Angeles County Sheriff's Department, founded a new group called the Association of White Male Peace Officers, with a stated mission to oppose affirmative action in law enforcement hirings, promotions, and assignments. Kirste was following right along in the footsteps of Detective Mark Fuhrman, who had founded the group Men Against Women in the West Los Angeles Division of the LAPD in the 1980s.

In November 1995, six blacks filed a suit against the City of Beverly Hills, the mayor, and the police chief for ignoring repeated complaints against the local police force for targeting and harassing African-American males between the ages of thirteen and thirty-five for "illegal investigative stops" in the City of the Stars.

In February 1996, the U.S. Supreme Court held a hearing on an appeal of a ruling by the Ninth Circuit Court of Appeals, which upheld the decision of a Los Angeles federal district judge to dismiss indictments against five black defendants on charges of conspiring to distribute crack. When the public defender's office submitted its study suggesting selective prosecution of black defendants in Los Angeles, the judge ordered federal prosecutors to justify this pattern of overrepresentation of blacks for prosecution, but the prosecutors refused to divulge these data. Nonetheless, a recent study of prosecutions for crack in Los Angeles County showed that nearly 90 percent of the defendants in federal cases were black, compared to only about half of the defendants in state cases. Since the 1993 National

Household Survey on Drug Abuse reported that 46 percent of all crack users were white, something is clearly wrong with the federal prosecution statistics in Los Angeles County.

The prosecutions for crack in Los Angeles simply mirror the racial disparities in federal sentencing, which mandates a minimum five-year prison sentence for possessing five grams of crack cocaine (used mostly by blacks) versus five hundred grams of powdered cocaine (used mostly by whites). In 1996, the U.S. Congress rejected a recommendation that would have removed this glaring inequity, which has resulted in harsher penalties and longer prison sentences for small-time black offenders while major white dealers of powdered cocaine are charged with misdemeanors in California and the rest of the nation.

In February 1996, the Center on Juvenile and Criminal Justice in San Francisco issued a report showing that nearly 40 percent of black males aged twenty to twenty-nine in California were involved in the criminal justice system—in prison, on probation, or on parole—a rate nearly eight times higher than for white males. The report dramatically documents the racial inequities in California's criminal justice system, where white males are given preferential treatment at almost every stage of the process, from their lower rate of drug arrests to their higher rate of obtaining reduced charges as first offenders. The report notes that in Los Angeles, black male offenders are seventeen times more likely than whites to be charged under the new California "three strikes" law. The authors offer a particularly relevant perspective on these discouraging statistics: "There have been several watershed events in race relations in America emanating from California. From the uprising following the decision in the Rodney King case, to the polls showing a sharp racial division in public opinion on the guilt or innocence of O. J. Simpson, the already broad chasm between blacks and whites over the fairness of the criminal justice system is widening."

On April 1, the nation watched another videotape of two sheriff's deputies, this time from Riverside County, wield their batons like baseball bats on two defenseless Mexican nationals, part of a group of as many as nineteen illegal aliens in a van chased for speeding on a Los Angeles County freeway. With the specter of Rodney King hovering over the familiar scene, it was tragically clear that this was not an April Fool's Day prank or an "aberration" by "a few bad apples" but yet another example of the color of justice, Southern California style.

On June 13, 1996, in a unanimous decision, the Supreme Court overruled the Ninth Circuit Court of Appeals, finding that Judge Davies had properly taken into account Rodney King's own misconduct in reducing the sentences of Koon and Powell. In ordering the Circuit Court to return the case to the District Court for a resentencing hearing, the Supreme Court strongly endorsed judicial discretion and further legitimized the victimization of Rodney King.

In the southwest corner of America at the end of the twentieth century, justice is not color-blind; it is color-coded.

The spirits of the *pobladores* who founded Los Angeles in 1781 must be very troubled and very discouraged as they witness the resurgent racial tensions, the chronic cultural conflicts, and the persistent economic inequalities plaguing their City of the Angels. After two centuries of living together in this city, the descendants of the *pobladores*—the Mexicans, the blacks, the Indians, the mestizos, and the whites—have still not learned how to get along with one another or with the newer settlers streaming in from Asia, Africa, South America, Europe, the Middle East, and the Caribbean, all seeking to fulfill their own dreams for a better life. And their leaders have still not learned that a color-coded system of justice is a system that will corrupt and contaminate all the institutions of the society that it is pledged to protect and serve.

Appendix A

Research Note

The five chapters in Part One of this book are based on a research project to investigate the impact of the Rodney King police brutality case and the subsequent civil disturbances on African-Americans between the ages of fifteen and thirty in South Central Los Angeles. The study, conducted by the author over a fifteen-month period in 1993 and 1994, focused on the attitudes and experiences of these youth and young adults in four major institutional systems: education, employment, health care, and criminal justice. The study used a combined qualitative-quantitative research design involving interviews with a diverse group of African-American young people and community leaders, visits to community institutions and social agencies, and participation in a range of community activities.

The sample of participants was recruited by first contacting established African-American community leaders and institutions in South Central Los Angeles, including churches, schools, youth development organizations, social agencies, job-training programs, and gang prevention programs, yielding a total of 175 young African-Americans interviewed in seventeen focus groups and thirty-two in individual interviews. In addition, sixty-seven leaders of organizations and programs serving the South Central community were interviewed, fifty-seven of them black. Focus group and individual interviews were semistructured and lasted from one and one-half to two and one-half hours. In addition, we conducted one six-hour session with an eighteenth focus group of twelve black professional adults who had been teenagers during the Watts riots of 1965 and subsequently became alumni of California State University, Northridge. All interviews were tape-recorded and transcribed.

Demographic information about the population in South Central and data on employment, education, health care, and crime were obtained, respectively, from census reports, the State of California Economic Development Department, the Los Angeles Unified School District, the Los Angeles County Health Department, and the Los Angeles Police Department. Additional sources of information on specific social indicators for the South Central area were obtained from social agencies, nonprofit community groups, civil rights organizations, and scholarly publications.

The first five chapters of this book incorporate findings from that study, with a particular emphasis on the participants' attitudes and experiences with the police and the criminal justice system. Quotes from the interviews with the leaders and the young adults are also included in later chapters in the book where they are relevant.

For the chapters in Part Two, which deal with the O. J. Simpson case and its aftermath, contemporaneous sources were used for most of the information. These sources included three daily newspapers, two weekly newsmagazines, and dozens of monthly magazines and other publications containing feature articles on the trial and the major personalities and issues involved in the case. In addition to extensive print media sources, I watched or videotaped daily summaries of the trial, television programs, and talk shows about the case and listened to radio talk shows and commentaries on the case as I commuted to work several times per week. I also read several books about the case that were published while I was writing this manuscript, as well as other biographical books and profiles about Simpson's early life and football career. Considering that the reports in different newspapers and magazines were frequently incomplete or contradictory, I was fortunately able to check the accuracy of the daily trial reports through the actual transcripts available on the Internet through the Netscape computer web site. This research reinforced my skepticism about the excesses and deficits of an increasingly monopolistic press.

From July through September 1995, as the trial entered its final phase, I conducted a series of face-to-face and telephone interviews with twelve of the original Los Angeles leaders who participated in my Rodney King study and twelve African-American adults in the San Francisco Bay Area, where Simpson had grown up and achieved his early fame as a high school and college athlete. In addition to these twenty-four adults, ranging in age from twenty-five to sixty-eight, I conducted informal interviews with approximately forty people at social gatherings, political events, and professional conferences in Los Angeles, San Francisco, Oakland, and Berkeley. The brief interview focused on the person's attitudes about Simpson before and after his arrest, opinions about his knowledge of or involvement in the crime, opinions about the strengths and weaknesses of the prosecution and defense cases, and predictions about the verdict in the case. Immediately after the verdict, during the week of October 3–10, I contacted sixteen of the original twenty-four interviewees to ascertain their reaction to Simpson's acquittal. Some of these comments are incorporated in the chapters on the Simpson trial and its aftermath to parallel the comments by the participants in the original study about the trial of Rodney King's assailants and the South Central civil disorder.

Although most of the leaders gave their consent to be identified and quoted in this book, a few preferred to offer their comments anonymously. I am indebted to them all, named and unnamed, for their generous participation in this project, as their observations and opinions have contributed immensely to my understanding of and insights into both of these significant cases.

Both phases of this research were supported by generous grants from the Zellerbach Family Fund of San Francisco. I am grateful to this foundation for its continuing encouragement and support of my efforts to articulate the alienation and aspirations of urban minority youth with the ultimate aim of increasing the understanding and empathy of those who have the resources to improve their lives.

Appendix B

People Interviewed

The following people from the African-American, Hispanic, Korean, and white communities were interviewed during the first phase of this study from September 1993 to September 1994. Although only twenty-seven are quoted in the text, I am indebted to all of them for their valuable information, opinions, and insights about the impact of the Rodney King beating, the acquittal of his police assailants, and the subsequent civil disturbances on the City of Los Angeles, especially on the multiethnic community of South Central Los Angeles.

Note that the participants are listed with their organizational or professional affiliations at the time they were interviewed. As of October 1995, several were no longer in these positions and could not be located for follow-up interviews.

Sandra Bankhead
Program Coordinator
El Nido Family Centers

Stacy Banks
Social Worker
El Nido Family Centers

John Bryant
President and CEO
Operation Hope

Duane B. Bremond
Public Relations Director
AIDS Project/Los Angeles

All private individuals identified by name have granted me authorization to do so; all other individuals have been disguised, identified in the text only with arbitrary initials entirely unrelated to their true identities.

Janet Clark
Administrator
Maxine Waters Employment Preparation Center

Kenneth Collins
Director of Communications
Brotherhood Crusade

Joycelyn M. Crumpton
Assistant Director
Center on Child Welfare
University of California, Los Angeles

Lou Dantzler
Administrator
Challenger Boys and Girls Club

Jimmy Dobson
Owner-Manager
Banjo's Yogurt Deli

Joseph Duff
President, Los Angeles Chapter
National Association for the Advancement of Colored People

Jarvis Emerson
Director, Teen Clinic Services
Watts Health Foundation

John Finn
Vice Principal
Daniel Murphy High School

Rev. Kenneth Flowers
Senior Pastor
Messiah Baptist Church

Sandra Guine
Social Worker
Los Angeles Department of Health

Joseph R. Hicks
Executive Director
Southern Christian Leadership Conference

Arlene Holt
Area Director, International Union
American Federation of State, County and Municipal Employees Union

Boyd James, M.D.
Department of Psychiatry
Charles Drew University of Medicine and Science

Ronald Johnson
Executive Director
National Family Life and Education Center

Herbert A. Jones
Director, Black Education Commission
Los Angeles Unified School District

Paul Jones
Executive Director
Community Youth Gang Services

Joseph Keys
Administrator
Hubert Humphrey Health Center

Bong Hwan Kim
Executive Director
Korean-American Youth and Community Services

Meehee Kim
Executive Director
Korean Grocers Victims
Association

Mikyong Kim-Goh, Ph.D.
Assistant Professor of Social Work
California State University,
Northridge

Bernard Kinsey
Executive Director
Rebuild L.A.

Donzella Lee
Administrator
Watts Health Foundation

Monica Lozano
Editor, *La Opinión*

John W. Mack
President
Los Angeles Urban League

George Mallory
Attorney-at-Law

Rev. Eugene H. Marzette
Interim Pastor
Trinity Baptist Church

Everetta Marzette
Teacher
Dorsey High School

Lorenzo Merritt
Executive Director
Project Heavy West

Lillian Mobley
Executive Director
South Central Multipurpose
Senior Citizens Center

Hon. H. Randolph Moore
Supervising Judge
Kenyon Juvenile Justice
Center

Rev. Cecil L. Murray
Senior Pastor
First African Methodist
Episcopal Church

Angela Oh
Attorney-at-Law

Nelson Offley
Administrator
Los Angeles County Probation
Department

Bernard C. Parks
Assistant Chief
Los Angeles Police Department

Gale L. Pauley, Ph.D.
Director
Youth Intervention Alternative
School

Juanita Pinion
Retired Probation Officer
Los Angeles County Probation
Department

Julio Ramirez
Adminsitrative Assistant
Los Angeles Public Defender's
Office

Roger Reed
Actor

Mark Ridley-Thomas
Council Member, Eighth
District
Los Angeles City Council

Leonard Robinette
Chair, Board of Trustees
Watts Labor Community Action Committee

Norman Rouillier
Captain, Southwest Division
Los Angeles Police Department

William Ruffin
Executive Director
Black Employees Association

Kathy Sanders-Phillips, Ph.D.
Psychologist
Charles Drew University of Medicine and Science

Glen Scott
Deputy Director
Community Youth Sports and Arts Foundation

Dennis Schatzman
Journalist
Los Angeles Sentinel

Brenda Schockley
Executive Director
Community Build

William Shearer
President
East-West Broadcasting Company

Tavis Smiley
Radio Show Host
KABC-AM, Los Angeles

Barbara Solomon
Dean of the Graduate School
University of Southern California

Gayle Pollard Terry
Journalist
Los Angeles Times

James Thomas
Director of Community Relations
West Angeles Church of Christ

Reed Tuckson, M.D.
President
Charles Drew University of Medicine and Science

Alice Walker Duff
Executive Director
Crystal Stairs Agency

Rita M. Walters
Council Member, Ninth District
Los Angeles City Council

Gary Watson
Attorney-at-Law

Martha Watson
Social Worker
Kaiser-Watts Counseling Center

Jerelene Wells, Ph.D.
Principal
Dorsey High School

Mark Whitlock
Executive Director
FAME Renaissance

Linda Williams
Director, Milken Training Center
Los Angeles Urban League

Medria Williams, Ph.D.
Psychologist, Teen Health Clinic
Jordan High School

Rev. Robert Wilkins
Executive Director
Weingart Urban YMCA

Jerry C. Yu
Executive Director
Korean-American Coalition

Arturo Ybarra
Administrator
Watts-Century Latino Organization

Notes

Prologue

Pp. xix–xx: This account of the history of the founding of Los Angeles is taken from three major sources: Antonio Rios-Bustamante and Pedro Castillo, *An Illustrated History of Mexican Los Angeles, 1781–1985* (Los Angeles: Chicano Studies Research Center, University of California, 1986); James M. Quinn, *A History of California and an Extended History of Los Angeles and Environs*, Vol. 1 (Los Angeles: Cole-Holmquist Press, 1915); and William W. Robinson, *Los Angeles from the Days of the Pueblo* (Los Angeles: California Historical Society, 1981). There is a controversy among historians over the exact number of settlers who founded the city from the expedition who had traveled by boat across the Gulf of California, then by land to arrive at the Porciuncula River (now the Los Angeles River) on September 4, 1781. But the consensus of the experts is that there were forty-four in that first group of *pobladores*, eleven families consisting of twenty-three adults and twenty-one children. The group reflected the ethnic diversity of Sonora and Sinaloa, the two Mexican towns from which they were recruited; thus the adults included ten blacks and mulattos, eight Indians, three mestizos (mixed Indian and Spanish or Indian and mulatto), and only two Spanish (only one of whom was actually born in Spain). Of the twenty-one children in the group, nineteen were racially mixed and two were Indians.

However, in 1782, three of the founding families left the small settlement, leaving a total of eight families with thirty-two members who would be recorded as the official charter members of the City of Los Angeles. Six of these remaining adults and twelve of their children, over half of the group, were black or mulatto.

Pp. xix–xx: Two quotes are from Andrew F. Rolle in *California: A History*, 3rd ed. (Arlington Heights, Illinois: AHM Publishing Corporation, 1980), p. 77.

Chapter One

P. 3: Quote is from the *Report of the National Advisory Commission on Civil Disorders* (Washington, D.C.: U.S. Government Printing Office, 1968). Otto Kerner, governor of Illinois, served as the commission's chairman at the time, so the report is often referred to as the Kerner Report.

P. 4: The waves of migrants and immigrants to Los Angeles are described in many accounts by social historians, including Carey McWilliams, *Southern California Country: Island on the Land* (New York: Duell, Sloan, & Pierce, 1946); James Gregory, *American Exodus: The Dust Bowl Migration and Okie Culture in California* (New York: Oxford University Press, 1989); Robert Fogelson, *The Fragmented Metropolis: Los Angeles, 1850–1930* (Cambridge, Mass.: Harvard University Press, 1967); and John Modell, *The Economics and Politics of Racial Accommodation: The Japanese of Los Angeles, 1900–1942* (Urbana: University of Illinois Press, 1977).

Pp. 5–6: Quote is from W.E.B. DuBois in the catalogue *Black Angelenos: The Afro-American in Los Angeles, 1850–1950* (Los Angeles: California Afro-American Museum Foundation, 1988).

P. 6: The phrase "Golden Era" and the population statistics are from *ibid.*, pp. 20–29.

P. 6: Quote is from *ibid.*, p. 36.

P. 7: The ghettoization of the black community in Los Angeles before and during World War II is well documented in books by Douglas A. Glasgow, *The Black Underclass: Poverty, Unemployment, and Entrapment of Ghetto Youth* (San Francisco: Jossey-Bass, 1980), and Gerald Horne, *Fire This Time: The Watts Uprising and the 1960s* (Charlottesville: University Press of Virginia, 1995).

P. 7: The tenure of Chief James Davis is described in a book by Jerome H. Skolnick and James J. Fyfe, *Above the Law: Police and the Excessive Use of Force* (New York: Free Press, 1993).

P. 7: The positive impact of President Roosevelt's 1941 Executive Order 8802 on June 25, 1941, outlawing discrimination in companies with government contracts is described in John Hope Franklin, *From Slavery to Freedom: A History of Negro Americans*, 5th ed. (New York: McGraw-Hill, 1979).

P. 8: Quote from interview with L. V., a black female elementary school teacher in Los Angeles, conducted on May 15, 1994.

P. 9: Quote from interview with Joycelyn M. Crumpton conducted on January 12, 1994.

Pp. 9–12: The impact of deindustrialization and ghettoization in Watts and adjacent communities is described by D. A. Glasgow, *op. cit.*, and G. Horne, *op. cit.*

P. 9: The tenure of Chief William Parker is described in books by G. Horne, *op. cit.*, and J. H. Skolnick and J. J. Fyfe, *op. cit.*

P. 9: The impact of the civil rights movement on civil rights judicial and legislative actions is described in books by Taylor Branch, *Parting the Waters* (New York: Simon & Schuster, 1988), and Peter Albright and Ronald Hoffman (eds.), *We Shall Overcome: Martin Luther King, Jr., and the Black Freedom Struggle* (New York: Pantheon Books, 1990).

P. 10: Quote from G. J., black male youth worker in Northridge Alumni Focus Group at Charles R. Drew University of Medicine and Science on November 20, 1993.

P. 11: Quote from the American Civil Liberties Report, cited in G. Horne, *op. cit.*, p. 140.

Pp. 11–12: Quote from E. B., black male probation officer, in Northridge Alumni Focus Group at Charles R. Drew University of Medicine and Science on November 20, 1993.

P. 12: Quote cited in G. Horne, *op. cit.*, p. 135.

P. 12: Quote from C. A., black female social worker, in Northridge Alumni Focus Group at Charles R. Drew University of Medicine and Science on November 20, 1993.

Pp. 13–16: Description of factors contributing to the Watts riots are drawn primarily from three sources: D. A. Glasgow, *op. cit.*; G. Horne, *op. cit.*; and the McCone Commission Report, *Violence in the City: An End or a Beginning?* (Sacramento, Calif.: Office of the Governor, 1965).

P. 15: Quote from interview with Ronald Johnson conducted on November 20, 1993.

P. 16: The official toll of damage, fatalities, and arrests are from the McCone Commission Report, pp. 22–24.

Pp. 16–18: This summary of the commission's recommendations is taken directly from the McCone Commission Report.

P. 18: The boundaries of South Central are defined differently by various individuals and groups in the communities. These two definitions reflect a consensus of the black leaders interviewed for the original Rodney King research project, as well as from descriptions in the mass media during and after the civil disorders in April and May 1992.

P. 18: Population estimates for 1965 and 1992 are from the U.S. Census estimates for Los Angeles County for those years.

Pp. 19–20: Racial, social, and economic changes in the community between 1965 and 1992 are documented in the following books: Robert Gooding-Williams (ed.), *Reading Rodney King/Reading Urban Uprising* (New York: Routledge, 1993); Haki R. Madhubuti (ed.), *Why L.A. Happened* (Chicago: Third World Press, 1993); Mike Davis, *City of Quartz* (New York: Vintage Books, 1992); and David Rieff, *Los Angeles: Capital of the Third World* (New York: Simon & Schuster, 1991).

P. 20: Quote from interview with Herbert A. Jones conducted on June 1, 1994.

Pp. 20–21: Accounts of the relationship of the black community and the LAPD, 1965–1992, are found in M. Davis, *op. cit.*; R. Gooding-Williams, *op. cit.*; G. Horne, *op. cit.*; and H. R. Madhubuti, *op. cit.*

P. 21: The comment by Chief Daryl Gates about the relationship between the anatomy of black males and the high rate of deaths from police choke holds is cited in M. Davis, *op. cit.*, p. 272.

Chapter Two

P. 22: Quote by Wade Henderson is cited by Ellis Cose, "Larger than Life," *Newsweek*, April 26, 1993, p. 30.

P. 22: Quote from interview with Ronald Johnson conducted November 20, 1993.

P. 23: Information on Rodney King's family and elementary school years is summarized from two newspaper profiles: Ashley Dunn and Andrea Ford, "The Man Swept Up in the Furor," *Los Angeles Times*, March 17, 1991, p. B1; and Avis Thomas-Lester, "Uneasy Celebrity for 'Gentle Giant,'" *Washington Post*, May 3, 1992, p. A25.

Pp. 23–24: Quote from interview with Herbert Jones conducted on June 1, 1994.

P. 24: Information on Rodney King's adolescent years, high school placement, and sports activities is also drawn from A. Dunn and A. Ford, *op. cit.*, and A. Thomas-Lester, *op. cit.*

P. 25: Quote from interview with Dr. Gale Pauley conducted on January 13, 1994.

P. 25: Information on Rodney King's jobs after he dropped out of high school is drawn from A. Thomas-Lester, *op. cit.*

Pp. 25–26: Information on Rodney King's two marriages is drawn from A. Dunn and A. Ford, *op. cit.*, and A. Thomas-Lester, *op. cit.*

P. 26: Information on Rodney King's robbery in 1989 is drawn from A. Thomas-Lester, *op. cit.*

Pp. 26–27: Quote from interview with Hon. H. Randolph Moore conducted on June 16, 1994.

P. 27: Quote from Rodney King's letter cited in A. Dunn and A. Ford, *op. cit.*, p. B14.

P. 27: Information about King's postprison job and the comments of his supervisor are drawn from A. Dunn and A. Ford, *op. cit.*

Pp. 28–29: Description of the police pursuit and arrest of Rodney King is drawn from accounts in the *Los Angeles Times* and the *New York Times* and from the description in the *Report of the Independent Commission on the Los Angeles Police Department* (1991), known as the Christopher Commission Report.

P. 28: Quote from Curtis R. Tucker, Jr., cited by Richard W. Stevenson, "Los Angeles Chief Taunted at Hearing," *New York Times*, March 15, 1991, p. A16.

Pp. 29–30: Information about the videotaping by George Holliday is drawn from newspaper articles in the *Los Angeles Times*, March 5, 1991; articles in two weekly magazines, *Time*, March 16, 1991, p. 33, and *Newsweek*, April 1, 1991, pp. 18–19; and the Christopher Commission Report, pp. 6–11.

P. 31: Quote from H. R., participant in Focus Group interview conducted March 18, 1994.

P. 31: Quote from Sgt. Stacey Koon cited in Christopher Commission Report, p. 14.

Pp. 31–32: Nurses' comments reported in "Police Joked About King, Nurses Say," *Los Angeles Times*, March 14, 1992, p. B1.

P. 32: Rodney King's injuries, results of his lab tests, and the prosecutor's decision to release him from jail are detailed in the Christopher Commission Report, p. 8. Dr. Edmund Chein is quoted in the *Los Angeles Times*, March 17, 1991, p. B1.

P. 32: King's comment about his father is from John L. Mitchell, "King Jurors Searching for the Man Behind the Symbol," *Los Angeles Times*, April 16, 1994, p. A1.

Pp. 32–33: Sequence of George Holliday's call and Paul King's visit to the Foothill Police Station on March 4 was reported in the Christopher Commission Report, pp. 9–11.

P. 33: Holliday's decision to give a copy of his videotape to KTLA-TV is reported in the Christopher Commission Report, p. 11.

P. 33: Response to the videotape of King's beating on CNN on March 5 was widely reported in the media; cf. *Los Angeles Times*, March 6, 1991, p. 1; *New York Times*, March 6, 1991, p. 1; *Time*, March 16, 1991, p. 33; and *Newsweek*, April 1, 1991, pp. 18–19.

P. 33: Quote by John W. Mack cited in R. W. Stevenson, *op. cit.*

P. 34: Quote by Sen. Bradley from his speech on the floor of the U.S. Senate, April 30, 1992.

P. 35: The grand jury's indictment was reported in the *Los Angeles Times*, March 16, 1991, p. 1.

P. 35: Statement issued by the Los Angeles Police Protective League reported by Bill Turque, "Damned but Defiant: A Scorching Report of a Violent and Racist LAPD," *Newsweek*, July 22, 1991, p. 22.

P. 36: The grand jury's decision and Ira Reiner's statement are reported in the *Los Angeles Times*, May 11, 1991, p. 1.

P. 36: Quote by Ramona Ripston is cited in J. H. Skolnick and J. J. Fyfe, *op. cit.*, p. 9.

P. 36: Judge Weisberg's decision to change the venue in the case is reported in the *Los Angeles Times*, July 24, 1991, p. 1.

P. 37: Quote from Barry Scheck, "Following Orders," *New Republic*, May 25, 1992, p. 17.

P. 37: Pro and con arguments about the change of venue can be found in Marcia Chambers, "It Is Always Difficult to Convict a Cop, Especially in the Suburbs," *National Law Journal*, May 18, 1992; Darlene Ricker, "Holding Out: Juries vs. Public Pressure," *American Bar Association Journal*, August 1992, pp. 48–53; NAACP Legal Defense and Education Fund, "The Color of Justice," *American Bar Association Journal*, August 1992, pp. 62–63; and Ira Reiner, "Don't Castigate Jury: They Did Their Civic Job," *National Law Journal*, May 18, 1992, pp. 13–16.

P. 37: The decision to remove Judge Kamins from the case is discussed in John D. Barnett, "An Attorney's Frontline View in Los Angeles," *National Law Journal*, May 18, 1992, pp. 13–14.

P. 37: The prosecution's failure to appeal the change of venue decision was criticized by Johnnie L. Cochran, Jr., "Assessing the Verdict and Its Legal Fallout," *National Law Journal*, May 11, 1992, pp. 15–16.

Chapter Three

P. 38: Quote from interview with Rev. Eugene Marzette conducted on March 17, 1994.

Pp. 38–39: Description of Simi Valley from articles by Carlos Lozano, "Crush of Media Raises Simi's Profile," *Los Angeles Times*, February 4, 1992, p. A3; Richard Lacayo, "Anatomy of an Acquittal," *Time*, May 11, 1992, pp. 30–32; and Jane Gross, "In Simi Valley, Defense of a Shared Way of Life," *New York Times*, May 4, 1992, p. A9.

P. 39: Population estimate of 33 percent nonwhites in Ventura County from B. Scheck, *op. cit.*, pp. 17–19.

P. 39: Composition of the jury described by B. Scheck, *ibid.*, and R. Lacayo, *op. cit.*

P. 39: Prosecutor's decision not to use Rodney King as a witness is discussed by R. Lacayo, *ibid.*; J. Cochran, *op. cit.*; and Houston A. Baker, "Scene—Not Heard," in R. Gooding-Williams, *op. cit.*, pp. 38–48.

Pp. 39–40: Descriptions of the four police officers are drawn from their photographs and biographical information during their second trial in Tom Mathews and David A. Kaplan, "Looking Past the Verdict," *Newsweek*, April 26, 1993, pp. 20–28.

P. 40: Quote by B. Scheck, *op. cit.*, p. 19.

P. 40: Quote by J. Cochran, *op. cit.*, p. 16.

Pp. 40–41: Prosecution's case is described and analyzed by R. Lacayo, *op. cit.*; B. Scheck, *op. cit.*; and M. Chambers, *op. cit.*

P. 42: Quote by M. Chambers, *op. cit.*, p. 13.

P. 42: Prosecutor Terry White's concern over the race issue in this case is discussed by R. Lacayo, *op. cit.*, and B. Scheck, *op. cit.*

P. 42: Laurence Powell's comment on "gorillas in the mist" reported by B. Scheck, *op. cit.*, p. 17; and R. Lacayo, *op. cit.*, p. 31.

Pp. 42–43: Defense testimony challenging the cause of Rodney King's physical injuries is discussed by R. Lacayo, *op. cit.*, and B. Scheck, *op. cit.*

P. 43: Quote from interview with Bernard C. Parks conducted on March 18, 1994.

P. 44: Briseno's testimony that his fellow officers were "out of control" was reported by R. Lacayo, *op. cit.*, p. 31.

P. 44: Discrepancy between police testimony and the car manufacturer's testimony about the car's maximum speed is discussed in the Christopher Commission Report, p. 4, and in Tom Owens, *Lying Eyes: The Truth Behind the Corruption and Brutality of the LAPD and the Beating of Rodney King* (New York: Thunder's Mouth Press, 1994).

P. 44: Police testimony that Rodney King was on "angel dust" was never refuted by lab results during the first trial. See Bill Girdner, "Different Result in New Cop Trial," *American Bar Association Journal*, June 1993, p. 16; and R. Lacayo, *op. cit.*, p. 31.

P. 45: Quote from interview with Dennis Schatzman, reporter for the *Los Angeles Sentinel*, a black-owned weekly newspaper, conducted on March 17, 1994.

Pp. 46–47: See analysis of the impact of showing this videotape in slow motion and freezing the frame of the action in H. A. Baker, *op. cit.*; Kimberlé Crenshaw and Gary Peller, "Reel Time/Reel Justice," in R. Gooding-Williams, *op. cit.*, pp. 56–70; T. Mathews and D. A. Kaplan, *op. cit.*; *Newsweek*, May 11, 1992, pp. 36–38; R. Lacayo, *op. cit.*, p. 32; and Bill Kovatch, "The Rodney King Video Revisited," *Nieman Reports*, Winter 1992, pp. 2–3.

P. 47: Accounts of the officers' verbal comments during the beating of Rodney King are in dispute since King has made contradictory statements about what he heard. See discussion in Christopher Commission Report, p. 8; B. Scheck, *op. cit.*; and R. Lacayo, *op. cit.*

P. 47: Quote from interview with Bernard C. Parks conducted on March 18, 1994.

Pp. 47–48: Testimony of Sgt. Charles Duke is described by B. Scheck, *op. cit.*, p. 17.

P. 48: Defense arguments that King "controlled the action" are critically analyzed by R. Lacayo, *op. cit.*

P. 48: Regarding defense photo of King showing few major bodily injuries, see R. Lacayo, *op. cit.*, p. 31.

P. 49: Quote by Michael Stone cited by R. Lacayo, *op. cit.*, p. 32.

P. 49: Description of the jury members' backgrounds is drawn from B. Scheck, *op. cit.*, and R. Lacayo, *op. cit.*

P. 50: Quote by Paul De Pasquale cited in R. Lacayo, *op. cit.*, p. 32.

P. 50: Quote by Jerome A. Skolnick cited in *ibid.*

P. 50: Chart displayed by prosecutor Terry White is described by B. Scheck, *op. cit.*, p. 17.

P. 51: Defense argument about the "thin blue line" was analyzed by Vittorio Zucconi, "Holding the 'Thin Blue Line,'" *World Press Review*, August 1991, p. 46; and H. A. Baker, *op. cit.*

P. 51: Defense use of animal labels to describe Rodney King is analyzed by Robert Gooding-Williams, "Look, a Negro!" in R. Gooding-Williams, *op. cit.*, pp. 157–177.

P. 52: Quote by white female juror cited in R. Lacayo, *op. cit.*, p. 32.

P. 52: Gathering of community leaders at the First African Methodist Episcopal Church is described in the *Los Angeles Times*, April 30, 1992, p. A1.

P. 52: Public response to the jury's decision was described in the *Los Angeles Times*, April 30 1992, p. 1; the *New York Times*, April 30, 1992, p. 1; and *Time*, May 11, 1992, pp. 10–11.

Chapter Four

P. 54: Quote from interview with John W. Mack conducted on October 29, 1993.

P. 55: Quote from interview with Rev. Cecil L. Murray conducted on June 17, 1994.

P. 55: Quote from interview with John W. Mack conducted on October 29, 1993.

Pp. 55–56: Quote from T. W., participant in Youth Gang Services Focus Group conducted on February 18, 1994.

P. 56: Quote from interview with Rev. Kenneth Flowers conducted on October 29, 1993.

Pp. 56–57: Quote from interview with Duane B. Bremond conducted on May 12, 1994.

Pp. 57–59: Description of the civil disorder from April 29 to May 3, 1992, is drawn from several sources, including the *Los Angeles Times*, April 30–May 4, 1992; the *New York*

Times, May 1–5, 1992; *Newsweek*, May 11, 1992, pp. 26–33; and *Time*, May 11, 1992, pp. 18–25.

P. 58: Quote from interview with Gayle Pollard Terry conducted on October 29, 1993.

P. 58: Quote from D. N., black male salesman, participant in Northridge Alumni Focus Group at Charles R. Drew University of Medicine and Science on November 20, 1993.

Pp. 58–59: Quote from C. C., black male junior college student participant in Weingart Urban YMCA Focus Group conducted on January 13, 1994.

P. 59: Quote from interview with Rev. Cecil L. Murray conducted on June 17, 1994.

P. 60: Quote from N. D., black male former gang member, participant in Youth Gang Services Focus Group conducted on February 18, 1994.

P. 60: Quote from interview with Joycelyn M. Crumpton conducted on January 12, 1994.

P. 60: Quote from interview with L. F., black female elementary school teacher, conducted on June 6, 1994.

P. 61: Quote from V. O., black female participant in the Youth Intervention Alternative School Focus Group conducted on March 18, 1994.

P. 61: Quote from K. J., black female participant in Weingart Urban YMCA Focus Group conducted on January 13, 1994.

P. 61: Quote from interview with Joycelyn M. Crumpton conducted on January 12, 1994.

Pp. 61–62: Quote from L. B., probation officer, participant in Northridge Alumni Focus Group at Charles R. Drew University of Medicine and Science on November 20, 1993.

P. 62: Quote from S. T., black community college instructor, participant in Northridge Alumni Focus Group at Charles R. Drew University of Medicine and Science on November 20, 1993.

P. 62: Quote from interview with Sandra Bankhead conducted on October 28, 1993.

P. 63: Quote from interview with Donzella P. Lee conducted on February 17, 1994.

Pp. 63–64: The killing of Latasha Harlins is described in the *Los Angeles Times*, March 19, 1991, p. B1, and by Wanda Coleman, "Blacks, Immigrants, and America: Remembering Latasha," *Nation*, February 15, 1993, pp. 187–191.

P. 64: Quote from interview with Sandra Bankhead conducted on October 28, 1993.

P. 64: Quote from K. J., black female participant in Weingart Urban YMCA Focus Group conducted on January 13, 1994.

P. 65: The police assault on Donald Jackson, an off-duty black policeman in Long Beach, is described by Charles E. Simmons, "The Los Angeles Rebellion: Class, Race and Misinformation," in H. R. Madhubuti, *op. cit.*, pp. 141–155.

P. 65: The history of police brutality against blacks in Los Angeles has been well documented by D. A. Glasgow, *op. cit.*; M. Davis, op. cit.; G. Horne, *op. cit.*; and J. A. Skolnick and J. J. Fyfe, *op. cit.*; and dozens of articles in newspapers, magazines, and edited collections.

P. 66: Quote from interview with William Shearer conducted on March 18, 1994.

P. 66: Quote from interview with Dr. Kathy Sanders-Phillips conducted on January 14, 1994.

P. 66: Quote from interview with John W. Mack conducted on October 29, 1993.

P. 66: Quote from interview with Prof. Barbara Solomon conducted on September 24, 1993.

P. 67: Quote from interview with Rev. Kenneth Flowers conducted on October 29, 1993.

P. 67: The riots spread from South Central to several other sections of Los Angeles over the four-day period. There are conflicting accounts about the scope and severity of the damage and the ethnic breakdown of the persons arrested during the riots. The statistics cited are from three major sources: Los Angeles Police Department, *1992 Annual Report* (Los Angeles: Los Angeles Police Department, 1993); Tom Larson and Miles Finney, *Rebuilding South Central Los Angeles: Myths, Realities, and Opportunities* (Los Angeles: California State University, 1990); and Editors of the *Los Angeles Times*, *Understanding the Riots* (Los Angeles: Los Angeles Times, 1992).

Police reported the ethnic breakdown of persons arrested for looting, vandalism, or assault to be 36.9 percent Latino, 29.9 percent black, 6.8 percent white, and 26.4 percent "other." See Melvin Oliver, in R. Gooding-Williams, *op. cit.*, pp. 117–141.

P. 68: Quote from interview with Dr. Alice Walker Duff conducted on January 14, 1994.

P. 69: Estimates of damage and destruction are cited in the *Report of the Special Committee on the Los Angeles Crisis of the California State Assembly*, published in September 1992.

P. 69: Mental health professionals who were interviewed for the initial study, including Dr. Boyd James, Dr. Kathy Sanders-Phillips, Dr. Reed Tuckson, and Dr. Medria Williams, reported increased rates of psychological distress among black patients at hospitals and clinics in the South Central–Watts area.

P. 70: Quote from interview with Gayle Pollard Terry conducted on October 29, 1993.

P. 70: Quote from H. M., black male junior college student participant in the Weingart Urban YMCA Focus Group conducted on January 13, 1994.

P. 71: Quote from W. A., black male small business owner, participant in the Northridge Alumni Focus Group at Charles R. Drew University of Medicine and Science on November 20, 1993.

P. 71: Quote from interview with Mark Ridley-Thomas conducted on February 17, 1994.

P. 72: Quote from B. B., black male gang prevention counselor, participant in Youth Gang Services Focus Group conducted on February 18, 1994.

P. 72: Quote from interview with Sandra Bankhead conducted on October 28, 1993.

P. 73: Quote from interview with Dr. Reed Tuckson conducted on October 29, 1993.

P. 75: Poem by Langston Hughes is from *Selected Poems of Langston Hughes* (New York: Knopf, 1951).

Chapter Five

P. 76: Quote from the Christopher Commission Report, p. xii.

P. 76: The background, membership, and charge of the Christopher Commission are described in Appendix One of the report.

P. 77: The two black members of the commission were Dr. John Slaughter, president of Occidental College, and Willie R. Barnes, a corporate lawyer.

Pp. 77–79: Testimony of the many witnesses at the public hearings was reported in the Christopher Commission Report, the *Los Angeles Times*, and the *New York Times*, and on the local and national radio and television networks during the hearings.

Pp. 78–79: Chief Gates's absence from Parker Center when the civil disorder broke out was a source of criticism by the media and his political foes. See Sumi K. Cho, "Korean Americans vs. African Americans: Conflict and Construction," in R. Gooding-

Williams, *op. cit.*, pp. 196–211; J. A. Skolnick and J. J. Fyfe, *op. cit.*; and Rick Connell, "Gates Absence Early in Riot to Be Examined," *Los Angeles Times*, May 4, 1992, p. A3.

P. 79: The response to the reading of the city charter provision by Geoffrey T. Gibbs was reported by Ronald J. Ostrow, "U.S. to Review Complaints of Brutality," *Los Angeles Times*, March 15, 1991, p. A3, and on CNN's *Morning News Show*, March 15, 1991. Gibbs was the spokesman for the John M. Langston Bar Association of Black Lawyers in Los Angeles.

Pp. 79–80: The forty-four police officers are identified anonymously, but several of their case histories of misconduct and abuse are summarized from personnel records in the Christopher Commission Report, pp. 39–48.

P. 80: The police shooting of Eulia Love on January 3, 1979, is briefly described in the Christopher Commission Report, p. 194; J. A. Skolnick and J. J. Fyfe, *op. cit.*, p. 14; and M. Davis, *op. cit.*, p. 271.

P. 80: Love's killing resulted in some reforms concerning policies and procedures on the use of guns and excessive force in the LAPD, but these reforms were never fully supported or implemented by the department, as noted in the Christopher Commission Report, p. 194.

Pp. 80–81: Quote about lax discipline in the LAPD is from the Christopher Commission Report, p. 57.

P. 81: Examples of racial epithets and insensitive terms for minorities in police radio transmissions are given in the Christopher Commission Report, pp. 71–74.

Pp. 81–83: Recommendations of the Christopher Commission are summarized on pp. xiv–xxiii of the report.

Pp. 83–84: The African-American members of the California State Assembly all supported the formation of the special committee, particularly since most of them represented districts in Los Angeles County. See article by Carla Rivera, "Riots' Causes Same as in '60s, State Panel Says," *Los Angeles Times*, October 2, 1992, p. A1.

Pp. 84–85: *Report of the Assembly Special Committee on the Los Angeles Crisis, California State Assembly* (Sacramento: Assembly Publications Office, September 1992).

P. 85: Quote from the Christopher Commission Report, p. 16.

P. 86: The Justice Department was subjected to intense pressure from civil rights groups and counterpressures from civil libertarians about intervening in the Rodney King beating case. See comments by Benjamin L. Hooks, "National NAACP Office Speaks Out on Rodney King Verdict," *Crisis*, April-May 1992, pp. 2–3; and Stephanie B. Goldberg, "Force of Law: Federal Lawsuits for Rodney King Raise New Issues," *American Bar Association Journal*, July 1992, pp. 76–77; Richard N. Ostling, "ACLU: Not All That Civil," *Time*, April 26, 1993, p. 31; Darlene Ricker, "Double Exposure: Did the Second Rodney King Trial Violate Double Jeopardy?" *American Bar Association Journal*, August 1993, pp. 66–69.

P. 86: The initial phase of jury selection in the civil rights trial against the police officers is described by Jim Newton, "Riots Shadow Hangs over King Jury Selection," *Los Angeles Times*, January 31, 1993, p. 2.

P. 87: Quote by Sgt. Stacey Koon cited in William A. Henry, "Putting Justice in the Dock," *Time*, April 19, 1993, pp. 32–33.

P. 87: The racial composition of the jury is described in *ibid.*, p. 33.

P. 88: See David A. Kaplan's description of King in *ibid.*, p. 26.

P. 88: Koon's testimony is reported by Bill Girdner, "Different Result in New Cop Trial," *American Bar Association Journal*, June 1993, p. 16.

P. 89: Singer's testimony is reported in W. A. Henry, *op. cit.*, p. 33.

P. 89: See the critique of Michael Stone's cross-examination of King in Girdner, *op. cit.*, p. 16.

Pp. 90–91: Details about the trial are summarized by B. Girdner, *ibid.*; George Church, "Cries of Relief," *Time*, April 26, 1993, pp. 18–19; and W. A. Henry, *op. cit.*, pp. 32–33.

P. 90: Details about the tactical alert and the authorization to call up the National Guard are described in T. Mathews and D. A. Kaplan, *op. cit.*

P. 91: Quote by Ira Salzman is cited in *ibid.*, p. 22.

P. 91: A photograph and description of the response of the crowd at Rev. Murray's church are featured in *ibid.*, pp. 20–21.

P. 91: Divergent opinions about the split verdicts are discussed in articles by E. Cose, *op. cit.*, and in an editorial in the *National Review*, May 10, 1993, pp. 13–15.

Pp. 91–92: Quote by the white male juror is cited by B. Girdner, *op. cit.*, p. 16.

Pp. 92–93: Judge Davies's memorandum on his decision to impose sentences less than the mandatory guidelines for Stacey Koon and Laurence Powell is reported in the *National Law Journal*, August 16, 1993, pp. 18–19.

P. 93: Criticism of Judge Davies's lenient sentences for the two police officers can be found in the *Economist*, August 7, 1993, p. A32, and the *Los Angeles Times*, August 5, 1993, pp. A1 and B7.

P. 93: Dred Scott, a Missouri slave who sued for his freedom after living in the free state of Illinois, had his suit thrown out by the U.S. Supreme Court in 1854 on the grounds that he was not a citizen and had no rights, allowing his master to retain ownership of him. See J. H. Franklin, *op. cit.*, p. 178.

Pp. 93–94: Quote from L. T., female youth member, participant in Weingart Urban YMCA Focus Group conducted on January 13, 1994.

P. 94: Chief Gates's raid to arrest the suspects in the Denny beating is described in "See the Sideshow," *Time*, May 25, 1992, pp. 17–18.

P. 94: The black gangs in Los Angeles are divided into two large loosely organized supergangs called the Crips and the Bloods. Each of these larger groups is divided into smaller "sets" of neighborhood gangs. For a fuller description of gang organization, see Leon Bing, *Do or Die* (New York: HarperCollins, 1991).

Pp. 94–95: There were more than four young black men arrested for assaultive behavior at the intersection of Florence and Normandie on the night of April 29, 1992, but these four defendants became known as the "L.A. Four" because their cases were initially linked together by the prosecutors. For a fuller discussion of the seven original defendants, see "Lessons in L.A. Law," *Time*, December 28, 1992, pp. 131–134; Peter J. Boyer, "Looking for Justice in L.A.," *New Yorker*, March 15, 1993, pp. 68–80; and Ashley Dunn,"More Tired than Angry, City Watches Denny Case," *Los Angeles Times*, August 28, 1993, p. A1.

P. 95: This demonstration for the L.A. Four is described in "Lessons in L.A. Law," *op. cit.*

P. 96: Judge Ouderkirk's complex rulings in the pretrial stage of this case are described by Tom Morgenthau, "The Denny Trial: L.A.'s Next Big Test," *Newsweek*, April 26, 1993, p. 28.

P. 96: Disparities in bail for the four police officers and the L.A. Four defendants caused considerable debate, as reported in "Lessons in L.A. Law," *op. cit.*

P. 97: The composition of the jury is described by Ashley Dunn and Edward J. Boyer, "Clear-Cut Legal Issues at Heart of Denny Beating Case," *Los Angeles Times*, August 19, 1993, p. A1.

Pp. 97–98: Quote from Judge Ouderkirk is cited in *ibid.*, p. A22.

P. 98: Descriptions of Damian Williams and Henry Watson are drawn from *Time*, May 25, 1992, pp. 17–18; and A. Dunn, *op. cit.*, p. A1.

Pp. 98–99: The attack on Reginald Denny is described by Edward J. Boyer, "Three Cameramen Testify in Denny Case," *Los Angeles Times*, September 3, 1993, p. B3.

P. 99: Dr. Leslie Geiger's testimony is reported by Edward J. Boyer, "Cause of Denny's Injuries Disputed by Defense Attorneys," *Los Angeles Times*, August 31, 1993, p. B3.

P. 100: Judge Ouderkirk's ruling to limit access of the defense lawyers to the prosecution witnesses is reported by Edward J. Boyer, "Denny Testifies, Hugs Mothers of Defendants," August 26, 1993, p. A24.

P. 100: The efforts of these four people to rescue Reginald Denny are described by Edward J. Boyer, "Rescuers Describe Saving Beaten and Bloody Denny," *Los Angeles Times*, September 21, 1993, p. A1, and Meg Greenfield, "Ignoring the Why Nots," *Washington Post*, September 7, 1993, p. A17.

P. 101: The expert testimony on the videotaped beating of Reginald Denny is reported by Richard Lacayo, "A Slap for a Broken Head," *Time*, November 1, 1993, pp. 46–47.

P. 101: Quote by trial observer cited by John Taylor, "L.A. Blues," *New York*, September 20, 1993, p. 43.

P. 102: See information on Edi Faal's background in William Hamilton, "The Man Who Turned the Denny Case Around," *Washington Post*, October 23, 1993, p. D1; and John L. Mitchell and David Ferrell, "Faal Emerging from Denny Case as Rising Legal Star," *Los Angeles Times*, October 20, 1993, p. A1.

P. 102: Faal's demonstration that Williams did not have a gap in his teeth is described by Edward J. Boyer, "Denny Case May Hinge on Clashing Testimony," *Los Angeles Times*, September 20, 1993, p. B1.

Pp. 102–103: The defense's strategy in this case is described by Edward J. Boyer, "Tough Law, Tough Cases: Defense Rests in Denny Case," *Los Angeles Times*, September 24, 1993, p. B1.

Pp. 103–104: The closing arguments of the prosecution and the defense are summarized, respectively, in Edward J. Boyer, "Williams, Watson Meant to Kill Denny," *Los Angeles Times*, September 29, 1993, p. A1, and Edward J. Boyer, "Attorney Depicts Williams as a Scapegoat for the Riots," *Los Angeles Times*, September 30, 1993, p. A1.

P. 104: Judge Ouderkirk's decision to dismiss or replace five jurors and nullify two early verdicts in the case are reported by Seth Mydans, "Second Juror Removed by Judge in Trial on Riot Assaults: Two Verdicts Are Nullified," *New York Times*, October 13, 1993, p. A1; Christine Spolar and William Hamilton, "In Denny Beating Trial, Jury Saga Is the Subplot," *Washington Post*, October 20, 1993, p. A3; and Mark Hansen, "Juror's Dismissal Debated," *American Bar Association Journal*, January 1994, p. 26.

P. 104: The jury's difficulties in deliberating and their final verdicts are described by Jan Hoffman, "When 12 People Can't Get Along," *New York Times*, October 16, 1993, p. 8; Ashley Dunn and Penelope McMillan, "Jury's Ordeal: Two Harrowing Weeks," *Los Angeles Times*, October 21, 1993, p. A1; Edward J. Boyer and Jesse Katz, "Jury

Convicts Defendants on Reduced Charges, Acquits on Others," October 19, 1993, p. A1.

P. 105: Denny's quote and response to the verdict are reported by Amy Wallace and John Hurst, "'Let's Get On with Life,' Denny Says After Verdict," *Los Angeles Times*, October 19, 1993, p. A19.

Pp. 105–106: Criticism of the verdicts was reported by columnists and editorial writers in the *Los Angeles Times*, October 20, 1993, p. B7; the *New York Times*, October 22, 1993, p. A14; the *Washington Post*, October 21, 1993, p. A30; and the *Wall Street Journal*, October 21, 1993, p. A16.

P. 106: Reactions to Joseph Duff's criticism of the defendants are reported by John L. Mitchell, "NAACP Official Stands By Controversial Remarks," *Los Angeles Times*, September 12, 1993, p. B1.

P. 107: Reactions of some jurors to the charge of racial bias and jury nullification are reported by Seth Mydans, "Leader Denies Bias or Fear on Riot Jury," *New York Times*, October 26, 1993, p. A10, and Edward J. Boyer, "Denny Juror Says Riot Fears Did Not Influence Verdicts," *Los Angeles Times*, October 26, 1993, p. A1.

P. 107: See R. Lacayo, "Slap," *op. cit.*

P. 107: Quote from Jerome A. Skolnick, "The People's Jury Did Its Job," *Los Angeles Times*, October 22, 1993, p. B7.

P. 107: Judge Ouderkirk's sentence of Williams is described in Edward J. Boyer and Andrea Ford, "Williams Given Maximum Ten Years in Denny Beating," *Los Angeles Times*, December 8, 1993, p. A1, and in *Time*, December 20, 1993, p. 16.

Pp. 108–109: Rodney King's series of arrests are described in *Time*, July 24, 1995, p. 19.

P. 109: Failure to reach a negotiated settlement in the assault case is discussed by Jim Newton, "Lawyers Given 30 Days to Settle King Civil Suit," *Los Angeles Times*, August 10, 1993, p. B1.

P. 109: The strategies of Rodney King's lawyers in the civil suit are described by John L. Mitchell, "King Reenacts Beating at Trial of Suit Against City," *Los Angeles Times*, March 29, 1994, p. A1.

P. 110: Quote from interview with John Burris conducted on March 11, 1996.

P. 110: Powell's refusal to testify and the strategies of the defense lawyers are described in the *New York Times*, April 22, 1994, p. A7; and the *Los Angeles Times*, May 13, 1994, p. A18.

P. 111: Jury's decision against punitive damages for King is reported in *Facts on File*, June 9, 1994, p. 415.

P. 111: Compare the theme of victimization in the novel by Toni Morrison, *Beloved* (New York: Knopf, 1987).

Chapter Six

P. 115: Quote by Harry Edwards, "We Must Let O. J. Go: Separating Fact from Image," *Sport*, February 1995, p. 80.

P. 115: Description of the Potrero Hill area drawn from Margot Patterson Doss, *San Francisco at Your Feet* (New York: Grove Press, 1964), pp. 162–164.

P. 116: Quote by Ellis Cose, "Caught Between Two Worlds: Why Simpson Can't Overcome the Barriers of Race," *Newsweek*, July 11, 1994, p. 28.

Pp. 116–119: Description of O. J. Simpson's early life from several sources including Larry Fox, *The O. J. Simpson Story: Born to Run* (New York: Dodd, Mead, 1974); Sheila Weller, *Raging Heart* (New York: Pocket Books, 1995); W. C. Rhoden, "O. J. Simpson," *Ebony*, January 1976, pp. 57–58; and Teresa Carpenter, "The Man Behind the Mask," *Esquire*, November 1994, pp. 84–85.

P. 117: Quote by Eunice Simpson from Evan Thomas, "Day and Night: He Lived Two Lives," *Newsweek*, August 29, 1994, p. 44.

P. 118: Simpson's juvenile arrest and subsequent meeting with Willie Mays and quote are recounted in *ibid.* and in Lynn Hirschberg, "The White World of O. J. Simpson," *New York*, September 26, 1994, pp. 40–46.

P. 119: Quote by O. J. Simpson is cited by E. Thomas, *op. cit.*, p. 43.

P. 120: Simpson's high school and junior college football records are described in L. Fox and O. J. Simpson, *op. cit.*, and H. Edwards, *op. cit.*, p. 80.

P. 120: Quote by Dr. Sharon Collins, a black sociologist from the University of Illinois, cited by E. Cose, *op. cit.*, p. 28.

P. 121: Quote from W. C. Rhoden, "The Simpson Saga Leaves Us All As Victims," *Emerge: Black America's Newsmagazine*, September 1994, p. 73.

P. 121: Simpson's football record at USC and Heisman Trophy award are described by Ron Fimrite, "A Look Back at the Glory Days," *Sports Illustrated*, June 27, 1994, pp. 32–35.

P. 122: Simpson's early years with the Buffalo Bills and his growing family are described in L. Fox and O. J. Simpson, *op. cit.*; S. Weller, *op. cit.*; and in W. C. Rhoden, "O. J."

P. 123: Quote from H. Edwards, *op. cit.*, p. 80.

P. 123: Simpson's records with the Buffalo Bills are recounted by R. Fimrite, *op. cit.*

Pp. 123–124: Quote from S. Weller, *op. cit*, p. 60.

Pp. 124–125: Descriptions of Simpson's private and public life as a celebrity are recounted by S. Weller, *op. cit.*; T. Carpenter, *op. cit.*; L. Hirschberg, *op. cit.*; and John Gregory Dunne, "The Simpsons," *New York Review of Books*, August 25, 1994, pp. 34–39.

P. 125: Quote from T. Carpenter, *op. cit.*, p. 88.

Pp. 125–126: Details of the purchase of his home in Brentwood are recounted by S. Weller, *op. cit.*; L. Hirschberg, *op. cit.*; and Jeffrey Toobin, "Drop-Dead Gorgeous," *New Yorker*, September 18, 1995, pp. 44–51.

P. 126: Quote from interview with Monique Jones conducted on August 24, 1995.

Pp. 126–127: Details of the meeting between O. J. Simpson and Nicole Brown and information on her background are described by S. Weller, *op. cit.*, and T. Carpenter, *op. cit.*

P. 128: Quote cited in S. Weller, *op. cit.*, p. 119.

P. 128: Details of the separation of O. J. and Marguerite Simpson and the drowning of their baby daughter Aaren are recounted by S. Weller, *op. cit.*, and T. Carpenter, *op. cit.*

P. 129: Simpson's business investments are described by T. Carpenter, *op. cit.*; Richard Hoffer, "Fatal Attraction?" *Sports Illustrated*, June 25, 1994, pp. 16–29; S. Weller, *op. cit.*; and E. Thomas, *op. cit.*

P. 129: Quote from W. C. Rhoden, "Simpson Saga," p. 73.

P. 130: Rumors of Simpson's affairs during his two marriages are discussed by S. Weller, *op. cit.*; L. Hirschberg, *op. cit.*; T. Carpenter, *op. cit.*; and Nancy Gibbs, "End of the Run," *Time*, June 27, 1994, pp. 28–35.

P. 130: Quote from W. C. Rhoden, "Simpson Saga," p. 73.

Pp. 130–131: Details of the wedding and the birth of Sydney are described by S. Weller, *op. cit.*; T. Carpenter, *op. cit.*; and R. Hoffer, *op. cit.* Simpson testified later in his civil trial that Nicole had had two abortions during their relationship and one after they separated in 1992. See Tim Rutten and Henry Weinstein, "Simpson Recounts Stormy Relationship with Ex-Wife," *Los Angeles Times*, March 2, 1996, p. A1.

P. 131: Simpson's acting career is described by S. Weller, *op. cit.*; T. Carpenter, *op. cit.*; E. Thomas, *op. cit.*; and W. C. Rhoden, "O. J."

P. 131: Quote from R. Hoffer, *op. cit.*, p. 21.

P. 132: Simpson's father's death from AIDS is reported by S. Weller, *op. cit.*, and Lance Loud, "Queen for a Dad," *Advocate*, September 6, 1994, p. 64.

P. 132: Quote by Cici Shahian cited in S. Weller, *op. cit.*, p. 21.

Pp. 132–134: Simpson's abuse of Nicole and his relations with her family are described by S. Weller, *op. cit.*; T. Carpenter, *op. cit.*; L. Hirschberg, *op. cit.*; and R. Hoffer, *op. cit.*

P. 135: Simpson's concern about being "colorless" and his attitudes about his children's racial identity are discussed by S. Weller, *op. cit.*; L. Hirschberg, *op. cit.*; E. Thomas, *op. cit.*; E. Cose, *op. cit.*; and E. R. Shipp, "O. J. and the Black Media," *Columbia Journalism Review*, November-December 1994, pp. 39–41.

Pp. 135–136: Nicole's call to the police and O. J.'s subsequent arrest were widely reported in the trial transcript, the news media, and in T. Carpenter, *op. cit.*; L. Hirschberg, *op. cit.*; R. Hoffer, *op. cit.*; and Josh Meyer, "Police Records Detail 1989 Beating That Led to Charge," *Los Angeles Times*, June 17, 1994, p. A24.

Pp. 136–137: The Simpsons' separation, O. J.'s reaction to Nicole's relations with other men, and Nicole's involvement in therapy are described by S. Weller, *op. cit.*; T. Carpenter, *op. cit.*; and L. Hirschberg, *op. cit.*

P. 137: Details of the divorce settlement are reported by S. Weller, *op. cit.*; T. Carpenter, *op. cit.*; and L. Hirschberg, *op. cit.*

P. 138: Quote from S. Weller, *op. cit.*, p. 21.

Pp. 138–139: Details of the couple's final separation and interactions on Sunday, June 12, 1994, are reported by S. Weller, *op. cit.*; T. Carpenter, *op. cit.*; R. Hoffer, *op. cit.*; and N. Gibbs, *op. cit.* The events of June 12 are also reported in testimony during the preliminary hearing at the Los Angeles Municipal Court, June 30–July 8, 1994; see summary in the *Los Angeles Times*, July 9, 1994, p. A1.

Chapter Seven

Pp. 140–142: Description of the crime and the events leading up to the day of Nicole's funeral are drawn from accounts in the *Los Angeles Times*, June 15, 16, and 17, 1994; the *New York Times*, June 15 and 17, 1994; *Time*, June 27, 1994; and *Newsweek*, June 27, 1994.

P. 141: Quote from W. C. Rhoden, "Simpson Saga," p. 73.

P. 143: CNN-Gallup Poll results reported on *Early Prime*, CNN, June 22, 1994.

Pp. 143–144: The police chase of O. J. and Al Cowlings on June 17, 1994, was widely shown on television and widely reported in the local and national media, including articles by Jim Newton and Shawn Hubler, "Simpson Held After Wild Chase: He's Charged with Murder of Ex-Wife, Friend," *Los Angeles Times*, June 18, 1994, p. A1;

Time, June 27, 1994; and *Newsweek*, June 27, 1994. O. J.'s booking number after his arrest was included with his photo in *Time*.

Pp. 144–145: The *Los Angeles Times* poll was reported in the *Los Angeles Times*, June 28, 1994, p. A1; the *Newsweek* poll was reported in *Newsweek*, June 27, 1994; the Gallup Poll was reported in *Gallup Poll Monthly*, July 1994, pp. 2–8.

P. 145: The convening of the grand jury and its disbanding are reported by Jesse Katz and Stephen Braun, "Grand Jury Reportedly Probing Simpson Alibi," *Los Angeles Times*, June 22, 1994, p. A1; and Andrea Ford, Richard Simon, and Rich Connell, "Judge, in Stunning Move, Voids Grand Jury Probe of Simpson," *Los Angeles Times*, June 25, 1994, p. A1.

P. 146: The preliminary hearing and the judge's decision to indict O. J. are reported by Paul Feldman and Ted Rohrlich, "With Dress Rehearsal Over, Case Prepares for the Trial," *Los Angeles Times*, July 9, 1994, p. A16.

P. 147: See contrast between cover photographs of O. J. Simpson in *Time* and *Newsweek* for the week of June 27, 1994. Also see articles on O. J. as murder suspect by R. Hoffer, *op. cit.*; Richard Rodriguez, "Is It Really Because O. J. Simpson Is Black?" *Emerge*, February 1995, pp. 28–31; Arion Berger, "Frozen O. J.: Why His Running Days Are Over," *New Republic*, July 11, 1994, pp. 10–12; and E. R. Shipp, *op. cit.*

Pp. 147–148: See John Hoffman, "Defending Men Who Kill Their Loved Ones," *New York Times*, July 10, 1994, p. E3; Lynn Smith, "Calls to L.A. Domestic Abuse Hot Lines Soar," *Los Angeles Times*, June 24, 1994, p. A1; T. Carpenter, *op. cit.*; L. Hirschberg, *op. cit.*; J. G. Dunne, *op. cit.*; Barbara G. Harrison, "Killing Love: A Personal Essay," *Mother Jones*, September-October, 1994, pp. 52–55; and Randall Sullivan, "Unreasonable Doubt" (Parts 1 and 2), *Rolling Stone*, December 15 and 29, 1994.

Chapter Eight

P. 149: Quote from E. R. Shipp, *op. cit.*, p. 41.

P. 150: Major television and radio networks, including CBS, NBC, ABC, and CNN, hired panels of lawyers to comment daily on the case; local stations in major cities had their own legal experts.

Pp. 150–151: Information about Judge Ito's background was drawn from accounts by Mike Tharp, "Ito's Fairness Doctrine," *U.S. News and World Report*, October 31, 1994, pp. 80–81, and Mark Miller, "The Celebrity on the Bench," *Newsweek*, November 28, 1994, p. 35.

P. 151: Quote from William Kunstler on *Talk Back Live*, CNN, July 10, 1995.

Pp. 151–153: Description of the jury selection process and final composition was drawn from reports by Andrea Ford and Jim Newton, "12 Simpson Jurors Are Sworn In," *Los Angeles Times*, November 4, 1994, p. A1; Andrea Ford and Jim Newton, "Jury Selection in Simpson Trial Ends in 11 Weeks," *Los Angeles Times*, December 9, 1994, p. A1; Christine Spolar, "Majority-Black Jury Selected on O. J. Simpson Murder Trial," *Washington Post*, November 4, 1994, p. A2; and "Experts Debate Composition of Simpson Jury," *New York Times*, November 5, 1994, p. 9.

P. 154: Quote from interview with S. R. conducted on June 17, 1994.

P. 155: Quote from black male caller, *Evening Talk Show*, KPIX Radio, San Francisco, July 6, 1995.

P. 156: Quote by Christopher Darden cited in "Blood Trail Ties Simpson to Murder, Court Hears," *New York Times*, January 25, 1995, p. A10.

P. 157: Quote from interview with black clergyman conducted on June 17, 1994.

P. 158: Quote by Sara McNeil Boyd from telephone interview conducted on September 6, 1995.

P. 158: Quote by P. H. from telephone interview conducted on September 11, 1994.

Pp. 158–161: Testimony from Ron Shipp, Brian "Kato" Kaelin, and Rosa Lopez was reported in the *New York Times*, February 5 and 6, 1995, March 22–24, 1995, and February 25–March 4, 1995, respectively.

P. 162: Information about Mark Fuhrman's racial attitudes, including a request for early retirement due to the stress of working in minority areas, is reported by Elizabeth Gleick, "The Tale of the Tapes," *Time*, August 28, 1995, pp. 28–32; Larry Reibstein, "The Detective's Story," *Newsweek*, March 20, 1995, p. 57; and Stryker McGuire, "Fuhrman in the Cross Hairs," *Newsweek*, March 6, 1995, p. 54.

Pp. 163–164: Dennis Fung's testimony is reported by Mark Miller, "A Powerful Damaging Cross," *Newsweek*, April 24, 1995, p. 36, and Jim Newton and Andrea Ford, "Criminalist Concedes Errors," *Los Angeles Times*, April 6, 1995, p. A1.

Pp. 164–165: A critique of Judge Ito's conduct of the trial and the racial tensions on the jury can be found in "Lance Ito's Circus," *Economist*, April 22, 1995, p. A32; Larry Reibstein, "Disorder in the Court," *Newsweek*, April 17, 1995, pp. 26–32; Christopher Farley, "Jury of the Century," *Time*, May 1, 1995, pp. 76–77; and Peter Huber, "The Simpson Circus," *Forbes*, July 3, 1995, p. 6.

Pp. 165–166: The DNA testimony was highly technical, but a clear summary can be found in John Horgan, "High Profile: The Simpson Case Raises the Issue of DNA Readability," *Scientific American*, October 1994, pp. 33–34; and Rachel Nowak, "Forensic DNA Goes to Court with O. J." *Science*, September 2, 1994, pp. 1352–1354.

P. 165: Quote by B. R. Crenshaw from interview conducted on September 12, 1995.

P. 167: The many errors in the coroner's report are described in Kenneth B. Noble, "Times of Death in Simpson Case Are Uncertain, Coroner Testifies," *New York Times*, June 15, 1995, p. A14, and *Newsweek*, May 29, 1995, pp. 70–72.

Pp. 167–168: The glove demonstration is described by Stephanie Simon and Bill Boyarsky, "Jury Rapt As Simpson Tries on Bloody Gloves," *Los Angeles Times*, June 16, 1995, p. A1, and Larry Reibstein, "A Size Too Small," *Newsweek*, June 26, 1995, pp. 60–61.

P. 168: The legal issues involved in "discovery violations" are explained by Andrea Ford and Jim Newton, "Lopez Ends Her Testimony: Two Simpson Lawyers Fired," *Los Angeles Times*, March 4, 1995, p. A1.

P. 169: Quote by Harland Braun cited in David Margolick, "After 92 Days of Testimony, Simpson Prosecution Rests," *New York Times*, July 7, 1995, p. A1.

P. 169: Quote by Jeffrey Toobin, journalist interviewed on *The Charlie Rose Show*, KQED-TV, July 7, 1995.

Pp. 170–171: The strategy of the defense case is discussed by David Margolick, "Simpson Defense Focuses on Three Key Themes As Its Campaign Opens Today," *New York Times*, July 10, 1995, p. A8; and Christopher J. Farley, "The Case Is Made for Now," *Time*, July 17, 1995, pp. 36–38.

P. 171: Quote by Dr. Robert Huizenga, Beverly Hills internist, from the *Los Angeles Times*, July 17, p. A1.

P. 172: Quote by Johnnie Cochran, interviewed by Ted Koppel on *Nightline*, ABC-TV, July 7, 1995.

Pp. 172–173: The controversy over EDTA is reported in the *Los Angeles Times*, July 25 and 26, 1995, p. A1.

Pp. 173–174: Quote by black male caller on *Evening Talk Show*, KPIX Radio, San Francisco, July 6, 1995.

P. 174: Judge Ito's fine of Marcia Clark and the increasing level of incivility in the courtroom is reported by David Margolick, "Judge Stymies Simpson Lawyers' Effort to Build Case for a Conspiracy," *New York Times*, July 21, 1995, p. A1.

P. 175: Judge Wood's decision in the hearing in North Carolina to subpoena the Fuhrman tapes is reported by David Margolick, "Simpson Defense Changes Glove Tactics," *New York Times*, August 1, 1995, p. B1.

Pp. 175–176: Issues of the shield law's applicability to Tracie Savage's testimony in this case are discussed by William Carlsen, "Prosecution Counters Sock Scenario," *San Francisco Chronicle*, August 1, 1995, p. A6, and "Defense Won't Be Allowed to See News Leak Files," *San Francisco Chronicle*, August 10, 1995, p. A1.

P. 176: Quote by Mike Tyson, interviewed by Larry King on his show on CNN, August 17, 1995.

P. 177: Criticism by Dr. John Gerdes of the LAPD forensic laboratory is described by David Margolick, "Simpson Witness Tells of Shoddy Lab Work," *New York Times*, August 4, 1995, p. 1, and William Carlsen, "Cloud Cast over DNA Evidence," *San Francisco Chronicle*, August 3, 1995, p. A3.

P. 177: Quote by Mark Fuhrman in taped interview with Laura Hart McKinny, cited by David Margolick, "Simpson Detective's Racial Epithets Fill Court As the Lawyers Debate the Tapes," *New York Times*, August 30, 1995, p. C16.

P. 177: Quote by Mark Fuhrman, cited in *ibid*.

P. 178: Excerpts of the Fuhrman tapes were published in the *Los Angeles Times*, August 17 and 30, 1995, p. A1; the *New York Times*, August 17, 1995, p. A9; *Time*, August 28, 1995, pp. 28–32; and *Newsweek*, August 28, 1995.

P. 178: Judge Ito's comments about his wife are reported in the *Los Angeles Times*, August 16, 1995, p. A1, and *Time*, August 28, 1995, p. 30.

P. 178: Judge John Reid's ruling about Captain York's relevance to the case is reported in "Wife Need Not Testify, So Judge Ito Can Stay," *San Francisco Chronicle*, August 19, 1995, p. A1.

P. 179: Judge Ito's criticism of the defense and the prosecution lawyers is described by David Margolick, "For Now, Judge Ito Defers Defense Request on Tapes," *New York Times*, August 22, 1995, p. A7; *Los Angeles Times*, August 23, 1995, p. A1; and *New York Times*, August 23, 1995, p. A1.

Chapter Nine

P. 180: Quote by Jeffrey Toobin, journalist, interviewed on *The Charlie Rose Show*, KQED-TV, July 7, 1995.

P. 180: Chief Willie Williams was under investigation by the Los Angeles Police Commission on charges that he accepted gifts from a Las Vegas hotel. See report in Peter Maas, "Can He Hang Tough?" *Parade*, January 14, 1996, pp. 4–6.

P. 180: Information about the failure to discipline LAPD officers is reported by Elizabeth Gleick, "The Crooked Blue Line," *Time*, September 11, 1995, pp. 38–42.

Pp. 180–181: Comments by Peter Keane, legal commentator for KPIX Radio, on an evening talk show on August 22, 1995.

P. 181: Quote by Jeanine Ferris-Pirro on *Larry King Live*, CNN, August 23, 1995.

P. 181: Judge Ito's quote about Dr. Lee's professional reputation from *San Francisco Chronicle*, August 26, 1995, p. A4.

P. 182: Quote by Gerald Uelmen from William Carlsen, "Fuhrman Tapes Rock Courtroom," August 30, 1995, p. A1.

P. 182: Quote by Marcia Clark from *ibid*.

P. 182: Gerald Uelmen's characterization of Mark Fuhrman is reported by David Margolick, "Simpson Detective's Racial Epithets Fill Court As the Lawyers Debate the Tapes," *New York Times*, August 30, 1995, p. C16.

P. 183: Quote by Marcia Clark in *ibid*.

P. 183: Quote by Gil Garcetti in *ibid*.

P. 183: Quote by Fred Goldman in *ibid*.

P. 184: Quote by Judge Ito and discussion of his decision on the Fuhrman tapes are reported by Andrea Ford and Jim Newton, "Jury to Hear Two Short Excerpts of Fuhrman Tapes, Ito Rules," *Los Angeles Times*, September 1, 1995, p. A1; Kenneth B. Noble, "Ruling on Fuhrman Tapes Intrigues Legal Experts," *New York Times*, September 6, 1995, p. A8; and David Margolick, "Jurors Will Hear Two Racial Epithets," *New York Times*, September 1, 1995, p. A1.

P. 184: Quote by Johnnie Cochran from A. Ford and J. Newton, "Jury to Hear Excerpts," p. A26.

P. 184: Quote from brief filed by the American Civil Liberties Union in *ibid.*, p. A27.

P. 184: Quote by Governor Pete Wilson in *ibid.*, p. A27.

Pp. 184–185: Testimony by Kathleen Bell, Natalie Singer, and Roderick Hodge is reported by David Margolick, "Simpson Jury Hears of Racist Incidents," September 6, 1995, p. A8; William Carlsen, "Fuhrman Takes the Fifth; Jury Is Out," *San Francisco Chronicle*, September 7, 1995, p. A1; and Elizabeth Gleick, "Is the End Nigh?" *Time*, September 18, 1995, p. 54.

P. 185: Quote by Christopher Darden in D. Margolick, "Simpson Jury Hears of Racist Incidents," p. A8.

P. 186: Laura Hart McKinny's comments about "police cover-ups" are reported by David Margolick, "Simpson Case Detective Refuses to Answer Questions by Defense," *New York Times*, September 7, 1995, p. A9.

P. 186: Mark Fuhrman's invoking of the Fifth Amendment is reported in *ibid.*, p. A1.

Pp. 186–187: Judge Ito's proposed instructions and the responses of Marcia Clark and Johnnie Cochran are reported by David Margolick, "Judge Ito's Ruling on Detective Incites Appeal from Prosecution," September 8, 1995, pp. A1, A8.

P. 187: Reasons for the reversal of Judge Ito's ruling by the state court of appeals are cited by David Margolick, "California Court Overturns Ruling in Simpson Trial," *New York Times*, September 9, 1995, p. A1.

P. 188: Quote by Richard Rubin from William Carlsen, "Expert Says Gloves Are Alike," *San Francisco Chronicle*, September 13, 1995, p. A1.

P. 188: Gil Garcetti's reaction to Judge Ito's fines against the district attorney's office is described by William Carlsen, "Judge Fines Angry DA; Defense Hints at Subterfuge," *San Francisco Chronicle*, September 14, 1995, p. A6.

Pp. 189–190: Quote by Dr. Henry Lee from David Margolick, "Simpson Case Expert Debates Footprints," *New York Times*, September 16, 1995, p. A9.

P. 190: Stipulation about the moon is reported by David Margolick, "Simpson Trial, Near Its End, Stands on the Brink of Chaos," *New York Times*, September 19, 1995, p. A15.

P. 190: Quote by Johnnie Cochran from Matt Spetalnick, "Jurors Growing Edgy As Trial Nears End," *San Francisco Chronicle*, September 18, 1995, p. A1.

Pp. 190–191: Description of the Fiato brothers and their testimony is drawn from accounts in the *New York Times*, September 20, 1995, p. 6, and the *Los Angeles Times*, September 20, 1995, p. A1.

P. 191: Label of "Dumb and Dumber" for Detectives Lange and Vannatter is reported in *Time*, October 16, 1995, p. 50.

P. 191: Protest of the court stenographer is described in "Rapid Rebellion over Rapid Talk," *Los Angeles Times*, September 21, 1995, p. A9.

P. 192: Responses of the defense team to Judge Ito's two major rulings are reported by David Margolick, "Choice on Charge for Simpson Jury," *New York Times*, September 22, 1995, p. A1.

P. 192: Quotes from O. J. Simpson from his statement to the court from David Margolick, "Simpson Tells Why He Declined to Testify As Two Sides Rest Case," *New York Times*, September 23, 1995, p. 1.

P. 193: Quote by Fred Goldman from *ibid.*, p. 10.

P. 193: Judge Ito's instructions to the jury are summarized in *ibid.*

Pp. 194–195: Poll results reported in the *San Francisco Chronicle*, September 24, 1995, p. A10. Result of national polls conducted by the major television and radio networks and the Gallup Organization were also reported during the week of September 25 to October 2, 1995.

P. 195: Quote by Marcia Clark from David Margolick, "Jury Is Asked to Ignore Sideshow and Look at Simpson Evidence," *New York Times*, September 27, 1995, p. A1; and Richard Lacayo, "An Ugly End to It All," *Time*, October 9, 1995, pp. 30–35.

Pp. 195–196: Statistics on the case are reported in the *New York Times*, September 23, 1995, p. 1. Marcia Clark's colored chart and puzzle are described by D. Margolick, "Jury Is Asked," p. A1; and *New York Times*, September 27, 1995, p. A1.

P. 196: Christopher Darden's direct accusation of O. J. Simpson is described in *Los Angeles Times*, September 28, 1995, p. A1.

P. 197: J. Cochran's closing argument and colorful rhetoric are described by David Margolick, "With Tale of Racism and Error, Simpson Lawyers Seek Acquittal," *New York Times*, September 29, 1995, p. A1; and R. Lacayo, "An Ugly End."

Pp. 197–198: Quotes by Barry Scheck and his critique of the evidence are reported in D. Margolick, *ibid.*, p. A10.

Pp. 198–199: Quotes by Johnnie Cochran and comments on his performance are reported by D. Margolick, "With Tale of Racism," p. A10.

P. 199: Quote by Fred Goldman in *ibid.*

P. 200: Quote by Shirley Baker about the Nation of Islam in *ibid*.

P. 200: Media comments about Cochran's "playing the race card" were widespread during the weekend of September 29 to October 1, 1995. See *Los Angeles Times*, October 1, 1995, p. A1; *Time*, October 9, 1995, pp. 38–39; and Rob Morse, "12 Exhausted Persons," *San Francisco Examiner*, October 1, 1995, p. A18.

Pp. 201–202: Quotes by Christopher Darden and summary of closing statement reported by David Margolick, "Simpson Case Ends As Victim's Voice Fills Courtroom," *New York Times*, September 30, 1995, p. 8.

Pp. 202–203: Quotes by Marcia Clark and summary of closing statement reported in *ibid.*, p. 1.

P. 203: Sheriff's tactical alert announcement reported by Kenneth B. Noble, "At the Courthouse, a Ban on Vendors, Preachers, and Paparazzi," *New York Times*, September 30, 1995, p. 8.

Chapter Ten

P. 204: Quote by Johnnie Cochran cited in Sylvester Monroe, "Race Matters: Johnnie Cochran, Jr., Makes the Case," *Emerge*, December 1995–January 1996, p. 36.

P. 204: Quote by Robert Shapiro cited in David Margolick, "Jury Clears Simpson in Double Murder," *New York Times*, October 4, 1995, p. 1A.

P. 205: The Goldman family's reactions to Johnnie Cochran's closing argument is reported by D. Margolick, "With Tale of Racism," p. A10.

P. 205: Polls taken after the closing arguments and before the verdict revealed deep racial splits over the verdict, as reported in *Los Angeles Times*, October 2, 1995, p. A1; *San Francisco Examiner*, October 2, 1995, p. A4; and *New York Times*, October 2, 1995, p. A9.

P. 205: Quote from interview with Arthur B. Walker conducted on September 3, 1995.

P. 206: The media coverage predicting the verdict was intense on the talk shows on radio and television on the evening of October 2 and in daily newspapers on the morning of October 3, 1995.

P. 207: Poll results reported by Janet Elder, "Racial Divide on Simpson," *New York Times*, October 2, 1995, p. A9.

Pp. 207–208: Descriptions of people waiting for the verdict are reported in *New York Times*, October 4, 1995, p. A1; *Los Angeles Times*, October 4, 1995, p. A1; *Time*, October 16, 1995, pp. 40–45; and *Newsweek*, October 16, 1995, pp. 28–35.

P. 208: Quote by Deirdre Robertson from *Los Angeles Times*, October 4, 1995, p. A1.

Pp. 208–209: Reactions of the defendant, the lawyers, and the family members to the verdict were visible on CNN newscasts and in photographs published on October 4, 1995, in the daily press and thereafter in the weekly newsmagazines.

P. 209: Quote by John W. Mack from Kenneth B. Noble, "In the City of Beautiful People, Trial Hinged on Uglier Issues," *New York Times*, October 4, 1995, p. A15.

P. 209: Quote by Myles Goodson from *ibid*.

Pp. 209–211: Reactions from groups in cities around the nation were captured on CNN immediately after the verdict on October 3, 1995.

P. 210: Quote by Howard University Law student on CNN news coverage of the Simpson verdict, October 4, 1995.

P. 210: Quote by Ben Stein in Frank Rich, "The L.A. Shock Treatment," *New York Times*, October 4, 1995, p. A19.

P. 210: Quote by Steven Yagman in K. B. Noble, "In the City of Beautiful People," p. A15.

P. 211: Quotes by Johnnie Cochran and Eunice Simpson in D. Margolick, "Jury Clears Simpson," pp. A12, A13.

P. 212: O. J. Simpson's statement reported in *Los Angeles Times*, October 4, 1995, p. A3.

Pp. 212–213: Robert Shapiro's disaffection from the defense team is described by Seth Mydans, "In the Joy of Victory, Defense Team Is in Discord," *New York Times*, October 4, 1995, p. A13; Howard Chua-Eoan and Elizabeth Gleick, "Making the Case," *Time*, October 16, 1995, pp. 48–61; and Mark Miller, Donna Foote, and Vern E. Smith, "After the Game, a Bunch of Sore Winners," *Newsweek*, October 16, 1995, p. 42.

P. 213: Quote by Fred Goldman in Charisse Jones, "In the Seats Reserved for Relatives, Joy and Pain, Relief and Disbelief," *New York Times*, October 4, 1995, p. A13.

P. 213: Quote by Christopher Darden in S. Mydans, *op. cit.*, p. A13.

Pp. 213–214: Reactions of the district attorney, prosecutors, and the Goldman family were shown live on CNN, October 3, 1995, and reported in C. Jones, *op. cit.*, p. A13; and H. Chua-Eoan and E. Gleick, "Making the Case."

P. 214: Quote from telephone interview with Sara McNeil Boyd conducted on October 6, 1995.

P. 215: Scene of police driving O. J. home was shown on CNN on October 3, 1995.

P. 215: Quote by Mary Tillotson, host of *CNN and Company*, CNN, October 3, 1995.

Pp. 215–216: Quote by Z. G. from telephone interview conducted on October 4, 1995.

Pp. 216–217: Debate over the verdict divided along racial lines was reported in the *Los Angeles Times*, October 4–11, 1995; the *New York Times*, October 4–11, 1995; *Time*, October 16, 1995, pp. 40–45; and *Newsweek*, October 16, 1995, pp. 38–35; and S. Monroe, *op. cit.*, pp. 30–36.

P. 216: Poll results reported by Mark Whitaker, "Whites vs. Blacks," *Newsweek*, October 16, 1995, p. 29. Other polls with similar results were reported by Martin Gottlieb, "Deep Split in Reactions to the Verdict," *New York Times*, October 4, 1995, p. A1; a CNN poll, October 3, 1995; and an ABC-TV poll, October 3, 1995.

P. 217: Quote by N. Don Wycliff in M. Whitaker, *op. cit.*, p. 34.

Pp. 217–220: Criticism of the jury and its decision was widely reported in the media for several weeks after the verdict. See John Wildermuth, "O. J. Case Verdict Rankles Whites," *San Francisco Chronicle*, October 7, 1995, p. A1; A. M. Rosenthal, "Verdict on a Trial," *New York Times*, October 6, 1995, p. A23; Mark Miller and Donna Foote, "How the Jury Saw It," *Time*, October 16, 1995, pp. 37–39; James Walsh, "The Lessons of the Trial," *Newsweek*, October 16, 1995, pp. 62–64; Henry L. Gates, Jr., "Thirteen Ways of Looking at a Black Man," *New Yorker*, October 23, 1995, pp. 56–65; and Neal Gabler, "History: The 13th Juror," *Los Angeles Times*, October 8, 1995, p. M1.

P. 218: Quote from phone interview with Shirlee T. Haizlip conducted on October 5, 1995.

P. 219: Analysis of the jurors' screening questionnaire is reported by M. Miller and D. Foote, *op. cit.*

P. 219: Quote from Debra J. Saunders, "Another Bad Verdict—Only in L.A.," *San Francisco Chronicle*, October 4, 1995, p. A13.

Pp. 219–220: Quote from George Will, "People Get Away with Murder," *Washington Post*, October 4, 1995, p. A16.

Pp. 220–221: Quote from Anita Hill cited in "One Verdict, Clashing Voices," *Newsweek*, October 16, 1995, p. 51.

P. 221: Quote by Susan Reverby cited by Isabel Wilkerson, "Whose Side to Take: Women, Outrage, and the Verdict on O. J. Simpson," *New York Times*, October 8, 1995, p. E1.

P. 221: Quote by Deb Spangler in *ibid.*, p. E4.

P. 222: Quote by Brenda Moran cited by H. Chua-Eoan and E. Gleick, "Making the Case," p. 61.

P. 222: Quote by David A. Aldana cited by Julia Campbell, "At First Shy of Publicity, Juror No. 4 Speaks Out," *New York Times*, October 10, 1995, p. A12.

Pp. 222–223: Comments by juror Moran are summarized in H. Chua-Eoan and E. Gleick, "Making the Case," p. 61; and M. Miller and D. Foote, *op. cit.*, p. 39.

P. 223: Material on David Aldana from J. Campbell, *op. cit.*

P. 224: Quote from Brenda Moran from "Stunned Legal Experts Ask Why," *San Francisco Chronicle*, October 4, 1995, p. A3.

P. 224: Quote from telephone interview with H. G. conducted on October 5, 1995.

Pp. 225–226: Simpson jurors' negative experiences with the police are reported in M. Miller and D. Foote, *op. cit.*, p. 39.

Pp. 226–227: Quote from telephone interview with Barbara Solomon conducted on October 6, 1995.

P. 227: The principle of cognitive dissonance is explained in all introductory social psychology textbooks; see, for example, Philip G. Zimbardo, *Psychology and Life*, 10th ed. (Glenview, Ill.: Scott, Foresman, 1979), pp. 651–653.

P. 228: Quote from interview with James Lowell Gibbs, Jr., conducted on October 4, 1995.

P. 229: Quote by Eric Adams from *Newsweek*, October 16, 1995, p. 51.

P. 229: Quote from telephone interview with T. N. conducted on October 6, 1995.

P. 230: Quote by Lani Guinier cited in "One Verdict, Clashing Voices," p. 46.

P. 231: Quote by Judge Leon A. Higginbotham cited in H. L. Gates, Jr., *op. cit.*, p. 59.

Pp. 231–232: Comments by legal analysts about the verdict can be found in H. L. Gates, Jr., *ibid.*; *Newsweek*, October 16, 1995, pp. 46–52; J. Walsh, *op. cit.*; and Barbara A. Babcock, "Protect the Jury System, Judge Was the Problem," *Los Angeles Times*, October 8, 1995, p. M6.

Chapter Eleven

P. 235: Quote from Andrew Hacker, *Two Nations: Black and White, Separate, Hostile, Unequal* (New York: Scribner, 1992), p. 49.

Pp. 236–239: The evolution of conspiracy theories is discussed in Patricia A. Turner, *I Heard It Through the Grapevine: Rumor in African-American Culture* (Berkeley: University of California Press, 1993); Theodore Sasson, "African-American Conspiracy Theories and the Social Construction of Crime," *Sociological Inquiry*, November 1995, pp. 265–285; Gary A. Fine, *Manufacturing Tales* (Knoxville: University of Tennessee Press, 1992); and Terry Ann Knopf, *Rumors, Race, and Riots* (New Brunswick, N.J.: Transaction Books, 1975).

P. 238: The Tuskegee study is discussed in James H. Jones, *Bad Blood: The Tuskegee Syphilis Experiment* (New York: Free Press, 1982). *Miss Evers' Boys*, a 1989 play about Nurse Rivers and the Tuskegee study by Cornell University professor David Feldshuh, was nominated for a Pulitzer Prize in 1992. A videotape, *Susceptible to Kindness: Miss Evers' Boys and the Tuskegee Syphilis Study* (Ithaca, N.Y.: Cornell University, 1994), is also available.

P. 238: The Noriega conspiracy charges are discussed by C. J. Robinson, "Race, Capitalism, and the Antidemocracy," in R. Gooding-Williams, *op. cit.*, pp. 73–81.

P. 238: The criminalization of young black males is discussed in Jewelle Taylor Gibbs (ed.), *Young, Black, and Male in America: An Endangered Species* (Westport, Conn.: Greenwood Press, 1988); Michael Tonry, *Race, Crime, and Punishment in America* (New York: Oxford University Press, 1995); and Marc Mauer, *Young Black Men and the Criminal Justice System: A Growing National Problem* (Washington, D.C.: Sentencing Project, 1990).

P. 239: The Cointelpro program is discussed by Mike Davis, "Uprising and Repression in L.A.," in R. Gooding-Williams, *op. cit.*, pp. 142–154; and Charles E. Simmons, "The Los Angeles Rebellion: Class, Race, and Misinformation" in H. R. Madhubuti, *op. cit.*, pp. 141–155.

P. 239: Lynchings of blacks are discussed in John Hope Franklin, *From Slavery to Freedom: A History of Negro Americans*, 5th ed. (New York: Knopf, 1979), and Mary F. Berry, *Black Resistance/White Law: A History of Constitutional Racism in America* (New York: Viking Penguin, 1994).

P. 240: Arrests of celebrity athletes and entertainers are described in R. Gooding-Williams, *op. cit.*, and H. R. Madhubuti, *op. cit.*

P. 241: Quote from J. H. Jones, *op. cit.*, p. 13.

Pp. 241–244: This summary of the Tuskegee study and its impact is drawn from the account in *ibid.*

P. 244: Quote from Haki R. Madhubuti, *Black Men: Obsolete, Single, Dangerous?* (Chicago: Third World Press, 1990), p. 67.

P. 245: The assassination of Medgar Evers is described in T. Branch, *op. cit.*, pp. 824–827, and Myrlie Evers, *For Us, the Living* (New York: Doubleday, 1967),pp. 302–309.

P. 245: The March 1994 conviction and sentencing of Byron de la Beckwith for the murder of Medgar Evers is reported by Eric Harrison, "Beckwith Is Convicted of Killing Medgar Evers," *Los Angeles Times*, February 6, 1994, p. A1.

P. 246: The assassination of Malcolm X is described by Bruce Perry, *Malcolm: The Life of a Man Who Changed Black America* (New York: Station Hill, 1991).

P. 246: Charges of FBI involvement in Malcolm X's murder are reported by George E. Curry, "The Last Days of Malcolm X, Part II," *Emerge*, March 1995, pp. 38–42, and Kenneth O'Reilly, *Black Americans: The FBI Files* (New York: Carroll & Graf, 1994).

Pp. 246–247: The arrest and charges against Qubilah Shabazz are reported by Don Terry, "Daughter of Malcolm X Charged with Trying to Kill Farrakhan," *New York Times*, January 13, 1995, p. A1.

Pp. 247–248: The assassination of Martin Luther King, Jr., is described by David J. Garrow, *The FBI and Martin Luther King, Jr.* (New York: Viking Penguin, 1983).

P. 248: Charges of FBI involvement in King's murder are reported in *ibid.*

P. 249: Quote by E. J. from interview conducted on June 15, 1994.

Pp. 249–250: See discussion of political and corporate conspiracy theories in P. A. Turner, *op. cit.*, pp. 108–136, and T. Sasson, *op. cit.*

P. 250: Quote by George Curry from E. R. Shipp, *op. cit.*, p. 41.

P. 250: Quote by B. R. from interview conducted on August 10, 1995.

P. 251: See critique of FBI response to the civil rights movement in Branch, *op. cit.*, and Garrow, *op. cit.*

P. 251: See critique of FBI response to the Black Panthers in M. Davis, *City of Quartz*, pp. 297–300.

Pp. 251–252: Johnnie Cochran's defense of Geronimo Pratt is described in Mary A. Fischer, "The Wrong Man," *Gentleman's Quarterly*, March 1995, pp. 202–209.

P. 252: Since 1992, accounts of police misconduct or brutality have been reported in Detroit, New Orleans, New York, Philadelphia, and Washington, D.C. See E. Gleick, "Crooked Blue Line"; Neil A. Lewis, "Police Brutality Under Wide Review by Justice Department," *New York Times*, March 5, 1991, p. A1; and National Association for the Advancement of Colored People, *Beyond the Rodney King Story: An Investigation of Police Conduct in Minority Communities* (Boston: Northwestern University Press, 1995).

P. 252: See the account of the attack on protesters against the Ku Klux Klan in Greensboro, North Carolina, by Bill Peterson, "Civil Trial Opens on Greensboro Clash," *New York Times*, March 16, 1985, p. A4.

Pp. 252–253: Quote from National Black Police Association letter in Nick Charles and Chrisana Coleman, "Criminally Suspect," *Emerge*, September 1995, p. 80.

P. 253: Accidental shootings of undercover black police officers are documented in *ibid.*

P. 253: The case of William Lozano is reported by Jeffrey Schmalz, "Miami Officer Guilty in Two Killings That Prompted Riots by Blacks," *New York Times*, December 8, 1989, p. A1.

P. 254: The case of Malice Green is reported by Dovon P. Levin, "Detroit Suspends Policemen in Fatal Beating of Motorist," *New York Times*, November 7, 1992, p. A1.

Pp. 254–255: See detailed account of Freedom Riders in the summer of 1961 by T. Branch, *op. cit.*, pp. 451–491.

P. 255: See the account of the bombing of the Sixteenth Street Baptist Church in *ibid.*, pp. 889–896.

P. 255: Quote by P. A. Turner, *op. cit.*, p. 208.

Pp. 255–256: See the account of Emmett Till's lynching by George E. Curry, "The Death That Won't Die," *Emerge*, July-August 1995, pp. 24–32.

P. 256: Quote by P. A. Turner, *op. cit.*, p. 162.

Pp. 256–257: Conspiracy theory about AIDS and blacks is reported in *ibid.*, pp. 151–163; Karen G. Bates, "Is It Genocide?" *Essence*, September 1990, pp. 76–79; Cindy Patton, *Sex and Germs: The Politics of AIDS* (Boston: South End Press, 1985); and J. H. Jones, *op. cit.*, pp. 220–241.

P. 257: Results of Sandra Crouse Quinn's survey of black churches is reported in the *Boston Globe*, November 2, 1995, p. 15.

P. 258: Quote by John W. Mack from Kenneth B. Noble, "Los Angeles Racial Tensions Fanned by Tapes," *New York Times*, August 31, 1995, p. A1.

P. 258: The case of Leonard Deadwyler is summarized in M. A. Fischer, *op. cit.*, and Bartley L. McSwine, "L.A. 1992: Race, Class, and Spiritual Poverty in the American Empire," in H. R. Madhubuti, *Why L.A. Happened*, pp. 247–257.

Pp. 258–259: The case of Ron Settles is reported by Sylvester Monroe, "Race Man: Johnnie Cochran, Jr.," *Emerge*, January 1996, pp. 30–36.

P. 259: The wrongful death suit in Settles's case is reported in *ibid.*, p. 35.

P. 259: The case of Donald Jackson is reported in C. E. Simmons, *op. cit.*, p. 144.

Pp. 259–260: The raid on the apartments is described in Christopher Commission Report, p. 196; M. Davis, *City of Quartz*, pp. 275–276; J. A. Skolnick and J. J. Fyfe, *op. cit.*, pp. 107–108; and David Ferrell, "LAPD Actions on Trial in 39th and Dalton Case," *Los Angeles Times*, May 12, 1991, p. A1.

P. 260: Quote by Christopher Darden from D. Ferrell, *op. cit.*, p. A24.

P. 260: Civil award in the Thirty-Ninth and Dalton case is reported by Terry Pristin and David Ferrell, "3 Officers Acquitted in 39th and Dalton Drug Raid," *Los Angeles Times*, June 20, 1991, p. A1.

P. 260: Quote by Dr. Frances Cress Welsing, medical researcher, from "The Symbolism, Logic, and Meaning of 'Justifiable Homicide' in the 1980s," in H. R. Madhubuti, *Why L.A. Happened*, p. 84.

P. 260: Deaths of young black males from police choke holds are documented by M. Davis, *City of Quartz*, and M. Oliver and others, *op. cit.*, p. 121.

Pp. 260–261: "Operation Hammer" is described by M. Davis, *City of Quartz*, pp. 274–277.

P. 261: Information on the Los Angeles County Sheriff's Department is from the *Report on the Los Angeles County Sheriff's Department*, July 28, 1992. See Hector Tobar and Kenneth Reich, "Probe Finds Pattern of Excess Force, Brutality by Deputies," *Los Angeles Times*, July 21, 1992, p. A1.

Pp. 261–262: Efforts of the LAPD to sabotage the gang truce were reported to me in several interviews with former gang members and are documented in accounts by M. Davis, "Uprising and Repression," *op. cit.*, and Luis J. Rodriguez, "From These Black and Brown Streets: L.A. Revisited," in H. R. Madhubuti, *Why L.A. Happened*, pp. 221–228.

P. 262: Quote by Mark Fuhrman is reported by David Margolick, "Simpson Detective's Racial Epithets."

P. 263: Quote by O. L. from interview conducted on June 15, 1994.

P. 263: See statistics on differential rates of arrests, dispositions, and duration of incarceration for black and white males in Vincent Schiraldi, Sue Kuyper, and Sharon Hewitt, *Young African-Americans and the Criminal Justice System in California: Five Years Later* (San Francisco: Center on Juvenile and Criminal Justice, February 1996).

P. 263: For statistics on comparative incarceration rates, see M. Mauer, *op. cit.*; M. Tonry, "Beyond the Rodney King Story"; and M. F. Berry, *op. cit.*

P. 264: Quote by A. B. from telephone interview conducted on September 15, 1995.

Chapter Twelve

P. 265: Quote from Abraham Lincoln's speech to the Republication state convention, Springfield, Ill., June 16, 1858.

P. 265: Quote from Cornel West, *Race Matters* (New York: Vintage Books, 1993), p. 159. Copyright held by Beacon Press.

Pp. 265–266: *Waiting to Exhale*, a movie based on a novel by the same name by Terry McMillan, was a surprise hit, as noted by Jane Ganahl, "*Waiting to Exhale* Touches a Nerve for African-American Women," *San Francisco Examiner*, January 2, 1996, p. B1.

P. 266: Quote from C. West, *op. cit.*, p. 155.

P. 266: See comments on "rich man's justice" in Elizabeth Gleick, "Rich Justice, Poor Justice," *Time,* June 19, 1995, pp. 40–47, and John Langhein, "Money Talks, Clients Walk," *Newsweek,* April 17, 1995, pp. 32–33.

P. 268: The theme of O. J. Simpson as the "prodigal son" for the black community was expressed in S. Monroe, *op. cit.;* H. L. Gates, Jr., *op. cit.;* and E. R. Shipp, *op. cit.*

P. 268: Quote from interview with Duane B. Bremond conducted on May 12, 1994.

P. 269: See discussions of the role of the police as agents of social control in J. A. Skolnick and J. J. Fyfe, *op. cit.*; M. Davis, "Uprising and Repression"; ; M. Tonry, *op. cit.;* and M. F. Berry, *op. cit.*

P. 270: Quote by Chief Willie Williams from P. Maas, *op. cit.*, p. 6.

P. 271: Resistance to Chief Williams's tenure and reforms is discussed in *ibid;* "L.A. Police Chief in Hot Seat," *San Francisco Chronicle,* February 19, 1996, p. A17; Patrick McGreevy, "L.A. Split on How Top Cop Is Faring," *San Francisco Examiner and Chronicle,* March 5, 1995, p. B4; and Eric Pooley, "Heat on the Beat," *Time,* October 16, 1995, pp. 66–67.

P. 272: Quote from interview with Lillian Mobley conducted on March 18, 1994.

P. 272: An example of the retreat from government programs to support the most vulnerable and economically disadvantaged groups is the "Contract with America" promoted by the Republican majority in the U.S. Congress after the 1994 midterm congressional elections.

Pp. 272–273: For documentation of these institutional inequities, see Reynolds Farley and Walter R. Allen, *The Color Line and the Quality of Life in America* (New York: Oxford University Press, 1989); J. T. Gibbs, *op. cit.;* A. Hacker, *op. cit.;* Gerald D. Jaynes and Robin M. Williams, Jr. (eds.), *A Common Destiny: Blacks and American Society* (Washington, D.C.: National Academy Press, 1989); and William J. Wilson, *The Truly Disadvantaged* (Chicago: University of Chicago Press, 1987).

P. 273: Quote from interview with John W. Mack conducted on October 29, 1993. Also see Jannette L. Dates and William Barlow (eds.), *Split Image: African-Americans in the Mass Media* (Washington, D.C.: Howard University Press, 1990).

P. 274: See critiques of media coverage of Watts riots in G. Horne, *op. cit.*, and of South Central riots in Howard Kurtz, "Media Coverage of Los Angeles Tensions Face Mounting Criticism," *Washington Post,* April 10, 1993, p. A11, and Steve Weinstein, "New TV Poll Sets Off Debate," *Los Angeles Times*, June 6, 1992, p. F1.

P. 274: See critiques of media coverage of the O. J. Simpson case in Barry Tarlow, "Try It in Court, Not in the Press," *Los Angeles Times*, June 28, 1994, p. B7; Don J. De Benedictis, "The National Verdict," *American Bar Association Journal,* October 1994, pp. 52–55; and R. Rodriguez, *op. cit.*

P. 274: See discussion of the impact of "three strikes" laws on black males in Fox Butterfield, "California's Courts Clogging Under Its 'Three Strikes Law,'" *New York Times*, March 23, 1995, p. A1.

P. 275: Quote from interview with Rev. Cecil L. Murray conducted on June 17, 1994.

P. 276: See impact of the Million Man March on black men in Los Angeles in Melinda Beck, "Beyond the Moment, What Can One Day Do?" *Newsweek,* October 30, 1995, pp. 38–39; and Edward J. Boyer, "Black Leaders Seek to Enlist Men for Rally," *Los Angeles Times*, September 1, 1995, p. B1.

P. 276: Quote by Martin Luther King, Jr., from his commencement speech "The American Dream" at Lincoln University on June 6, 1961. Cited in James M. Washington (ed.),

The Essential Writings and Speeches of Martin Luther King, Jr. (San Francisco: HarperSanFrancisco, 1986).

P. 277: Census projections from S. H. Holmes, "Census Sees a Profound Ethnic Shift in U.S.," *New York Times*, March 14, 1996, p. A8.

P. 277: Los Angeles has been portrayed as the "city of the future" in M. Davis, *City of Quartz*, and David Rieff, *op. cit.*

Epilogue

Pp. 279–280: On the Supreme Court case, see "Latest Legal Question in Rodney King Case," *San Francisco Chronicle*, February 19, 1996, p. A1.

P. 280: The videotape's release is noted in "Simpson Videos on the Way—He Seeks Cash, Forgiveness," *San Francisco Chronicle*, February 17, 1996, p. A1.

Pp. 280–281: See Jonathan Kellerman, "Don Juan in Hell," *Los Angeles Magazine*, July 1, 1995, pp. 52–58.

P. 281: Rodney King's problems with his wife are detailed in Kenneth B. Noble, "The Endless Rodney King Case," *New York Times*, February 4, 1996.

P. 282: On Stacey Koon, see Ralph Frammolino, "2 Die As Gunman Seeks Koon at Halfway House," *Los Angeles Times*, November 24, 1995, p. A1, and "Cop Convicted of Rodney King Beating Due for Halfway House," *Los Angeles Times*, October 15, 1995, p. A1.

P. 283: On Laurence Powell, see "Rodney King Rejects Idea That Officer Was a Victim," *San Francisco Chronicle*, November 20, 1995, p. A14.

P. 283: On Timothy Wind, see Mary Moore, "Despite Opposition, Figure in King Case Hired for Police Job," *Los Angeles Times*, October 12, 1994, p. B3.

Pp. 283–284: On Ted Briseno, see "Officer in King Case Is Dismissed," *New York Times*, July 17, 1994, p. 8; and Dwayne Bray, "Probe Finds It Likely Briseno Lied Under Oath," *Los Angeles Times*, December 20, 1994, p. B1.

P. 284: On Ira Reiner, see Sheryl Stolberg, "Garcetti Vows to Take 'Larger Role' as D.A.," *Los Angeles Times*, September 19, 1992, p. A1.

P. 285: See Steven Lerman, "A King's Ransom," *Harper's*, April 1995, pp. 20–22; and John L. Mitchell, "Judge Grants Reduced Fees to King's Attorneys," *Los Angeles Times*, January 18, 1995, p. B1.

P. 285: On John Burris, see Reynolds Holding, "Simpson Case Boosts Savvy Oakland Lawyer's Status," *San Francisco Chronicle*, October 6, 1995, p. A1.

P. 285: See Daryl F. Gates, *Chief: My Life in the LAPD* (New York: Bantam Books, 1992).

Pp. 285–286: On Willie Williams, see P. McGreevy, *op. cit.*; "L.A. Police Chief in Hot Seat," *op. cit.*; and Jim Impoco and Mike Tharp, "Under Siege at the LAPD," *U.S. News and World Report*, October 16, 1995, pp. 44–45.

P. 287: On Rebuild L.A., see Tom Larson and Miles Finney, *Rebuilding South Central Los Angeles: Myths, Realities, and Opportunities* (Los Angeles: School of Business, California State University, 1995).

P. 288: On O. J. Simpson's testimony, see Kenneth B. Noble, "Simpson Begins Depositions in Civil Lawsuit on Slayings," *New York Times*, January 23, 1996, p. A6, and T. Rutten and H. Weinstein, *op. cit.*, p. A1.

P. 288: See "Simpson Guest Gives Testimony in Civil Lawsuit," *New York Times*, February 15, 1996, p. C21, and "Kato Tells of Nicole's Fears," *San Francisco Chronicle*, February 28, 1996, p. A1.

P. 289: See "Judge Puts Off Simpson Trial till September," *San Francisco Chronicle*, March 1, 1996, p. B1.

Pp. 289–290: See "Simpson Videos," *op. cit.*, and Richard Zoglin, "Testifying for Dollars," *Time*, January 22, 1996, p. 34.

P. 290: Regarding the Black Entertainment Network interview, see Walter Goodman, "Simpson Interviewer: Striking a Balance," *New York Times*, January 27, 1996, p. A14.

Pp. 291–292: On Mark Fuhrman, see Fox Butterfield, "A Portrait of the Detective in the 'O. J. Whirlpool,'" *New York Times*, March 2, 1996, p. A1.

P. 292: See Faye Resnick, *Shattered: In the Eye of the Storm* (Beverly Hills: Dove Books, 1995).

P. 292: Regarding Susan Forward, see "Account of Therapy for Nicole Simpson Brings Suspension," *New York Times*, November 24, 1995, p. B16.

P. 293: On Gil Garcetti's campaign, see Martin Berg, "Are We Lucky or What?" *Los Angeles Magazine*, March 1996, pp. 18–20.

Pp. 293–294: Regarding Marcia Clark's book deal, see Mary B. W. Tabor, "Viking to Pay $4.2 Million for Book by Marcia Clark," *New York Times*, November 10, 1995, p. C1.

P. 294: On Christopher Darden, see Frank Rich, "One Night Stand," *New York Times*, November 22, 1995, p. A15. Book is Christopher Darden with Jess Walter, *In Contempt* (New York: HarperCollins, 1996).

P. 295: On Johnnie Cochran, see Alan Abrahamson, "Looking Ahead for the Lawyers," *Los Angeles Times*, October 8, 1995, and "Lawyer of the Year: Johnnie L. Cochran, Jr.," *National Law Review*, December 25, 1995, p. C4. Cochran's book deal is described in Tim Rutten, "Cochran Tops $4.2 Million Clark Book Deal," *Los Angeles Times*, November 15, 1995, p. A1.

P. 295: On Robert Shapiro, see A. Abrahamson, *op. cit.*; and M. Miller, D. Foote, and V. E. Smith, *op. cit.* Book is Robert L. Shapiro with Larkin Warren, *The Search for Justice* (New York: Warner Books, 1996).

Pp. 295–296: On F. Lee Bailey, see Mireya Navarro, "Bailey Is Jailed in Dispute over Former Client's Assets," *New York Times*, March 7, 1996, p. A10, and "F. Lee Bailey Freed from Jail in Dispute over Drug Money," *New York Times*, April 20, 1996, p. 9.

P. 296: See Alan M. Dershowitz, *Reasonable Doubts: The O. J. Simpson Case and the Criminal Justice System* (New York: Simon & Schuster, 1996).

Pp. 296–297: On Scheck and Neufeld, see A. Abrahamson, *op. cit.*

P. 297: On the jurors, see "2 Jurors Say O. J. Probably Was the Killer," *San Francisco Chronicle*, January 17, 1996, p. A1.

P. 297: See Michael Knox, *The Private Diary of an O. J. Juror* (New York: Viking Penguin, 1995).

P. 298: Regarding Tracy Hampton, see "The O. J. Juror with a Difference: Her Story, Her Photos," *Playboy*, March 1996.

P. 298: Regarding O. J. Simpson's calls, see W. Carlsen and J. Wildermuth, "O. J. Calls In While Jurors Speak Out," *San Francisco Chronicle*, October 5, 1996, p. A1.

P. 299: On Tammy Bruce, see Elizabeth Gleick, "Fighting Words," *Time*, January 8, 1996, p. 41.

Pp. 299–300: On the LAPD, see "2 L.A. Cops Suspended for Falsifying Reports," *San Francisco Chronicle*, September 2, 1995, p. A4.

P. 300: On Ed Kirste, see "L.A. Sheriff's Whites Group Is Disavowed," *San Francisco Chronicle*, November 18, 1995, p. A20.

P. 300: See Kenneth B. Noble, "Several Blacks Sue Beverly Hills, Asserting Bias by the Police," *New York Times*, November 26, 1995, p. A1.

Pp. 300–301: On disparities in sentences for cocaine possession, see Linda Greenhouse, "Justices Hear Case on Disparity in Cocaine Sentences," *New York Times*, February 26, 1996, p. A10, and Jeffrey Ambramson, "Making the Law Colorblind," *New York Times*, October 16, 1995, p. A19.

P. 301: On blacks in the criminal justice system, see V. Schiraldi and others, *op. cit.* Quote is from pp. 1–2.

Pp. 301–302: On the immigrant beating incident, see Aurelio Rojas, "FBI Probes Beatings near L.A.," *San Francisco Chronicle*, April 3, 1996.

Index

A

Adams, Eric, 229
Aldana, David A., 222, 223
Allred, Gloria, 281
Aschenbach, Anise, 223
Assembly Special Committee on the Los Angeles Crisis, 286, 287

B

Bailey, F. Lee, 145, 162, 295–296
Baker, Robert, 289
Baker, Shirley, 200
Bankhead, Sandra, 62, 64, 72
Barnett, Terri, 100, 101
Bell, Kathleen, 184
Black community: media portrayal of, 273–275; and mixed-race marriages, 158. *See also* Conspiracy theories of black community; Los Angeles black community
Black Panthers, 251
Blasier, Robert, 172, 173, 188
Bodziak, William, 189
Boyd, Sara McNeil, 158, 214
Bradley, Bill, 34
Bradley, Tom, 76
Braun, Harland, 169
Bremond, Duane B., 57, 268
Briseno, Ted, 35, 40, 43–44, 49, 52, 88, 90, 283–284
Broady, Earl C., Jr., 103
Brown, Denise, 134, 157–158, 190, 290
Brown, Edmund G., 16
Brown, Juditha, 133–134, 140, 158, 169, 214
Brown, Lou, 133, 158
Brown family: civil suit of, 288–289; reaction to verdict, 208–209; relations with O. J. Simpson, 157–158
Bruce, Tammy, 299
Burris, John, 109, 110, 285

C

Carpenter, Teresa, 125
Centers for Disease Control, and Tuskegee Study, 242, 243
Chambers, Marcia, 42
Chein, Edmund, 32
Christopher, Warren, 17, 76, 286–287
Christopher Commission, 77–83, 271
Clark, Marcia, 154, 172–173, 174, 179, 185, 187, 188, 190, 193, 194, 195, 208, 213; and Fuhrman tapes, 182–183; opening statement of, 155–156; posttrial, 293–294; summation of, 196, 201, 202–203
Clarke, George, 177
Clymer, Steven, 87, 284
Cochran, Johnnie, 40, 151, 168, 170, 171, 172, 179, 188, 191, 193, 200, 204, 208, 211, 212; early cases of,

251, 258, 259; and Fuhrman tapes, 175, 177, 184, 186; posttrial, 295; response to opening statement, 156–157; summation and closing arguments, 197, 198–199, 205
Collins, Sharon, 120
Community policing, 270, 286
Conspiracy theories of black community, 235–264; AIDS origin stories, 238, 256–257; and civil rights and protest groups, 251–252; harrassment and destruction of black leaders, 237, 244–250; and Los Angeles Police Department, 257–264; and police killings of unarmed black males, 252–254; and urban myths and collective memories, 239–241, 255
Cooley, Amanda, 297
Cose, Ellis, 116
Cowlings, Al, 118–119, 143–144
Crenshaw, B. R., 165
Criminal justice system: expectations of, whites versus blacks, 106–107; racism and racial inequities in, 225–228, 299–302; weaknesses and strengths of, 150. *See also* Los Angeles Police Department
Crumpton, Joycelyn M., 60, 61
Curry, George, 250

D

Darden, Christopher, 154, 161, 208, 260; closing statement of, 196–197, 201–202; and Fuhrman tapes, 185–186; and glove episode, 167–168; posttrial, 294; reaction to verdict, 213–214
Davies, John G., 86, 92–93, 285
Davis, Edward, 20
Davis, James, 7
De Pasquale, Paul, 50
Deadwyler, Leonard, 258
Deedrick, Douglas, 169, 189
Denny, Reginald: assault on, 57–58; attitude toward attackers, 105; rescue of, 100–101
Denny assault trial, 94–108; charges and defendants in, 94–96, 98, 101, 103; verdict and sentencing in, 104–108; white reaction to verdict, 106–107
Dershowitz, Alan, 296
Domestic violence, and Simpson trial verdict, 221–222, 223
Douglas, Carl, 160
DuBois, W.E.B., 6
Duff, Alice Walker, 68
Duff, Joseph, 106
Duke, Charles, 47
Durio, Carmelita, 170

E

Edwards, Harry, 115, 123
Entertainment industry, dehumanization and demonization of blacks by, 273–275
Evers, Medgar, assassination of, 245

F

Faal, Edi O. M., 96, 100, 101, 102–103
Farrakhan, Louis, 246
Federal Bureau of Investigation (FBI), and conspiracy theories of black Americans, 245–248, 251
Ferris-Pirro, Jeanine, 181
First African Methodist Episcopal Church (FAME), 54–55, 207, 209
Flowers, Kenneth, 56, 66–67
Forward, Susan, 137, 292
Frye, Marquette, 13
Fuhrman, Mark, 141, 160–162, 175, 195, 291–292, 300; discrediting of, 185, 186–187; tapes of, 177–179, 182–184
Fung, Dennis, 163–164

G

Garcetti, Gil, 126, 145–146, 178, 183, 188, 284, 293
Gates, Daryl, 20, 21, 52, 94, 260, 285; efforts to oust, 78–79, 83; reaction to assault on Rodney King, 34–35

Geiger, Leslie, 99
Gerdes, John, 176–177
Gibbs, James Lowell, Jr., 228
Goldberg, Hank, 154
Golden, Irwin, 167
Goldman, Fred, 183, 193, 199, 201, 213, 291
Goldman, Ron, 137; murder of, 140–142
Goldman family: civil suit against O. J. Simpson, 288–289; reaction to verdict, 205, 208, 213–214
Gordon, Ed, 290
Green, Bobby, 99, 100
Green, Malice, 254
Grimes, Milton, 109
Guinier, Lani, 230

H

Hacker, Andres, 235
Haizlip, Shirlee T., 218
Hampton, Tracy, 298
Harlins, Latasha, 62–64
Henderson, Wade, 22
Hertz, 124, 136
Higginbotham, Leon A., 231
Hill, Anita, 220–221
Hodge, Roderick, 185
Hodgman, William, 154–155, 156, 157
Hoffer, Richard, 131
Holliday, George, 30, 32, 33, 41
Horne, Gerald, 12
Hughes, Langston, 75
Huizenga, Robert, 171

I

Ito, Lance, 164, 168–169, 174, 176, 177, 178–179, 181, 186, 187, 188, 191, 192, 193–194, 204, 206, 208; background of, 150–151

J

Jackson, Donald, 65, 259
Johnson, Magic, 265–266
Johnson, Ronald, 15, 22
Jones, Donald, 100
Jones, Herbert A., 20, 24
Jones, James H., 241
Jones, Monique, 126

K

Kaelin, Kato, 136–137, 139, 141, 158–159, 288–289
Kardashian, Robert, 143
Karlin, Joyce A., 64
Kelberg, Brian, 154, 171
Kennedy, Tracy, 297
Kennedy-Powell, Kathleen, 146
King, Larry, 298–299
King, Martin Luther, Jr., 276; and the FBI, 247–248
King, Paul, 33
King, Rodney, 22–37; arrest and assault of, 28–32; assault injuries of, 31–32, 48; childhood and adolescence of, 23–25; criminal record of, 26–28; marriages of, 25–26; police and grand jury response to assault, 35–36; post-assault arrests and problems of, 108–109, 281–282; videotape of, public response to, 29–31, 41. *See also People* v. *Powell et al.; Rodney King* v. *City of Los Angeles; United States* v. *Los Angeles Police Department*
Kinsey, Bernard, 287
Kirste, Ed, 300
Knox, Michael, 297
Koon, Stacey, 31, 40, 48, 52, 87, 88, 90; conviction and sentencing of, 91–93, 266, 282–283; final appeal of, 279–280
Kowalski, Barry, 87
Kunstler, William, 151

L

Lacayo, Richard, 107
Lange, Tom, 141, 191
Lee, Donzella P., 63
Lee, Henry, 181, 189–190
Lerman, Steven, 108, 285
Lopez, Rosa, 160–161
Los Angeles, multiethnic history of, 4–5

Los Angeles black community: ghettoization and economic devastation of, 7, 9–11; history of, 5–16; responses to Simpson trial verdict in, 214–217, 224–230; selective prosecution of, 300–301; Watts riots in, 12–18. *See also* South Central Los Angeles
Los Angeles City Council, Gates' support and opposition on, 79
Los Angeles County Sheriff's Department, 261
Los Angeles Police Department (LAPD): and black gangs, 261–262; brutality and misconduct toward blacks by, 7, 9, 11, 14–15, 20–21, 65, 76, 77–78, 79–81, 258–264, 299–301; Christopher Commission hearings on, 77–83; and conspiracy theories of black community, 257–264; failure to reform racist policies, 180, 271, 299; reaction to assault on Rodney King, 34–35; stop and search practice of, 7, 78, 300. *See also United States* v. *Los Angeles Police Department*
Love, Eulia, 80
Lozano, William, 253

M

Mack, John W., 33, 54, 55, 66, 258, 273
Madhubuti, Haki R., 244
Malcolm X, assassination of, 246–247
Markel, Charles, 299–300
Martz, Roger, 173–174
Marzette, Eugene, 38
Mazzola, Andrea, 167
McCone, John A., 17
McDonell, Herbert, 174
McKinny, Laura Hart, 175, 182, 185–186
Media: dehumanization and demonization of blacks by, 273–275; leaks of Fuhrman tapes by, 178; post-acquittal coverage of O. J. Simpson, 289–290, 298–299; Simpson case rush to judgment, 154, 219–220
Miller, Antoine, 94, 96
Mobley, Lillian, 272
Moore, H. Randolph, 27
Moran, Brenda, 216, 222–223, 224, 297–298
Morrison, Lawrence, 99
Murphy, Titus, 100
Murray, Cecil L., 52, 54, 91, 207, 209, 275

N

Nation of Islam, 199–200
NBC Sports, 136
Neufeld, Peter, 165–166, 296–297

O

O. J. Simpson: The Interview (videotape), 280, 289–290
Ouderkirk, Judge, 97–98, 100, 104, 106, 107

P

Paratis, Thano, 189
Park, Alan, 205
Parker, William, 9, 11, 12, 20
Parks, Bernard C., 43, 47
Pauley, Gale L., 25
People v. *Powell et al.*, 38–53; closing arguments in, 50–52; defense in, 43–48, 145; jury in, 49–50, 51–52; prosecution case in, 40–43; Simi Valley location of, 36–37, 38–39; verdicts and reactions, 52–56
People of State of California v. *Orenthal James Simpson*, 149–203; aftermath, 215–224, 287–299; blood evidence in, 172–174, 175, 189; closing arguments in, 194–203; and conspiracy stories of black community, 239–241; and coroner's office errors, 167; defense's race card in, 180–187, 200–201, 204; DNA evidence in, 165–167, 176–177; EDTA controversy in, 172–173; and Fuhrman tapes, 177–179, 182–184; glove fiasco in, 167–168, 187–188; grand jury and prelimi-

nary hearings, 144–146; jurors' characteristics and racial experiences, 151–153, 217–219, 225–228; jurors' post-verdict behavior, 222–224, 297–298; jurors' revolt in, 164–165; and media, 154, 219–220; police conspiracy theory in, 159, 162, 163–164, 168, 169, 170, 171, 174, 191, 197, 199, 223; post-trial publications/public appearances, 293–294, 295–299; prosecution case in, 154–169; prosecution team in, 154–155, 168–169, 213–214; public reponse to, 209–211; and the Rodney King case, 181, 200–201; verdict, 207–215, 222, 228–229; verdict, response to, 209–211, 213–214, 216–217, 231–232
Phillips, Ron, 141
Powell, Laurence, 35, 40, 42, 50, 52, 88, 90, 110, 283; conviction and sentencing of, 91–93; final appeal of, 279–280
Pratt, Geronimo, 251–252

Q

Quintana, Gabriel, 99, 101

R

Race, and Simpson trial verdict, 216–217, 220–221
Racism: and criminal justice system, 225–229, 299–302; as endemic to American society, 273; of Los Angeles Police Department, 7, 9, 11, 14–15, 20–21, 65, 76, 77–78, 79–81, 258–264, 299–301; and Los Angeles riots, 71–73
Reiner, Ira, 35, 36, 39, 284
Resnick, Faye, 136, 156, 292
Reverby, Susan, 221
Rhoden, W. C., 121, 129, 130, 141
Ridley-Thomas, Mark, 71
Rieders, Frederic, 172–173
Riordan, Richard, 285
Ripston, Ramona, 36
Rivers, Eunice, 242
Robertson, Deirdre, 208
Rodney King v. *City of Los Angeles* (civil suit), 86–87, 108–111; verdicts and awards in, 110, 111
Rubin, Richard, 188
Rufo, Sharon, 288

S

Salzman, Ira, 88, 91
Sanders-Phillips, Kathy, 66
Sathyavagiswaran, L., 167
Saunders, Debra J., 219
Savage, Tracie, 175–176
Schatzman, Dennis, 45
Scheck, Barry, 37, 40, 163–164, 165–166, 189, 198, 199, 296–297
Settles, Ron, 258–259
Shabazz, Betty, 246
Shabazz, Qubilah, 246
Shahian, Cici, 132
Shapiro, Robert, 142, 143, 145, 164, 167, 204, 212–213, 295, 296
Shearer, William, 66
Shipp, E. R., 149
Shipp, Ron, 159–160, 170–171
Simi Valley jurors, 225–226, 227
Simpson, Arnelle, 121, 141–142, 170
Simpson, Eunice, 116, 117, 170, 211, 212
Simpson, Jason, 134, 212
Simpson, Jimmy, 116–117, 132
Simpson, Marguerite Whitley, 119, 121, 124–125, 127, 128
Simpson, Nicole Brown: abuse of, 134, 135; early relationship with O. J. Simpson, 126–127; marriage and motherhood of, 130–131; murder of, 140–142; separation and divorce from O. J. Simpson, 136–138
Simpson, Orenthal James: arrest for spousal abuse, 135–136; as celebrity spokesman, 124; childhood and adolescence of, 116–119; children of, 128, 134–135; civil suit against, 288–289; college and professional football career of, 119–123; as crossover celebrity, 129–130; freeway chase and arrest of, 143–144;

marital problems with Nicole, 132–133; marriage to Marguerite Whitley, 124–125; marriage to Nicole Brown, 130–131; as media and movie star, 131–132; opinions as playboy, 123–124, 125, 130; post-acquittal media treatment of, 280–281, 289–290; public opinion polls on, black versus white views, 144–145, 194–195, 205, 206–207; separation and divorce from Nicole, 136–138; spousal abuse of Nicole, 124–125, 133–134, 135–136; statements during trial by, 192–193; trial by media of, 146–148. *See also People of the State of California* v. *Orenthal James Simpson*
Sims, Gary, 189
Singer, Melanie, 88–89, 90
Singer, Natalie, 185
Skolnick, Jerome, 50, 107
Solomon, Barbara, 66, 227
South Central Los Angeles: community organizations in, 275–276; "culture of hopelessness" in, 59–62; deterioration of, 18–20; Korean merchants in, 62, 63–64; "Operation Hammer" in, 260–261; reaction to Denny assault verdicts, 106; Rebuild L.A. (nonprofit corporation) in, 83, 287; as synonym for black America, 267–268
South Central riots, 56–75; aftermath of, 68–69, 73–74; committee and public hearings on, 77–83, 83–85; and conspiracy theories, 70–71; labeling of, 66–67; looting in, 67–68, 69; motives and causes, 59–65, 71–72
Spangler, Deb, 221
Stone, Michael, 49, 88, 89

T

Teague, Andrew, 299–300
Terry, Gayle Pollard, 58, 70
Tillotson, Mary, 215
Toobin, Jeffrey, 169, 180
Tucker, Curtis R., Jr., 28, 287
Tucker, Walter, Jr., 83
Tuckson, Reed, 72–73
Turner, Patricia, 236, 255, 256
Tuskegee Study, 238, 241–244
Tyson, Mike, 176

U

Ueberroth, Peter, 287
Uelmen, Gerald, 186
United States v. *Los Angeles Police Department*, 85–93; defense case in, 88–90; King's testimony in, 89–90; prosecution case in, 87–88; verdict and sentencing in, 90–93

V

Vannatter, Phillip, 141, 190–191

W

Waiting to Exhale, 265–266
Walker, Arthur B., 205
Watson, Henry, 94, 96, 98, 103, 105
Watts riots, 12–16; and McCone Commission report, 16–18
Weir, Bruce, 166
Weisberg, Stanley, 36, 39, 44
Weitzman, Howard, 142, 145
Weller, Sheila, 124, 138
Welsing, Frances, 260
West, Cornel, 265, 266
White, Terry, 40, 42, 50
Will, George, 219–220
Williams, Damian, 94, 96, 98, 101, 103, 105
Williams, Gary, 94, 95–96
Williams, Willie, 83, 95, 180, 270, 271, 285–286
Wilson, Pete, 184
Wind, Timothy, 35, 52, 88, 90
Wycliff, N. Don, 217

Y

Yochelson, Alan, 40
York, Margaret, 151, 178
Yuille, Lei, 100

Z

Zellerbach Family Fund of San Francisco, 305

About the Author

Jewelle Taylor Gibbs, who received her M.S.W. and Ph.D. degrees from the University of California, Berkeley, is the Zellerbach Family Fund professor of social policy, community change, and practice at the School of Social Welfare at Berkeley. She is also a licensed clinical psychologist who specializes in the social and mental health issues of low-income and minority youth.

A graduate of Radcliffe College, Gibbs is the editor of *Young, Black, and Male in America: An Endangered Species* (1988) and coauthor of *Children of Color: Psychological Interventions with Minority Youth* (1989), as well as numerous book chapters, articles, and essays. She has received several awards for her work, including the McCormick Award from the American Association of Suicidology for her research on minority youth suicide. Gibbs has been a distinguished scholar at the Joint Center for Political and Economic Studies in Washington, D.C., a visiting professor at the University of Toronto, and a visiting scholar at the University of London, the National Institute of Social Work in England, McGill University, Wayne State University, and the Claremont College system.